·KARMA·

Sponsored by the
JOINT COMMITTEE ON SOUTH ASIA
of the
SOCIAL SCIENCE RESEARCH COUNCIL
and the
AMERICAN COUNCIL OF LEARNED SOCIETIES

·KARMA·

AN ANTHROPOLOGICAL INQUIRY

EDITED BY

Charles F. Keyes

AND

E. Valentine Daniel

UNIVERSITY OF CALIFORNIA PRESS

Berkeley • Los Angeles • London

University of California Press
Berkeley and Los Angeles, California
University of California Press, Ltd.
London, England

Printed in the United States of America

1 2 3 4 5 6 7 8 9

Library of Congress Cataloging in Publication Data

Main entry under title:

Karma: an anthropological inquiry.

Includes index.
1. Karma—Addresses, essays, lectures. 2. South Asia—Religious life and customs—Addresses, essays, lectures. 3. Asia, Southeast—Religious life and customs—Addresses, essays, lectures. I. Keyes, Charles F. II. Daniel, E. Valentine.
BL2015.K3K36 291.2'2 81-19719
ISBN 0-520-04429-0 AACR2

Contents

Preface

This work has grown out of a project on "Karma and Rebirth" sponsored by the Joint Committee on South Asia of the American Council of Learned Societies and the Social Science Research Council. As the initial step in this project, Karl Potter organized a workshop held at Lake Wilderness, Washington, in October 1976. At the conclusion of this workshop, Charles Keyes and Paul Hiebert were asked to coordinate studies of the ideas of karma and rebirth as found in contemporary traditions in South and Southeast Asia. Their effort was seen as complementing that of Potter and Wendy O'Flaherty, who undertook the task of bringing together studies concerned with accounts of karma and rebirth in the classical literature.

Following the workshop, Keyes and Hiebert organized a symposium on the topic "Texts in Context: Ideas of Karma in Popular Texts in South and Southeast Asia," for the annual meeting of the American Anthropological Association held in Houston in October 1977. Preliminary versions of several of the essays in this book (those by Beck, Sheryl Daniel, Pugh, Lichter and Epstein, and Keyes) were presented as papers at this symposium. Reflections on these papers were stimulated at the symposium by the critiques that Owen Lynch made of them.

In January 1978 a second workshop on karma was held in Pasadena, again under the sponsorship of the Joint Committee on South Asia. At this time the papers that had been presented at the American Anthropological Association symposium were again discussed in conjunction with other papers prepared for other related symposia and with those specifically prepared for the workshop. The first essay by E.V. Daniel in this book was presented for the first time at Pasadena.

At the conclusion of this workshop, Keyes and Hiebert reviewed the papers and determined that a volume on the subject of ideas of karma in the popular traditions of South and Southeast Asia would need several additional essays to give it coherence. Keyes then commissioned the essays by Babb and Boon. Babb was asked to provide an overview of ideas of karma in the religion of rural peoples in India, drawing upon the existing literature, including the essays on India contained herein. Boon was asked to address himself to the place of karma in the popular religion of Bali. As Balinese religion is reputed to be a form of Hinduism, it seemed of particular interest to inquire as to what place the idea of karma had in this tradition far removed from the Indian subcontinent.

A change of editorship was undertaken in the volume after Hiebert had moved to California and Daniel joined the faculty at the University of Washington. In final preparation of the volume, we have shared editorial responsibility, and Daniel has written the conclusion, Keyes the introduction.

This volume is linked by common origins in the project on Karma and Rebirth with the volume edited by Wendy O'Flaherty, *Karma and Rebirth in Classical Indian Traditions* (Berkeley: University of California Press, 1980). As we complete our work, we look forward to a third volume on Karma to come out of a workshop held in Philadelphia in April 1980, organized by Guy Welbon and A. K. Ramanujan. The third volume will give consideration to ideas of karma and rebirth in the post-classical traditions.

A work such as this volume with its ramified connections has been accomplished only by incurring many debts. We can acknowledge only the most obvious. In the first instance we should like to thank Karl Potter, who has been the guiding light throughout the karma and rebirth enterprise. Paul Hiebert has contributed far more to this work than is apparent; the final product reflects the many hours that he has given to helping one or both of us. Not only has David Szanton looked after the Joint Committee's interest by applying a gentle goad from time to time, his ideas expressed at the workshop have been of substantive significance in our own thinking. Wendy O'Flaherty has provided encouragement from the vantage of her own successful endeavor. We should like to express our appreciation to Agehanada Bharati, whose perspective on certain ethnographic aspects of karma, presented in discussions at the Pasadena symposium as well as in a working paper, have enriched this volume in several meaningful ways. To Larry Epstein we are much indebted for having read several versions of our editorial essays and provided many useful comments that have contributed significantly to their coherence and clarity; Larry has also generously given a helping hand in preparing the index for the volume. While we gratefully acknowledge his and others' help, the responsibility for any errors of interpretation or representation lies entirely with us. We thank several of the secretaries of the Department of Anthropology at the University of Washington, and especially Cora Murphy and Leslie Irey, for their help in typing our own contributions to this volume. The greater part of the final manuscript was typed by Rowena de Saram, to whom we owe a special word of thanks.

Contributors

LAWRENCE A. BABB, Professor of Anthropology, Amherst College

BRENDA E. F. BECK, Professor of Anthropology, University of British Columbia

JAMES A. BOON, Professor of Anthropology, Cornell University

SHERYL B. DANIEL, Ph.D. in Anthropology, University of Chicago

E. VALENTINE DANIEL, Assistant Professor of Anthropology, University of Washington

LAWRENCE EPSTEIN, Research Associate, Department of Anthropology, University of Washington

PAUL HIEBERT, Professor of Anthropology, Fuller Theological Seminary

CHARLES F. KEYES, Professor of Anthropology, University of Washington

DAVID LICHTER, Ph.D. in Anthropology, Stanford University

JUDY F. PUGH, Assistant Professor of Anthropology, University of British Columbia

SUSAN S. WADLEY, Professor of Anthropology, University of Syracuse

Introduction: The Study of Popular Ideas of Karma

Charles F. Keyes

Interpretation of Karmic Ideas in Practice

The authors of the contributions to this volume are concerned, each in their own ways, to interpret how those who follow popular forms of Hinduism and Buddhism in several South and Southeast Asian societies make use of (or, as in the case of Bali, do not make use of) ideas of karma (Pāli *kamma*). In approaching the problem of interpreting the practical meanings that are associated with ideas of karma, one is faced with having to find an appropriate language within which to couch one's interpretation. As Horton has said, "A first step in the analysis of an alien religious system must always be the search for an area of discourse in one's own language which can appropriately serve as a translation instrument" (Horton 1979:284). In this essay, as well as in E. V. Daniel's concluding essay, explicit consideration is given to the "instruments" that appear to have utility in translating the ideas of karma found in the popular traditions of South and Southeast Asia.

The meanings to which the label "karma" has been attached find expression among South and Southeast Asians in concrete forms, that is, associated with vehicles that have an immediacy for those who encounter them; they are also expressed in abstract forms, that is, removed from the integument of actuality and situated among other

I am much indebted to F. K. Lehman, who subjected an earlier incarnation of this essay to an intensive critique. He proved to have a keen nose for sniffing out weaknesses in my argument, and although I have often not adopted the substance of his criticisms, I have rarely left unchanged the points that he found to be questionably formulated. I am also grateful to Val Daniel and Larry Epstein, who were willing to discuss at rather interminable length the thoughts that were eventually shaped into my essay.

abstractions. E.V. Daniel, in his concluding review of the ethnographic materials presented by the various contributors, has centered his attention more on the concrete forms, and he approaches the problem of translation of karmic ideas with such tropological tools as metaphor, metonym, and synecdoche. I will be more concerned here with the abstract forms in which karmic ideas are expressed and will employ as my tools those concepts that lead one to see ideas as belonging to systems of meaning. While both approaches are necessary in an endeavor to interpret the practical meanings that karmic ideas hold for the peoples in South and Southeast Asia, it is worth noting that our choices of approach may reflect, at least in part, the different emphases in the modes used to express karmic ideas in the particular cultures that we have individually studied. Whereas Daniel's Tamils, like the other Hindus discussed in this book, tend to treat karma in markedly concrete ways, conceiving of it as an actual substance, the Thai Buddhists with whom I worked (as also, apparently, the Tibetan Buddhists whom Lichter and Epstein have studied) are much more prone to discuss karma abstractly—indeed, it is difficult to find Thai or other Buddhists who will discuss karma without referring to the "law of karma" (*karmaniyama*; Thai *kot haeng kam*). Abstract ideas lend themselves much better than do concrete ideas to what Weber called "rationalization," and it is clear, I believe, that Buddhism—even (or perhaps especially) at the popular level—is a more rationalized religion than is Hinduism. The reasons for this will become clearer later in this essay.

One suggestion regarding the class of abstractions to which karmic ideas belong was made by Max Weber in his study *The Religion of India*. In Weber's words:

> Hinduism is unusually tolerant of doctrine (*mata*) while placing greatest emphasis on ritual duties (*dharma*). Nevertheless, Hinduism has certain dogmas... if by dogma one means credal truths whose denial is considered heretical and places the group if not the individual outside the Hindu community. (1958:117–118)

He then goes on to specify the dogmas of Hinduism: "the *samsara* belief in the transmigration of souls and the related *karman* doctrine of compensation" (Weber 1958:118). There is clearly some distortion in employing the concept of dogma with its Christian connotations to interpret Hindu ideas, although the problems do not appear so great insofar as Buddhism, or at least Theravāda Buddhism, is concerned (cf. Gombrich 1971:4–8; 40–56).[1] If, however, we take dogma to mean the fundamental premises or axioms of a system of meaning that are authoritatively asserted and do not insist that these premises or axioms be consciously embraced or even recognized, then I believe that something can be gained by considering karmic ideas as dogmas.

Religious dogmas provide those who accept them with authoritative truths with which to confront what Weber called problems of meaning and what are talked about by others as problems of suffering, evil, and intellectual despair. The existential situations in which people turn to religious ideas, as distinct from other kinds of ideas, are those in which they become conscious of afflictions that cannot be cured by any known means, of the power of some humans to interfere arbitrarily or illegitimately in their lives such that their happiness is seriously impaired, or of fundamental contradictions between principles of social life that are susceptible to no logical resolution.[2] In the face of those experiences that appear to open up an endless chasm into which all meaning disappears, humans can turn to religious dogmas and find in them assertions that provide a bedrock of ultimate meaning upon which all other meaning rests.

It is when faced with the ultimate conditions of existence that peoples of South and Southeast Asia are most likely to find karmic ideas meaningful. As Babb has noted for Hindus below: "Whatever else the doctrine of karma might be, it is a theory of causation that supplies reasons for human fortune, good or bad, and that at least in theory it can provide convincing explanations for human misfortune." Lichter and Epstein observe that for Tibetan Buddhists karma begins to provide meaning "where the exigencies, the little joys and sorrows, of simply living leave off." And I report that "among practicing Theravāda Buddhists, karma is invoked as an explanation of conditions that have emerged in one's lifetime only on rare occasions... conditions that must be accepted because there is nothing one can do about them." Wendy O'Flaherty in her study "Karma and Rebirth in

[1] Lawrence A. Babb (private communication) has queried my interpretation of karmic ideas as dogma, suggesting that there is a Christian connotation to the concept that is not applicable to Hindu ideas. It is my intent to use the concept in a more universalistic sense, and I have attempted to formulate it to match my intent. Lehman also offered a critique of my discussion of karma as dogma in an earlier version of this essay; I am indebted to him for some of the language I have used in the present formulation.

[2] I have been led in the foregoing by Geertz's (1973:98–108) discussion of problems of meaning.

the Vedas and Purāṇas" has suggested that "the sadness of death and the inability to accept it as final" constitute "sentiments which must lie very near the heart of the spirit that created the karma doctrine" (O'Flaherty 1980c:15).

Religious dogmas, including karmic dogmas, are not merely asserted; they are clothed "with such an aura of factuality" that the moods and motivations that they engender "seem uniquely realistic" (Geertz 1973:90). Dogmas are accepted on *faith*, and such faith is engendered because one is willing to commit oneself unequivocally to some religious authority. The legitimacy of this authority must, if it is to be accepted, be known in other than simply a rational sense because faith always involves going beyond the confines of any system of rationalization for the premises of that system.

The authority for karmic dogmas that immediately suggests itself is that of the sacred texts of Hinduism and Buddhism. While such texts often do provide the form wherein karmic ideas are expressed, as the essays herein attest, these ideas are accepted as ultimate truths only when the "word" has been linked with powerful emotional experiences. The authority from which springs faith in dogmas is always, for popular religions at least, an experienced authority. Typically, for most South and Southeast Asians—as for most people, whether they adhere to religious traditions lacking sacred texts or to historic religions with such texts—submission to the authority of the word occurs as a consequence of participation in what Turner has called the ritual process (1969; see also Turner 1967, 1975, 1978). In rituals, traditional interpretations of karmic ideas, encoded in symbols or expounded upon in the sermons of ritual specialists, are linked to the emotionally disturbing experiences attendant upon meteorological uncertainties, familial crises, illness, and death. Important as the authority of tradition manifest in ritual is, there are alternatives whereby the truth of karmic dogmas may be known. Hindus and Buddhists have long had before them the model of seeking religious truth through the conscious undertaking of a spiritual discipline that ends in mystical experience. In practice, few Buddhists or Hindus choose to subject themselves to such a discipline, and the authority of the directly experienced truth that is mystical insight has had but a peripheral place within the popular traditions of South and Southeast Asia.[3] Related to the authority of mystical experience following the

[3]This said, it would still be of value if attention were to be given to the interpretation of karmic ideas held by Hindu *saṃnyāsins* and Buddhist ascetic monks.

practice of spiritual discipline is the authority that attaches to those who claim to have insights into fundamental truths that are not dependent upon traditional ritual-based interpretations and demonstrate the power of their insights through enhanced efficacy of action within the world. The interpretations of karmic dogmas by Hindu and Buddhist charismatics, if they may be so termed, have not been given attention in any of the essays in this volume, although they have figured in my analyses in other contexts of charismatic authority in Theravāda Buddhist societies (Keyes 1977, 1978, 1981).

Although the authority with which karmic ideas are asserted may rest in the actions of ritual specialists or, more rarely, in the mystical experiences of world-renouncers or in the actions and pronouncements of Hindu and Buddhist charismatics, the form that these ideas are given still typically derives from a textual source. Ideas of karma may have their origins, as Obeyesekere (1980) has suggested, in the localized religions of preliterate peoples in South Asia.[4] However this may be, they were given more universal cast in an Indian literature generated at least six centuries before the Christian era by religious founders and their followers. With literacy, the drive toward what Weber termed "rationalization" was given a marked impetus in the Indian traditions, for these ideas, as well as other cultural meanings, could be detached from their pragmatic contexts to be scrutinized and reflected upon with reference to other meanings. Insofar as karmic ideas were subjected to hermeneutical processes by Indian (or other South and Southeast Asian) theologians, they tended to be rationalized with reference to standards of logical consistency comparable to those used in the construction of scientific theories; that is, like scientific theories they serve to explain "the diversity and complexity of observed phenomena as the product of an underlying unity, simplicity, and regularity" (Horton 1979:250–251). Again, like scientific theories, the karmic ideas of theology have both explanatory and predictive aspects in that they make intelligible certain types of experiences (even if these are not structured experiments) and also serve to orient people toward certain courses of action because they believe themselves capable of predicting the outcome of these courses.[5]

The comparison between karmic theories and scientific theories

[4] On this point, see also O'Flaherty's comments (1980b:xi–xviii).

[5] The explanatory and predictive aspects of theories correspond to Geertz's distinction (1973:93–94, 124) between "model of" and "model for" aspects of meaning in general.

cannot be pushed too far, however.[6] The efforts of the theologians who developed karmic theories were not subjected to "any guiding body of explicit acceptance/rejection criteria" (Horton 1979:251). Indeed, it is not possible that such criteria might be employed, because karmic theories—like all religious dogmas—are not conjectural propositions about some particular domain of experience, but are taken as given truths about the ultimate conditions of human existence. The claims—sometimes explicit, but usually implicit—made by those who developed theories of karma were that these theories applied not to a narrow range of experience but to the totality of experience.

The hermeneutical process to which karmic ideas were subjected by theologians was seen by Weber as resulting in the production of a highly rationalized and ethicized doctrine: "*Karma* doctrine transformed the world into a strictly rational, ethically-determined cosmos; it represents the most consistent theodicy ever produced by history" (Weber 1958:121). By theodicy, Weber here means a resolution to "the incongruity between destiny and merit" (Weber 1946:275),[7] that is, a resolution to the problem of unequal suffering. Weber, we now know, glossed over (in part because of literature available to him) significant differences between several varying theories of karma developed in the classical Indian traditions. Weber also tended to misrepresent the place of karmic ideas in the religion of the general populace, either by presuming that popular ideas of karma were the same as those of the ideal type that he had constructed, or else by assuming that actual practices that did not accord with the ideas in the typification reflected lapses into magic. It is now apparent, as can be seen from a perusal of recent studies made of karmic theories in the classical traditions of India (O'Flaherty 1980a), that the degree to which karmic ideas have been rationalized and ethicized with reference to other religious ideas in the hermeneutic traditions of South and Southeast Asia is open to question. It is also problematic as to how, if at all, rationalized and ethicized ideas of karmic dogmas from one or another of the hermeneutic traditions have been incorporated into the popular religions of the region. As the essays in this volume demonstrate, karmic ideas that can be said to be refractions of theological theories are to be found in some South and Southeast Asian religions

[6] For further consideration of this comparison, see O'Flaherty (1980b:xxi).

[7] For a discussion of Weber's different usages of the concept of theodicy, see Gananath Obeyesekere's (1968) essay, "Theodicy, Sin and Salvation in a Sociology of Buddhism."

and not in others (Bali being an example of the latter case); and even when found, these refractions are often articulated with religious meanings that have no place in the karmic theories of the hermeneuticians. The question of how popular understanding of religious dogmas relates to theological interpretations is clearly central to the concerns of this volume.

Texts and Popular Religion

The distinction that I have made between theology and popular religion, between the hermeneutic process and the ritual process, would appear to correspond, at least on first blush, with the Redfieldian distinction between "great tradition" and "little tradition." Given the apparent similarity, it is of value to review briefly the Redfieldian model and the critiques that have been made of it. In *Peasant Society and Culture*, Redfield wrote:

> In a civilization there is a great tradition of the reflective few, and there is a little tradition of the largely unreflective many. The great tradition is cultivated in schools or temples; the little tradition works itself out and keeps itself going in the lives of the unlettered in their village communities. The tradition of the philosopher, theologian, and literary man is a tradition consciously cultivated and handed down; that of the little people is for the most part taken for granted and not submitted to much scrutiny or considered refinement and improvement. (1956:70)

Redfield's own thinking was stimulated, in part, by a study by M. N. Srinivas (1952), *Religion and Society among the Coorgs of South India* (cf. Redfield 1956:92–93). Srinivas argued that the Coorgs, a people previously marginal to the literary culture of India, had consciously attempted to upgrade their social status by adopting practices or reinterpreting existing practices with reference to various Sanskritic texts, thereby leading Srinivas to call the process "Sanskritization." To Redfield, this process was evidence of social change brought about by the penetration of the high tradition into village life: "So far does the great tradition reach and so much does it yet do in India to change the cultures of depressed or marginal peoples" (1956:93).

Marriott, another student of village life in India, argued that there is constant interchange between little and great traditions. On the one hand, he argued, "an indigenous civilization is one whose great tradition originates by a 'universalization,' or a carrying-forward of materials which are already present in the little traditions which encompass it" (1955:202). On the other hand, once a civilization exists, it may not only serve to provide a literary tradition that can be used to provide universal standards for local practices, such as Srinivas found, it may also provide elements that are reinterpreted and given a specifically local interpretation. Marriott called this process "parochialization. . . a process of localization, of limitation upon the scope of intelligibility, of deprivation of literary form, of reduction to less systematic and less reflective dimensions. The process of parochialization constitutes the characteristic creative work of little communities within India's indigenous civilization" (1955:205–206).

Redfield, Srinivas, and Marriott all posit a disjunction between the little tradition and the great tradition within a single civilization—a civilization defined with reference to its religious aspect. They also argue that there is a dynamic relationship between little and great traditions. The first aspect of their formulation has been strongly criticized, whereas the second has essentially been ignored by the critics. Perhaps the most radical critique of the little tradition/great tradition model has been offered by two anthropologists who attempted to create a new sociology of India encompassing the study both of texts and of popular religion. In a series of articles, Louis Dumont and David Pocock argued that there is an underlying unity in the textual and popular traditions. For them, "'Sanskritization' does not consist in the imposition of a different system upon an old one, but in the acceptance of a more distinguished or prestigious way of saying the same thing" (Dumont and Pocock 1959:45; also see Dumont and Pocock 1957, and Dumont 1960 and 1970). Their approach leads, in the end, to a fundamentally ahistorical interpretation of Indian civilization. This ahistoricity notwithstanding, Dumont and Pocock have clearly demonstrated in their work that for the civilization of India, if not for other civilizations, it is not possible to draw a sharp distinction, even for analytical purposes, between the tradition based upon interpretations of texts and the popular tradition based upon ritual action of people living in small communities.

Tambiah has offered a somewhat different critique of the two-traditions model in a study carried out on the popular Buddhist tradition found in a village in northeastern Thailand. Tambiah argues:

> I submit that the idea of two levels [of tradition] is an invention of the anthropologist dictated not so much by the reality he studies as by his professional perspective. By definition an anthropologist goes into the field to study live action, and for the observations made over a short period of time

> he tries to derive a systemic pattern or order.... Because he is already committed to an anthropological level of reality and social facts, the anthropologist who works in complex "historical" societies is likely to view the literary culture of that society as constituting another "level" or order equivalent to the level of "live action" he has managed to record. (1970:371)

Tambiah goes on to argue that one should see ritual and textual traditions not as belonging to different levels of reality but as coexisting and interdependent within a single tradition. This juxtaposition of ritual and textual sources of authority is effected by the local ritual specialist, the person who is at once educated through study of selected texts and their theological interpretation and, at the same time, responsible for the performance of rituals. As Tambiah says:

> It seems to me that if anthropologists in India had been oriented to the collection and recording of ritual texts and the literature used by rural specialists, they might have formulated the question [regarding the relationship between little and great traditions] differently. (1970: 372)

If we reformulate what Tambiah has said with reference to the source of religious dogma, we can say that the authority for particular dogmas within local communities of South and Southeast Asia—indeed, of any civilization—may derive from texts, but only insofar as these texts have been brought to life in the ritual process and other modes wherein meaning is socially communicated.

A number of the authors in this book comment on how the "word" of texts is brought to life in the social worlds in which South and Southeast Asians live. For example, Lichter and Epstein report that the "subtleties and nuances of the Tibetan world view" as found in texts are also expressed in "rituals, conversations, quarrels, complaints, jokes, and so on." Wadley points to the use of colloquial texts, printed as pamphlets, by those who perform the life-transforming *vrat* rituals in rural northern India. I also discuss the use of ritual texts in my study of popular Theravādin ideas of merit-transference, and I have made a general methodological point with reference to my findings, concluding that "there often exists a dialectical interconnection between texts and rituals in traditional societies that is comparable to the dialectical interrelationship between oral myth and ritual in preliterate societies."[8]

[8] My argument has been developed, in part, with reference to the seminal discussion by Tambiah (1968) on the use of literacy in traditional rural northeastern Thailand.

For most of the peoples discussed in this book, ideas of karma have been established as dogmas (in the sense specified above) and accepted on faith as ultimate truths as the consequence of linking the "word" of texts with experience of communitas in the ritual process. The existence of texts containing ideas of karma within a culture is not sufficient, however, in and of itself to establish the authority of the "word," as Boon has shown so well in his study of Bali. Although Balinese culture is linked with the "specialized institutions of writing, reading. . ., and text-based performances," and although karmic ideas can be found in some of the texts that are utilized by Balinese literati, these ideas have not been fitted into the total religious field of meaning that is Balinese religion. On the contrary, "like tribal cultures, symbolic totality in Bali obtains from a fertility of variant extremes." The existence of a textual tradition within Balinese culture has created a tension that appears to impel some current reformist tendencies; yet these tendencies notwithstanding, the dogmas established through the ritual process in Bali remain predicated upon a primitive polarity, albeit clothed in Indian forms (thus leading Boon to label Balinese religion as "tantric" rather than "tribal"), rather than upon ethicized ideas of karma.[9]

The Balinese case provides an excellent example of a religion which in many of its outward forms looks like "Hinduism" but which in the dogmas that underlie these forms is clearly radically different from other popular religions that bear the Hindu label. The Balinese case underscores a methodological point for those who would study popular religions that are linked with a tradition in which there are sacred texts. It is always problematic whether dogmas contained in texts are accepted as authoritative by any particular community of people. And if they are so accepted, there is the problem of how they have been vested with authority.

The peoples of South and Southeast Asia, as is attested to in the essays in this volume, demonstrate a marked preference for textual versions of karmic ideas that come clothed in the language of myth. One recalls, in this connection, the distinction that Lévi-Strauss has made between mythical (or magical) thinking and scientific (analytical) thinking (Lévi-Strauss 1966, esp. chap. 1). The concrete language of mythical thought—even when derived from texts that have come

[9] See, in this regard, not only Boon's essay herein, but also his book *The Anthropological Romance of Bali, 1597–1972* (1977). Geertz in his essay "'Internal Conversion' in Contemporary Bali" (1973, chap. 7), would appear to be more optimistic about reformist efforts in Bali than is Boon.

to a community from some distant place—gives meaning an immediacy that is not true of cold analytical abstractions. The very concreteness of mythical language, however, leads to the structuring of meaning in ways quite different from that found in scientific—or theological—discourse: "Mythical thought for its part is imprisoned in the events and experiences which it never tires of ordering and reordering in its search to find them a meaning" (Lévi-Strauss 1966:22).

The rich mythical language utilized by all the South and Southeast Asians discussed in this volume as a means to grasp fundamental religious truths is not characteristic of popular religion, in contrast to the religion found in texts written by literati. On the contrary, many textual sources provide the mythical language for the rituals, dramas, and other modes of expression of religious ideas in the rural communities of the area.[10] Although the fact cannot be denied that texts that hold popular appeal are often those that have been composed–or, more likely, simply recorded—by literate *bricoleurs* (to use Lévi-Strauss's image of the mythmaker), it is also important to note that more abstract and analytical versions of karmic theories developed by theologians are also known in at least some rural communities in South and Southeast Asia. Hiebert found "village philosophers" in the south Indian village of Konduru who carried out debates about "the philosophical issues common to the Hindu great tradition." These village philosophers, he notes, drew upon "Upanishadic and bhakti texts" for the grist for their debates.

The village philosophers of the Hindu tradition find their counterparts in the Buddhist tradition primarily in the guise of local monks (and, in Southeast Asia at least, ex-monks). Boon has pointed to the revolutionary significance of the introduction of monasticism:

> If one assumes [he writes in his essay below] with believers that religious merit is vital to society's perpetuation as well as to ultimate release, then monasticism achieves what Durkheim called "organic solidarity" with an incremental level of differentiation: reciprocity between two specialist sectors or categories, one producing merit and release, the other producing successors and subsistence. Neither lay nor monk alone can reproduce the socioreligious totality.

[10] Wendy O'Flaherty in a number of studies (1973, 1976, 1980d) has given particular attention to the mythical formulations of religious ideas in Hindu texts. Her approach provides a useful corrective to the image of texts in the Hindu tradition as consisting primarily of philosophical treatises. Too often anthropologists have accepted such an image, in part led by the students of textual sources in historic religions who tend to dismiss as less valuable those texts that are constructed in mythical rather than philosophical modes.

And, he continues: "monasticism totalizes cosmic order through the organizing power of specialized writing, chanting, liturgical canons." With fully developed monasticism, such as one finds in the Buddhist traditions of both Theravāda and Tibet, the abstract theories of karma worked out by theologians acquire a significance for communities that support the monastics which is lacking in traditions in which monasticism is undeveloped or lacking. The monastic, by his rejection of a sexual and materially productive role, is inclined to adopt a critical stance toward the world. In the Buddhist traditions, this stance has been associated with the responsibility to communicate the *dharma* (Pāli *dhamma*), the teachings of the Buddha, as interpreted by theologians. While the communities in which Buddhism is a practical religion still draw heavily on mythical language, this language has been constrained by more abstract understandings of Buddhist theology. Monasticism adds a new dimension of authority to the texts from which religious meanings are drawn. This authority appears to attach much less to the village philosophers in India and the religious literati of Bali, even if Brahmin by caste. Indeed, in Bali, the role of religious literati appears confined to that of being a manipulator of ritual forms rather than an interpreter of dogmatic truth.

There is another difference between the popular Hindu and the popular Buddhist tradition that needs to be stressed in this connection as well. Whereas Buddhist hermeneutics—at least within Tibetan or Theravādin traditions—appear to have generated texts that are remarkably consistent through time and space in their interpretation of fundamental dogmas, Hindu texts display less consistency. The reason for this clearly lies in the fact that Hinduism cannot be traced to a single founder and an authoritative canon. There is a degree of eclecticism in the dogmatic formulations of popular Hinduism that reflects an eclecticism of formulations in the Hindu theological literature. In short, there is no single great tradition expressed in reflections on the ultimate conditions of existence in Hinduism in a way that it could plausibly be said that there is in Buddhism. It is not surprising, thus, that popular Buddhist ideas of karma appear to be more rationalized than do popular Hindu ideas.

Karmic Ideas in Context

The construal of karmic ideas in popular religion depends not only on the nature of the texts within which these ideas are expressed, but also on the larger field of practical meanings within which they are accorded a place. Each of the essays in this volume addresses, to some extent, the contextualization of karmic ideas. In the extreme instance, as Boon demonstrates for Bali, some popular religions for which sources of karmic ideas are available offer no place whatsoever within their system of meanings for these ideas. The Balinese case is not alone in this regard; many peoples living on the peripheries of South and Southeast Asian civilizations have long had access to sources of ideas of karma and yet have not incorporated these ideas into their religious worldviews. Other peoples—like the Coorgs described by Srinivas—have begun to orient themselves toward such sources and have adopted some elements of karmic theory. While this volume does not include any study of religions in which karmic ideas are in the process of being adopted, some insight into such a process can be obtained from Boon's discussion of the reformist efforts (unsuccessful to date) in Bali.

All other essays herein deal with religions in which karmic ideas, such as they are, have been hallowed by tradition. That is, in the various communities in which the authors have carried out field work, some version of karmic ideas has been accepted as dogma. This is not to say that there is no tension between these karmic ideas and other meanings; that there is, is evident in several of the essays. Before we consider these tensions, it is necessary to draw some fundamental comparisons between the different karmic ideas found in the popular traditions of South and Southeast Asia.

The dogma of karma, in whatever form it is found, "posits," as Babb observes, "a distinctive connection between moral responsibility and destiny." That is to say, popular doctrines of karma, like their theological counterparts, serve to explain certain dimensions of one's present existential circumstances in terms of a predetermined destiny *and also* serve to define the nature of the responsibility that one should assume for one's actions in order to attain positive (including post-death) ends. The popular traditions in South and Southeast Asia differ in the relative stress they place on these two aspects of karmic doctrine.

What Lichter and Epstein report for Tibetan Buddhists applies equally well to Theravādins: "Tibetans seem to speculate more about karmic prospects than they do about retrospects." In my essay, I discuss the emphasis that Theravādins give to the actions that are believed to enhance one's karmic prospects, that is, to actions that produce "merit." In contrast to the Buddhists, all Hindus discussed in this book (save those of the Balinese stripe) appear much more concerned with the constraints placed on their freedom of action determined by fate and karma. The incident described by S. Daniel in which Tamil villagers debated whether thieves were morally responsible for their actions or were victims of their fate could not, I suspect, be replicated in any Buddhist community. In all popular traditions of Buddhism, one assumes that one is responsible for one's actions unless there is convincing evidence that some exogenous power (that may be karma or may be some less ultimate agent) has intruded into one's life. In popular Hinduism, on the other hand, one has to begin by determining the constraints of fate (what E.V. Daniel calls the *kuṇam* complex) before one can decide what action (Daniel's *karmam* complex) is appropriate.[11]

Despite the stress that Buddhists place upon their ability to take moral responsibility for their actions, they still find themselves in certain circumstances faced with misfortunes that they cannot explain as being the direct consequences of their actions. In such circumstances, Buddhists, like their Hindu counterparts in India, may invoke karmic destiny as an explanation for why misfortune has befallen them. In rationalized theories of karma such as those found in both Hindu and Buddhist theological treatises, to invoke karmic destiny as an explanation for the vicissitudes for which one can not find the cause in one's moral actions in the present lifetime does not, however, eliminate moral responsibility as a cause. Rather, one's

[11] In connection with the discussion here regarding the relationship between karmic determination and moral responsibility, Lehman (personal communication) writes as follows:

> [I]f sentient beings can make moral choices, it follows that they can be taught and persuaded to do or not do something "wrong." In turn, then, if a being [human, "spirit," whatever] injures me, it is all very well for me to claim that my *kamma* is responsible for my injury and suffering [in a sense "I" am responsible], and yet, if I take this unambiguously, I eliminate moral choice even for myself, since I eliminate it for sentient beings generally, as agents of wicked action towards others. In fact, we are canonically in Buddhism under some obligation to try to persuade other sentient beings to refrain from doing harm, and they are responsible for harm they do others. This is a genuine doctrinal paradox, the paradox of agency, one that Spiro and others miss totally. In addition, and here is where the Hindus seem to grasp the problem, I believe, if what happens to me in this life is the *vipāka* ["fruit"] of my acts in earlier lives, then how am I morally responsible for that if, indeed, my previous life course was morally determined by the one before that and so on, recursively? This does not go unrecognized even in Theravāda Buddhism. For example, a *preta* (*peta*) ["spirit"] is often held to be so inherently bad that it cannot be dissuaded from evil; all we can do is share merit with it so that it eventually escapes *petaloka* ["the realm of spirits"]. Here, notice, the acts of a sentient being are fully determined by past *kamma*, indeed!

karmic legacy is seen as the consequence of moral actions in a previous existence. In practice, karmic explanation of present misfortunes carries, both for Buddhists and for Hindus, few if any connotations of personal responsibility.

No practicing Buddhists, whether Tibetan or Theravādin, have been reported as showing interest in whether it was some previous "self" who performed the actions whose consequences are now being felt; rather the karma that may be invoked to explain suffering or other misfortunes is construed as an impersonal force—the law of karma—over which one has no control.[12] For practicing Hindus, it is widely believed (as can be seen from the essays in this volume as well as from other sources) that "god" (Bhagvān, Kaṭavuḷ, Śiva, and so on) has "written" one's karmic destiny on one's forehead at birth. While Hindus—both in theological discussions (see, in this connection, several of the essays in O'Flaherty 1980a) and in practice (as reported by S. Daniel, Beck, and Wadley in their essays)—believe that under certain circumstances one's karmic destiny can be altered, or at least channeled along more positive lines, there still remain those consequences of karma that are absolute and final. Hindus do not believe that God is responsible for these consequences, for He composed each person's "headwriting" blindly. Thus, whether the karma that is identified as the *causa finalis* of unchangeable human suffering is construed, as by Buddhists, as an impersonal "Law" or, as by Hindus, as the "headwriting" of God, there is no agent to whom responsibility for one's irrevocable karmic destiny can be traced. Karma in the popular traditions of Buddhism and Hinduism cannot be said, as Weber claimed, to be a logical solution to theodicy, since it points to an ultimate force that cannot be comprehended in logical terms.

It is in this sense that we can now consider the Tibetan concept of *la-yogs*, "a karma-like conception of causation" but without "karma's justice and optimism." In fact, there is no moral justice in karmic destiny, even as understood by Tibetans. Rather, we can see that when Tibetans (like other Buddhists and Hindus) invoke karmic destiny as an ultimate explanation for suffering, they are pointing to a force that lies beyond human ability to control or manipulate. What then is *la-yogs*? After exploring the significance of this concept, and its relation-

[12] I owe this conclusion to discussions that Larry Epstein and I have carried out regarding the similarities and differences between Theravādin and Tibetan popular Buddhism based on our knowledge of the ethnographic literature for the two traditions.

ship to karmic ideas, Lichter and Epstein conclude that *la-yogs* "resembles nothing so much as the Suffering of Change, or Conditioned Suffering." In other words, to assert that some misfortune is *la-yogs* is really to point to the underlying Buddhist dogma that all is suffering (*duḥkha*). It is not always necessary in the Buddhist tradition—and perhaps in the Hindu tradition, as E.V. Daniel argues in his conclusion regarding the implicit presence of a *la-yogs* concept in that tradition—to explain suffering when one acknowledges that ultimately all existence is suffering. When an explanation is called for, Tibetans, like other Buddhists and Hindus, do draw upon available karmic notions.

When practicing Buddhists and Hindus experience suffering for which they believe that they were not themselves responsible, they may not immediately invoke karmic destiny as an explanation of their circumstances. Rather, they may point to a variety of other potential causes of their suffering, such as the acts of spirits or gods, the unsettledness of one's vital essence, the conjunction of cosmic influences as manifest in astrological codes, the aggressive actions of others expressed directly or through such indirect means as witchcraft and sorcery, and, for those exposed to modern scientific knowledge, viruses, infections, and other natural forces.

When a Hindu or a Buddhist chooses to explain his or her misfortunes in terms of one of these non-karmic theories of causation—particularly if the theory implies the belief in a supernatural power—does he or she compromise his or her belief in karmic destiny? M. E. Spiro, writing of beliefs among Burmese Buddhists in the supernatural beings known as *nats*, argues that such compromise does occur: "To attribute . . . vicissitudes to the *nats* and to believe that their propitiation (or lack of propitiation) can in any manner influence one's life-fate, is to implicitly deny the omnipotence of karma, a doctrine which constitutes the very core of Buddhist teaching" (1978:254). Such a conclusion is misleading, although not entirely wrong.

Theories of karmic destiny and other theories that serve to explain misfortunes that are not the consequences of one's own actions belong, for most practicing Buddhists, as for practicing Hindus (see, in this connection, Hiebert's essay), to two different levels of explanation. In one sense, it can be said that any human, simply by virtue of being human, has been preordained by karma to be subject to the slings and arrows of many different kinds of outrageous fortune. Concomitantly, one has been given, by virtue of one's karmic destiny, the ability to identify these varieties of forces and the concomitant knowledge of how to attempt to alleviate or protect oneself against the sufferings they bring. If one does not act in accordance with this ability and knowledge, one will most certainly suffer. Yet, one's actions may be of no avail. A Tamil may undertake the appropriate *pūjās* to gods believed powerful enough to reverse one's decline in material fortunes, and yet continue to fall into greater poverty. In northern India, one may undertake a *vrat*, a vow, probably in association with a *pūjā*, as Wadley observes, "to influence some deity to come to one's aid" by providing "some kind of boon," and yet the boon never materializes. Almost anywhere in South or Southeast Asia (as Pugh has described it for northern India), one may have an astrologer determine how one is to orient oneself with reference to cosmic influences in order to escape the consequences of ill fate, and yet those consequences may persist. A Tibetan may perform the proper rituals to safeguard one's *bla*, "a sort of personal life force," and yet one may die. A woman in Buddhist Burma or Thailand may make offerings to local deities or make a vow at a Buddhist shrine in order to be infused with fertility, and yet she may remain infertile. In many areas, one woman may employ counter-magic against another woman who is attempting by means of witchcraft to woo away the first woman's husband, and yet he leaves her. It is precisely in such circumstances, when one's efforts fail to rectify misfortunes presumably caused by forces that are part of ordinary mundane existence (and it should be noted that, for most South and Southeast Asians, "spirits" are as much part of this existence as "germs" are), that one turns to an explanation in terms of an ultimate, absolute, irrevocable force, a force that is conceived of as karmic destiny.

Not all South and Southeast Asian Hindus and Buddhists maintain a clear distinction between ultimate explanation in terms of karmic destiny and efficient explanations in terms of other mundane forces; it is for this reason that there is some truth in Spiro's conclusion regarding the compromised character of karmic ideas in popular religion. Some concepts—such as the Tamil notions of *viti*, *yōkam*, and *kuṇam*, as E. V. Daniel shows—may denote karmic destiny in some circumstances while implicating sub-karmic forces in others. I found a similar ambiguity surrounding the northern Thai concept of *chātā*, a concept that I have translated as "fate" and discussed in another context (Keyes 1975). Many Hindus, as has already been noted, believe that it is possible to alter one's karmic destiny; insofar as they believe themselves successful in their efforts to effect such changes, then karmic destiny becomes something less than an ultimate force. In the "pragmatic relativism," to use S. Daniel's term, of practicing Hindus and Buddhists, ideas that have explanatory and predictive value are not always used with the logical consistency of theology.

While the practical idea of karmic destiny is not related to other ideas of causation in a totally consistent manner, and while this idea does not constitute a logical solution to theodicy—to the problem of unjust suffering—as Weber claimed it did, it remains one of the dogmatic foundations of popular Buddhism and popular Hinduism in all cases discussed in this book save that of Bali. To invoke karma when one is confronted with suffering about which one can do nothing but suffer, with injustice which one can do nothing to rectify, or with existential paradoxes that yield to no logical solution is to assert that there is an ultimate order within which these experiences are meaningful. People may not accept—and most do not—an "heroic" version of karma wherein they are in some sense personally responsible for the karmic consequences they experience; but they do, nonetheless, posit that somehow these consequences are morally justified.

To South and Southeast Asian Hindus and Buddhists, karmic theory defines not only a moral universe within which problems of ultimate meaning can be confronted, but also a mode of action whereby it becomes possible to augment the positive moral element of karma that adheres to one. This moral element of karma has a tangible quality. For Tamils, as S. Daniel reports, karma "in addition to being a kind or kinds of particular substance, is contained in . . . and may only be transmitted by bodily substances." Wendy O'Flaherty has noted that such ideas point to an implicit "hydraulic analogy" in karmic theory, "the reification of moral qualities into a transferable substance" (O'Flaherty 1980c:14). Among practicing Buddhists, this analogy is not carried to the same extremes that it is in Hinduism; nonetheless, Buddhists also think of positive karma—that is, "merit"—as having a tangible character, and in my essay below I have suggested, following Gombrich, that an analogy with currency might be appropriate in talking of merit in the Buddhist sense. On reflection, I think that electricity might be a better analogy, and it is one that I have heard educated Buddhists use. While acknowledging the differences between Hindus and Buddhists in the ways in which they transform the moral element of karma into a tangible quality, I must stress the point that both Hindus and Buddhists derive from their various versions of karmic theory, not an abstract set of ideas to use in orienting themselves in their actions, but assumptions about concrete qualities that adhere to persons.

Among practicing Buddhists much time is given over to actions that are believed to be productive of additional amounts of positive karma; among practicing Hindus such activities are much less stressed, although they are not unknown, owing to the importance in Hinduism of caste *dharma*. This difference reflects the fundamental distinction between popular Buddhist and popular Hindu theories of karma, namely, that among Buddhists much greater emphasis is laid upon the moral responsibilities that one assumes for one's actions than upon the constraints of karmic destiny, whereas among Hindus the emphasis is reversed.

Whether karmic qualities are derived from one's karmic legacy or from merit-making—to use a translation of the Thai idea (*tham bun*) of merit accumulation—Hindus and Buddhists both believe that karmic qualities can be transferred from one person to another. As O'Flaherty has pointed out, drawing upon Marriott's (1970) work, karmic transfers among Hindus are "particularly likely to arise in relation to transactions involving food and sex, the two bases of Hindu social activity and caste interactions" (O'Flaherty 1980c:29). Among Buddhists as I have discussed at some length in my essay, karmic transfers do not require that any substance actually be exchanged. The merit that one receives from the act of offering alms to monks may be represented in nothing more than the words of a chant, and the merit that a son transfers to his parents through his act of becoming a member of the monkhood passes without being associated with a visible vehicle. Among Buddhists there seems to be little concern about the transfer of negative karma, whereas among Hindus such transfers are, apparently, more common and are linked with the idea of pollution (see, in this connection, O'Flaherty 1980c:28ff.).

The ideas of karmic transference, in whatever form these ideas have been couched, and those of caste *dharma* within the Hindu tradition have implications that are clearly counter to those of a fully ethicized karmic theory predicated upon the assumption that each person is solely responsible for his or her own actions and their consequences. The reason for this lies in the point which I also take up in my essay that a fully ethicized theory of karma is ill suited to the practical exigencies of those who have committed themselves to the social imperative of living within a social order. In the popular Hindu tradition, karmic theory has been accommodated to the social imperative by playing down the moral-responsibility dimension of karmic theory and stressing that one is bound by karmic destiny and concomitant caste *dharma*. Ideas of karmic transference are also known, but are far less developed than they are in popular Buddhism. In popular Buddhism, moral responsibility is stressed far more than in popular Hinduism, but the tendency toward greater ethicization is checked by elaborate ideas regarding merit-transference.

In this review of karmic ideas in context, I have identified a number of significant departures from a fully rationalized and ethicized theory of karma. While these departures take different forms in popular Hinduism and popular Buddhism, there is an underlying structural similarity to a number of them. First, while the idea of karmic destiny does implicate a moral order within which problems of meaning can be confronted, this idea has not been formulated in popular Hinduism or popular Buddhism with reference to an idea that one has, in some sense, personal moral responsibility for one's destiny. Second, ideas regarding karmic destiny have not been articulated in a fully consistent and logical way with reference to other ideas regarding the causes of misfortunes. Finally, the idea of moral responsibility for one's present actions has been adapted to other notions deriving from what I call the social imperative, that is, the imperative to commit oneself to the demands of a social order. These deviations from a fully rationalized and ethicized version of karma may reflect, to a certain extent, an inadequate acquaintance of rural peoples with the theological subtleties of karmic theory. And, as the case of Bali demonstrates, theological versions of karmic theories contained in available texts need not be accepted as the basis for dogmatic formulations in a popular tradition. Yet, even when one allows for theological unsophistication on the part of practicing Hindus and Buddhists, there remains, I maintain, a more fundamental reason for the departure in popular ideas of karma from theories that have been made logically consistent and from which unequivocal ethical orientations have been derived.

I maintain that *any* karmic theory that is put into practice—that is, one that is articulated with actual social experience—will manifest structurally similar deviations, albeit expressed in different particulars, as have been found in the cases reviewed here. In the first instance, unless one is omniscient and can know the details of one's past existences, there is no practical way whereby karmic destiny could in any meaningful way be linked to one's personal actions or to actions of some previous "self." It is not simply that there is a "psychological uncertainty" about one's previous karma, as Obeyesekere (1968:21) has observed, but there is also cognitive uncertainty; one cannot know why one has the karmic destiny that one has come to realize, through experience, that one has. Moreover, as F. K. Lehman (personal communication) reminds us, even if one could know the past with perfect certainty, one could still do nothing about it. However one may trace one's present circumstances to the past, one still must accept that past as a given. Second, there is rarely an affliction that lends itself to unequivocal explanation in karmic terms. While karmic destiny may provide a *causa finalis*, the *causa efficiens* is sought in other theories about the natural and supernatural forces that are believed to impinge upon humans. Moreover, relationships of different theories of causality are judged by those interested in their practical applications, not with reference to logical consistency but with reference to experienced effectiveness. Take the example of the Tamils discussed in S. Daniel's paper. Karmic dogma is fundamental to the worldview of the Tamils with whom she worked; but this dogma is not articulated with their other beliefs in a fully consistent way. The same individual may oscillate among different theories, searching for the one that is most satisfactory for her or him; and, within the same community, people may explain the same event with reference to different causal theories as befits their own involvement in the event. Finally, if it were accepted that moral responsibility devolved solely upon the individual, all social interactions would become totally ego-centered; no legitimate social demands could be made that would supersede the responsibility that the individual had to himself or herself. Since those who have accepted karmic dogma have committed themselves to living within social orders, it is to be expected that such dogma has been construed in such a way as to allow for social imperatives to condition the manner in which one undertakes moral action.

The value of the essays in this volume—all by anthropologists rather than textual scholars—lies not in their demonstration that ordinary practicing Buddhists and Hindus hold to rather degenerate versions of karmic theories when compared with versions found in theological treatises. Quite the contrary: the essays, save for that by Boon, demonstrate how karmic dogmas as construed in abstract theology have been reworked to have practical significance. If such reworking had never taken place, karmic ideas would hold, at best, academic interest for a tiny band of philosophers. Instead, karmic dogmas have been made fundamental to the worldviews of millions of people living in South and Southeast Asia. The power of an idea has been proven in its practical application.

References Cited

Boon, James A.

1977 The Anthropological Romance of Bali, 1597–1972. Cambridge: Cambridge University Press.

Dumont, Louis

1960 World Renunciation in Indian Religion. Contributions to Indian Sociology 4:43–62.

1970 Homo Hierarchicus: The Caste System and Its Implications. Mark Sainsbury, trans. Chicago: University of Chicago Press.

Dumont, Louis, and David F. Pocock

1957 Village Studies. Contributions to Indian Sociology 1:23–41.

1959 On the Different Aspects of Levels in Hinduism. Contributions to Indian Sociology 3:40–54.

Geertz, Clifford

1973 The Interpretation of Cultures. New York: Basic Books.

Gombrich, Richard F.

1971 Precept and Practice: Traditional Buddhism in the Rural Highlands of Ceylon. Oxford: Clarendon Press.

Horton, Robin

1979 Ritual Man in Africa. *In* Reader in Comparative Religion. William A. Lessa and Evon Z. Vogt, eds. 4th ed. Pp. 243–254. New York: Harper and Row. Originally published in Africa 34:85–104 (1964).

Keyes, Charles F.

1975 Buddhist Pilgrimage Centers and the Twelve-Year Cycle: Northern Thai Moral Orders in Space and Time. History of Religions 15:71–89.

1977 Millennialism, Theravāda Buddhism, and Thai Society. Journal of Asian Studies 36:283–302.

1978 Political Crisis and Militant Buddhism in Contemporary Thailand. *In* Religion and Legitimation of Power in Thailand, Laos, and Burma. Bardwell L. Smith, ed. Chambersburg, Pa.: Anima Books. Pp. 147–164.

1981 Death of Two Buddhist Saints in Thailand. *In* Charisma and Sacred Biography. Michael Williams, ed. Chico, Calif.: Scholars Press. Pp. 149–180.

Lévi-Strauss, Claude

1966 The Savage Mind. Chicago: University of Chicago Press.

Marriott, McKim

1955 Little Communities in an Indigenous Civilization. *In* Village India. McKim Marriott, ed. Chicago: University of Chicago Press. Pp. 175–227.

1976 Hindu Transactions: Diversity without Dualism. *In* Transaction and

Meaning: Directions in the Anthropology of Exchange and Symbolic Behavior. Bruce Kapferer, ed. Philadelphia: Institute for the Study of Human Issues. Pp. 109–142.

Obeyesekere, Gananath

1968 Theodicy, Sin and Salvation in a Sociology of Buddhism. *In* Dialectic in Practical Religion. E. R. Leach, ed. Cambridge: Cambridge University Press. Pp. 7–40.

1980 The Rebirth Eschatology and Its Transformations: A Contribution to the Sociology of Early Buddhism. *In* Karma and Rebirth in Classical Indian Traditions. Wendy Doniger O'Flaherty, ed. Berkeley: University of California Press. Pp. 137–164.

O'Flaherty, Wendy Doniger

1973 Asceticism and Eroticism in the Mythology of Śiva. London: Oxford University Press.

1976 The Origins of Evil in Hindu Mythology. Berkeley: University of California Press.

1980a Karma and Rebirth in Classical Indian Traditions. Wendy Doniger O'Flaherty, ed. Berkeley: University of California Press.

1980b Introduction. *In* Karma and Rebirth in Classical Indian Traditions. Wendy Doniger O'Flaherty, ed. Berkeley: University of California Press. Pp. ix–xxv.

1980c Karma and Rebirth in the Vedas and Purāṇas. *In* Karma and Rebirth in Classical Indian Traditions. Wendy Doniger O'Flaherty, ed. Berkeley: University of California Press. Pp. 3–37.

1980d Women, Androgynes, and Other Mythical Beasts. Chicago: University of Chicago Press.

Redfield, Robert

1956 Peasant Society and Culture. Chicago: University of Chicago Press.

Spiro, Melford E.

1978 Burmese Supernaturalism. Expanded ed. Philadelphia: Institute for the Study of Human Issues.

Srinivas, M. N.

1952 Religion and Society among the Coorgs of South India. London: Oxford University Press.

Tambiah, S. J.

1968 Literacy in a Buddhist Village in North-East Thailand. *In* Literacy in Traditional Societies. Jack Goody, ed. Cambridge: Cambridge University Press. Pp. 86–131.

1970 Buddhism and the Spirit Cults of North-East Thailand. Cambridge: Cambridge University Press.

Turner, Victor

1967 The Forest of Symbols: Aspects of Ndembu Ritual. Ithaca, N.Y.: Cornell University Press.

1969 The Ritual Process. Chicago: Aldine.

1975 Revelation and Divination in Ndembu Ritual. Ithaca, N.Y.: Cornell University Press.

Turner, Victor, and Edith Turner
1978 Image and Pilgrimage in Christian Culture. New York: Columbia University Press.
Weber, Max
1946 The Social Psychology of World Religions. *In* From Max Weber. H. H. Gerth and C. Wright Mills, trans. and eds. New York: Oxford University Press.
1958 The Religion of India. Hans H. Gerth and Don Martindale, eds. and trans. New York: Free Press.

· Part One ·

INDIA

· 1 ·

The Tool Box Approach of the Tamil to the Issues of Moral Responsibility and Human Destiny

Sheryl B. Daniel

The question of whether a person is free to determine the ethical quality of his actions and to control his own destiny is one to which Hindu culture gives not one answer but many. Among the Tamils of Kalappūr, South India, these multiple responses occupy a range that spans the perspective of Free Will on the one hand and Determinism on the other. According to the former, man, although influenced by a preordained fate, can alter it and redirect his own destiny. According to the latter, fate is absolutely unalterable and therefore man is not free to make his own choices.

This essay will not only present the content of these diverse beliefs and examples of their use in varying contexts, it will also explore the cultural premises that underlie certain patterns that emerge in a Tamil's contextual choices from among the wide range of cultural alternatives available to him. I will begin with an examination of the cluster of ideas concerning fate that have a bearing on the issue of moral responsibility.

Fate

Villagers believe that in the beginning Śiva (Kaṭavuḷ) created the vast

The field research on which this essay is based was carried out in 1974–1976 primarily in the village of Kalappūr (pseudonym), north of the town of Tiruchirappalli in the state of Tamil Nadu. Informants were predominantly of the Āru Nāṭṭu Veḷḷāḷa caste, the dominant caste in Kalappūr. However, many valuable informants were of the Brahmin, Paṇṭāram, Kavuṇṭar, and Āsāri castes. Less-intensive interviews were conducted with members of the other minority castes of Kalappūr and with informants from neighboring villages and the nearby town of Tiruchirappalli. I gratefully acknowledge the generous grant from the National Science Foundation that made this research possible.

array of living beings out of his own bodily substance. He molded each creature and determined its nature, be it good or evil, strong or weak. He then wrote upon the head of each entity its "headwriting" (*talai eṛuttu*), which was an exact and very detailed specification of every act it would perform, of all the thoughts it would have in its life, and of every event, good or bad, that would befall it. After creation the activities of the world began with each order of creation impelled to act in accordance with its own headwriting as specified by Kaṭavuḷ. As each entity began to act it began to generate good and bad karma according to the nature of its actions (*karmams*). At the end of each entity's life, Kaṭavuḷ reviewed that entity's karma, and on this record, caused it to be reincarnated in a new form with a new headwriting. The entity then acted according to its new headwriting, generated more karma upon which its headwriting in the next birth was determined, and so on through the cycle of births and deaths.

While it is believed that the headwriting in all except the "first" incarnation is based on a person's past deeds (karma), it is also believed that the headwriting is based as well on the past deeds of relatives or even chance acquaintances from whom the person acquired karmic substance. Let me explain.

When we employ the word "action" to render the concept of karma in translation, we unwittingly introduce into the karma concept the connotation of non-substantiveness or non-materialness which we habitually associate with the abstract noun "action." However, to treat karma thus, as a mere abstraction, is to miss the crucial ethnosociological point that karma, in addition to being a kind or kinds of particular substance, is contained in (Marriott and Inden 1977) and may only be transmitted by bodily substances. Informants schooled in the theory of the five body sheaths will readily locate karmic substance in the third outermost body called the causal body or *kāraṇa uṭal*. The *kāraṇa uṭal* is part of the subtle as opposed to the gross body (*pūta uṭal*) and therefore is constituted of a substance which is as substantive as its gross counterpart.

We do not have to go to the few educated Tamils who are schooled in body-sheath theories to encounter the substantive conceptualization of karma. Almost any Tamil villager will tell you that karma is inevitably transmitted from one generation to the next in the blood (*rattam*). Some also claim that cooked food is capable of transmitting one person's karma to another. Let us look closely at some examples.

Periyaswamy, a wealthy Veḷḷāḷā of Kalappūr, was a lecher of much notoriety and a moneylender who dealt ruthlessly with those unfortunates who became indebted to him. Villagers believed that his flagrant sins had resulted in bad karma, which caused him to be afflicted in later life with leprosy and rheumatism. They also believed that his bad karma had blighted the lives of his son and married daughter. The son, although himself a religious man and an outstanding member of the community, was thought to suffer from skin diseases and childlessness because of the bad karma that he had inherited from his father through their shared blood.

Periyaswamy's daughter, although a member of her husband's lineage after marriage, retained ties of shared bodily substance with her natal family. Through this shared substance she also incorporated his bad karma. She in turn passed on this karma to her husband, with whom she shared bodily substance, and he, as the result of this transfer, died at an early age. Thus, for the sins of the father both the children and their own families suffered childlessness, ill health, and even death.

In another case, a Veḷḷāḷa boy of about eight years fell seriously ill and died. His family could not trace his death to any sin of his own or of the known family members, but they confided to me that it must have been the result of the bad karma resulting from the sin of an ancestor two or three generations earlier.

Other types of karma exchange are said to occur when a person accepts cooked food from another person. It is for this reason that Tamils are eager to accept the cooked food and even leftovers (*mīti*) of gods, Brahmins, and holy men: they believe that they are acquiring some of their good karma and will gain greater prosperity as a result. For the same reason, they are selective about accepting food from undesirables such as thieves and prostitutes who will transfer a measure of their bad karma in the food which they cook.

Many types of karma exchanges occur through casual or accidental associations. For example, there was a case in which two college roommates in Tiruchirappalli parted company when the health of one boy declined and transfers of bad karma from his roommate (who was of the same caste) were blamed for the illness. The sharing of karma in this case was said to have occurred through co-residence, since the boys did not share food. Fear of karma transfers from mere physical proximity makes villagers cautious about whom they allow to enter their homes. A holy man or a well-respected villager is, of course, always welcome, since the presence of such a person in a house will have a beneficial effect on all the members of the household. The same cannot be said of widows or barren women.

It is beyond the scope of this essay to elaborate on the logic and rules of all such transfers. Suffice it to say that from all this flurry of exchanges of karma, some voluntary and some involuntary, it is clear that the individual does not have complete control over the karma that he accumulates and for which he must reap the benefits and punishments. Although it is believed that a person will be punished and rewarded for the acts which he himself initiates, so, it is believed, will his wife and his child. Similarly, he will be punished and rewarded for the acts of his ancestors, living kinsmen, and chance acquaintances, although he has no voluntary control over these acts.

As was noted earlier, the headwriting functions to determine all the events, thoughts, desires, and actions of a person within a particular life-span. It does this by coordinating the life circumstances and events of a person with the desires and willed actions on his part that fulfill what is foreordained in the headwriting. To take a hypothetical example, if it is in Rangasamy's headwriting that on such and such a day he is destined to murder his Kavuṇṭa (a goatherding *jāti*) neighbor, his headwriting will coordinate his inner nature (*kuṇams*, psychobiological qualities) and the particular emotions and decisions of that day with the appropriate environmental setting which provokes and accommodates the act. Thus, Rangasamy will be filled with a murderous rage that overrides his reason and results in his passionate decision to murder Kandan, the goatherd, who on this occasion is caught in bed with Rangasamy's wife. Kandan's headwriting in turn will orchestrate the events of his life and his inner nature and desires so that he commits adultery and is caught by Rangasamy and killed.

The effect of the headwriting on the "will" (on the processes of volition) are particularly important to our concern with the issue of moral responsibility. I will, therefore, briefly outline the Tamil villager's understanding of the functioning of the psychobiological "person" and deal specifically with the interaction of the will and the headwriting.

Headwriting and the Will

In Kalappūr culture, a person (*āḷ*), like everything else in the phenomenal universe, is constituted of substance. This substance is "ontogenetically" one but qualitatively many. The qualitative differentiation of the primordial or of any substance into different kinds of substances does follow cultural rules that often do not concur with non-Indian cultural expectations. For instance, the substance of a person is not distinguished in terms of psychological as opposed to physiological qualities. Thus, *kuṇams*, which suffuse an entity's body, are coded with dispositions or qualities that are both psychological and biological at the same time, from a Western point of view. If a person is of a predominately *cātvīkakkuṇam* (Skt. *sattva guṇa*), his bodily substance as a whole is refined and pure. This basic quality reflects itself in the nature and functioning of the various aspects of the person. For example, the *manam*, which is thought to be the seat of emotions and desires, gives rise, in such a person, to primarily *dharmic* (appropriate) desires. The *manam* of a person of *cātvīkakkuṇam* would not even conceive the desire to commit a base crime, unlike the *manam* of a person of a predominately *tāmata kuṇam* (Skt. *tamas guṇa*), which is known to be filled with excessive and improper desires. Further, the *mūḷai* (literally, brain) of a *cātvīka* person would be of a similarly refined substance, which would reveal itself in its ability to function in a disciplined manner when it performs its basic tasks of judging the desires of the *manam* and deciding which desires are to be censored and which are to be enacted. The *mūḷai* is the reality-testing organ of the body, which attempts to deal effectively with the internal needs and pressures of the *manam* and the external influences of the environment. In a person of a *cātvīkakkuṇam*, the *mūḷai* is able to deal calmly and rationally with these internal and external pressures. In contrast, a *tāmata mūḷai* is characterized by a lack of control, alertness, and intelligence and hence by an inability to function as effectively.

The *mūḷai* is the seat of decision making and the center of the "will." The English term is used to refer to the decision-making aspect of the *mūḷai*. The term *sittam* can be translated as "will," but it is not frequently used by villagers. The term *iṣṭam* (wish) is the more commonly used word, as for example, when a villager says that so and so did such and such because it was his wish (will, decision) to do so. Insight into the Tamil notion of "will" (as decision making, intention) can perhaps best be obtained by examining the function of *putti*. The *putti* is that part of the *mūḷai* which is associated with intellect and intelligence, and with a person's general mental disposition, which expresses itself as a tendency to will certain acts. When Tamils say that a person has a scheming *putti*, they mean not only that the general disposition of the *putti* is that of a schemer but that the *putti* intentionally schemes. This implies that the *putti* functions to will actions. The desire to scheme (referred to as *iṣṭam*, wish) may be thought of as the end product of the intent of the *putti*.

Consider this statement uttered by the *kōṭanki*, the village diviner, when I interviewed him following a divination. On this occasion he had advised his client that the latter's problems had been the result of his failure (for the sixth time) to make a pilgrimage to his ancestral shrine in a distant village and to celebrate a *pūjā* with an accompanying feast for the poor. The client appeared very contrite and penitent and swore with all earnestness and conviction that this time he would most certainly fulfill the wishes of his ancestral deity. There was very little room to doubt the sincerity of his intent. I shared this latter observation of mine with the *kōṭanki* as we left the house. I asked him whether he thought his client was only a very convincing liar. To this the *kōṭanki*'s response was as follows:

> There isn't a lie in what he says when he opens his heart and cries. The vows he opens his mouth and makes are all true. But even though he wants [to do something] in his heart, his *putti* doesn't let him. Without the *putti* allowing what can one do?
>
> Avẽ manõ viṭṭu aṛutu sattiõ paṇṇuratile oru poiyũ illinka. Vāi terantu sattiyõ paṇṇuratu attaynayũ uṇmatānunka. Ānā manatila virumbinālũ putti viṭātunka. Putti viṭāṭṭi enna tã seiyalã?

In any event, the *kuṇam* permeates every organ and every aspect of the body, including the *mūḷai* and the *manam*. But the *kuṇams* of people are highly resistant to change. I was told by one villager that "for every 10,000 physicians or magicians who know a mantra to change bile into phlegm or phlegm into wind there is only one who knows a mantra powerful enough to change a person's *kuṇam*."

In fact, the *mūḷai*, besides being composed of the relatively immutable *kuṇams*, is also made up of more mutable substances such as the humors. Thus, if a person eats food that is too "heating," his body may produce an excessive amount of the humor bile (*pittam*). This bile will enter the *mūḷai* and will affect the *putti*, producing a kind of disorganization and madness (*pittam*). It is worthy of note here that the *putti* itself is on the one hand conceptualized as a particular expression of the brain's quality while on the other hand it is thought of as being a particular (substantial) composite of an aspect of the brain itself. The *putti* as a substantial entity is far less immune to change and transformation than one's *kuṇam* (E. V. Daniel 1979).

As in the above example, the *mūḷai* and the *putti* are affected by the substances from the environment which a person assimilates through food intake, residence, and so forth (Marriott 1976). For instance, if a person of a very calm *kuṇam* (*sāntakkuṇam*) marries and shares, through shared food and exchanged *indirium* (sexual fluid), the bodily substance of a person of a very excitable and hot-tempered *kuṇam* (*munkōpakkuṇam*), the *putti* of the calm person will be affected by the incoming *munkōpakkuṇam* of the hot-tempered person. The result will be a loss of some of the calm and level-headed functioning of the *putti*. The *sāntakkuṇam* on its part will continue to mix with the changeable *putti* and thus qualitatively affect it, but the effect of the incoming *munkōpakkuṇam* substance will offset some of the influence of the *sāntakkuṇam*. Likewise, the hot-tempered spouse will undergo a change of *putti* because of the incoming *sāntakkuṇam* and will become calmer and more controlled than before. (See E. V. Daniel 1979 for an elaboration of *putti-kuṇam* interaction.)

In order to complete this brief sketch of the Tamil villager's understanding of psychobiological functioning, it is necessary to consider the way in which karma and headwriting affect the *manam* and the *mūḷai*.

To begin, it is important to consider the exact nature of headwriting vis-à-vis the substance of the *kuṇams*, humors, and so forth. To the Tamil, headwriting is not merely an abstract "fate" in the mind of God (Kaṭavuḷ). It is a coded substance which is inseparably conjoined to the bodily substance of an entity at the time of birth. This fusion of substances occurs when Kaṭavuḷ writes on the entity's forehead his headwriting, which, from that moment onward until the gross and subtle bodies of that incarnation cease to exist, will exert a controlling influence on the destiny of that entity. It is the headwriting itself and not an intervening Kaṭavuḷ that effects the internal and environmental changes that are necessary to fulfill the encoded fate of the said entity.

One's headwriting is one of the most indelible and unalterable entities. It is far more resistant to mutation than one's *kuṇam*. The headwriting is said to determine when, where, and how a certain strand of karmic substance is activated. In the words of the local *pūcāri*:

> [As to] how, when and where [a certain] *karmam* will come to fruition is written in one's headwriting.
>
> Oru karmam eppaṭi, enkē, eppō paṛukkū enpatu talai eṛuttil eṛutiyirukku.

To continue to quote the same informant:

> ... the peculiarities of the *kuṇams*, and the dependent whims of the *manam*, the maladies of the brain, [and all such things], are none other than the products [results] of this *karman*.

> ... kuṇappētankaḷ, ataiyoṭṭi manampōrapōkku, mūḷaikkōḷarukaḷ, itellā antakkarmattai oṛiya vēra onnũ illa.

It is the karmic substance then, under the control of the headwriting, that determines the nature of a person's *kuṇams* and hence of the general functioning of the *manam* and *mūḷai*. In addition, *karmam* acts simultaneously both upon the external environment and upon the desires of the *manam* and the decisions of the *mūḷai* (*putti*) to coordinate a sequence of motivations and actions with the appropriate environmental setting.

Just such a predetermined sequence of events was described to me by a Kavuṇṭā informant. The story had the flavor of a favorite anecdote about the power of a Brahmin's curse. According to the story, a Parayan laborer worked for a wealthy Brahmin landowner who had for years goaded the Parayan into silent hatred by the ruthless and unjust exploitation of his labor. One night when the moon was full, the Brahmin and the Parayan chanced to be out late together in the fields. The Brahmin began to disparage the work of the Parayan, and a quarrel ensued. The Parayan, seeing his chance to avenge himself, seized a stick and savagely beat the Brahmin to death. Before the Brahmin died, however, he cursed the Parayan, saying that with the moon as his witness, the Parayan would suffer for his sin of Brahminicide. The Parayan was so shaken by the curse that he went home and confessed his crime to his wife.

Life went on as before, and no one suspected the Parayan. The Brahmin had had so many enemies that no one in particular could be linked to the murder. Then one day the Parayan and his wife began to quarrel and he took a stick and began to beat her. In her anger she shouted, "And so are you going to kill me like you killed the Brahmin?" The neighbors who had come to intervene in the connubial dispute chanced upon the wife's remark as well. They bound the Parayan and turned him over to the police. He was later convicted for the crime.

"So you see," continued my informant, "you cannot escape the curse of a Brahmin. Neither can you escape that which is written in your headwriting." When I questioned him in more detail, he indicated that it was the Parayan's fate to have the *kuṇam* to kill and to be born into that village and to become the laborer of that particular Brahmin. The headwriting also arranged it so that he met the Brahmin on that night and that his rage overcame the restraint of his *mūḷai*. Similarly, it was his fate to tell his wife his secret and for her to reveal this secret. The curse of the Brahmin was the immediate precipitating cause of the quarrel of the Parayan and his wife and of her revelation of his secret. However, it was the headwriting which ordained the entire sequence of events. Similarly, it was the headwriting of the Brahmin to be of such an irascible nature that one of his own laborers would eventually beat him to death.

I turn now to consider the import of the beliefs concerning fate presented thus far. We have seen that headwriting has pervasive control over a person's destiny. It not only orchestrates the setting and events that "happen" to him, it also controls his own internal nature (*kuṇams*) and influences the ongoing psychobiological functioning of the *mūḷai* in its interactions with the *manam*. It thus controls his "will" and therefore controls his actions. The headwriting causes an individual to experience rewards or punishments according to his karma or past deeds. As was noted earlier, this karma consists not only of a person's own past deeds but of the deeds of others from whom the person has received karma through shared blood, food, and so forth. Thus, a person's headwriting insures punishments and rewards for the deeds of others over whom he has no control. To add to the external constraints on a person, there is the problem of the original, arbitrarily assigned headwriting which skewed the fate of all entities in a positive or a negative direction. This first headwriting had no basis in former deeds and hence decreed events which were in some sense "undeserved."

Given the powerful influence of fate, one must ask whether a person ever has a chance to alter his headwriting, to correct a negative trend initiated by the first headwriting, to override bad karma assimilated from others or to simply resist the influence of the headwriting in order to chart a destiny which he desires and controls. The answer to this question hinges on the beliefs concerning the mutability of the headwriting itself.

Is Headwriting Mutable?

Although it is a generally accepted belief that headwriting is the most permanent of all coded substances, in reality all substances are in flux and therefore are capable of change under certain conditions. Tamils hold two opposed beliefs concerning the conditions under which headwriting can change. On the one hand it is held that headwriting is subject to the powers of the will. I shall call this point of view, the "Free Will perspective." On the other hand, there is a somewhat opposed belief according to which the "will" has little or no power to alter one's headwriting. This, I shall call, the "Deterministic perspective." Let me elaborate on the latter perspective first. From this perspective, headwriting cannot be altered within the lifespan of an entity. Even death may not release a being from its headwriting, since a prolonged existence as a ghost or a demon (*picācu*) might be part of the headwriting. The headwriting does undergo change, but it does this through the internal processes of its own fulfillment. When all the events of the headwriting have occurred, the headwriting will have exhausted itself and become deactivated. According to this belief, "will" even if it is believed to possess some degree of independence from control by the headwriting (i.e., to desire a contrary fate and even to attempt to resist the headwriting), can have no effect on it and cannot change the headwriting no matter how intense the willed *karmams* (actions) performed (such as rituals to avert a predicted disaster).

In support of this view of the ineffectuality of will and karma (action) to alter headwriting, there are myths such as the Kāmuṇṭi myth which is enacted as a drama once a year in a village adjacent to Kalappūr.

In this myth, Śiva, in his capacity as the impartial instrument of fate, is obliged to write the fate of his own daughter. It is her fate, because of her past karma, to be widowed on her wedding day. Further, according to Śiva's own headwriting and that of the groom, Kāma (the god of desire), Śiva himself is to kill the groom cum son-in-law and thus widow his own daughter. Although gravely distressed by the fate which he is forced to write, Śiva is unable to alter it and thereby spare his beloved daughter the much-dreaded lot of a widow. The wedding occurs, and Kāma is burned to death by the fire of Śiva's third eye. The daughter is angry and distraught and rails against her father for having executed such an evil fate. Śiva tries to explain to her that one's fate is based on one's former deeds (i.e., on one's karma) and that not only is he powerless to avoid writing a bad headwriting in the first place, but he is unable to alter the headwriting once it has been written. She does not believe that her father is in fact helpless, and she goes insane with grief and despair, circling round and round the ashes of her dead husband.

In desperation Śiva decides that although the headwriting could not be altered and Kāma had to die, there is yet a chance to alleviate some of the pain of such a fate. Using his powers as a creator, he recreates Kāma in a subtle body which cannot be seen by anyone except his wife, Radhi. Thus Radhi remains, socially, a widow, and Kāma is officially dead, yet they live as husband and wife. Śiva was unable to alter their headwriting, but he could mitigate somewhat its harsher aspects.

The myth is cited by villagers, not for its hope of divine assistance in coping with the unalterable edicts of fate, but to illustrate the often quoted saying that "one cannot change what God (Śiva) has written" (*Kaṭavuḷ eṛutinatai manuṣanāl māttamuṭiyātu*). Informants interviewed during the Kāmuṇṭi festival cited the drama as an illustration of the fact that even the almighty Śiva is powerless to save a woman from predestined widowhood. "If he could not save his own daughter, how can he deliver us from an evil fate? What is destined to happen will happen. Nothing can change fate."

It is also of interest, however, that this myth can also be used to support the opposite aphorism that "Fate can be vanquished by wit" (*vitiyai matiyāl vellalām*). In the Kāmuṇṭi myth the headwriting itself could not be altered by wit, but wit could alter the "spirit" of the headwriting. Thus Radhi and Kāma were able to live as husband and wife even though their headwritings decreed Kāma's death and Radhi's widowhood. This would indicate a slight shift away from the "Deterministic perspective" toward the "Free Will perspective."

Belief in the power of "wit" to alter fate goes much beyond this limited application when Tamils adopt the view that headwriting can be altered, even within one life-span, by correctly executed *karmams* initiated by the will. In this view, the "Free Will perspective" is given predominance wherein the "will" (*putti*) is treated as relatively independent of the headwriting. Granted, this independence is within the context of pervasive influences both from the headwriting and from the involuntary effects mentioned earlier of karma intake, *putti* changes due to humor imbalances, substance exchanges with other persons, and so forth. Yet, the *putti* can effectively plan a course of action to counteract some of these influences. It does this by performing *karmams* which qualitatively affect the nature of the given or "inherent" *karmam* substance, which in turn can change the headwriting, which is based on the *karmam* substance.

Myths that support this perspective of the nature of "will" and "headwriting" are such as the story of Markeṇṭēya, a Purāṇic myth frequently recounted in the oral tradition of the village.

Markeṇṭēya was a Brahmin boy who discovered at an early age (through astrological prediction) that he was destined to die at the age of sixteen. Determined to thwart this adverse fate, he set about performing *pūjās* to Śiva in order to win the boon of a prolonged life. When the time came for his predestined death, Yama, the god of death, came to take him away. However, so tightly did he cling to the Śiva *liṅgam* that Yama was unable to drag him away. This caused quite a disturbance in the three worlds, and Śiva himself was called upon to enforce the fate he had written. Śiva, caught between conflicting duties as the author and executor of fate and as the grantor of boons to deserving devotees, responded in favor of the boy. His reason was that the devotion (itself a *karmam*) of the boy was so powerful that it had, in effect, overcome fate (i.e., altered the headwriting). The headwriting, thus changed, had no further control over the boy, and he was free to live beyond his originally preordained life span.

The Markeṇṭēya myth supports the basic thesis that *karmams* can alter headwriting, but it implies that this requires *karmams* of an extraordinary kind. There is, in fact, a wide range of beliefs concerning the exact strength of the *karmams* needed to alter headwriting. An example of less intense *karmams* being used to alter fate is that given by E. V. Daniel in his discussion of the flower ritual (in this volume). He cites the case of a father who believed that his prayers, *pūjās*, and pilgrimages had changed the fate of his daughter, who was predestined to die at the age of six. The flower ritual itself, while aimed at altering a person's *kuṇam* and not his or her headwriting, affirms the efficacy of the will to plan and perform *karmams* to alter aspects of one's inherent nature (which is determined by one's *karmam* substance and ultimately by one's headwriting). Although it can always be argued by a Tamil that such minor alterations of the *kuṇams* were actually foreordained in the headwriting, this does not detract from the faith in action and initiative that such rituals reveal.

The mechanics of how the "will" generates *karmams* which in turn impinge upon and alter the headwriting are understood in two different ways, depending on which theory of karma encoding is adopted by a Tamil.

The first theory is what one English-speaking informant, Milraj, called the "bank balance" theory of karma. According to Milraj, a person gains points for a good deed and loses points for a bad deed. For example, if X commits the sin of cheating his brother, he loses 25 points and thus depletes his overall bank balance by this amount. He can restore and improve his balance, however, by performing a number of meritorious deeds that total or exceed 25 points, thus, in effect, canceling out his sinful deed. After explaining this, Milraj laughed and said, "So you see, you can still afford to commit quite a lot of sins as long as you perform enough meritorious acts to counterbalance them." Speaking of his own case, he quite openly discussed his already well-known propensity for extramarital affairs and said that he felt that the meritorious *pūjās* which he performed routinely as the priest (*pūcāri*) of the local temple were sufficient not only to offset these sins but to leave him with a surplus of merit (*puṇyam*) in his karma bank account.

A person's headwriting is based on the total balance in his karma account. If he has a balance of 60 points out of a possible 100 points, then he will have a headwriting with 60 percent good events and 40 percent bad events. According to the Free Will interpretation of the bank balance theory, even within the span of one headwriting, if the karma balance is radically altered in terms of either an increase or a decrease, this will affect the headwriting. Thus, an evil fate can be avoided if sufficient good *karmams* are accumulated to raise the bank balance, or a good fate may not be realized if the bank balance drops because of sins. There is a wide range of opinion concerning how much effort is required to generate the requisite amount of merit to tip one's bank balance in one's favor. Some say it requires extraordinary effort like that of Markeṇṭēya, and others, such as Milraj, are quite casual about it, feeling that one's destiny can be controlled much as a shrewd man manages his finances, carefully calculating his gains and losses.

The second theory of karma encoding is what I shall call the "tit for tat" theory. Here every deed is recorded separately, and each must result in a reaction (reward or punishment) suited to the nature of the deed. Good deeds cannot cancel bad deeds, although the greater the number of good deeds, the greater the number of pleasant events to be ordained by the headwriting. The role of the headwriting, in this theory, is to determine what karma will be activated, that is, attain fruition, in a particular lifetime. Not all deeds performed in one lifetime bear karmic fruit in the next lifetime. Some are deferred for several lifetimes.

The strategy employed to alter headwriting under this view of karma (presuming, of course, that one has adopted a Free Will perspective), is one that aims at the ritual blocking or deactivating of a particular karmic result. Thus, if a man is told that his wife is to die in the third year of their marriage, he will perform *pūjās* to the deities, give alms to the poor, fast, promise to perform a certain elaborate or costly ritual or to give a certain amount of money to a temple if a deity will intervene and prevent the fruition of that part of his wife's headwriting. Such measures do not eradicate the bad karma; rather, they defer its fruition until a later birth. In time, every *karmam* will bear fruit.

In summary, the difference between the Deterministic and Free Will perspectives can be highlighted through likening life to a drama and people to actors in the drama. According to this analogy, Śiva is the playwright who, for his own amusement and in accordance with the laws of karma, writes the script of the play and determines the role of each of the actors (headwriting). In the Deterministic perspective, the actors can be likened to marionettes pulled to and fro by the strings of fate. They have no choice but to enact their script (headwriting). In the Free Will perspective, the actors, although constrained by the setting and the script, are yet able to improvise and to prevail upon the playwright-director to make alterations in their scripts.

I turn now to the question of moral responsibility. First of all, I shall address myself to the way in which the Deterministic and Free Will perspectives rule on the issue of the responsibility (*poruppu*) of an individual for his actions.

Moral Responsibility

The Deterministic perspective generally treats an individual as responsible only in the sense that, because he is the agent of the deed and there is no one else to blame or reward, he must bear the circumstantial responsibility for the action. Yet, this perspective usually elicits pity for those who suffer or commit crimes and supports summary dismissals of the accomplishments of those who have been successful. It is the headwriting that is ultimately responsible, since the good or bad intentions of the person are only the by-product of the influence of the headwriting.

The Free Will perspective, in contrast, rests the responsibility with the individual, for it is believed that he has the ability to resist the control of the headwriting over his "will" and to initiate *karmams* that can reverse unfavorable events. If unexpected sufferings befall him because of his headwriting, he is still considered responsible, because they are thought to represent a just punishment for deeds freely willed in a former lifetime.

Let us consider now the most complex aspect of the issue of moral responsibility. This is: How do Tamils choose from among the wide spectrum of beliefs concerning the alterability of fate to decide questions of moral responsibility? Do they adopt a Deterministic or a Free Will perspective? The answer is that they rarely choose to consistently favor one perspective to the exclusion of the other. Rather, the choice of perspective is a context-sensitive one determined by needs and biases, among other factors. In one context, a villager may espouse the perspective he then favors as if it were the final and only correct judgment, and yet in another context, if it suits his need, he will support the opposing perspective. Often he will support first one perspective and then the other even within the same context—for example, in discussing the moral responsibility of a particular individual. The result is not only what appears to be conflicting perspectives of reality but conflicting judgments concerning the moral responsibility of the individual in question.

To illustrate this contextual usage, I shall present a series of examples. The first category of examples concerns those instances in which the headwriting must work through the desires and actions of a person in order to be fulfilled. The second category consists of those cases in which the headwriting does not have to work through a person's volition but can cause events through controlling the things that "happen" to a person.

In the case of fate that must be fulfilled through willed actions, I shall take the example of a debate over an issue of ethics: in this case, the moral responsibility of a thief for his crime.

In Kalappūr, three Kavuṇṭā men stole five chickens from the village schoolmaster. They feasted in secret on the chickens but carelessly left the telltale feathers scattered around their houses. The schoolmaster soon traced the theft to them and reported the incident to the village *munsif* (village policeman). The three men were called before the *munsif* and each was fined fifty rupees, a staggering sum for such poverty-stricken men. The schoolmaster's son, however, was not satisfied with the punishment and publicly complained that they had not also been whipped in the village square.

The wives and relatives of the men pawned their jewelry to come up with the money to pay the fine. Kandasamy, one of the thieves, was reportedly upbraided by his wife, who denounced him as an irresponsible fool who gave no thought to his responsibilities toward his wife and three children. She, however, did eventually help him pay the fine.

The next day Kandasamy's wife and mother left as usual to work in the fields. In their absence Kandasamy, who felt utterly humiliated by the incident, ate nerium-seed paste, a poison. When his wife and mother returned from the fields at midday they discovered him unconscious and frothing at the mouth. The mother ran for assistance and managed to find a few men to help carry her son to the local hospital. There, unattended by the village doctor, who was having her afternoon siesta, he died half an hour later.

A crowd of villagers had gathered around the hospital and in the street outside. They openly discussed the case with little regard for the feelings of the family and for friends who were present. An elderly Veḷḷāḷa man, who was also a friend of the wronged schoolmaster, called Kandasamy an arrogant bastard and said that he should have thought of the shame of being caught and punished before he committed the theft. He clearly supported the schoolmaster's son in his view that Kandasamy had committed the theft and the suicide out of his own free will, and that the folly of such disgraceful behavior was adequate proof that Kandasamy was a worthless wretch. An old Veḷḷāḷa woman, who was not aligned on either the side of the schoolmaster or the side of the friends and supporters of the thieves, denounced Kandasamy, clearly blaming him for his sins. ("What a thieving wretch of an ass he is. He lived in disgrace and now he dies in disgrace. At least our committing suicide at our ripe old age is excusable. There is absolutely no excuse in his case.") Her husband vacillated between excusing Kandasamy at one moment, saying that he was a victim of his fate, and vehemently denouncing him as a man whose arrogance (*timir*) was responsible for his crime. One old woman explained to me that Kandasamy was to be pitied, since after all no one can prevent oneself from acting out one's headwriting. But, she added, he had, nonetheless, committed a crime, and it was only right that he was punished for that crime.

Family members quarreled with some of the detractors and defended Kandasamy as a man who had suffered from the harsh edicts of fate and who could not have prevented either his participation in the theft or his own suicide. Yet, like many others present, even his family members vacillated between the Deterministic and Free Will positions in their reaction to Kandasamy's crimes. In the quarrel between Kandasamy and his wife over the fine, the wife seemed to treat him as a free agent who could and should have resisted the temptation to steal the chickens. Later, however, she was to defend him as a victim of fate. His mother, likewise, clearly addressed herself to him as if he were responsible for his actions and could have chosen not to commit suicide when she, as he lay dying, scolded him for killing himself and leaving his family behind. Yet, when he was dead, she was a staunch defender, saying that he was a good man who, because of the cruel *līlā* (play, sport) of Kaṭavuḷ (Śiva), had suffered a terrible lot. She denounced Śiva for his senseless sport and vowed that she would never again enter his temple or offer food for his worship.

The incident of the theft and suicide reveals the way in which the perspectives of Free Will and Determinism are used to accommodate the biases of the villager at any given moment. Kandasamy's supporters tended to favor the Deterministic perspective when arguing in defense of Kandasamy against his detractors (the schoolmaster's friends), who adopted the Free Will perspective, according to which Kandasamy was morally responsible because he could have acted otherwise. Yet these same supporters also adopted the Free Will perspective when they thought of the way in which they had been individually wronged by Kandasamy's actions. Neutral bystanders voiced both perspectives, evidencing no concern for the contradictory ethical judgments to which such statements gave rise.

The opposed nature of the two perspectives was, however, clearly recognized by the villagers when a detractor advanced a Free Will perspective and was countered by a supporter with a Deterministic interpretation of Kandasamy's responsibility for his actions. Within the limited context of such a debate a villager consistently applied the perspective which he then favored. Further, he implied that this perspective was the only accurate view of fate and that the ethical judgment that was based on it was the only correct one. He would, however, imply the same exclusive truth value for the opposite perspective if, in another context, he chose to favor it. The tendency to shift support from one perspective to another seemed to hinge on the discussant's shifting moods, as for example, when Kandasamy's mother wanted to defend him or alternately to blame him for abandoning her. Each perspective seemed to represent a true and valid evaluation of the moral responsibility of Kandasamy for the discussant at the moment at which the judgment was advanced. It seemed to matter little to the discussant or to the others present that "inconsistent" moral judgments were made and defended.

It is interesting to note that while some villagers also blamed the excessive fine and Kandasamy's quarrel with his wife for his suicide, these incidents were seen as only the precipitating causes. The real issue was whether Kandasamy was morally responsible for his suicide—that is, whether he could have and should have prevented himself from responding in this extreme way to these humiliations. This reasoning is similar to that in the story recounted earlier in which the Parayan laborer kills his Brahmin master. While the exploitation and the quarrel that occurred on that particular night were the immediate causal events for the murder, to the village informant who told me the story the real cause was fate (headwriting). Fate had caused the events that created the hatred and provided the circumstances in which the Parayan could get his revenge. The question that could be asked of this case as well as that of Kandasamy's case is whether it is possible to use one's *putti* to override the influence of one's headwriting. Put in specific terms, why did Kandasamy respond to the heavy fine by commiting suicide when his co-thieves did not? Was he morally weak, or was it his fate alone to commit suicide, with the humiliation he suffered just the instrumental cause of this fated outcome?

A good example of an instance in which the issue of responsibility pivots around a person's ability to alter the events that fate causes to "happen" to him, rather than around the desires it conjures up within his *putti*, is that of an astrological prediction of disaster.

In these instances there are usually two phases to the debate over moral responsibility for control over one's fate. During the anxious days prior to a predicted disaster the person uses the perspectives of both Free Will and Determinism according to his shifts in mood. Applying the perspective of Determinism, he hopes that the astrological prediction is wrong. Since astrology is only an approximate reflection of the unknowable headwriting, there is always a chance that a prediction is inaccurate. Or he may begin to prepare himself for the disaster, adopting an attitude of resignation to a fate beyond his understanding or control. Yet, at other moments he feels that it is intolerable to wait for the worst to befall him, and so he frantically clings to the belief in Free Will and sets about performing a range of ritual actions designed to alter his headwriting should it in fact spell disaster.

After the crisis is past and the results are known, the responsibility of the individual for his fate is again debated from the viewpoint of the two perspectives. From the perspective of Free Will, the person can be blamed for not having prevented the disaster, particularly since hindsight usually reveals the practical measures that could have been taken to avoid it. The individual may feel guilty and despondent, blaming himself for the misfortune. Other villagers are also quick to criticize and either blame some lack of practical effort or say that the individual is suffering for sins freely willed and committed in former births. If, however, the disaster predicted did not occur, the person may claim credit for having altered his headwriting. In practice, however, this claim is rarely made, since it is hard to substantiate. It is generally believed that the events that occur are those ordained in the headwriting. Therefore, it is easier to discredit astrological predictions than to defend the view that the headwriting itself has been changed.

The individual who has suffered the disaster generally seeks refuge in the Deterministic perspective, which offers him solace by depicting him as the helpless victim of an unalterable fate. Even though he may be deemed responsible, he is judged less harshly, and pity and sympathy are more naturally given him than criticism and blame.

In this type of situation, a person rather self-consciously shifts between perspectives, choosing that perspective which fits his changing moods and motivations (to fight or give up; blame himself or escape blame). He is aware of the moral dilemma over whether he is to be responsible and suffer anxiety and possible blame or whether he is to hold the headwriting responsible for whatever happens to him. Yet, he does not respond to the crisis by choosing one perspective and deciding the issue of his own responsibility once and for all. Rather, he continues to believe in whatever perspective is pragmatically meaningful. At the moment of his belief, it appears to be *the* final revelation of truth to him. But, moments later, he may believe equally fervently in the opposite perspective. At times he is aware of his inconsistency, but he is not generally troubled enough by it to try to make a lasting choice between the alternate perspectives of fate. Instead, he responds by yet another temporary shift to the perspective that he happens to favor at that moment. To illustrate this sort of contextual adaptation of the perspectives, let me relate the story of Subiya, a Paṇṭāram *pūcāri* of Kalappūr.[1]

Subiya owned land and a house and had the right to run the village Māriyamman temple and collect the offerings. He was not a wealthy man but was considered to be reasonably prosperous. Several years ago, a number of astrologers predicted that Subiya would lose all his property, including his ancestral house. He sought to avoid this fate by praying daily to the goddess Māriyamman for protection. He also sought the counsel and advice of a Veḷḷāḷa *pūcāri* (Milraj), who was a very wealthy man and who was the privileged devotee of the powerful goddess Kāmākṣi in whose temple he served in the capacity of primary *pūcāri*.

Milraj had been a family friend for years and was a trusted ally. When Subiya needed a 500-rupee advance for his daughter's marriage, he asked his friend Milraj to make the loan, which was to be returned within one week. He said that, of course, he was a man of property and that his property stood as collateral behind the loan. Milraj agreed and the loan was made. In one week's time Subiya came to return the money as promised, but Milraj publicly denounced him and said that the 500 rupees had not been a loan but an advance for the sale of all of Subiya's property. Subiya protested, but Milraj said that there were witnesses, and he produced a bill of sale on which Subiya (who was illiterate) was said to have made his mark.

Subiya took the matter to court, but he was no match for the wealthy Milraj, who spent thousands on bribes to false witnesses, to lawyers, and even to judges. In the meantime, Milraj sent men to harass Subiya and prevent him from farming his fields, thus cutting the income that Subiya could spend on the court expenses. As of this writing, the court case is still going on and has now reached the Madras court. Subiya is bankrupt and deeply in debt to his wife's family. It is very likely that Milraj will win the case by simply delaying so long that Subiya's money for court costs is exhausted.

Subiya, like most other villagers, draws on both Free Will and Deterministic perspectives according to which is useful to him. In his effort to avert the predicted disaster, he told me that he hoped that either the astrological prediction that he would lose his property was

[1] The Paṇṭāram *jāti* is a *jāti* of non-Brahmin temple priests and temple servants. They are a "clean" *jāti* and unlike the Veḷḷāḷas of Kalappūr are vegetarians. However, they rank lower than the Veḷḷāḷas in the local caste-hierarchy.

erroneous or his *pūjās* to the goddess Māriyamman would win her support and that she would change his headwriting. In despondent moods, however, he told me that headwriting cannot be changed and that if the astrological prediction was correct his only hope was that the goddess would look after him when he was reduced to poverty.

This case has, as have many others that involve things that "happen" to people, an element of the control of the headwriting over the "will" as well as over other events. Subiya's wife and relatives frequently mocked and chided him for his stupidity in trusting Milraj in the first place. Sometimes Subiya would retort that it was the headwriting that had made him trust Milraj. At other times he would say that his trust in Milraj was fully warranted by the latter's previous behavior and that some strange twist in Milraj's own headwriting had caused him to turn against him. In this defense, Subiya was essentially insisting on classifying this misfortune as one that did not involve the headwriting's control over his judgments.

It is interesting to note that no one to whom I spoke suggested that perhaps Milraj, who had been the close friend of Subiya and who probably had heard of the prophecy, might have gotten the idea of exploiting him from the astrologer's prediction. It is conceivable that Milraj could have decided to take advantage of Subiya's fate by becoming the instrumental cause of his misfortunes, believing that, if it all was fated, then his scheme was sure to be successful in the end. This aspect of the case will have to remain a mystery, however, because Milraj was unwilling to discuss the incident with me, since he was in the midst of the litigation and suspicious of my association with Subiya.

Another interesting example of the fated incidents that "happen" to a person is the following story recounted or reconstructed for me by the parents of the young man concerned and sworn to be true by villagers familiar with the incident.

This story recalls the case of a young Veḷḷāḷa boy who was predicted to die of a snakebite when he was sixteen. The boy himself was said to have been skeptical about the traditional beliefs in astrology, headwriting, and so forth. His parents were orthodox Hindus who took this prediction very seriously. On the day on which it was predicted that he would be bitten, his parents locked him up in a room with no opening through which a snake could creep. They stationed servants as guards near the door and would not permit anyone to enter or leave. The boy, who was somewhat annoyed and amused by all this fuss, spent the day studying. Then, as a private joke, he got up and drew a snake on the wall and said, "So you are supposed to kill me, are you?" With that he jabbed his finger at the snake's fang. A rusty nail happened to be slightly protruding from the wall at that point. It pierced his finger and infected him with tetanus. He died within a few days' time.

Neither the plausibility or the implausibility of the story nor its striking similarity to a Tamil folktale recorded by A. K. Ramanujan (personal communication) are of significance to me here. What is of interest is the way in which reconstruction of the event (however mythologized) by the villagers, including the dead boy's parents, is relevant to the general point I am making here. From the villagers' point of view, granted somewhat retrospectively constructed, it is impossible to change one's headwriting no matter how hard one tries. Some minor details might be altered, such as dying of the poisonous fang of a picture snake rather than of a real snake, but in the end, the headwriting is fulfilled. As the parents see it, it is clear that prior to the death, they had shifted between a belief in Free Will, which prompted their attempt to thwart fate, and a fear of Determinism. After the boy's death they adopted a Deterministic perspective of the incident and ruled out the Free Will perspective, since they thought that they had done all that was humanly possible. There was more consistency in their final preference for the Deterministic perspective than in many of the examples thus far cited.

In the examples given above, the perspectives of Free Will and Determinism have been used by villagers according to their own advantage. If it was to their advantage to shift rapidly between the perspectives, they did so. If, as in the snakebite example, it was to their advantage to stick to one particular perspective, they did so. What seemed to govern the choice of the perspective and the consistency with which it was used was the contextual bias of the discussant rather than any allegiance to an ideology that one must be consistent in the use of explanation.

This personal bias can, in some cases, be rooted in more deep-seated needs rather than in those dictated by more fleeting contextual expediency. For example, many Tamils have a rather consistent sense of what their own headwriting is and often make decisions and interpret past events in terms of this "script." Some people also seem to be more consistent in their preference for a particular perspective when they consider their own fate and whether or not they, personally, can alter it. Some tend to favor a Free Will perspective and seem to fight to shape their own destiny against contrary astrological predictions and at great odds. Others favor a Deterministic perspective and give up and let what will happen, happen. Such acquiescence is not always passive, however. In many cases a person's decisions in life are affected by his concept of his fate. He will tend to give in to those events and desires which he feels are dictated by his headwriting and cannot be resisted, while resisting desires and turning down opportunities that he feels are destined to be thwarted anyway.[2]

This kind of preference is based on a sense of self which is deeply rooted and long lasting. For example, a positive sense of self may be behind one person's confidence in his ability to change even fate itself, whereas a negative sense of self may be what leads a person to believe that his is to be a life of suffering. The consistency with which the perspectives of Free Will or Determinism are applied in these cases appears also, as in the cases of more superficical contextual biases, to be the result of the persistence of the need or bias behind the choice of the perspective rather than in the person's conscious attempt to choose between perspectives in order to answer to some ideal of consistency and non-contradiction. Let me illustrate this type of consistent choice of a perspective through the example of Kamalam, a poverty-stricken Veḷḷāḷa widow whose tendency to favor the Deterministic perspective had a profound effect on her life.

Her mother died when Kamalam was six years old, and she and her infant brother were raised by her mother's sister who, even before the death of her mother, had become the mistress of her father. The mother's sister was a woman noted for her vicious temper. She frequently beat Kamalam and rubbed chili powder into her eyes. The father did not intercede on Kamalam's behalf and instead treated her as a domestic servant to be overworked and neglected. Kamalam said that no one ever spent money to have her horoscope drawn up by an astrologer, but that she had no need of a horoscope, for she "knew" at an early age that her headwriting had destined her for a life of suffering.

When she came of age, her father insisted that she marry a forty-year-old man who was a cripple and who lived openly with a low-

[2]The belief in a life script written in the headwriting has interesting parallels with Eric Berne's concept of "scripting." Here the Tamil beliefs concerning an actual, substantial script add a new twist to the universal scripting process posited by Berne (1972).

caste mistress. Kamalam refused and was beaten by her father and chased from the house. While wandering alone in the fields, however, she said that she came to realize that it was her fate (headwriting) to marry this man, that Kaṭavuḷ had chosen him to be her husband. She knew that such a marriage would mean a lifetime of suffering, but she was convinced that this was her destiny and that no amount of rebellion on her part could alter it. She returned and agreed to the marriage. The husband, predictably, neglected and abused her. He continued to live with his mistress and never contributed toward the financial support of Kamalam or the two children born of the marriage.

When I asked her about her life she wept and cursed Kaṭavuḷ for having given her such an evil fate, but she never believed that she could have avoided any of the suffering. Her fellow villagers, however, were not as sympathetic. They believed that her poverty and hard lot were just punishment for some sin in this life or in a previous life and also, alternatively, that she could have done better; how, they did not specify.

This case is a good example of the power of the belief in headwriting and the extent to which an individual's tendency to favor a particular perspective, in this case the Deterministic perspective, can shape the events of a lifetime. Although Kamalam was no exception in her belief in Free Will as well as in Determinism, she never applied the Free Will perspective in the context of talking of her own life events. Although a Deterministic perspective did work to her advantage in excusing her for her sufferings, it was also, however, instrumental in leading her to accept and even cause much of this suffering.

Contextual Variability and *Līlā*

Thus far I have sought to establish the fact that Tamil culture supports a wide range of acceptable viewpoints concerning the freedom of the individual to control his own thoughts and actions. At the two extremes are the positions of absolute Determinism and of Free Will, with a variety of positions within the Free Will perspective concerning the amount of effort required to change the headwriting. I also illustrated the use of these divergent beliefs in contexts in which the villager must choose among them in order to decide an issue of moral responsibility. Several features of this contextual usage are of particular interest here.

(1) Tamils clearly perceive the Deterministic and Free Will positions as mutually exclusive and will argue for either one or the other in instances such as the debate over the moral responsibility of the chicken thief for his theft and suicide. (2) When they choose to support a particular perspective they argue with dogmatic fervor that the perspective which they then favor is the one and only "true" description of fate, implying that, therefore, it is the only perspective which should be utilized in contexts in which fate is an issue. (3) Yet, despite the emphasis on an either/or choice and the ethic of consistency implied in the assertion that one perspective is "true" across the board, Tamils, in practice, seem to be little concerned when they vacillate in their support of the two perspectives and make inconsistent and contradictory ethical judgments based on these perspectives. Thus, as we saw in the examples cited, it was a common occurrence for villagers to shift rapidly from favoring a view of absolute Determinism to favoring one of Free Will, and further, for others who witness such inconsistency to take it as a matter of course.

I noticed a similar lack of concern on the part of the persons themselves when I confronted them with their inconsistent responses and asked them to explain why they were saying apparently contradictory things about the mutability of headwriting. One Tamil, a more educated woman, said to me: "So what's so virtuous about consistency?" A Veḷḷāḷa informant responded by saying, "All these things are the result of the *līlā* of Śiva." When I asked her why it was Śiva's *līlā* to change headwriting in the Markeṇṭēya incident but to say that it was impossible to alter headwriting in the case of his own daughter (Kāmuṇṭi myth), she replied: "It is Śiva's *līlā* to do all these things. How am I to know such things? Only Śiva understands such *līlā*." An old Veḷḷāḷa man responded more cynically: "What do you expect in the Kali Yuga? Just look at Śiva's family life. One son is a womanizer and the other refuses to marry. Śiva and Pārvatī can never stop quarreling. If even the gods behave like this, what do you expect of men? Who are we to question such *līlā*?"

A Brahmin informant, however, viewed Śiva's *līlā* in a more positive light: "We are mere human beings. It is hard for us to understand the *līlā* of the gods. After all, aren't they far wiser than we?"

The implication of their responses is that the inconsistencies of men are nothing when compared with the inconsistencies of the gods. If such behavior on the part of the gods is defensible as their *līlā*, who is it that can rightfully censor this behavior in god or man? In short, if Śiva did not feel it necessary to choose once and for all between the view that headwriting can be changed and the view that it cannot be changed, although he favors one or the other view in different contexts, then how were they, mere ignorant mortals, to be expected to choose consistently between them? Here the contextual dogmatic adherence to a particular perspective obviously did not bind Śiva or the villager to follow through on its exclusive claims to truth by espousing that perspective alone in all contexts. Rather, the ethic of consistency seemed to be set within a larger cultural context in which inconsistent responses across contexts were acceptable and reflected a more overarching truth: that the world itself is complex and that it is Śiva's *līlā* to sustain multiplicity and opposition rather than to "resolve" it. As Wendy O'Flaherty has written concerning the *Purāṇas*, oppositions are "suspended" rather than "resolved."

> These fleeting moments of balance provide no "solution" to the paradox of the myth, for indeed, Hindu mythology does not seek any true synthesis. Where Western thought insists on forcing a compromise of or synthesis of opposites, Hinduism is content to keep each as it is; in chemical terms, one might say that the conflicting elements are resolved into a suspension rather than a solution. (1973:317–318)

This tendency to suspend diverse beliefs rather than to seek to synthesize or to make an exclusive and lasting choice between them seems to be characteristic of Śiva's *līlā* and of the villager's response to cultural alternatives.

In Beals's ethnographic work he has also noted a similar tendency on the part of his informants. He has described it as the propensity to collect cultural beliefs like pieces of a puzzle, which are assumed to go together in some way to form a unified whole (1976:185). Kundstater (1975) has touched upon a related point, that in many societies the average person simply makes use of the cultural alternatives available to him without concerning himself with the logical compatibility of the systems of thought to which they belong. (His point was with reference to the acceptance of Western and indigenous medical systems as alternate forms of treatment with little concern for the underlying incompatibility of the theories of illness and of the body which these systems represent. Amarasingham [1980] has made a similar observation about the use of medical help of diverse sorts in Sri Lanka.)

Yet there is more to the approach of the Tamil to cultural alternatives than just a tendency to avoid dealing with complex philosophical problems and making exclusive choices. The difference lies in the fact that villagers justify their inconsistent behavior by citing the example of Śiva's *līlā*. To understand the significance of this reference to *līlā*, it is necessary to consider the meaning and relevance of Śiva's *līlā* to the villager.

To the gods, life itself is a game. They engage even in apparently serious endeavors such as war or marriage all in the spirit of fun. As one informant put it, "For the gods, it is all *līlā*. Everything is Śiva's sport."

Yet in all games there are rules by which one must play. For example, soccer is a type of play for the villager, but it also has rules which the players must follow to sustain the game itself. While Śiva's *līlā* is considerably more spontaneous and unpredictable than a game of soccer, it nevertheless also conforms to some basic rules. To decode the rules of Śiva's game, let us consider a Kalappūr variant of a well-known Hindu creation myth.

According to the myth, there was a time when nothing existed in the universe except God (Kaṭavuḷ). He was in a totally peaceful, undisturbed, meditative state. Then one day there was a disturbance in his body caused by *kāma* (desire). This disturbance caused the three *kuṇams*, the three humors, and the five elements to separate and become distinct. The humors, *kuṇams*, and elements in turn recombined and became redistributed in different proportions. This process was compared by one informant to a massive "turning of the stomach" (*vaittu peraṭṭal*). The god's stomach exploded, and out from it came all manner of creatures (*jātis*), such as gods, demons, humans, animals, plants. The process of recombination and redifferentiation continues, resulting in degeneration and regeneration. God still exists, but not as before. He is, however, still closer than the rest of creation to that primordial state of perfect equilibrium (*amaitinilai*) in which all the *kuṇams*, humors, and elements were balanced. As a result of this more equilibrated condition God enjoys a more healthy state than do less equilibrated entities such as humans.

> But even in Him the elements, the humors and the *kuṇams* move around, try as He might to keep them in equilibrium [*ōṭāmal āṭāmal*]. That is why He is unable to do the same kind of thing for too long. If He meditates for more than a certain number of years, the amount of *cātvīkam* begins to increase. So then Kāma comes and disturbs Him and then He goes after Śakti...or the

> Asuras. . . . This results in an increase in His *rajasa kuṇam*. When *rajasa kuṇam* increases beyond a certain limit He must return to meditating. But most of the time, He is involved in *līlā*. . . . All our ups and downs are due to His *līlās*. But that is the only way He can maintain a balance [*samanilai paṭuttalām*]. (E. V. Daniel 1979:5)

This brief allusion to *līlā*, the play of Kaṭavuḷ, indicates quite clearly that *līlā* is far more than mere caprice. *Līlā* is a way to achieve some measure of balance in a world that is beset by the disequilibrating activities of desire (*kāma*). Specifically, *līlā* is necessary to balance the various substances (*kuṇams*, humors, and elements) of which Śiva is composed.

According to a Veḷḷāḷa informant, Śiva's *līlā*, which involves shifts between life as a householder and life as a yogi, not only balances his *kuṇams*; it allows him to enjoy the pleasures of the world and yet to enjoy the pleasure of meditating on his *ātman*. He added, "That is why I also meditate even though I am a householder."

Thus, while Śiva's *līlā* appears to be utterly erratic play, with Śiva at one moment playing the role of the archetypal ascetic and at another moment playing the part of a frenzied lover, this seemingly inconsistent behavior conforms to the underlying logic of Śiva's game. This is, that anything taken to excess is disequilibrating and that, therefore, it is necessary for Śiva to alternate his enjoyment of the various pleasures of his creation.

The notion that *līlā* is what one does to enjoy diverse pleasures and yet maintain a balance between one's various diversions is a theme expressed not only by the villager but in the *Purāṇas*. While only a few villagers were noted for their mastery of Purāṇic stories, these storytellers drew crowds of interested villagers during festivals such as Śivarātri and amused their family and neighbors during the course of many a late evening gathering on the veranda of their houses. The *Tiruviḷayāṭal Purāṇam* was a particular favorite, which was read in the home by the educated villager on occasions such as Śivarātri when the family must keep awake during the all-night vigil. In addition, popular Tamil movies to which many villagers went portrayed mythological themes. These movies, which often were shown in thatched-hut movie theaters, brought to the village the textual tradition which was the focus of more serious study by the more educated villager.

A central theme in these Purāṇic stories and movies is the *līlā* of Śiva. All of Śiva's actions are, in fact, said to be his *līlā* (sport). Thus, whether he quarrels with Pārvatī, incarnates as a local deity, or grants a boon to a devotee, it is all a function of his *līlā*.

To gain some insight into the *līlā* of Śiva, it might be useful to consider the type of sport in which Śiva engages. In the *Śiva Purāṇa*, which was the subject of my M.A. thesis (1974), I studied four volumes of mythology on the *līlā* of Śiva, and I referred to a wider range of *Purāṇas* illuminated by the work of Wendy O'Flaherty (1968, 1969, 1971). From my study of these *Purāṇas*, it became apparent that Śiva rather predictably intervened whenever anyone became too embroiled in a certain type of action. Thus, in the Pine Forest myth, Śiva seduces the wives of sages who are overly involved in their meditation on the *ātman*. He awakens in them desires and jealousies which link them once again to the temporal world. Conversely, he censors those who are overly embroiled in the concerns of the world and who value their limited virtues above the wisdom of the ascetic who knows the *ātman*. Typically, a householder such as Brahmā or Viṣṇu becomes smug and self-righteous about his status and virtue. Śiva then deludes him with *māyā* (illusion) and causes him to enact suppressed aggressive or adulterous desires. When the householder is humbled, Śiva reveals to the offender the higher truth that all the distinctions of the particularistic world are irrelevant from a more enlightened perspective, according to which the wise know that all of creation is but an illusory emanation of Śiva's expansive nature. Yet, it is Śiva's *līlā* to sportively create and sustain the illusion, and it is his *līlā* to qualify it by a higher wisdom. His *līlā* is thus an enlightened "transcendent perspective" that balances the "dualistic perspective," according to which the distinctions of the world seem real, and the "monistic perspective," according to which there are no distinctions to be experienced. It is Śiva's *līlā* to sustain both perspectives so that he may enjoy both the pleasures of the world and the *mōṭccam*-like (salvation-like) states of his ascetic interludes. His *līlā* thus balances the temporal world and the *ātman* and strikes a balance between desire and restraint (S. Daniel 1974).

In summary, *līlā* in the textual tradition and in Kalappūr culture is a mixture of a playful orientation toward the world and a measure of restraint. To the gods, life itself is a game-drama. While the main purpose is play (*līlā*, *kūttu*, *viḷayāṭṭu*), it is also necessary for one to live in accordance with the rules of the game. For god and man alike, this means maintaining a certain degree of balance without which there is no well-being and consequently no enjoyment.

There are in Kalappūr culture, however, two very divergent perspectives on the degree to which gods and men are tempering their desire in order to keep to the basic rules of the game of life. According to what I shall call the Kali Yuga perspective, the world is so degenerate in this final *yuga* that neither man nor god is capable of exercising much restraint. The Kali Yuga is an epoch in which desire has gotten out of hand and it is no longer possible to even hope for any satisfactory degree of stability. Śiva's *līlā* is the result more of caprice than of any attempt to balance out all the multiple and opposed aspects of the cosmos. He does manage to achieve some measure of balance as the result of his *līlā*, but it is the type of balance that comes when an immediate desire is gratified and there is momentary relief from excess desire. In the short term this is equilibrating, but in the long term it leads to other complications. Thus, in a popular Tamil movie Śiva destroys Pārvatī in a quarrel over who is more important, only to find himself without a wife. Such shortsighted solutions are the essence of Śiva's *līlā*, according to the Kali Yuga perspective.

According to what I shall term the "Ideal" perspective, god and man alike, despite the degeneracy of the Kali Yuga, are yet thought to be capable of exercising restraint and of seeking to achieve long-term substantial well-being. Śiva's *līlā* when judged by this Ideal perspective is seen as an enlightened relativism. His apparently inconsistent behavior in various contexts is in the service of a consistent, higher-order code for conduct: *līlā*. Thus, according to this perspective, Śiva's *līlā* is playful, but it balances desire and restraint and facilitates equilibrium not only within Śiva's own body but in the universe as a whole.

Śiva's *līlā*, as a model for achieving substantial equilibrium, is significant to the villager in different ways, depending on his point of view. According to one perspective, which emphasizes the separation of gods and men, the codes for conduct that are appropriate for gods are not appropriate for men. Gods and men are seen as separate orders of creation or rather as belonging to two distinct levels in the degenerative process of creation (see E. V. Daniel 1979). Stated simply, gods have many more entities or forms into which they can degenerate than do human beings, and they also have more powers than humans to effect such transformations. Thus, gods can assume human forms with ease, whereas it is practically impossible for humans to regenerate into godly forms with the appropriate divine powers. From such a perspective, then, Śiva's *līlā* becomes a code for conduct that enjoins a level of caprice which is appropriate for gods but excessive for men.

No sooner than such a distinction between gods and men is established, it is challenged at the level of ideology by the more encompassing view of nondualism (to be dealt with below) and at the level of praxis by the *jāti* hierarchy among and between humans. In the village of Kalappūr the terms of address used by lower *jātis* toward higher ones, Brahmins and Veḷḷāḷās in particular, were the same that devotees used toward their deities. The same held true in food transacting behaviors, and in much of the deference and demeanor coded in proxemic and kinesic conventions. On more than one occasion an informant from a lower *jāti* has excused or explained away the "eccentric" activities of members of the higher castes—especially the licentious and drunken behavior of some Veḷḷāḷās—as being the privilege of gods. In other words, what may clearly be seen as "excessive" to and for a Parayan or a stonecutter may be deemed appropriate for a Veḷḷāḷā. The disequilibrating conduct to be avoided as excess for one *jāti* becomes the equilibrating sport to be engaged in by another. That the *jātis* of gods and men belong in the same continuum is quite clear. The essential component of *līlā* (its concern with achieving balance through avoiding excesses) is as much a part of the human privilege, need, and quest as it is that of the divine. The *līlā* of Śiva, in so far as it is displayed with such engaging abandon and lavishness, is but an extreme expression of a culturally valued means for achieving substantial wellbeing.

The breakdown of the clear dichotomy and its corollary perspective is carried to its limit in the nondualistic ideology alluded to above. The latter introduces a quite different perspective on the relationship of gods and men; it collapses all traces of the distinctions that seem to separate them. This perspective is said to express the more enlightened view that all of creation is but a manifestation of different aspects of Śiva and Pārvatī. Thus, even as local deities are said to be incarnations of Pārvatī and Śiva, so human beings as well are thought to be incarnations of the divine couple. The belief that every man is Śiva and every woman is Pārvatī is not only a familiar theme in Purāṇic mythology (S. Daniel 1974) it is celebrated in the Veḷḷāḷa marriage ritual when the groom and bride are explicitly said to be incarnations of Śiva and Pārvatī (see Allison 1980).

It is said to be the *līlā* of Śiva and Pārvatī tc incarnate in more delimited forms. Although they choose to experience some limitations in these forms, it is all in the spirit of their sport. The wise are not fooled by such disguises and recognize the more encompassing and expansive nature of Śiva and Pārvatī in whatever form they assume.

From this perspective then, *līlā* is Śiva's code for conduct in all his manifestations. The range of his sport may be limited by his incarnation in a human form, but his *līlā* remains essentially the same; it expresses the same relativistic inconsistency in search of balance and harmony.

In summary, Śiva engages in *līlā* in order not only to stabilize his own *kuṇams* and humors but to achieve some stability in the three worlds. The degree of stability he is thought to achieve depends upon one's perspective. If one adopts a Kali Yuga perspective, then Śiva's *līlā* achieves balance only in the short term. If, on the other hand, an Ideal perspective is favored, then Śiva's *līlā* is thought to be necessary to achieve long-term stability. From either a Kali Yuga or an Ideal perspective, Śiva's *līlā* is paradigmatic for the villager either as a relevant art or as an expression of a code for conduct that is appropriate for Śiva in both his divine and his human manifestations.

Let us return now to the references made by villagers to *līlā*. When the villager cites *līlā* to justify his own tolerance for multiplicity and opposition (i.e., his tendency to suspend rather than to resolve opposition) and his inconsistent preference for one perspective or another in different contexts, he is in effect likening his behavior to the *līlā* of Śiva.

Like *līlā*, his behavior can be judged by either a Kali Yuga or an Ideal perspective. For example, in a context in which villagers observe a person change his beliefs to cast himself in a positive light, they might favor a Kali Yuga interpretation of his behavior. According to this perspective, he is judged to be just another crass opportunist, another Kali Yuga degenerate. Rarely is this opportunism severely criticized. It is tolerated as a product of a degenerate age. On the other hand, the villager himself and his supporters might choose to view his inconsistencies in the light of the Ideal perspective. By defending his behavior with reference to Śiva's *līlā* they imply that there is good reason for apparent nonsensical and contradictory behavior. It is all in the service of maintaining one's balance. It expresses a more enlightened awareness of the relativity of all beliefs and perspectives.

I wish to make it clear at this point that I do not intend to imply that the inconsistent and contradictory responses that first caught my attention are peculiar to the people of Kalappūr. I suspect that in every culture people are inconsistent and tend to contradict themselves. In fact, recent research on the behavior of individuals in different contexts lends support to the view that people are a great deal less consistent than our expectations of consistency would lead us to suspect (Shweder 1979).

What is of interest is the fact that the villager justified or explained his behavior with reference to the culturally validated ethic of *līlā*. *Līlā* is, in essence, a culturally patterned mode for ordering the multiplicity of the Hindu world view. It enjoins a certain relativistic and consequently an inconsistent pattern of choosing among the various options available within the culture. It legitimizes a "contextualized" approach to decision making and discourages trans-contextual, consistent preferences. The latter may be good for a time, but they are ultimately disequlibrating.

It would perhaps be useful to consider an analogy. The villager can be likened to a man who has before him a tool box that contains all the beliefs of his culture about what he is and what he ought to be doing. He is to pick and choose among the cultural beliefs (tools) available to him to make sense of the life circumstances and dilemmas with which he is faced. In Kalappūr culture he is free to pick whatever tool fits his immediate contextual need, knowing that such contextual choices can be justified in terms of either the Kali Yuga or the Ideal interpretations of *līlā*. Thus, an ethic of *līlā* encourages him to tinker in a playful and inconsistent way with the distinctions of the particularistic world. This style of tinkering is what I shall call the "Tool Box approach" of the Tamil. The Tool Box approach is a culturally validated style which emphasizes contextuality and which sanctions inconsistency in the light of a search for substantial equilibrium.

The Tool Box approach, as a construct is, I submit, more generative and culturally meaningful than several other concepts that have been suggested for handling apparent intracultural inconsistencies. Milton Singer's well-known concept of "compartmentalization" employed to explain the shift between the traditional-familial and the modern-industrial behavior of Madrasee industrialists is a case in point (1972). Compartmentalization is certainly an interesting analytic category. However, it retains its focus on behavior and does not provide the underlying cultural explanation of this behavior. A. K. Ramanujan's adaptation from linguistics of the notion of context sensitivity comes closer to what I have tried to present here (personal communication). I believe, however, that I have gone a step further in trying to discover what in Tamil culture makes context sensitivity a "culturally" meaningful response.

I also wish to make it clear that I am not assuming that the ethic of *līlā* necessarily motivates villagers to behave in an inconsistent manner. It is quite possible that their behavior is motivated by an opportunistic exploitation of the cultural options available to them. However, to conceive of the Tool Box approach as being merely an expression of the general human propensity for opportunism is to miss the point. In one sense, in a trivial sense, the Tool Box approach may be an instantiation of a generalized opportunism. But to elevate an opportunism thus conceived to the status of a practical logic upon which the cultural variable depends is to commit a fallacy similar to the material reductionism so cogently argued against by Sahlins (1976:206). To deny an opportunism based on a supposed universal practical logic the status of all-moving force is not to deny the real effects that some form of opportunism may have on the cultural order. The point being made is homologous to the one made by Sahlins.

> [T]he nature of the effects cannot be read from the nature of the forces, for the material [practical] effects depend on their cultural encompassment.... The force may...be significant—but significance, precisely is a symbolic quality. At the same time, this symbolic scheme is not itself the mode of expression of an instrumental logic, for in fact there is no other logic in the sense of a meaningful order save that imposed by culture on the instrumental process. (1976:206)

In my treatment of the Tool Box approach of the Kalappūr villager to the multiple options of his culture, it is the texture of this encompassment, the form and shape of this symbolic logic that I have tried to represent. What gives the villager's Tool Box approach its cultural distinctiveness is the ethic of *līlā* which pervades it, an ethic which makes defensible inconsistent, contextually advantageous choices.

In conclusion, although I began with an apparently simple problem—to explicate the villager's beliefs concerning fate—I discovered not just one composite cultural understanding of "fate" but diverse perspectives and variations on these perspectives. Further, my analysis of the way in which my informants pick and choose among these perspectives led me to explore a culturally patterned attitude toward multiplicity itself (the Tool Box approach), which I found reflected the larger Hindu world view and evidenced in particular the significant influence of the culturally valued ethic of *līlā*. Such a culturally patterned mode of orientation is, I would suggest, as interesting and worthy of further research as the particular beliefs concerning fate themselves. It is essential to an understanding not only of what Tamils believe but of how they use their beliefs to explain, justify, and judge their own actions and those of others.

References Cited

Allison, Charlene Jones
1980 Belief and Symbolic Action: A Cultural Analysis of a Non-Brahmin Marriage Ritual Cycle. Ph.D. dissertation, Department of Anthropology, University of Washington.
Amarasingham, Lorna Rhodes
1980 Movement Among Multiple Healing Practices in Sri Lanka: A Case Study. Culture, Medicine and Psychiatry, vol. 4.
Beals, A. R.
1976 Strategies of Resort to Curers in South India. *In* Asian Medical Systems. C. Lesley, ed. Berkeley: University of California Press.
Berne, Eric
1975 What Do You Say After You Say Hello?: The Psychology of Human Destiny. London: Transworld Publishers.
Daniel, E. Valentine
1979 From Compatibility to Equipoise: The Nature of Substance in Tamil Culture. Ph.D. dissertation, Department of Anthropology, University of Chicago.
Daniel, Sheryl B.
1974 The Spirit of *Līlā*: An Anthropological Study of the *Śiva Purāṇa*. M.A. thesis, Department of Anthropology, University of Chicago.
Kundstater, Peter
1975 Do Cultural Differences Make Any Difference? Choice Points in Medical Systems Available in Northern Thailand. *In* Medicine in Chinese Cultures. A. Kleineman, ed. Washington: NIMH, DHEW #75-653.
Marriott, McKim
1976 Hindu Transactions: Diversity without Dualism. *In* Transaction and Meaning. Bruce Kapferer, ed. Philadelphia: Institute for the Study of Human Issues.
Marriott, McKim, and Ronald B. Inden
1977 Toward an Ethnosociology of South Asian Caste Systems. *In* The New Wind: Changing Identities in South Asia. Kenneth David, ed. The Hague: Mouton.
O'Flaherty, Wendy Doniger
1968 Asceticism and Sexuality in the Mythology of Śiva in the Sanskrit Purāṇas. Ph.D. dissertation, Department of Sanskrit and Indian Studies, Harvard University.
1969a Asceticism and Sexuality in the Mythology of Siva, Part I. History of Religions Journal 8(4).
1969b Asceticism and Sexuality in the Mythology of Siva, Part II. History of Religions Journal 9(1).
1971 The Symbolism of Ashes in the Mythology of Siva. Purāṇa 13(1). Varanasi, India: All-India Kashiraj Trust.
1973 Asceticism and Eroticism in the Mythology of Siva. London: Oxford University Press.

Sahlins, Marshall
1976 Culture and Practical Reason. Chicago: University of Chicago Press.
Shweder, Richard A.
1979 Rethinking Culture and Personality Theory, Part I: A Critical Examination of Two Classical Postulates. Ethos 7(3).
Singer, Milton
1972 When a Great Tradition Modernizes: An Anthropological Approach to Indian Civilization. New York: Praeger Publishers.

· 2 ·

Fate, Karma, and Cursing in a Local Epic Milieu

Brenda E. F. Beck

Looking at folk literature can be a very useful way of deepening our knowledge of folk concepts. Basic ideas about causation and about the ethical underpinnings of human life are often expressed in folk stories. The folk epic is a particularly appropriate place to look for such concepts because epic accounts attempt to mirror actual human life more closely than do shorter forms of story. Tamil folktales often deal with fanciful events and focus on magicians, talking animals, or trickster figures. By contrast, Tamil folk epics claim to link up with actual local history. They depict a rich social order that is full of local, caste-specific characters. These local epic heroes also embody a moral perspective. They often depict the overthrow of the unjust. Though the heroes and heroines of such epics may be idealized figures, their very purpose seems to be to challenge some wider framework or destiny. By studying the actions of these epic figures we can come to a better understanding of what such larger concepts of fate may be.

The data for this essay are drawn from the text of a local epic called *The Brothers' Story*, which is currently popular in the Coimbatore District of Tamilnadu.[1] This regional legend draws heavily on patterns and images found in traditional *Mahābhārata* accounts. At the same time it is thoroughly local in terms of its basic descriptive format. The subtle overlap between events and patterns in this regional story and in that celebrated pan-Indian epic are usually lost on casual observers. This is particularly true of spontaneous commentaries on oral versions, less so where interpretations are offered of written

[1] It is locally called the *Annanmarcāmi Katai* or the *Ponnaraka Rennum Kallaraka Ammānai*. This epic-length legend does not seem to be known in the southern and eastern parts of Tamilnadu.

variants. For this reason, a study of oral variants helps clarify which classical epic themes and conceptual structures are thought to be important, even in truly local versions of a folk legend.

This essay will explore the extent to which fate and karma, two key concepts in the *Mahābhārata*, are also important in the *Brothers' Story*. This local epic speaks of a fate (*viti*) that is written on each human forehead.[2] As the actions of the heroes make clear, individuals at best only glimpse what that personal fate consists of. No one, of course, can see his own forehead, except with the aid of a mirror. More commonly, people turn to fortune-tellers for help, since even with magical mirrors one cannot (oneself) read what has been written. The gods, it is felt, reveal themselves through such soothsayers. They often read from books or almanacs that serve as some kind of earthly equivalent of the great account books kept by the gods. The words in these books seem to lay out the future, but they need interpretation. Specific instructions about how to act, and about what to expect, must always be worked out through discussion between a specific divine seer and his local client.

Fate and the Fortune-Teller

In one scene drawn from the *Brothers' Story*, Lord Viṣṇu arrives in the disguise of an old man so that the mother of the heroes can consult him about the reasons for her barrenness. As he approaches, this man calls out to her with a description of his appearance:

> I have grown grey, like *nānal* flowers
> I am a little grey, like a flowering *kōrai*
> I am grey, as the *tumpai* plant does
> Or like the [white] flowers of the *tūtuvilām*
> There are no teeth in my mouth
> There is no substance to my [concave] belly
> My eyes are like [small, black] *kīrai* seeds
> My ears do not hear well
> I am like a dried up old man
> Who has lived ninety years plus ten
> The skin and veins of this old man sag
> This man holds in his hands
> An old, worm-eaten almanac.

[2] It is significant that this image of what is "fixed" or immutable lies in the act of writing it down. We may read into this, perhaps, a significant attitude regarding the difference between oral and written texts more generally.

The woman in question next addresses this fortune-teller as though he were Viṣṇu himself. First she asks for the boon of a child. But the old man answers that he is not Śiva, and that he has no direct power to grant her life. However, he does promise to read his almanac and to provide her with some understanding of her barren condition. He first demands that she bathe, that she call her husband so they can listen together, and that she place a set of offerings in front of him. All these gestures follow closely the expected forms for interaction between an astrologer and a client in contemporary life. Finally, the old man consults his book, turning to a page that deals with luck (*atiṭṭam*). There he reads that there will be no children for this woman until she has endured seven rebirths. She is predictably upset at this revelation and inquires next about what human fault has occasioned this enormous ill fate. She now asks if this misfortune is due to her own incorrect actions in the past, or to those of her husband, or to one of their ancestors.

When the fortune-teller speaks again he seems to look up from his book and to begin the task of personal interpretation. He now speaks of her husband's father and of his grave error in once allowing the death of seven sacred cows. When these cows begged Śiva for justice the great god obliged by cursing the family to barrenness for three times seven (twenty-one) generations. The fortune-teller also reveals, however, that Viṣṇu (with whom he now admits a common identity) was able to soften Śiva's resolve by performing a twenty-one-year penance at the gates of his great residence. Next, the woman is told that her husband was born of Śiva's creative will, but only as a result of Viṣṇu's special pleas. Yet the sin of the death of the seven cows must still be compensated for. That fate has fallen upon her shoulders.

Through a careful look at this passage in the local epic, one can see that concepts about the causes of human suffering are commonly portrayed. One's family, one's ancestors, behavior toward animals, and the will or sympathy of the gods can all be involved. The mother of the heroes now pursues the problem of her barrenness and, logically, asks what she can do about it. The fortune-teller advises that she spend considerable sums of money doing various pious deeds, such as worshipping the gods, constructing public works, and feeding the poor. Finally, she will have to perform a great penance herself, in which she will symbolically pass through seven deaths. Only that, finally, will compensate for the lives of the cows that were carelessly lost. Hence personal effort, devotionalism, and self-sacrifice can here be seen to blend with a more material formula for redressing wrong with equal amounts of right conduct.

Reincarnation

Popular epic images related to incarnation provide a further way into the complex problem of how fate is seen to operate in this epic context. Consider the scene in the *Brothers' Story* where the mother of the legend's twin heroes is first impregnated with their spirit essences. This event occurs just after this heroine has completed the lengthy penance the soothsayer prescribed.[3] Successful, she is now entitled to ask for a boon. The mother-to-be tells Śiva of her wish for two sons. She also wants each one to have the strength of a great elephant. Śiva orders his account-keeper to search for the spirits of two persons already deceased who might fulfill this special condition. Two Pāṇḍava brothers who figure prominently in the *Mahābhārata* are found to suit the woman's demand. The bodiless life essences of these two heroic figures are then retrieved by one of Śiva's assistants from a heavenly storage area not far from this god's home. The great lord explains to each spirit that his essence is about to be returned to earth in a new body. Lastly, Śiva places both of these life-seeds inside a lemon, which the supplicant mother is asked to ingest.[4] The implication is that the epic's heroes-to-be are reincarnations of already existing spirits who will now grow new bodies. Significantly, Śiva himself is seen as the moving force behind this impregnation and the several transformations it will entail.

The physical union of a receptive body and a formless spirit is engineered by the greatest of gods at the very moment of the local heroes' conception. In parallel fashion, a separation of these two occurs at the moment of the heroes' physical death. At that very instant Śiva sends his messenger, Yama, to carry the spirits of the deceased heroes back to heaven in a tiny golden box. In between these two points in time the life essence of the hero is free to act within the

[3] The penance is performed on a pillar made of seven needles. On the tips of these needles are balanced seven spouted cups. On the cups rest seven beads. On the beads rest seven more copper needles. On these seven red oleander flowers are placed. The heroine sits balanced on top of this entire edifice, with one leg folded, one leg hanging down, and both arms extended.

[4] The bardic versions of the epic are the most concrete in their imagery. The printed versions of the story skip this reference to a lesson. The spirits of these persons are there placed in the heroine's belly directly.

body it has been given and must be guided by its own sense of judgment. Even the advice of astrologers and soothsayers must be personally evaluated. The ultimate life-span of each local character is thus preset (for the heroes this period is sixteen years), as are certain other parameters of action, like the whole set of births that occur in a particular family. If penance or atonement for previous misdeeds is seen as an effective way to compensate for and eventually overcome such personal suffering, the exact mix of one's personal past actions with the misdeeds of other family members in determining one's fate is never clear. There is considerable flexibility here, as in so many other aspects of folk belief. In other words, blame for misfortunes can be placed on one's own prior actions, or on the misdeeds of others, whichever is more appropriate given a particular context.

Suffering

Suffering experienced in everyday life is therefore seen to stem from past misdeeds, whether they are one's own or those of someone to whom one is inexorably connected. But physical suffering may also occur between those periods, while the soul participates in worldly events. For example, on the way to heaven the heroes' mother encounters a frightening scene that rivets her attention. Viṣṇu, who is accompanying her on this journey, tells her not to look to either side. However, the heroine cannot help but turn her head at the sound of screams. Suddenly she sees human bodies before her which are being held upside down and whipped. She also sees human bodies being thrown into pits and trampled. The lady asks her divine companion the cause of these events. He explains that in each case the person undergoing torture was selfish in his previous life. One woman refused to pay the doctor or the barber for his services. Another had refused her husband the family cot and told him to lie on the floor. A man is also seen suffering. Viṣṇu explains that he once left his wife for the pleasures of a prostitute. By implication, of course, the heroine has also misbehaved. She looked when she heard the screams, despite Viṣṇu's clear order to keep her eyes averted. In this case the mere discomfort and terror she experiences as an onlooker seem to constitute her punishment. Hence, a character's own misbehavior can lead either to direct or to more indirect forms of torture. All such expiation, however, takes place near the gates of Śiva's palace.

The picture of suffering this local epic provides, therefore, is both rich and logically complex. Pain, anguish, and the denial of one's deepest desires can occur in the ordinary world or in some sort of liminal space where the spirit essence of a person maintains something of its bodily form. But in the liminal space encountered on a journey to Śiva's heaven, characters suffer only from the effects of their own past actions. Like a (negative) pilgrimage, a person is here temporarily relieved of the demands and responsibilities of normal life. It seems that one can suffer from the misdeeds of others only while he is embedded in a normal social milieu. One's own misdeeds, however, continue to affect a person's well-being even when he is alone.

Rewards

The concept of rewards for good behavior is far less developed in the *Brothers' Story*. What is clear is that the benefits of correct and dutiful action come both in the form of ordinary successes in life and in the form of extraordinary boons granted under liminal conditions. The heroes' mother, for example, at one point makes a long trip to heaven to perform penance. It is there, after passing through death seven times, that she is finally granted her wish for pregnancy. At this time, the relationship between this woman's spirit and bodily forms becomes ambiguous. Near the beginning of her magical journey she leaves her husband behind, asleep under a tree. Viṣṇu then steps in as a substitute travel companion. This divine ally turns the woman into a fly in order to enable her to rise above and cross the Himālayas. Here, already, her spirit and her physical form are not as closely wedded as they were in ordinary life. Similarly, she has left the social responsibilities of a dutiful spouse behind. Later, this partial link between body and soul becomes further attenuated by her seven deaths, each of which involves some kind of dismemberment and the later reconstitution of her material self by Viṣṇu. Hence the heroes' mother never attains a perfectly free state of bodiless being. This latter condition is reserved for the life-essences of the *Mahābhārata* heroes who will be reborn as her sons. It would seem that a bodiless state is reserved for those who have no previous misdeeds to haunt them. These great men were totally freed of their bodies at death. Their reward is a chance to exist as spirits or minor divinities in some nether world (not described). Yet, even these beings may always be called upon by higher gods for further service.

Types of Misbehavior

Before we proceed to other issues, it is useful to look in a little more detail at lists of misdeeds described in a variety of folk epics. Written accounts often address the fact of the human condition openly through short philosophical monologs. The more heavily a story and its telling depend on the performative skills of the teller, however, and the more important its appeal to a peasant audience, the more concrete

Table 1
Lists of Misdeeds (Possible Breaches of Dharma That Reap Eventual Suffering)

Oral Text Collected from a Village Bard and Cast in a Performance Style	*Written Text Composed by a Local Urban Poet in a Semi-Folk Style*	*Written Text Composed by a Learned Court Poet*
Not compensating the washerman, barber, or doctor for services performed	Paying someone too little	Lacking gratitude (no expiation possible)
Sleeping on a cot while one's husband sleeps on the floor	Measuring out an incorrect amount	Leaving one's wife for another woman
Leaving one's wife for a prostitute	Telling a beggar to come back later	Misrule by a king who does not observe Manu's laws
	Beating someone who asks for food	Stealing the wealth of one's dependents or subjects
	Beating a mendicant	Harming those who surrender to one and request help
	Beating a Brahmin	Killing a cow, a child, or a Brahmin
	Dividing or destroying a kinsman's field	
	Selling things that belong to god and using the money oneself	
	Preventing someone else from doing works of charity	
	Demanding an exorbitant rate of interest	
	Betraying someone and receiving money for it	
	Taking a poor man's land by writing up fancy legal documents	
	Desiring someone else's goods or property	
Rāmacāmi, E. K. (bard), *Annanmarcāmi Katai* (recited version, pp. 128–129)	Paranacāmi (ed.), *Annanmarcāmi Katai* (p. 69)	Villiputturalavar, Villi Pāratam (Drone Parava, verses 41–43)

will be the imagery used. A good example of increasing degrees of abstraction employed to discuss such core ideas can be drawn from catalogs of misbehavior imbedded in such accounts. These lists occur with some regularity in Indian extended narratives. They also have the advantage of being easily comparable across versions.

The accompanying table compares catalogs of misbehavior drawn from three different epic texts, one oral and one written version of the *Brothers' Story*, and one important literary rendition (in Tamil) of the *Mahābhārata*.[5] These accounts are increasingly abstract in tone, yet virtually the same underlying idea is captured by all. At the most general level, this is the conviction that a misdeed stems from a lack of commitment to certain basic principles of social reciprocity. Such failures may be embodied in the overt breaking of some social contract, or may simply involve taking advantage of another unfairly. If the stipulation that one acknowledge indebtedness is a universal ethical norm, furthermore, the particulars by which that norm finds expression will always be context dependent. From the table one can see that such standards are somewhat more specific in oral- and performance-oriented variants of this epic tradition.

Types of Correct Behavior

Good deeds are rarely as colorfully depicted as are misdemeanors. The penance of the heroes' mother has already been described. This is one of the most vivid and painful scenes in the *Brothers' Story*, and it results in the heroine's winning a major divine blessing. Perhaps this is because her actions involve intense personal suffering. Other, more altruistic deeds which this woman performs, before she agrees to these personal austerities, include building rest points for travelers on public roads, feeding beggars, and financing a major temple festival. Even within the realm of dutiful conduct, the concept of personal sacrifice is never far from the surface. When a beggar appears in the *Brothers' Story*, for example, it is always a god in disguise. The true motive is always to test the person being approached. For an act to be charitable, one must give until it hurts, that is, until some personal sacrifice is involved. Even gestures of charity, however, do not reap key rewards by themselves. Śiva blesses the supplicant with fertility only after her

[5] Compare these with Lodo Rocher's (1980) excerpts from a list of the results of sinful acts provided by Manu in the *Dharmaśāstra*.

good deeds have been capped by this final act of extreme self-denial.

One further setting in which correct behavior is described occurs where merit is accrued less directly, simply by listening to an epic account. Because the *Brothers' Story* depicts the acts of moral men, an audience that attends to those actions itself becomes ethically elevated. The characters in the story themselves suffer at many points. In the end they make an ultimate sacrifice by laying down their own lives. Hence listening to such an epic provides a kind of vicarious experience. If listening to an epic does not involve personal suffering in the direct sense, it would seem to very clearly involve suffering through a psychological identification of members of the audience with particular story characters. Perhaps this is a major reason why the ritual reenactment of scenes from this and other popular epics entails physical hardships for enthusiastic participants. Various ritual behaviors popular in the context of such epic storytelling include walking on hot coals, beating oneself with chains or knives, holding flaming torches, walking barefoot, and even crossing a forest at night.

At the end of an epic recitation, the members of the audience normally receive a special blessing. The words in this benediction contain images of abundance, growth, and prosperity. The words are standardized:

> May you grow and multiply
> luxuriantly like the banyan tree
> May your roots spread out
> like the *aruhu* [grass] and
> May your kin and descendants
> cluster like [clumps of] bamboo.[6]

When angered by the accidental slaughter of seven sacred cows, Śiva cursed the mother of the heroes with barrenness. Now, when finally granting her the boon of pregnancy he also gives her a small pot of sacred water. She is to sprinkle this on everything she encounters in order to spread fertility throughout the kingdom. That imagery finds a resonance in the verses used to bless the audience (above). Further verses, used by local bards in their benedictions, reinforce these metaphoric parallels that hold between moisture, abundance, and fertility:

[6] The wording is apparently common to a great many Tamil ballads. The particular translation given here follows Arunachalam (1976), p. 17.

May your family be like
a milky spring
May there be water
that never dries up.

The Idea of Balanced Quantities

It should now be clear that there is some concept of balance at work in this popular epic. The rules of equivalence require that each misdeed be compensated for by an equal amount of suffering. Each failure seems to be measurable in quantitative terms. These calculations are particularly exacting where life and death are concerned. Hence the seven cows that died must be exactly matched by the seven trials and seven deaths which the heroes' mother must undergo before her infertility can be lifted from her. Prosperity, by contrast, is not granted in measured amounts. Instead of exact numerical estimates, one now finds a much looser imagery of expansion and overflow employed.

Personal Constraints

The two heroes of the *Brothers' Story* are constrained at birth by certain key factors that Śiva and Viṣṇu bargain about long before their lives ever became implanted in their mother's womb: they will only live to be sixteen years old,[7] they will be attacked by a boar, and Viṣṇu will not trouble Śiva with requests for aid during their earthbound lifetimes.[8] Certain more positive parameters of these heroes' lives have also been fixed by the gods. The two men are to be born along with one sister. She, too, will have superhuman powers. And the three of them are to have a low-caste helper. They will also ride great horses especially granted to them by the gods, and they will eventually kill

[7] This fixed period of sixteen years provides one of several links between these heroes and the Kuru dynasty of the *Mahābhārata*. Hiltebeitel (1972) discusses the possible correspondence of this number with the count of days in the light half of the lunar month and hence with lunar symbolism more generally. The son of the great *Mahābhārata* hero Arjuna (whom one of the local heroes is seen to reincarnate) is also fated to live for only sixteen years. He was, of course, a member of the lunar dynasty.

[8] The same idea has already been developed by Hiltebeitel (1976) with reference to Viṣṇu's absence from the dicing match in the *Mahābhārata*, and his absence from the victory camp on the evening of Aśvatthāman's terrible raid (1972). In the same context he also points out the absence of Viṣṇu's subordination to Śiva where life and death matters are concerned. Indeed, there is considerable evidence to suggest that the heroes are themselves seen as manifestations of Viṣṇu for the period of their brief sojourn on earth.

the boar that challenged them. These heroes have no clear understanding of their own life-constraining parameters, however. Instead, their personal destinies are a matter for slow revelation. Each divinity who talks to the heroes speaks in some kind of disguise. Thus such visionary words are never fully attended to, nor can their import be completely understood. Each hero and heroine must test these semi-revealed truths through their own actions and through reflection on those experiences.

The Role of the Gods

There are two levels of action depicted in a folk epic which can now be seen to combine in any given life situation. One level is that of divine ordainment, the other is one of human striving. From the first perspective Śiva preordains what will happen. From the second perspective an individual must himself flesh out that destiny and push it to its limits. If individuals do not know what has been written on their foreheads, much less what is recorded in the account books of the gods, neither do the gods really seem to know in detail what will happen to their protégés. Instead, the role of divinity seems largely to consist of testing human devotees. The more noble, heroic, and self-sacrificing a story character is in the face of the varied challenges that gods provide, the more beneficent and supportive those divine figures become.[9]

These two levels of action can be illustrated by the following lullaby. In this song a local goddess sings to the young heroes while they are still infants being raised under her care:

> You will be dark-complexioned farmers
> You were born as a result of penance
> You will be courageous farmers
> You will be lords, you will be elephant-like
> You will destroy the clansmen
> You will destroy Kompan [the boar]
> You will spear the boar my lords
> You will divide it into seven pieces.

The events described in this song have been preordained. But the two small boys do not really understand the import of the goddess's

[9] Hiltebeitel (1972, 1976) similarly discusses the complementarity of Śiva's and Viṣṇu's roles in the *Mahābhārata*.

visionary words. Later struggles must be directly experienced before the heroes' personal understanding can grow. At one point, for example, the two men do not recognize the destruction of their rice crop as a sign that the great boar has come to challenge them. Later, even after they commit themselves to a war where they are fated to die, these men wonder if they should back out. Just as Arjuna doubts the wisdom of his actions as he enters the great battle depicted in the *Mahābhārata*, so too these local heroes doubt their entry into violent combat. Heroes emerge from such an interaction with a notion of destiny and with the idea that each human must struggle and suffer for himself. The concept of destiny provides a necessary foil. Its function is to provide the individual with encompassing limits, so that there is something to struggle against.

Dice Play

One interesting representation of the contrasting planes of causation that operate in the *Brothers' Story* can be observed in scenes that describe dicing. In this local legend, dicing is a kind of ritual event. Each time the heroes play, Lord Viṣṇu himself stands as their combined opponent. Each time, these men lose. Each such loss, furthermore, directly presages some external political defeat. Hence, the gambling games with Viṣṇu are like contests between these two heroes and their own destiny. But this gambling contest has a special significance. Each throw of the dice allows the gods to "play" with a specific event in which the heroes give up their struggle and allow other forces to determine the outcome. Penance, on the other hand, and the correct worship of local gods can bring increased control over the family and the kingdom. If gambling and the loss of personal control bring political defeat, self-sacrifice and self-control bring victory.

The complementary roles of Śiva and Viṣṇu in this local epic provide additional reinforcement for this purposive, effort-filled view of causation.[10] Śiva, the greatest of all gods, is largely preoccupied with his own meditations, and does not like to be disturbed. For this reason, he rarely enters the epic directly. At points where Śiva does

[10] The portions are allocated to: (1) the elder twin, (2) the younger twin, (3) the younger sister, (4) Viṣṇu, (5) the revenue villages, (6) the little dog, and (7) the First Minister, respectively.

take action, he is shown to be concerned only about the basics of birth and death. Insofar as a person's fixed fate is seen to stem from anywhere in particular, then, it can be seen to derive from decisions taken by Lord Śiva himself.

Viṣṇu, the other great Hindu god, appears in a complementary role. This softer and more compassionate deity enters the action more frequently. He also appears to be more playful than Śiva. Viṣṇu likes to tease and to test his clientele. Furthermore, Viṣṇu is a kind of social worker. Unlike the detached Śiva, Viṣṇu expresses concern about his human devotees and arrives quickly when epic heroes or heroines call upon him. In one example he comes to earth to help a young orphan (the heroes' father). This hungry and abandoned child has decided to sell firewood to local peasants:

Orphan (thinking): I'll climb this tree, cut the wood, let it fall, and tie my takings in a large bundle. Then I will carry this parcel to the next town and deliver it to someone. In exchange I will ask for a good meal of curry and rice.

Narrator (describing): My Lord is riding on his Garuḍa vehicle. My Lord is flying in the center of the sky. My Lord is leaving the milk sea and approaching the earth.

Viṣṇu now arrives in the forest where the boy is seated. He then changes his form into a fly and sits on the chosen tree. As soon as the boy touches its trunk with his hand the branches fall off and form a neat pile. Next the boy climbs down. He now finds that he can bundle up and carry a headload of this firewood that is bigger than fifteen normal headloads would be.

In this incident, Viṣṇu is invisible. The orphan child only senses the god's presence. Furthermore, the boy achieves this state of success not through passive resignation but only through a combination of his own great efforts and his faith in the eventuality of divine assistance.

In other incidents where Viṣṇu teases other devotees, his divine role as a tester becomes even more clear. Only after the endurance and determination of a particular person have been stretched to their very limits, does this god respond. Viṣṇu's teasing of the heroes, then, can be viewed as a technique for building up psychological strength. Both the male and the female characters in the *Brothers' Story* have this personality characteristic. The heroes and heroines, both, continually strive against their self-perceived limits.

Male Courage

A severe test of the heroes' mother, through penance, has already been described. But what is the equivalent test of male courage? Epic males, it seems, meet their personal trials on the battlefield. Furthermore, a striking set of symbolic events presage these ultimate, personal incidents. Before the great war that the brothers fight, a wild boar first appears to destroy the family's rice fields. This animalistic behavior seems to embody all that is chaotic and evil. Local storytellers delight in describing the way in which this boar roots around in the fine seedlings of the paddy pond. He first drains it of all its life-giving water. Next this boar throws the fine young plants around at random. These provide clear inversions of the heroes' mother's actions when she sprinkles the land with water after being granted the divine boon of pregnancy. Here is the symbolic prelude to the impending death of the twin boys themselves. But failing to read these omens, the two heroes enter upon their final days unwittingly.

Sacrifice and Sacrificer

When the twins eventually do succeed in killing the wild boar, that scene serves as a kind of sacrificial ritual not unlike events that more often occur in local temple settings. Normally, a patron will provide some kind of sacrificial animal. The symbolism of such sacrifices is often said to have a metaphoric significance. The sacrificer, it can be argued, is giving up a symbolic equivalent of the self. In the epic studied here the twin heroes take their own lives just a few scenes after they have sacrificed the boar.

How is this ritual equivalence of the sacrificer and the sacrificed accomplished? Immediately after their successful kill the twin brothers skin their animal prize. They then divide the meat into seven portions. Each portion is allocated to a specific member of the heroes' family, to a faithful servant, or to members of the militia.[11] But Lord Viṣṇu is closely watching these events. He now arrives on the scene, disguised as a washerman, and requests a personal share of the sacrificial animal for his pregnant wife. The brothers respond to this stranger's plea for help by giving him the head of this great boar. When the washerman disappears with his prize, however, the twins quickly realize what they have just done. By making an outsider the subject of this important gift they now see that they symbolically prepared the way for a giving up of their own lives.

Younger brother: Oh, my! Instead of taking some allocated portion of meat, my brother, you let him have the head? Just as the boar's head has gone, so we are now about to relinquish our own lives.

It is too late, of course. There will soon be a great battle with nonkinsmen. The heroes now realize that the washerman was a disguise for Lord Viṣṇu himself announcing the end of their sixteenth year. They will soon be handing over their own bodies to the gods.

The fierce war goes against these heroes, and their army is decimated. They cannot return home without their loyal followers, so they instead decide to commit suicide. But this agreement to face death is not just a personal decision. It is also a matter of fate. Viṣṇu announces that their final moment has come by first breaking their sacred chest threads with a magical arrow. In the heroes' suicide, then, destiny and individual willpower are inextricably combined. This merger is diachronic as well as synchronic, furthermore, since the main characters of the story now return to heaven. A return to Śiva's realm, the very place from whence these characters first came, joins their lives with a longer Hindu perspective on cyclical world destruction and renewal.

Festival Rituals

The *Brothers' Story* is currently sung by a wide range of bards in the Salem, Tiruchirappalli, Coimbatore, and Madurai districts of Tamilnadu. In many local towns and villages of this area, festival rituals help

[11] In the *Mahābhārata* (Sukthankar 13.6.7), for example, Bhiṣma at one point speaks to his brother's grandson (Yudhiṣṭhira) saying, "It is not only destiny but also personal effort that determines human life." Bruce Long (1980) has observed, furthermore, that inquiries concerning the nature and destiny of man occur in the *Mahābhārata* at times of extreme distress. Similarly, in this local epic the main heroines (and to a lesser extent the heroes) blame their barrenness (or other misfortunes) on presumed acts of misbehavior in their previous lives, but only during extreme emotional outbursts where such characters burst into stylized (and musical) laments. One can also compare the causal reasons invoked for suffering in other circumstances. Both in Long's discussion of the *Mahābhārata* and in this local epic, these wider influences on one's personal condition include divine interference, inherited strengths and imperfections, support or misunderstanding on the part of various family members, and also planetary (astrological) events.

to enhance the basic story with special ritual proceedings. Indeed, this epic is most often performed at annual celebrations where its heroes can be honored as local divinities. Such dramatic local performances, furthermore, encourage audience participation in death-imitating experiences. Volunteers here lose themselves in a kind of trance that reenacts the death the heroes themselves undergo. Those who really wish to internalize this story relive this key episode as if they were taking the lives of the central characters upon their own bodies for a temporary period.

Female Courage and the Use of Curses

Passage through death provides an ultimate trial, both for the heroes of the story and for their audience of devotees. Cast in terms of a battle, this warrior-sacrifice is a male-oriented theme. It is thus reenacted only by males. Looked at more broadly, however, these same ideas apply equally well to the story's several heroines. In the mother's austere penance, for example, several death themes are evident. In performing her acts of renunciation this heroine suppresses a number of life functions. She does not eat, for example, and she tries not to breathe. At the apex of her efforts, this mother-to-be does not even move a muscle for twenty-one years. Furthermore, her body is intermittently dismembered in various ways. After each death that Śiva brings upon her, Viṣṇu must rescue the woman and reassemble her body pieces. Each time this happens she symbolically completes one more of the seven funerals she must undergo to compensate for the seven cows her father-in-law killed. Even if the concrete acts that demonstrate male and female courage are different, the underlying idea remains one: proof of selfless striving, and a focus on a worthy goal. Only at the possible cost of one's own life can one win ultimate freedom from desire and care. The heroine's goal in this is the search for the reproductive power to perpetuate her family. For the male heroes it is the protection of that same family from external attack and hence external control.

The partial link between suffering and events in the remote past has already been made clear. But the characters of the *Brothers' Story* also experience more immediate and manageable causes of misfortune. If Śiva once cursed the females in the heroes' family with barrenness, a spell of illness is also laid on the males by a little female dog. This cross-gender, cross-species, and size-inverting imagery deserves special attention. The heroines curse various males in the story at one time or another. But only a covert female, in the form of a tiny bitch, is seen to lay a curse on the great epic warriors themselves. For all such acts of malice the person uttering the spell must first have special power due to personal self-control. Furthermore, such curses can be lifted only when a divine soothsayer reveals the cause of suffering and when steps have been taken to compensate for whatever moral failure allowed the curse to work.

In the example above, the little (female) dog was first ignored by the heroes when they left on the great boar hunt. This dog had always been a loyal member of the household, and she felt that her rights had been unjustly overlooked. The heroes' moral oversight and the dog's stockpile of loyal service thus allowed her to curse these men at a crucial moment, as they prepared to hunt the great enemy. When the heroes notice a sudden inability to fight, they consult a fortune-teller. Discovering the true cause, they then send an apology to the little dog and invite her to join the hunting party. She lifts her curse, accompanies the men, and later plays an important role in capturing the enemy. Women are thus as powerful as men, though the forms of influence they wield are different. Men are seen to be this-worldly, physically imposing, and generally straightforward. Women are portrayed as more magical, small, and indirect.

Conclusion

In both the pan-Indian epic and the local milieu ideas about fate, karma and cursing are important. In both contexts, too, a concept of fixed destiny is balanced by a second theme: personal, heroic, and striving. We repeatedly witness how discipline and inner strength can overcome the inherited weaknesses and limits of individual characters. But such an overcoming always seems to involve a passage through death. The message would seem to be that death cannot be postponed. Instead, it must be conquered. When death is viewed as self-transformation, to meet it can become a personal challenge. The power of self-willed suicide can convert such an event into a symbolic triumph over self-limitations. The concept of fate or destiny, in sum, is the necessary challenge. A hero or a heroine requires a fixed (forehead) fate and a knowledge of certain death in order to have an opportunity for this self-transcending struggle.

In an article on conceptual differences between North and South India in such matters, George Hart has spoken of the importance of devotional thought in the South of India today. This Southern folk account, similarly, skillfully combines traditional pan-Indian epic themes with a modern, regional enthusiasm for devotional themes. The legendary heroes of the *Brothers' Story* often see their suffering in terms of a divine concern to test them. But this legend also incorporates much that is Brahmanical and Northern by its equal stress on the sociological, substantive, and positivistic causes of human suffering. In sum, this folk view of human destiny is not simple, either in basic conception or in overall structure. Instead, it represents a rich blend of many currents in traditional Hindu thought.

References Cited

Arunachalam, M.
1976 Peeps into Tamil Literature: Ballad Poetry. Tiruchitrambalam, Tanjore District: Gandhi Vidyalayam.
Beck, Brenda E. F.
1978a The Logical Appropriation of Kinship as a Political Metaphor: An Epic at the Civilizational and Regional Levels (India). Anthropologica 20(1–2):46–64.
1978b The Hero in a Contemporary Local Tamil Epic. Journal of Indian Folkloristics 1(1):26–39.
1978c The Personality of a King: Prerogatives and Dilemmas of Kingship as Portrayed in a Contemporary Epic from South India. *In* Kingship and Authority in South Asia. John Richards, ed. Madison: University of Wisconsin, Madison, Publication Series, No. 3, pp. 169–191.
Hart, George L. III
1980 The Theory of Reincarnation among the Tamils. *In* Karma and Rebirth in Classical Indian Traditions. Wendy Doniger O'Flaherty, ed. Berkeley: University of California Press. Pp. 116–133.
Hiltebeitel, Alf
1972 The Mahābhārata and Hindu Eschatology. History of Religions 12(2):95–135.
1976 The Ritual of Battle: Krishna in the Mahābhārata. Ithaca and London: Cornell University Press.
Long, Bruce J.
1980 The Concepts of Human Action and Rebirth in the Mahābhārata. *In* Karma and Rebirth in Classical Indian Traditions. Wendy Doniger O'Flaherty, ed. Berkeley: University of California Press. Pp. 38–60.
O'Flaherty, Wendy, ed.
1980 Karma and Rebirth in Classical Indian Traditions. Berkeley: University of California Press.
Paranacāmi, K. P., ed.
1971 Annanmarcāmi Katai (The Story of the Brothers). Coimbatore: Verrivel Patippakam (2nd ed., 1977).

Rāmacāmi, E. K. (bard)
1964 Annanmarcāmi Katai (The Story of the Brothers). Two texts are extant, one tape-recorded during a performance before a village audience, the other dictated to a scribe.
Rocher, Ludo
1980 Karma and Rebirth in the Dharmaśāstras. *In* Karma and Rebirth in Classical Indian Traditions. Wendy Doniger O'Flaherty, ed. Berkeley: University of California Press. Pp. 61–89.
Sukthankar, V. S., ed.
1935 The Mahābhārata (in Sanskrit, critical edition). Poona: Bhandarkar.
1959 Oriental Research Institute. (Mandakranta Bose helped to locate and translate the particular passage cited in this paper.)
Villiputturalavar, Sarava-Bhauma A.
1970 Villi Pāratam. Madras: Star Publications.

·3·

Karma Divined in a Ritual Capsule

E. Valentine Daniel

The "ritual of flowers," a colorful little rite of divination, may be encountered in almost any roadside shrine or temple courtyard all over South India and in the Tamil-speaking areas of Sri Lanka. Even though this rite is very commonplace, it has, by and large, gone uncelebrated if not unnoticed by the countless scholars whose interest in things "religious" and "ritualistic" has been more than perfunctory. Bishop Gustav Diehl, who has recorded this particular rite, has done so with so little pause that the reader hardly notices it (1956). It is not until Brenda Beck's paper on "Colour and Heat in South Indian Ritual" (1969) that we find a serious attempt to understand the structure and meaning of this rite.

In this essay I shall attempt to uncover the logic underlying this rite and in so doing will be led to differ with Beck on several points of analysis. While the greater part of these differences are due to the limited nature of the body of data that was available to her, some are

Most of the data on which this essay is based were gathered during field research carried out in the Tamil village of Kalappūr (pseudonym) in South India. This study was made possible by grants from three sources. The National Science Foundation met the greater part of the expenses of the project, and the Danforth Foundation, some of it. A grant from the Amherst Memorial Fellowship Fund enabled the author to carry out some essential ancillary field research in Sri Lanka among Āru Nāṭṭu Veḷḷāḷa expatriots. To all three sources of support, I am grateful. This essay benefited a great deal from comments made by the participants in the American Council of Learned Societies and the Social Science Research Council Joint Committee South Asian Seminar at the University of Chicago on "Persons and interpersonal relationships: An exploration of indigenous conceptual systems," where it was presented for the first time. A special debt is owed to the following individuals who read one or more earlier drafts of this essay and made valuable suggestions: Bernard Cohn, Veena Das, McKim Marriott, Terrence Turner, Victor Turner, Lee Schlesinger, and most important, my wife, Sherry.

due to the different types of questions which we have asked of the same data. In principle, however, her analysis is sound and was my original source of inspiration for studying this ritual more extensively and intensively. I shall not engage in a point-for-point comparison and contrast of Beck's analysis with mine except where such comparisons seem inevitable.

Before we get to the ritual per se, it is imperative that I introduce the reader to several cultural concepts that are indispensible for an understanding of the analysis that is to follow.

Hot and Cold

Hot and Cold Foods

Beck, in her paper "Colour and Heat in South Indian Ritual" (1969), has provided us with a list of foods classified according to whether they are 'hot' or 'cold'. At least five qualifications have to be made with respect to such a classification.

1. Foods are not lumped into a clearly defined 'hot' or 'cold' category. Rather, they are strung along a hot–cold gradient.
2. The classification of known foods according to 'hot' and 'cold' is not a generalized, translocal, pan-Indian or pan-South Asian one. Foods that are considered to be 'cold' in one region of South Asia may be thought of as being 'hot' in another region and vice versa. There is a variety of the plantain fruit known as *āna mālu*, for instance, which is considered to be 'hot' by the Sinhalese of southern Sri Lanka but to be 'cold' by some groups of Jaffna Tamils of the island's north.
3. Such variations in the classification of foods according to 'hot' and 'cold' may cut across caste lines in the same locality or village. Buffalo milk, for example, considered 'hot' by the Telugu Brahmins of Kalappūr, is thought of as being neither too 'hot' nor too 'cold' by the Paṟayans of the same village.
4. One can even become more centrifocal and say that there is a variation in food classification between one individual and another, and
5. With the same individual from one context to another.

Sunther is eighteen years old and the son of one of the wealthier Veḷḷāḷa landlords of Kalappūr. His father owns six milch cows. But Sunther has been unable to drink milk from the age of four, probably because of the absence of lactase in his system. Consequently, his mother has decided that cow's milk is too 'hot' for him even though ordinarily it is a 'cold' food and treated as such. This anecdote illustrates (4) above.

The variation according to context with respect to the same individual (5, above) was illustrated to me by a Siddha physician in Tiruchirappalli who maintained that even the same patient who is able to eat a particular food because of its being 'cold' on one day will not be able to eat the very same food on another day when for one reason or another it will turn out to be 'hot' for him.

The point being made here is that 'hot' and 'cold' are relative concepts: relative to locality, caste, individual, and even time. General criteria for the classification of foods as being either 'hot' or 'cold' are neither unequivocal nor consistent. The only incontrovertible statement that can be made regarding 'hot' and 'cold' foods is that foreign foods (including Western drugs) or foods whose origin is clearly marked as being alien are, without exception, 'hot'. The most pointed example being ice cream, which is thought of as being very 'hot', emphasizing the fact that the South Asian concepts of 'hot' and 'cold' have little if anything to do with temperature per se, that is, as we understand it thermometrically.

Hot and Cold Persons

Like foods, persons too may be seen to occupy places along a 'hot'–'cold' gradient. Some have 'hot' bodies and some have 'cold' ones—once again with the added qualification that 'cold' bodies can become 'hot' and 'hot' ones 'cold' under certain conditions in certain contexts. In general, it may be said, however, that the maximally transacting Veḷḷāḷās and the pessimally transacting Parayans have 'hotter' bodies than the optimally transacting Brahmins and the minimally transacting Āsāris, that is, the smiths and carpenters.[1] The 'hot' castes, it will be noted, more readily, willingly, and customarily eat 'hot' foods than do the 'cool' castes. Here, too, individual variation, such as Sunther,

[1] The terminology derives from Marriott's (1976) fourfold classification of transactional strategies:

(a) Minimal transactors are those who prefer, whenever possible, to refrain from both giving and receiving.
(b) Maximal transactors are those who both give and receive relatively freely.
(c) Optimal transactors are those who give but shy away from receiving.
(d) Pessimal transactors are those who, for one reason or another, end up receiving more than they give.

the Veḷḷāḷa lad whose prescribed diet had to be 'cooler' than even that of a Brahmin or an Āsāri, must be taken into account.

A healthy person then, is one who maintains an optimum balance between 'hot' and 'cold'. This optimal level, however, is caste specific and even person specific. What determines the optimal level is one's coded substance (Marriott and Inden 1974), or *kuṇam*.

Hot and Cold Humors and Kuṇams

While the stabilization of the easily upsettable humoral balance is a cumbersome task and calls for constant attention, it is not an impossible one. This is, in fact, the primary preoccupation of a skilled Ayurvedic or Siddha physician.[2] The proportion of humors in a body is alterable by several means, diet and drugs being the most common ones. The *kuṇams*, however, are exceedingly stable and cannot be altered as easily as the humors can.

In terms of the physician's concerns and priorities, humors are more directly related to states of illness and health than *kuṇams*. Humors, not *kuṇams*, belong to the diagnostician's and physician's expertise. The physician's primary aim is to get at the humor imbalance even though he may admit that humors and *kuṇams* are related and by exension that *kuṇams* too implicate conditions of health and illness even though less directly.

Of the three humors, bile (*pittam*) is 'hot', phlegm (*kapam*) is 'cold', and wind (*vāyu*) is middling, though more often than not tending toward 'heat'. In the village of Kalappūr, I was able to compile seventeen disorders attributed to bile, sixteen to wind, and only eight to phlegm. To this list must be added one bodily disorder resulting from the combined malfunctioning of bile and wind, one from that of phlegm and wind, and one from that of phlegm and bile. Of the entire catalog of humor-caused bodily disorders, only eight were seen as having been caused by or resulting in 'cold'-cum-sick bodily states. And all eight were caused by an imbalance in phlegm. The remaining thirty-seven were associated with 'heat' as either being caused by or resulting in the latter.

On a frequency table drawn up from a sample of ten local nonspecialist diagnosticians who translated illnesses in terms of the humors and 'hot' and 'cold', the ratio of 'heat'-associated disorders to 'cold'-

[2] One of the three major branches of indigenous medical systems practiced in India, the other two being Unani and Ayurveda. Siddha medicine is confined to the South.

associated ones was 25:1. About the same ratio held in the case of the Siddha specialist in Tiruchirappalli. The obvious point, of course, being that according to cultural categories 'heat' is far more likely to be implicated as causing bodily disorder than is 'cold'.

Both the native physician and the priest performing the divination are concerned with 'heat' and 'cold'. However, while the former is but secondarily concerned with a patient's *kuṇam*, for the divining priest (in the ritual of flowers) the *kuṇam* of his patient is of primary importance. If the priest is at all concerned with humors, it is only in terms of the humors' relationship to the patient's *kuṇam*. The physician deals with temporary conditions of 'heat' and 'cold' caused by the ever-changing humoral balance and imbalance. The priest is concerned with the more permanent conditions of 'heat' and 'cold' which are determined not so much by the fluctuating humors as by the relatively permanent *kuṇams* or dispositions. If one may make a cytogenetic analogy here, it may be said that the priest is interested in genotypy whereas the physician's primary interest is in phenotypy. I shall justify this analogy later in this essay.[3]

'Heat' is also associated with transformations, most obviously in cooking, less obviously in initiation rites, life-crises rituals, all manner of rites of passage, and menstruation (especially in a girl's first menstruation), to mention but a few. All these processes involve separation or mixing and transformation of bodily and nonbodily substances.

The following folk-poem illustrates the work of 'heat' in a maiden's first menstruation:

Potinta tāmarai pūttal kaṇṭu
Oṭiyatō mūṭupani—alla
Katiravan eṛutal kaṇṭu
Maraintatō kūren kaṇmaṇi

Tell me my precious one;
Has the mist run away
Seeing the lotus-bud unfurl
Or is it the sun's awakening
That has driven him into hiding?

[3] There are several points of congruence between my use of genotype and phenotype and that of Robert LeVine's (1973:121–124), in spite of LeVine's use of these concepts to explicate personality alone.

Here the heat generated by the blossoming (*pūttal*) of the lotus—symbolic of the vagina and the coming of age—is compared to that generated by the sun. More often, of course, menstrual 'heat' is spoken of in less poetic and more "dangerous" terms. In any event, it is natural for a girl's first menstruation to be a 'heat'-generating process. Furthermore, in spite of all the danger and vulnerability associated with puberty, it is, on the whole, a desired change from childhood (*kanni*) to a potentially fertile state (*kumari*), a change that brings a female to the threshold of what Babb aptly describes as "the supreme affirmation of her identity" as a woman and provides her a secure "place in the scheme of things" (Babb 1975:76).

The house-opening ceremony known as *graha pravēsam* is yet another example of a transformatory ritual believed to generate a great quantity of 'heat'. This is why Agni is fed 'cooling' ghee in the *hōma kuṇṭam* (the ritual hearth), and the nine planets are fed 'cooling' watermelons, the ancestral spirits (*pitrus*) are fed 'cooling' halved limes, and every room in the house is washed with turmeric water, which is considered to be 'cooling'.

Sexual intercourse, another process involving transformation through combining and separating (E.V. Daniel 1979, chap. 3) is described as a 'heat-caused' and 'heat-generating' process. 'Cold', on the contrary, seems to be associated with stabilized, sterile, and non-procreative states.

Hot and Cold Colors

'Heat' and 'cold' also have certain colors with which they are ordinarily associated. Black and red are 'hot', while green and white are usually thought of as being 'cool' and never as being 'hot'. Red in particular, by being associated with 'heat', is an auspicious color with respect to fertility, procreation, and motherhood, and consequently marriage itself. Thus we find that a Tamil Hindu bride would never consider wearing white, which is an infertile, unpassionate, 'cold' color, a color of widowhood, social disinterest, marginality, and even asceticism. The most popular color of the bridal sari is red or shades of red. I did ask one informant who told me about green being a 'cold' color why the bride in a wedding we attended together was wearing a green sari. First he explained it away by saying, "Ah! The green brings out the *jarukai* (the gold border); and gold is a fertile color." After awhile he said, "Well, green too is a fertile color. It reminds you of the green fields after the monsoons." White, I might add, does not have such a redeeming iconic or even indexical attribute in the context of a maiden's marriage.[4] Red in the same context is unequivocally auspicious.

Description of the Ritual of Flowers

This ritual is one of divination in which the temple priest, usually a non-Brahmin priest or *pūcāri*, takes six packets made of green leaves. Within three of these are concealed red flowers, and within the other three, white ones. When the supplicant has stated his question to the priest, the latter throws the six packets of concealed flowers on the floor of the temple after reciting a few incomprehensible *mantras*. When this is done, a bystander, preferably a little girl (or some such marginal individual), is asked to make a pick. The priest then divines the future of the supplicant or that of the subject for whom the ritual is being performed from the color of the flowers found in the packet thus chosen. The divination is phrased in the form of a direct statement as to what the future holds in store for the patient or else is stated as a conditional one in which he would say, "If you do x you will reap y," which is as much advice to the patient as it is a divination of the future.

In any event, to conclude one's divination from a single throw and pick is rare and may be considered to be the most elementary form of this ritual. More often than not, one or more additional throws are made, and the colors picked are sequentially added on to the color of the first pick before a final judgment is given. The most elaborate form of the ritual allows for a maximum of four throws and four picks. An important point to be remembered, however, is that when and if the divination is to be made on the basis of more than one pick, there must be a change of colors in the sequence at some point of the ritual. Only then is it deemed possible to answer the question posed for the divination.

Red Flowers = 'Heat'; White Flowers = 'Cold'

In our earlier discussion we established the equivalence between red and 'heat' and white and 'cold'. On the one hand, we saw that red, by

[4] I use "icon" and "index" as specifically intended by C. S. Peirce's trichotomy of signs: an icon being a sign in which representamen and object are related by shared quality; an index being a sign when the relationship between representamen and object is one of contiguity; a symbol being a sign defined by the arbitrary nature of the relationship that inheres between representamen and object. (See Peirce 2: 227–307 for a more elaborate and detailed classification of signs.)

being a warm and fertile color, was auspicious for anything that had to do with marriage. On the other hand, we saw that most illnesses are caused by excessive 'heat' and therefore it is only reasonable to assume that white, by being the equivalent of 'coolness', should be a desired or auspicious color with regards to most illnesses. This much is obvious.

However, we did take note of the fact that not all illnesses are 'heat'-caused, that there are some, admittedly a few, that may be caused by 'cold'. For this reason, to group questions presented to the priest for divination as those having to do with "illness" as opposed to those having to do with "marriage," as Beck seems to have implied in her categorization, can be misleading. As we take a closer look at the ritual of flowers it will become evident that a much broader definition of illness than that which Beck employs is warranted. Under such an expanded definition the protracted unmarried state itself may be said to be a condition of being ill regardless of whether the abnormality of the protracted maidenhood of the patient is the result of an imbalance of the humors or the result of Mars being in the seventh house or of some other astrological mishap (the latter itself potentially capable of expressing itself in humoral imbalance as one of many ways in which it could become manifest). The physician, as was stated earlier, is concerned with symptoms (such as dysmenorrhea or some such apparent disorder) and the causes that directly underlie them, which causes are invariably related to humoral imbalances. For this reason, for the average native physician, the unmarried state may not be an "illness" in the strict sense of that term unless, of course, there are symptomatic disorders such as the ones mentioned above. For the divining priest, however, the protracted state of maidenhood itself is symptomatic, not necessarily of a relatively surface phenomenon such as a humoral imbalance, but of a deeper undesirable condition of the patient's *kuṇam*. By this broader conception an abnormally protracted unmarried state becomes tantamount to an illness.

Even if we were to circumscribe our analysis by a narrow definition (a physician's definition) of illness, as Beck has done, and thereby remove marriage out of the province of sickness and health, two obvious problems persist in her categorization of questions presented to the diviner in the ritual of flowers. First, as was already indicated, there are some illnesses, few as they may be, that are 'cold'-caused and in which instances the warmth of red will be desirable. Thus to unequivocally identify red (warm) flowers in the ritual as inauspicious with regards to illnesses is not justified. Second, in the ritual of flowers there are questions presented to the diviner which have nothing whatsoever to do with marriage or illness per se—questions such as "Should I go to Madurai tomorrow?" or "Should I embark upon this new business venture?" However, these questions do have something to do with movement and stasis, instability and stability, restlessness and peacefulness, and desire and satiation—all these pairs in turn being various expressions of 'hot' and 'cold', respectively.

To return to our flowers, the criterion upon which the auspiciousness of a color is based is whether that color (red or white) is associated with that state which is desirable or not with respect to a particular condition of the subject for whom the ritual is being performed, this condition being determined as being either 'cold' or 'hot'.

It is also fallacious to classify illness-related questions, as Beck has explicitly done, as being "questions about the end of an undesirable condition existing at present" and marriage-related questions as being "those about the occurrence of a desirable event in the future" (Beck 1969:555). Even if we were to overlook the fact that there are so many questions that may be asked of the diviner which have nothing to do with marriage or illness per se, and if we were to limit ourselves to Beck's own catalog of marriage and illness-oriented questions, both classes of questions are at the same time about an undesirable present condition—either an unmarried state or the state of being ill—and about the occurrence of a desirable event in the future: marriage and health respectively. This brings us back to what I find to be the most satisfactory way of classifying the questions presented to the diviner, namely, as those relating to 'cold'-caused undesirable states and 'heat'-caused undesirable states.

In its most elementary form, the ritual of flowers consists of a single throw and a single pick. In this form, however, the meanings assigned to the flowers are quite arbitrary and have nothing to do with either 'hot' or 'cold', being merely a product of the whimsical choice of the moment made by either priest or supplicant. After the packages of concealed flowers are thrown on the ground, the supplicant or the priest makes up his mind as to what colored flower if picked would be a good omen. In this case the meaning attributed to any given colored flower is quite arbitrary in every sense of that term, and both Saussure (1959:69) and Peirce (1958:2:307)[5] would have agreed to call the

[5] All reference to Peirce's *Collected Papers* will appear in the text using the conventional volume and paragraph numbers.

meaning thus constituted, symbolic, even unconventionally symbolic.

Most diviners, however, base their divinations on a certain complexly structured logic of signification. This logic is iconic and indexical rather than symbolic. By iconic I refer to a signifying relationship in which the representamen and the object are qualitatively alike and which quality renders the representamen fit to be as such. Thus the redness of a red flower in being 'hot' is an icon (representamen) of the 'hot' state of a patient afflicted by a 'hot' disease (object), or correspondingly a white flower in being 'cold' is an icon of the 'cold' state of an inherently unmarriageable girl.

In the context of the ritual, the flower, be it 'cold-white' or 'hot-red', may also index the state of the patient. As an indexical sign the particular flower or flower-sequence qualifies as a sign because of some existential relation or connection to the object it represents and which connection then makes it an appropriate sign for calling attention to that object (see Fitzgerald 1966:61).

What follows is an analysis of the more elaborate, complex, and specialized iconic-cum-indexical mode of the ritual rather than the simple, nonspecialized symbolic form. The analysis of the iconic-indexical function itself may be carried out on four levels.

Analysis: Level 1

Table 1 displays in outline the colors and their sequences in picks ranging from one to four in number, which signify either affirmative or negative responses to two kinds of questions. It is quite clear that in the single-pick form of the ritual the decoding of the colors into their appropriate messages is done in terms of their iconic associations with either 'heat' or 'cold'.[6] Thus, to the question regarding a 'cold'-caused undesirable state of being unmarried, a red flower, by its association with 'heat' and fertility, spells out an auspicious answer. A white flower, on the other hand, portends a 'cold' and infertile state, hardly desirable for marriage.

We noted above the inadequacy of Beck's statement which classified illness-related questions as being "those about the end of an undesirable condition existing at present" and marriage-related questions as ones concerned "about the occurrence of a desirable event in

[6] It will be noted that this table omits the divination from a single pick which is based on pure arbitrariness.

Table 1
'Heat' and 'Cold'-Caused Undesirable States

	'Cold'-caused undesirable states Sample question: Will my daughter be married?				*'Heat'-caused undesirable states* Sample question: Will my son recover from smallpox?			
	Auspicious			*Inauspicious*	*Auspicious*			*Inauspicious*
Single pick	R			W	W			R
Double pick	RW			WR	WR			RW
				(WW)				(WW)
				(RR)				(RR)
		Karmam-complex				*Karmam*-complex		
Triple pick (a)[1]	WRR	Strong	Weak	WRW	RWW	Strong	Weak	RWR
(b)[2]	WWR	Present	Absent	WWW	WWR	Present	Absent	WWW
	RRW	Present	Absent	RRR	RRW	Present	Absent	RRR
Quadruple pick[1]	WWRR	Strong	Weak	WWRW	RRWW	Strong	Weak	RRWR

[1] These throws and picks are called "*pūcai palankaṇittal*," or "the evaluation of the strength of the *karmam-complex*."

[2] *This throw and pick is called "pūcai kaṇittal*," or "determining the existence of the *karmam*-complex."

the future." I maintained that all questions, regardless of whether they are marriage-related or illness-related, are about an undesirable present condition and a desirable future one. However, this is still inadequate in that it fails to be specific; it fails to delineate the sign-function and the signifying mechanism involved. Here again the double-sequence form of the ritual enables us to confront this question more squarely than we have done thus far.

Do the first and second flowers in a given sequence in any way stand for past, present, or future? Let us attempt to answer this riddle by looking at our sample 'hot'-state question, in which the supplicant wishes to know whether his son will recover from smallpox, a 'heat'-caused disease. There are three possible ordered pairs for the white–red sequence.

1. *White = Past* and *Red = Future*: This must be ruled out on the grounds that if red were to signify the future, the future is bound to be a 'hot' one and hardly a desirable state for a patient afflicted by smallpox, a disease caused and exacerbated by 'heat'.

2. *White = Present* and *Red = Future*: This must also be rejected for the same reason that (1) was rejected. Furthermore, to say that "white" symbolized the "present" would, at least on the face of it, contradict reality where the patient is anything but 'cool'.

3. *White = Past* and *Red = Present*: This makes little sense when

we remember that the whole purpose of this ritual is to divine the future and not so much to know about the past and the present, unless, of course, these can shed some light in some way on what might be. Moreover, if in the interest of consistency we were to apply the same rule to questions about marriage, it would be meaningless to speak of a past unmarried state and a present married one, or vice versa, given that the subject's past and present states are both that of being unmarried. Furthermore, if at all there were a flower-sequence that could meaningfully symbolize the unchanged, unmarried state, it would be a white–white sequence. But we have already noted that a non-alternating color-sequence is disallowed by the ground rules of the ritual, for such a non-alternating sequence is judged as being null and void, devoid of any intrinsic message other than that of its being null and void.

A clue to this riddle was provided for me by a supplicant named Karuppan, whom I met one day as he was returning after having had the ritual of flowers performed for him. Karuppan's daughter was twenty-three years old and had failed to secure herself a bridegroom. On this occasion the reading given by the flowers was a good one. The order of colors in a double-throw sequence had been red and then white, an auspicious response to a question related to a 'cold'-caused unstable state. On his way from the temple I asked Karuppan whether this had been the first time he had had the ritual of flowers performed in his behalf.

K: [Karuppan, henceforth K] No, sir. I've been doing this every January since my girl attained puberty at the age of fourteen.

A: [Anthropologist, henceforth A] Is this the first time Murugan [his favored deity] has given you a pleasing answer?

K: Oh, no! He has given me the good sign twice before.

A: Then why isn't Janaki married as yet?

K: Man is hasty. Always hasty. Murugan knows the right time. God never fails. . . . It is all written. It is one's *yōkam*. It is one's *viti* [both *viti* and *yōkam* can be translated variously as fate, luck, fortune, destiny, etc.]. It is one's *kuṇam*.

A: If it is one's *yōkam*, then why worry about it? Doesn't *viti* always fulfill itself?

K: Yes, sir. There is *viti*. But one can always prevent *viti* from happening or make *viti* happen [then quoting a common Tamil proverb]: *Vitiyai matiyāl vellalām* [*Viti* can be conquered by *mati*; *mati* meaning discernment, judgment, intelligence, etc.].

A: I don't understand.

K: If I had good *yōkam* and did not try, that good *yōkam* would never be fulfilled.
A: Can you stop bad *viti*?
K: Of course I can provided I do the right *karmam* [*murayāna karmam*].

Then he proceeded to relate the following incident:

> My youngest daughter was fated [*vitikkappaṭṭiruntatu*] to die before she was five. It was in her *jātakam* that she was to die of a snakebite. For five years I made vows, I visited Katirgāmam [a holy place in South Sri Lanka], and I prayed to Sivan and his son, Murugan, and they saved her. He never fails. God never fails. Right effort [*murayāna muyatcci*] never fails. After that her *viti* changed. Her *yōkam* changed and her *kuṇam* changed.

Two salient conceptual sets emerge from this dialogue. First, *viti*, *yōkam*, and *kuṇam* are used in a roughly interchangeable and equivalent manner connoting their relative permanence. Second, right effort (*murayāna muyatcci*) and proper action (*murayāna karmam*) and intellect, judgment, and discernment, collectively called *mati*, are used in a roughly paradigmatic manner. And it is shown that *viti-yokam-kuṇam* can be controlled and directed, suppressed or given expression, by *karmam-muyatcci-mati*. I am in no way minimizing the differences (semantic or pragmatic) that exist between and among *viti*, *yōkam*, and *kuṇam*, on the one hand, and the differences that exist between and among *karmam*, *muyatcci*, and *mati*, on the other. On a scale of determinism vs. indeterminism, *viti* is most deterministic, *yōkam* less so, and *kuṇam* least deterministic of the three. On a scale in which the degree of will or *sittam* is the criterion, *mati* and *muyatcci* would tend to have greater *sittam* than would *karmam*, and so on. But basically there is something that holds the former three members together in contradistinction to the latter three. *Viti*, *yōkam*, and *kuṇam* are primarily states or conditions, whereas *karmam*, *muyatcci*, and *mati* imply action and effort. At least in the context of the ritual this is how these terms have been used. But the important point must be made that this duality collapses in different contexts and even at different levels of analysis and exegesis of the ritual itself. It is only too well known that *karmam*, for instance, describes both action and state, as in "Have you performed all your *karmams*?" and in "Poor chap. He has to suffer so much. Such is his *karmam*."

Henceforth, for the sake of convenience I shall refer to *viti*, *yōkam*, and *kuṇam* collectively as the *kuṇam*-complex and the set of *karmam*, *muyatcci*, and *mati* as the *karmam*-complex.

The *kuṇam*-complex is believed to be inherent and unalterable in one's given lifetime. However, with the help of the *karmam*-complex one can bring about the realization or the non-realization of the *kuṇam*-complex. In other words, the *kuṇam*-complex is potentially fixed and permanent. However, this potential form can be converted into its kinetic counterpart. Such a conversion can be effected only by performing some manner of action upon it. This action, *karmam*-complex, or "appropriate effort," as Karuppan called it, may take the form of sacrifices, pilgrimages, vows, offerings, *pūjās*, prayers, or simply effort (*muyatcci*).

It is not unusual to hear a Tamil mother bemoaning the fact that her son failed to live up to her ideal, by saying, "My son's *viti* and *yōkam* was to become a doctor, but alas he never tried!" In other words, her son's potential *yōkam* or *kuṇam*-complex was that of becoming a doctor, but he never acted upon it in order to transform it from its potential to its kinetic form.

While action or right effort, or the *karmam*-complex, can aid in the actualization of the *kuṇam*-complex, it can also arrest the fulfillment of an evil *kuṇam*-complex. Thus the way Karuppan arrested the evil *viti* of his youngest daughter, who was fated to die of a snakebite at the age of five, was by performing the proper *karmam*-complex.

The duality being made here between the *kuṇam*-complex and the *karmam*-complex is analogous to the duality that holds between actor and action, product and process, or condition and operation. Am I really justified in making such a distinction? Yes and no. And I am afraid that the apparent contradiction is not mine—it is Tamilian; I dare say it is South Asian. In the final analysis it is a question of levels. As we take a closer look at the structure of this ritual of flowers we shall be able to see both the apparent contradiction and its resolution in an encapsulated form.

I shall continue my analysis of the ritual of flowers at the level in which the duality between the *karmam*-complex and the *kuṇam*-complex is maintained. I shall return later to the level in which this duality is negated.

My hypothesis about and a response to what we called "the riddle" of how the first and second flowers corresponded to the periods of time is that the flowers do not, in a simple one-to-one correspondence, symbolize past, present, or future. What the flowers in fact do is signify one's *kuṇam*-complex and one's *karmam*-complex. The two complexes, as has been established, are different both in form and in kind, analytically and semiotically,[7] at the level I am dealing with now. One is a state, the other is a process; one is a condition, the other is an instrument that is intended to act upon that condition. How is this duality signified by the ritual of flowers? The answer is quite clear. As you may recall, according to the rules by which the ritual is performed, *the colors must alternate*. The difference in color between the first and the second flower is what establishes this distinction between the *kuṇam*-complex and the *karmam*-complex.

The first flower picked, I hypothesize, is one's *kuṇam*-complex, which admittedly is an inherent, inalienable state. In the most elementary form of the ritual represented in Table 1, where only one pick is made, the color of the flower picked is iconically related to the "complexion" of the subject's *kuṇam*-complex as being either 'hot' or 'cold'. In response to a question regarding a 'cold'-caused undesirable state, a red flower is auspicious because it signifies a potentially favorable *kuṇam*-complex, suitable for marriage. The same would be true for the auspicious white flower picked in response to the question regarding a 'heat'-caused undesirable condition, such as being afflicted with smallpox.

Earlier I equated the *kuṇam*-complex with genotypy. I suppose that one could conceive of equating the *kuṇam*-complex with the cryptotype in Whorf's opposition of phenotype vs. cryptotype (1956:105) or else substitute terms such as "unmanifest," "covert," "latent," and so forth, as the analogue of the *kuṇam*-complex. Instead, I have chosen the word "genotypy" as it contrasts with "phenotypy" because I wish to stress the cultural idea of the *kuṇam*-complex's relative permanence and immutability, which are indeed the very qualities and attributes of genotypy.

The analogy's appropriateness becomes even more meaningful when we focus on the priest and his aim in the context of the ritual. What in fact the priest is interested in finding out in this ritual of divination is the relatively permanent "genotype" of his subject. "Phenotypy" is only of secondary importance to him. An unmarried girl may eat 'cold' foods because it is believed that 'cold' foods do keep one's passions under control, and the control of one's passions is tantamount to preserving one's chastity. These 'cold' foods, prescribed by cultural edicts, parental advice, or even a physician's counsel, are intended to address themselves to the girl's "phenotypy,"

[7]For a precise definition of semiotics, as the term is used here, see Milton Singer (1978).

real or imagined, potential or actual. The priest, however, is interested in finding out whether or not, regardless of "phenotypic" expressions, the "genotype" (the *kuṇam*-complex) itself is such that it destines the girl to live a 'cold', infertile, or unmarried life.

If a white flower is picked up when the question "Will my son recover from smallpox?" is asked, the message conveyed by the flower may be paraphrased as follows: "Fear not. Even though your son is 'phenotypically' 'hot' and sick, his 'genotype' is 'cool'. Therefore his chances of recovery are good."

The second flower in the double-pick sequence adds on to the message of the first. However, the second flower does not indicate the state of the subject through its iconicity to either 'hot' or 'cold' as did the first flower—at least not at the level of the sign function we are dealing with at the moment. Its only function here is to establish its distinctiveness by virtue of its color vis-à-vis the first flower and then to diagram this difference of form and kind into the relationship that holds between the *kuṇam*-complex and the *karmam*-complex. In other words, what is established is this: even as the second flower is different from the first, so is the *karmam*-complex different from the *kuṇam*-complex. However, this is not all. In establishing this difference, it also acknowledges the fact that the *karmam*-complex does exist; that the patient or supplicant has made some significant effort or performed some significant action, whether to repress or to express a preexisting *kuṇam*-complex.

Thus the red–white sequence relating to a question regarding a 'cold'-caused unstable state such as a protracted unmarried state, is auspicious, not only because the first (red) flower signifies a potentially good, 'hot' *kuṇam*-complex with respect to marriage, but also because there is a second flower which signifies the existence of a *karmam*-complex needed to bring about its fulfillment.

What of the white–red sequence with respect to a 'cold'-caused unstable state which our table tells us is an inauspicious sequence? Here too, the first color, in this case, white, establishes the fact that the *kuṇam*-complex of the subject is a 'cold' one and therefore not suited for a happy married life or even marriage itself. The second flower, by being different from the first, establishes the presence of the *karmam*-complex. The *karmam*-complex, however, is not adequate or sufficient for preventing the fulfillment or the persistence of the 'cold', inauspicious *kuṇam*-complex. In Hindu culture evil and decadence are taken to be the normal and the expected whereas goodness and virtue call for great effort to create and sustain. The tendency of the phenomenal world is to devolve rather than evolve; the bias is toward degeneration rather than creation.[8] In such a world the intensity, if you will, of the *karmam*-complex needed to arrest or suppress the activation of an evil *kuṇam*-complex must be double that of the *karmam*-complex required to effect the expression of a good *kuṇam*-complex.

This argument was illustrated to me by the priest in the following example:

> Take my rice fields. I sow high quality, Kaṇṇaki [a modern high-yield crop] paddy. Now nobody can deny that in each and every one of those seeds there is the best, *pakkā*, rice plant. But without the monsoons and the expensive chemical fertilizers nothing will come out of those seeds. Take that field [pointing]. All those weeds. Belongs to that lazy Paṇṭāram.[9] I saw him weed it once. Just once. And he thought that was it. That was enough. But look how the weeds have grown. A jungle. Without any help. No fertilizer, no water. Just the Paṇṭāram's laziness. You've got to weed fields like that not just once but several times. Must use chemical weed-killers too. It is hard to make good paddy grow, I grant you. But it is twice as hard to keep weeds from growing.

When we consider the more elaborate forms of the ritual of flowers, this argument will be clearly substantiated by the structure of the ritual itself. For now, suffice it to note that a single red flower is not sufficient for containing the inauspiciousness signified by a single white flower.

A non-alternating sequence of red–red or white–white is called *pūcaittavaru* (an abortive ritual) because the second flower fails to indicate the presence of the *karmam*-complex, whether the supplicant has performed pilgrimages, sacrifices, vows, or whatever. In so far as the flowers fail to acknowledge his "efforts" and "actions" the flowers are thought to "lie."

Therefore, the throwing and picking is repeated two or more times until the colors do alternate. If, however, after several throws the colors persist in repeating themselves, then either the supplicant is said

[8] See, for example, Wendy O'Flaherty (1976).

[9] Paṇṭārams belong to a traditional non-Brahmin priestly *jāti* that is slightly lower than Veḷḷāḷas in the hierarchy.

to be lying about having performed the various rites, vows, sacrifices he claims to have performed, or else the actions performed to date are deemed insignificant, insufficient, or irrelevant.[10]

Once I witnessed the priest make ten attempts before he finally obtained an alternating color sequence. On that occasion he had been so persistent because the supplicant was one who had come to the priest previously with the same problem and the priest at that time prescribed a course of offerings and rituals which then the priest himself administered or performed over a given period of time. This foreclosed the escape route of declaring to the supplicant that the latter was lying about having performed the prescribed course of action.

The Triple-Pick Sequence

The analysis thus far has centered on divination arising from only two picks. But it so happens that if an auspicious sequence is not picked up in the first two throws, one or even two additional throws will be made. The triple-pick sequence belongs to two sub-types, namely:

1. a third throw following an alternating inauspicious sequence, and
2. a third throw following a non-alternating inauspicious sequence.

Let us take these one at a time.

When a third throw is made in order to add on to an inauspicious alternating-color series, the purpose of this throw is described as *pūcai palankaṇittal*. Literally, this means the evaluation of the fruits or rewards of *pūcai*. *Pūcai* here refers to what we have called the *karmam*-complex, which includes pilgrimages, offerings, and so forth, along with any other efforts that have been made for the purpose of bringing about the fulfillment of a good *kuṇam*-complex or the suppression of a bad *kuṇam*-complex, as the case may be. The temple priest with a certain amount of etymological error translated *pūcai palankaṇittal* as "the evaluation or gauging of the strength of the rituals performed," that is, the gauging of the strength of the *karmam*-complex. In any event, the essential meaning is retained whether it is the "strength" or the "fruits" of the ritual that enters our translation. In fact, the folk etymology as given by the priest is culturally more meaningful than the actual etymology.

[10] The expression most often used is *karmam palikkavillai*, which is translated as "*karmam* which has not borne fruit."

In the third flower, then, one attempts to discover whether sufficient effort has been expended to prevent the fulfillment of a bad *kuṇam*-complex. If in a marriage-related question, or more generally, if in regards to a question posed in connection with a 'cold'-caused unstable state, an initially inauspicious sequence of white–red is followed by a red in the third pick, the latter adds on to the existing red, which has already signified the existence of a certain amount of *karmam*-complex, and strengthens the latter, so to speak. Thus a white–red–red sequence indicates not only the presence of a bad *kuṇam*-complex in the white but also the presence of a reinforced *karmam*-complex signified by the double red. From this the priest is able to conclude that the expression of the potentially bad *kuṇam*-complex will be effectively obstructed so that the patient will achieve his or her goal, which can be realized only in the absence of 'cold'. On the other hand, if the third pick yields a white flower, giving a sequence of white–red–white, then the last flower in being different from the second pick weakens the already existing but inadequate *karmam*-complex, like, in the words of one of my informants, "boring a hole through the wall of a dike which is already too weak to contain the waters of the monsoon rains." This sequence would assuredly result in the fulfillment of a bad *kuṇam*-complex caused by a 'cold' state. The argument for 'heat'-caused unstable states is the same with the color sequences reversed.

When a third pick is made in order to add on to an unalternating sequence of two picks of red–red or white–white, this pick's purpose is described as *pūcai kaṇittal*. Here the purpose is not to gauge the strength of an already existing *karmam*-complex, as in the case of *pūcai palankaṇittal*, but rather to see whether or not *karmam*-complex exists at all. If in this third throw a different colored flower is picked and added on to the first two isochromatic flowers, then this third flower is said to acknowledge that some kind of effort has been made toward solving the crisis in question. However, if the color sequence fails to change even after three throws, then this sequence is interpreted as indicating the absence of *karmam*-complex or else the flowers are said to lie and the whole ritual is repeated. More often than not a red–red–red or a white–white–white sequence is considered to have conclusively indicated that as of that moment there is no reason to believe that the patient's problem will be solved.

Relative to this conclusively negative response derived from the triple unchanging sequence, both red–red–white and white–

white–red are positive. However, only the red–red–white sequence is unequivocally positive with respect to questions relating to 'cold'-caused unstable states, whereas the white–white–red is still ambiguous and has to have a fourth pick made and its color added on to the existing sequence before a final judgment is given. This is so because, as was argued above, it is believed that a stronger *karmam*-complex is required to contain a bad *kuṇam*-complex than to bring about the realization of a good *kuṇam*-complex. Accordingly, the purpose of the fourth and final pick is also described as *pūcai palankaṇittal*, which the folk etymological translation renders roughly as "assessing or gauging the strength of ritual effort (*karmam*-complex) expended."

Before we move on to this final pick I shall make one more point regarding the unchanging sequence obtained in the first two throws. Unlike the white–red–red or red–white–white sequences in which the third flower by being similar to the second one reinforces the meaning and the message established by the second flower (i.e., implying a strengthening of the action-complex), in a red–red–white or a white–white–red sequence, the second flower by being of the same color as the first does in no way imply an intensification or doubling of the *kuṇam*-complex which the first flower establishes. The two initial consecutive reds or whites, as the case may be, are considered to be the same as a single red or a single white respectively.

I came to this conclusion after the following experience. When the priest and I, with pencil and paper in hand, were discussing and diagramming the various possible sequences in this divination rite, a curious thing happened. We would begin to consider, say, a red–red sequence. He would explain that

> a red flower follows a red flower. Now I make another throw and the little girl picks a white flower. Now we have a red–white sequence...

Or again when discussing a white–white sequence,

> Ah...first pick white, second pick also white. But third pick is red! Now what does this white–red sequence mean?

I kept correcting him by saying, "you mean a red–red–white sequence," or "you mean a white–white–red sequence." He would simply nod his head in agreement and then carry on as usual, repeating the omission of the "red–red" or the "white–white" part. Frustrated, I confronted him squarely with his persistent and obvious (to me) omission. In an extremely irritated tone he told me,

> Yes, red–red–white or red–white, it is the same. White–white–red or white–red, it is the same.

This was in keeping with the divination itself in which the priest considered a red–white positive response to be identical to a red–red–white positive response; and the same for a white–red and white–white–red sequence.

The Quadruple-Pick Sequence

The sequence that is subjected to a last addition is a white–white–red or a red–red–white sequence if either one of these does not spell out a conclusively positive response. If we were to take the white–white–red sequence as being the one obtained in response to a question posed regarding a 'cold'-caused illness, and if to this sequence another red is added as a fourth, it indicates that the double-red establishes the existence of a *karmam*-complex strong enough to contain the inherently unfavorable 'cold' *kuṇam*-complex. A fourth, white flower, on the other hand, would imply the presence of a weak *karmam*-complex, inadequate for the containment of the unfavorable, 'cold' *kuṇam*-complex.

Analysis: Level 2. "Blood in Milk and Milk in Blood"

In the analysis thus far, the distinctiveness of the *karmam*-complex as opposed to the *kuṇam*-complex was seen as being one of the first requirements of the ritual of flowers. This requirement was met by the syntax of alternating colors. But there is another level, once again a level of analysis generated by the ethnographic data itself.

The priest and I were discussing a question about an unmarried girl whose condition, to repeat, was believed to be the result of a 'cold' state. On that particular morning the sequence in a double-throw form of the ritual had been an auspicious red–white, indicating that her *kuṇam*-complex was inherently 'hot' despite the conclusion one might arrive at from the external evidence of her protracted unmarried state, and also that there was sufficient *karmam*-complex to bring about the expression of this favored *kuṇam*-complex. The priest also indicated that the girl's body was 'warm' (*vetuvetuppānatu*) rather than 'hot' (*cūṭu*) and that this was good. I questioned him as to what he meant by 'warm.' His response was:

Priest: What do you get when you add a pint of milk to twenty pints of blood?

A: What?

Priest: Pink (*iḷancivappu*). And that is warm (*iḷancūṭu*).

A: But you said that red is the best color for an unmarried girl because it meant that she was fertile and 'hot' for marriage. And so pink must mean that she is less fertile and does not have as much 'heat' for marriage as she would have had if the color had been pure red.

Priest: Yes. But too much 'heat' itself could prevent marriage from being successful. That was the matter with this girl's mother, who had three miscarriages because of too much 'heat' in her womb before her first son survived. And that is also why you see married men running around emaciated. Their wives have very 'hot' bodies (*trēkankaḷ*).

A: If that were the case then, red–white should be as good as white–red. So why did you consider white–red to be bad in this case?

Priest: Is it the same to pour a pint of milk into twenty pints of blood as it is to pour a pint of blood into twenty pints of milk? Well, that's the difference.

When I reread my notes after returning from the field, this "pinking" factor at least initially seemed to throw a spoke in the wheel of my First-Level analysis in which the action is clearly differentiated from the actor and his bodily state. However, I could not discard the analysis at that level because there was sufficient evidence to support it.

The question, then, is this: Are we to present both analyses of the ritual as they are and leave them as contradictions? I think not. The resolution is that at one level the *karmam*-complex (effort, pilgrimages, offerings, prayers, vows, etc.) is differentiated from the *kuṇam*-complex (the actor's bodily state, his *yōkam*, his fate, etc.). However, the moment it is thus differentiated, action becomes conjoined with actor, altering his *kuṇam*-complex. This, I believe, establishes in a capsular form the much-evidenced action-actor identity principle in Hindu culture.

Ever since Arnold Van Gennep (1908) identified the tripartite structure of rites of passage, anthropologists have built upon and elaborated this basic structure and in so doing have brought many relevant and interesting details of ritual from out of the shadows. Van Gennep's significant work was anticipated in his contemporaries' essay on sacrifice (Hubert and Mauss 1898) and continues to find creative elaboration in one of the more imaginative anthropologists of our time, Victor Turner (e.g., 1969, 1974, 1978). Hubert and Mauss's work on sacrifice and Turner's work on Ndembu ritual both center on sets of rituals that have all three phases of the processual form symbolically represented. That is, the pre-liminal, liminal, and post-liminal phases are symbolically enacted or portrayed in the rituals they have studied.

I believe that the ritual of flowers is also a processual ritual, in that it signifies a transformation of state. However, there is something that is distinctive about the ritual of flowers in that it has but two parts or phases of the ritual process represented. The first color, as has been noted, reveals the patient's *kuṇam*-complex, and the second color (and the colors that follow the second) reveals the presence and nature of the patient's *karmam*-complex. These two may be said to structurally correspond to the pre-liminal and the liminal phases respectively. But then comes the crucial twist of the processual rite. The limin is conjoined with the pre-liminal to form something new, a post-liminal state. But the post-liminal need not be signified in any way comparable to the distinctly enacted or symbolically represented tripartite forms described by Van Gennep and Turner, among others, because in Tamil culture, the union of the pre-liminal and liminal is itself considered to be the post-liminal state and therefore in no need of signification as such, and thereby implying the actor-action identity not present in most non-Indian ritual modes or cultural systems.

Elsewhere (1973) I have given a number of examples of this Tamil variation of the ritual process, but I did not have an adequate explanation for its peculiarity. I called these rites "implicatory" because the presence of the limin, I held, implied that the post-liminal state would follow and that the signification of this last state in the ritual process was deemed superfluous by the cultural logic and therefore omitted by the Tamils. Now, however, I am convinced that all those rituals which displayed the same structure were in fact consonant with the culture at large in which the action-actor identity is stressed.

In a recent study (1979) I examined in detail the territorial unit known as *ūr* in Tamil and most often translated into English as "village." There I noted that the term "frontier" or "threshold" more aptly described the territorial limits (*ellai*) in question than did the concept of a linear boundary. If we were to metaphorically transport this distinction into our discussion of limins, then limins too in the rituals of Tamils may be better understood as frontiers in the ritual process. Frontiers, unlike boundaries, are not merely distinct and sui generic entities. Frontiers are integrated with what they bound. This is what gives *ūr ellais* or *ūr* frontiers a fluid and elusive quality. To extend the geographical metaphor, limins in Tamil rituals of process do not stand for a "no man's land," as boundaries do; they, like frontiers, belong. This, in effect, is what Tambiah means when he speaks of boundaries "overflowing" (1973).

This brings us to a point that is very important to our understanding of the way in which Tamils perceive this coalescence of actor and action in the concluding phase of the ritual. I have hitherto referred to the *karmam*-complex because I wished to emphasize that complex of ideas that surround "action" (i.e., *karmam*, *muyatcci*, and *mati*). However, the word "complex" confers an abstract quality on *karmam*. To the Tamil, *karmam* as "action" is not solely abstract. It is a substance even as *kuṇams* are substances. This substantial aspect of *karmam* is clearly indicated in the *pūcāri*'s milk-into-blood analogy. Here the effect of *karmam* (action) on *kuṇam* substance (actor) is likened to the "mixing" of two substances, milk and blood, which flow into each other and create a new substance (i.e., the transformed substance of the person). The analogy of *karmam* as milk, a substance, and of the mixing itself reveals the Tamil's perception of the *kuṇam-karmam* interaction as the mixing of two substances.

The milk-into-blood analogy, however, leaves the impression that karmic substance is something external to the body substance, and in being introduced into the latter combines with the *kuṇam* substance. That *karmam* substance is not external to the body is made clear in several Indian philosophical traditions. The analogy of karma as *pala* or fruit is most clearly made in Jainism (Jaini 1980), but also occurs in several Hindu traditions including Śaiva Siddhānta. When a given *karmam* or karmic residue is activated, realized, or experienced, so to speak, it is said to have come to fruition or to have "ripened" (*palikkum* or *paṛukkum*). Following the *Upaniṣads*, Śaiva Siddhānta also locates karmic residue in the second innermost body (of the five bodies), known as the *kāraṇa uṭal*, encased by the body sheath, called the *vigñāna maya kōṣam*.[11] *Karmam* is thus an integral part of the body substance, a part of one of the innermost bodies, to be precise,

[11] See E.V. Daniel (1979) for a more detailed discussion of the body-sheath theory.

ripening at its own, predetermined rate, moving toward final realization.

There is one last snag that remains, with respect to the actor-action identity or the identity of the *kuṇam*-complex and *karmam*-complex. All that the ritual shows is that a given action alters or becomes a part of the actor in some measure after the said actor has performed the said action. However, the actor-action identity has two components to it. To phrase it in simple terms, we may say that (1) an actor is what he is because of what he does, and (2) an actor does what he does because of what he is. (Also see Marriott 1976:109, 110.)

The ritual discussed thus far substantiates but the first half of this claim. Have I evidence to support the claim that what actors do is predetermined by what they are? I think I have.

The incident I am about to relate happened, not in the village in which we carried out field work but in another village near the Kaveri River where I had gone to collect data on this same ritual of divination. The priest in this village asked me if I wanted something divined. As a matter of fact, I did want to know the future of my wife's chronic intestinal condition, which had been incorrigible from the first day of our arrival in India. Needless to say, most intestinal disorders are considered to be 'heat'-caused, and my wife's disorder, as diagnosed by this priest, was no exception. The flowers were thrown on the ground and the picks were made. The order was white and then red.

Priest: Good. There is no problem. She will be well. Your prayers will be answered. Only do keep your vows.

A: [I told him that I had neither prayed nor made any vows.] All I've done is fold my hands and wait.

Priest: It doesn't matter. The flowers show that good *karmam* exists. And that you will do good *karmam*. It is in your headwriting [*talai eṛuttu*]. That is what these flowers show. Maybe this supplication to the flowers itself is it. It was in your headwriting, otherwise why would you have come here in the first place?

The second flower, then, need not only signify an action that has been performed or one that is being performed; it records even a potential action, an action that will be executed. The analogy to a genetic template is most appropriate in which the temporal dimension is also coded. In other words, the second half of the proposition relating to actor-action identity, that a person does what he does because of what he is, is also established.

Analysis: Level 3

At the onset of the description of the ritual of flowers I chose to focus on what I called the iconic-indexical form or mode of the ritual and distinguished it from the simpler and purely symbolic form. From then onwards I have variously referred to the sign vehicles involved as icons, indices, and at times merely as signs, and correspondingly I have called the signifying mechanisms iconic, indexical, iconic-indexical, or else more generally, signification. This apparent over-fastidiousness is not without a purpose, a purpose that goes beyond the classification and labeling of categories of signs. It is to this point that I now turn.

I am in sympathy in general if not in detail with those who hold that culture is a symbolic system. I emphasize "detail" here both to acknowledge the differences among those whose articulation of the general position is best known (D.M. Schneider, C. Lévi-Strauss, C. Geertz, L. Dumont, and M. Sahlins, among others) and to make the point that I, in my turn, differ on some details with all of them. To amplify on these details is not my purpose in this brief essay. However, I do wish to make a case, prolegomena fashion, for refining our notion of "symbol" and by extension, "culture," along Peircean semiotic lines with the aim of presenting a more adequate description and understanding of a culture than is currently the case.

A given culture may well be a symbolic system. (I use the term "symbolic" here, not in the nonspecific sense generally used by anthropologists I have cited in the preceding paragraph, but rather in the precise Peircean sense, as a system of signs that are related to the objects they represent, arbitrarily). However, within the system so defined, within the culture, for and among those interpretants who or which make the relationship between object and representamen meaningful, further subsystems of signification may be identifiable. Minimally, the three basic sign types or significant modes, namely, the symbolic, the indexical, and the iconic, are operative in a culture. To rephrase this, cultural reality may present itself symbolically, indexically, or iconically, to individuals or groups of individuals in that culture.

When seen from outside the context of the ritual and from outside the culture, the signs employed in the ritual of flowers are symbolic, that is, general, conventional, and arbitrary. From this perspective, then, there is neither iconicity (isomorphism, identity, or likeness) nor indexicality (spatiotemporal contiguity) between sign (a particular colored flower) and object (a state of being 'hot' or 'cold'). A semiotic analysis or a cultural description that is merely symbolic fails to convey the specific manner in which signs or a system of signs achieve their significant effect, how they succeed in being emotionally and cognitively persuasive.

Within the ritual context, to the involved and informed participants in the ritual, the relationship between a white or a red flower and a 'cold' or a 'hot' patient is an indexical one, that is, a contiguous and causally necessary one. What is even more interesting from the point of view of South Asian culture is that the relationship is also iconic, a point which I wish to develop further below.

Before examining the purpose and place of iconicity in this ritual in particular and in the culture in general, let us spell out further some of the indexical functions present in the ritual of flowers. It ought to be self-evident that for any rite of divination to be worthy of its name, its major operational signs must be predominantly indexical in that the purpose of divination is to index, to point at, to direct one's attention toward, something concealed in space or time or both. It must be emphasized however, that from a cultural point of view, the sign focused on during divination is no less indexical, no less necessarily contiguous, and no less causally linked to its object than the color of a litmus paper is linked to the acidity of a solution in which it is immersed or a blood test is related to a given pathogen. Thus, the particular affliction of a patient, be it smallpox or an unmarried state, indexes the presence of the excess of 'heat' or 'cold' respectively in the patient. For as an index a sign is "a representamen which fulfills the function of a representamen by virtue of a character which it could not have if its object did not exist" (Peirce 5:73). To emphasize again, the relationship of 'hot' and 'cold' to affliction may not appear to those of us who are members of the "culture of science" to be anything like the relationship of litmus paper to acidity. For us the former is merely symbolic and the latter indubitably indexical. However, for those who share Tamil culture, for those steeped in its world view, it is the indexical mode of meaning that pragmatically gives the sign in question significance.

Another prominent indexical function we have encountered in the ritual of divination is what we have called the "pinking" effect. "Pinking" was seen to index a corresponding 'warmth' of the patient's *kuṇam*.

The crucial role that indexical signs play in the ritual of divination is what makes the whole ritual cognitively persuasive and affectively plausible for those who practice and partake in it. The clothing of our conceptions, to paraphrase Geertz (1973:90), with an aura of factuality so as to make the moods and motivations seem uniquely realistic is possible only because of indexical signs.

To the role played by indexical signs in the construction of cultural reality must be added the role played by iconicity. My hypothesis is that in South Asia the iconic function occupies a place of privilege in the construction of cultural reality. This should come as no surprise given that pervasive hold that its dominant non-dualistic cosmology has on so many facets of its culture. (See E. V. Daniel's concluding essay in this volume; S. Daniel, this volume; Marriott and Inden 1974; Inden 1976; Inden and Nicholas 1977; Davis 1976). If indeed ultimate reality and ultimate truth are to be found in the oneness of all things, it is not difficult to see that everything is an icon of everything else, given that icons are signs which act as signs by virtue of the fact that they share some quality with the object they represent. However, in this highly differentiated phenomenal world of *māyā* and dualism, the fact of iconicity is concealed under ignorance. "Ritual," however, is one of those domains in which the truth of iconicity is pointedly hinted at. The very truth of ritual in South Asia is constituted to a large extent in and through iconicity.

At the most general level of similarity, where the "shared quality" of iconicity is an abstract set of correspondences, we find iconicity expressed through the rule of alternating colors. By this rule, it is required that the second flower be different from the first in color so that the difference between the *kuṇam*-complex and the *karmam*-complex can be established. This is an instance where the overtly emphasized signifying relationship is iconic or diagrammatic (Peirce 2.282). That is, the shift from red to white or from white to red diagrams the shift from actor to action, from *kuṇam*-complex to *karmam*-complex. In Lévi-Strauss's succinct formula, "it is not the resemblances but the differences that resemble each other" (1963:77).

Iconicity, however, operates at a less abstract and more immediate level as well in the ritual of flowers. We saw how a given color indexed a corresponding *kuṇam*-type, either 'hot' or 'cold'. However, 'red' as an icon of 'hot' is 'hot', and 'white' as an icon of 'cold' is 'cold'. Thus, while a red flower functions as an index of heat just like a natural symptom (i.e., smallpox indexes the 'hot' state of the patient), it also functions as an icon in that it, in being red and 'hot', exhibits a "likeness" to the sick, 'hot' patient. It is this commonly shared *quality* that enables it to function as an iconic sign. Once again, in the "pinking" effect described by the priest, in addition to the indexical function already discussed an iconic function is operant as well. The quality of 'warmth' that is shared between "pink" and 'warm' *kuṇam* makes the relationship between sign and object an inherently iconic one.

To recapitulate the semiotic involved here, then, we find that indexicality along with iconicity plays crucial, I dare say indispensible, functions in making the ritual of divination real and convincing, on the one hand, and preeminently and characteristically cultural (South Asian), on the other.

Past, Present, and Future Reconsidered

From our analysis thus far, it is clear that the flowers do say something about one's past, present, and future. But they do not have a simple one-to-one correspondence, such as first flower–past, second flower–future, and so on. These flowers through a process of iconicity and indexicality indicate that one's past is part of one's present and that one's present and past together will be one's future, and that these transformations and transportations, as it were, of past into present and present into future are carried out by the cultural mechanism of the mutual identity that obtains between the *kuṇam*-complex and the *karmam*-complex, establishing the dictum that "a person is what he does and he does what he is."

One Last Detail

At the beginning of this essay I dissented from the position that the questions posed to the diviner are to be classified merely as either marriage-related or illness-related. Ethnographic facts indicate that a wide range of questions are entertained. The following is a sample:

Questions	*Positive Response*
1. Will my son be well?	W, WR, RWW, RRWW
2. Will my daughter recover from smallpox?	W, WR, RWW, RRWW

3. Will my mother's asthma get better?	R, RW, WRR, WWRR
4. Will my daughter be married this year?	R, RW, WRR, WWRR
5. Should I go on such and such a journey?	?
6. Should I accept this new job?	One of the sequences, not both
7. Will I recover my lost sheep?	W, WR, RWW, RRWW
8. Should my son marry this girl?	Either sequence

The clear-cut cases are (2), (3), and (4); (2) and (4) are the sample questions we considered in our analysis; (3) insofar as it is held that asthma is caused by a phlegmatic imbalance specifically requires a red *kuṇam*-complex or body state to be favorable.

If a question such as (1) is asked, the priest will, as a rule, require the subject to elaborate and will then diagnose the illness as being caused either by 'heat' or by 'cold'. In my experience, however, when the priest is not sure how to categorize the question according to the humor theory, or when he considers the supplicant's social status too insignificant for him to spend time probing for details, he will merely assume that the illness is 'heat'-caused—as most illnesses are—and then decide on W, WR, RWW sequences as being the auspicious ones.

Question (5) too would normally call for an elaboration, and more often than not the purpose of the journey will be given. In one instance, a certain supplicant did not wish to divulge the purpose of his proposed journey for fear that some of his fellow villagers who were around him might create trouble if they knew. On this occasion the positive sequence decided upon was the W, WR, RWW, RRWW sequence. The priest later explained to me that whatever reason impels him to go on this journey, it must be so that he may acquire a greater peace of mind than he presently has, and for this reason a 'white' sequence is good, since his present state of perturbation indicates that there is a lot of 'heat' resulting from and causing his restlessness. The W, WR, RWW, RRWW sequence for question (7) is decided upon as being the auspicious one for the same reason as in (5), because the recovery will restore "peace of mind."

Questions (6) and (8) present the widest room for interpretation. If the priest decides that the new job is intended to bring prosperity and indicates the leaving behind of a job that was nonproductive, humdrum, and routine, then he would choose the R, RW, WRR, WWRR sequence. On the other hand, if the present job is one which is causing the supplicant restlessness and a lack of peace of mind, the W, WR, RWW, RRWW sequence will be chosen to be the auspicious one.

Question (8) would also call for more information. A knowledge of the girl should help. If she has a reputation of being a *koṇṭi māṭu* (that is, a cow that has not been trained to be docile and obedient to man's commands; a grown cow or an ox that is skittish like a calf), then a W, WR, RWW, RRWW sequence will be an affirmative response forecasting that once married she will settle down. On the other hand, if the girl is known to have an astrological anomaly such as Mars being in the seventh house—which indicates infertility—then the R, RW, WRR, WWRR sequence would assure the supplicant that, in fact, after marriage, a 'red', 'hot', and fertile life is destined for the girl. Not all astrological anomalies are nullified or modified by the R, RW, WRR, WWRR sequence, however. If for instance, the ascendent falls in the *Trimsamsa* or the 1/30th division of a sign, it speaks of an adulterous nature, excessive heat. In this case, a W, WR, RWW, RRWW sequence will be the favored one.

In discussing question (8), the priest gave me an example. On a rare occasion he found himself at a loss when he was asked to divine the answer, because it so happened that the boy in question was madly in love with the girl. "He was literally a madman (*pittan*). But unfortunately, the girl had *sevvāi tōśam* forshadowing widowhood." He expressed his predicament in song:

> pasukkoṇṭiyillā sevvāyaṭā
> tiru nīr vārta trēkamaṭā
> kāḷai kontaṛappuṇṇōṭalayum
> kontaḷamē kontaḷam nātutaṭā

A poor translation (the only one I can offer) goes like this:

> Mars is ominous for this tame cow
> Whose body is covered with holy ashes
> The bull, restlessness personified, roams
> Like a fire with a raging wound
> Searching for her locks to singe.

The problem is, as you see, a difficult one. If he decided on a W, WR, RWW, RRWW sequence, it would be good for the boy and his 'heat'-caused state of "running around like a restless bull and raging fire with a wound in it," but it certainly would not suit the girl, who did not need to be told by the flowers too that she was going to be 'cold' and infertile, something she already knew from her horoscope. A R, RW, WRR, WWRR sequence would have been good news for the girl, promising her escape from her horoscope, but what good will it do the boy if he is going to remain unsatiated after marriage?

This is how the priest solved the problem: He first decided which one he would treat as patient, the boy or the girl. He decided that it was going to be the boy because the boy's father happened to be the supplicant. The sequence turned out to be W, WR, RWW, RRWW, so he gave his blessing and go ahead for the marriage. "The two have been married now for six years and have five sons. The horoscope was obviously wrong. But then it still could be right and she could become a widow."

Summary

The ritual of flowers is a problem-specific and person-specific ritual aimed at divining a person's past, present, and future at the same time. This is done by identifying the *kuṇam*-complex and the *karmam*-complex, and then collapsing the two to form a new *kuṇam*-complex. Or stated differently, the ritual of flowers helps to identify the quality of one's *kuṇam* substance vis-à-vis its 'hot'-'cold' aspect. Furthermore, it also helps in identifying the qualitative state, the fruition or non-fruition of *karmam* substance. When *karmam* substance is ripened, it is fully incorporated into the *kuṇam* substance, intrinsically altering the latter for better or for worse.

The red and white flowers through their iconic and indexical relationship with 'hot' and 'cold' body states are able to respond to a wide array of questions about sickness and health. The concepts of sickness and health, however, must be understood in their broadest sense, according to which even being overly anxious or worried about something is to be sick or ill.

What causes excessive 'heat' or excessive 'cold' on the phenotypic level are the three humors. The perfect humoral balance is peculiar to person and time. Any deviation from this perfect or ideal balance results in either a 'heat'-caused or a 'cold'-caused bodily disorder.

However, these "dis-eases" caused by the ever-fluctuating humors are no cause for serious concern, unless, of course, it is discovered through the ritual of flowers that the patient's *kuṇam* substance itself is isomorphic or sympathetic in some measure and conducive to the apparent disorders attributed to the humors; for this would indicate that the condition of the patient is more or less permanent and genotypic rather than merely phenotypic.

The signifying mechanism in the ritual of flowers operates most overtly by means of the indexical function. However, the culturally characteristic iconic relationship between the various signs and their objects is unmistakably present and is certainly at the surface of the consciousness of the participants in the ritual. Of all three functions, it is the symbolic mode that is least clearly represented to the consciousness of the interpretants.

Finally, it has been shown that there is considerable room for creative manipulation and interpretation in the hands of the priest. And the choices he makes can be understood only contextually, pragmatically.

References Cited

Babb, Lawrence A.
1975 The Divine Hierarchy: Popular Hinduism in Central India. New York: Columbia University Press.
Beck, Brenda E. F.
1969 Colour and Heat in South Indian Ritual. Man 4:553–572.
Daniel, E. Valentine
1973 A Penny for the Boatman. M.A. thesis, University of Chicago.
1979 From Compatibility to Equipoise: The Nature of Substance in Tamil Culture. Ph.D. dissertation, University of Chicago.
Davis, Marvin
1976 A Philosophy of Hindu Rank from Rural West Bengal. Journal of Asian Studies 3.
Diehl, Gustav
1956 Instrument and Purpose: Studies on Rites and Rituals in South India. Lund: Gleerup.
Fitzgerald, John J.
1966 Peirce's Theory of Signs as Foundation for Pragmatism. The Hague: Mouton and Company.

Geertz, Clifford
1973 The Interpretation of Culture. New York: Basic Books.
Gennep, Arnold Van
1908 The Rites of Passage. New edition. London: Routledge and Kegan Paul.
Hubert, Henri, and Marcel Mauss
1898 Sacrifice: Its Nature and Function. New edition. Chicago: University of Chicago Press.
Inden, Ronald B.
1976 Marriage and Rank in Bengali Culture: A History of Caste and Clan in Middle Period Bengal. New Delhi: Vikas Publishing House, PVT LTD.
Inden, Ronald B., and Ralph Nicholas
1977 Kinship in Bengali Culture. Chicago: University of Chicago Press.
Jaini, P. S.
1980 Karma and the Problem of Rebirth in Jainism. *In* Karma and Rebirth in Classical Indian Traditions. Wendy D. O'Flaherty, ed. Berkeley: University of California Press.
LeVine, Robert A.
1973 Culture, Behavior and Personality. Chicago: Aldine.
Lévi-Strauss, Claude
1963 Totemism. Boston: Beacon Press.
Marriott, McKim
1976 Hindu Transactions: Diversity without Dualism. *In* Transaction and Meaning. Bruce Kapferer, ed. Philadelphia: Institute for the Study of Human Issues.
Marriott, McKim, and R. B. Inden
1974 Caste Systems. Encyclopaedia Britannica, Macropaedia, 15th ed.
O'Flaherty, Wendy D.
1976 The Origin of Evil in Hindu Mythology. Berkeley: University of California Press.
Peirce, Charles S.
1958 Collected Papers. C. Hartshorne and P. Weiss, eds. Cambridge: Harvard University Press.
Saussure, Ferdinand de
1959 Course in General Linguistics. Charles Belly and Albert Sechehaye, eds. New York: Philosophical Library.
Singer, Milton
1979 For a Semiotic Anthropology. *In* Sight, Sound and Sense. T. A. Sebeok, ed. Bloomington: Indiana University Press.
Tambiah, S. J.
1973 From Varna to Caste Through Mixed Unions. *In* Character of Kinship. Jack Goody, ed. Cambridge: Cambridge University Press.
Turner, Victor W.
1969 The Ritual Process. Chicago: Aldine.
1974 Drama. Fields and Metaphors. Ithaca, N.Y.: Cornell University Press.

Turner, Victor W., and Edith Turner
1978 Image and Pilgrimage in Christian Culture. New York: Columbia University Press.
Whorf, Benjamin L.
1956 Language, Thought and Reality: Selected Writings of Benjamin Lee Whorf. John B. Carroll, ed. Cambridge: MIT Press.

·4·

Karma and Other Explanation Traditions in a South Indian Village

Paul G. Hiebert

There are many places an anthropologist can look in the South Indian village of Konduru to discover the meanings and uses of the concept of karma in the lives of the people.[1] One could turn to the village religious leaders and pandits who bridge the great and little traditions of Hinduism, and for whom karma is a key concept in ordering the events of life. For example, Goldsmith Lakshayya has published several religious tracts arguing that abstract meditation rather than asceticism is the best means to eliminate one's evil karma and achieve *mokṣa*. Brahmin Ramachari, the temple priest, while not directly disagreeing, contends that for most people the path of simple devotion and offerings to God is the best. Sambayya, also a Brahmin and a family priest, stresses the need for proper family rituals and devotional services.

Elsewhere one finds karma playing an important role in the numerous myths that form the heart of popular village Hinduism. These stories are reenacted in temple rituals, celebrated in village festivals, dramatized in street dramas, sung by bards in the street performances and by mothers to their children, and retold in the summer evenings. Here the meaning of karma is learned, not by philosophical discourse, but by illustration from the lives of gods and demons, saints and sinners.

[1] Konduru is the village in Southern Telengana, A.P., India where the author completed two and a half years of anthropological field research (1963–1965). Additional studies on the village are found in Paul Hiebert, *Konduru: Structure and Integration in a South Indian Village*, Minneapolis: University of Minneapolis, 1971; "Caste and Personal Rank in an Indian Village," *American Anthropologist* 71:434–453, 1969; "Friendship Patterns in a South Indian Village School," *Indian Journal of Comparative Sociology* 1:2:1–18, February 1975; and other articles by the author.

Finally, one may turn to real life situations that demand explanation and action, and listen to people as they deal with the incongruities and uncertainties of life. As Babb, Beck, and S. Daniel point out, elsewhere in this volume, karma is only one of a number of explanation traditions people use to account for and respond to the experiences of life. Here karma plays a surprisingly unimportant role even though it is deeply rooted in the world view of the people.

How can we account for this diversity in interpretation and use of karma in village life? To answer this we need first to develop a taxonomy outlining the various explanation traditions used in the village and the relationships between them.

Village Explanation Traditions

Konduru villagers use a number of explanation traditions to account for their experiences. These range from natural explanations, such as attributing pain to the dropping of a rock on the foot, to explanations involving planets, female goddesses, transcendent deities, fate, and karma. For analytical purposes we will use a two-dimensional model to examine both the differences and the relationships between these explanation traditions (Fig. 1).

The organic-mechanical continuum. Some village explanation traditions are based on organic analogies. In these the world is seen in terms of living beings of one or more kind in relationship to each other. Konduru and its vicinity is inhabited not only by people and animals, but also by ghosts, by *rākṣasas*, *dayamuḷu*, *apsaras*, and many other types of spirits, and by more than a hundred different female goddesses who reside in trees, wells, fields, and the nearby forest. In addition, Hindu gods and their consorts leave their heavenly abodes to minister to their devotees in the temples and shrines. All of these beings influence human affairs in certain ways. Spirits possess humans, driving them mad. Female *apsaras* lure men into their lairs and draw out their life forces. Goddesses bring plagues of disease, drought, and fire. And high gods punish people in their anger. Human responses to these beings are analogous to interpersonal relationships, and include offerings, confessions, supplications, and prayers.

Other village explanation systems are based on mechanical analogies. In these, impersonal forces, whether natural or supernatural, determine the course of events. These include the forces of stars and

Figure 1

Explanation and Therapy Traditions in Konduru

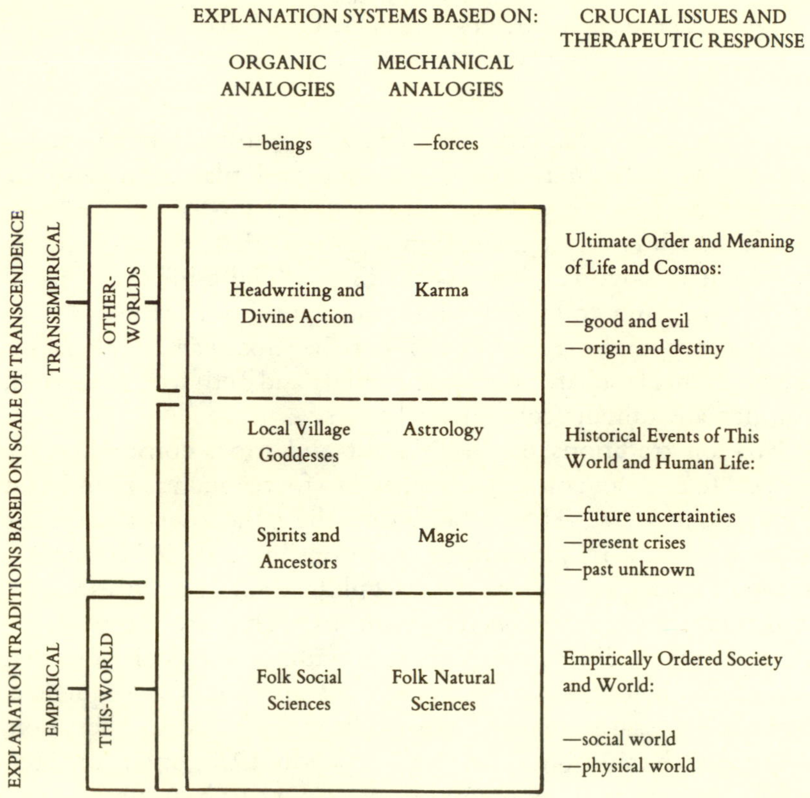

planets, magic, karma, and nature. In themselves these forces are deterministic and amoral, but people who know how to control them can use them for good or evil.

The immanent-transcendent continuum. Konduru explanation traditions distribute themselves along a second continuum, namely that of scale. On the lowest level are natural explanation systems that account for the world in terms of directly observed cause and effect. Villagers know that a fire untended can cause a house to burn, and that a cantankerous wife can ruin family relationships. These folk natural and social sciences are often codified in proverbs and aphorisms such as these:

> A reviling wife, a vengeful friend
> A proud and spiteful son, a house full of snakes
> These certainly lead to death.

For the most part, folk sciences deal with immediate events—immediate not only in the sense of time and place, but also of experience.

On a second level are explanation traditions that appeal to trans-empirical but this-wordly beings and forces. These include ghosts, spirits, and gods and goddesses whose ultimate abode is this earth, as well as planetary and magical forces. For the most part, explanation traditions on this level are codified in rituals and activities associated with immediate human problems and crises.

Explanation traditions on the highest and most comprehensive level appeal to gods and other worlds, and to forces such as karma that transcend this universe. They entail within them the lower systems of explanation. In folk religions these traditions are codified in myths, and among the religious elite in abstract philosophical treatises.

Relationships between explanation traditions. What are the relationships between these different explanatory traditions? It is obvious that they do not all belong to the same level of analysis. Consequently, they are not necessarily in direct competition with one another. Like different research traditions in science (cf. Laudin 1977), many of them bring different questions and methods of inquiry to bear on the same set of human experiences.

For the most part, the folk sciences deal with immediate problems in the empirical world which can be handled by natural means. Middle-level traditions (trans-empirical but this-worldy), as Pugh points out, often deal with problems related to the uncertainties of the future (should I marry my daughter to this man?), to knowns of the past (who stole the gold?), and to immediate crises that cannot be solved by natural means, such as plagues, droughts, earthquakes, and repeated misfortunes. High-level explanation traditions raise questions of the ultimate nature of the universe, and meaning and purpose of life. They provide answers by dealing with questions of origin and destiny, and by affirming the order of the universe.

Figure 2

The Role of Explanation Traditions
within Konduru Cognitive Structures

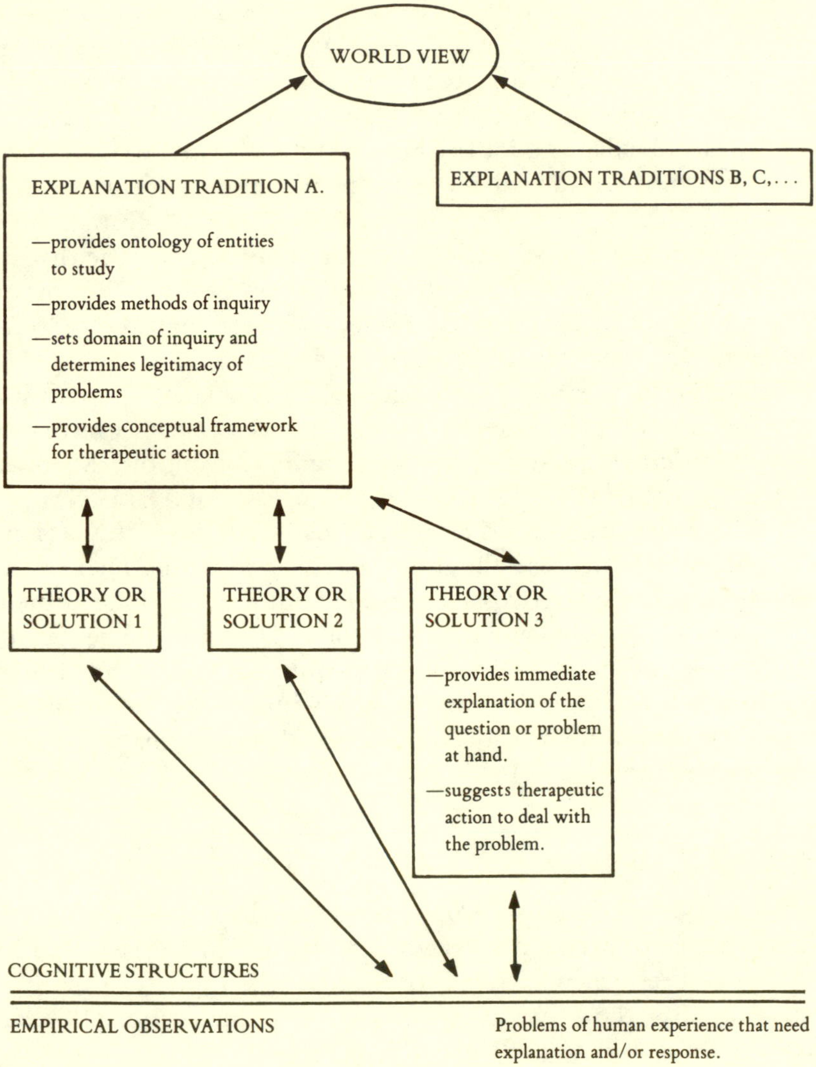

(adapted from Larry Laudin, *Progress and Its Problems,* 1977)

Villagers use one or another of the explanation traditions, depending upon the questions being asked and the purposes for which the answers are sought. Moreover, two or more may be used simultaneously without a sense of contradiction or cognitive dissonance. Where contradictions do exist between explanation traditions according to their purposes, villagers must choose between the alternative explanations that emerge within any given tradition, for it is on this level that direct confrontation occurs (Fig. 2). For example, if they agree that one of the local village goddesses played some role in the current crop failure, they must decide whether it was Maisamma, Mutyalamma, or Pōshamma if they are to take remedial action. As E. V. Daniel shows in his essay, it is on this level of selecting between specific theories within an explanation tradition that divination becomes important. Divination is normally not used to select between explanation traditions in the determination of cause or consequence.

Finally, villagers can and do use several explanation traditions simultaneously to account for human experiences, for as we have seen, they ask different questions of the data. For example, Shepherd Sayanna returned one day with a deep gash in his foot. His ax was dull, he said, and besides this, Maisamma was angry with him for not having given her a new sari though he gave his wife one. There are no contradictions in the two explanations, for one described the immediate or instrumental cause and the other the mediate or sufficient cause. With further questioning he would probably agree that the ultimate cause for both Maisamma's anger and his injury was either his bad karma earned in some previous life, or God's predestination written on his forehead (*talavratha*).

Karma as Folk Explanation Tradition

What specific function does karma serve in village life? We need to differentiate here between the two major functions of explanation traditions—between what Clifford Geertz calls models or explanation traditions *of* the universe, and models *for* human action (1979:81). We will look at the latter of these first.

Models for. One of the functions of explanation traditions is to provide people with directions for solving the problems of life. Babb refers to this as the "therapeutic" function of explanation traditions. For the most part, ordinary problems in the village are solved by natural means. A carpenter knows how to fit rims onto cart wheels, and a mother knows how to make her child obey. But there are crises that cannot be dealt with in this fashion. Frequently, in such situations, villagers turn to middle-level solutions—to the placation of spirits, ghosts, and goddesses, or to magic and astrology. The results of therapeutic actions on the lower and middle levels are generally direct and immediate.

Sometimes lower- and middle-level solutions fail, and the villager must turn to a higher-level explanation—to gods or karmic forces—to deal with crisis. Farmer Muggayya, the village magician, put it this way.

> When you run off the road to avoid a runaway cart and still get hit, or if you do everything you can and still have no children, that is your headwriting [divine predestination]. Only God can change that. But if you are careful, but have not done all you can, then you are in part to blame. For instance, if you only run to the side of the road and get hit by the cart, that is your karma, and karmic forces can be countered to some extent by magic and medicines.

But the use of karmic theory for therapeutic action has its problems. Actions designed to counter one's bad karma take time to come to fruition. By then the disaster may have occurred. Karmic action can change the general states and long-range directions of life. It is not surprising, therefore, that people turn to other therapeutic means to deal with the immediate crises of everyday life.

Models of. If karma is rarely mentioned as a solution to the immediate problems of life, it is common in the village lore that provides people with their models *of* the world. As we have seen, it provides the grist for the philosophical debates of Lakshayya, Ramachari, Sambayya, and the other village philosophers. For the most part, they draw upon Upaniṣadic and *bhakti* texts, and debate the philosophical issues common to the Hindu great tradition.

Karma is also a common theme in the village myths that are the cosmic charter for popular Hinduism in the village. Here the central question is not how karma is accrued and transmitted, but how it works itself out in the lives of people. The answers are given in the form of stories drawn from Purāṇic sources and from local histories. The former include a great many *Sthala-purāṇas* (mythical accounts of local towns and places). As Rajarao points out (1963:vii):

> There is no village in India, however mean, that has not a rich *sthala-purana*, or legendary history, of its own. Some god or godlike hero has passed

by the village—Rama might have rested under this pipal-tree, Sita might have dried her clothes, after her bath, on this yellow stone, or the Mahatma himself, on one of his many pilgrimages through the country, might have slept in this hut, the low one, by the village gate. In this way the past mingles with the present, and gods mingle with men.

An example of local history is the myth that has emerged in southern Telengana surrounding the 1956 accident in which a train plunged into a river and many were drowned. This is now published as a street drama and is cited as an example of karmic action.

One common theme in village myths is the corporate nature of karma. Philosophers tend to view karma in highly individualistic terms. Each person reaps the rewards of his or her own previous actions. Little is said about how events that happen to one person because of his karma affect those around him. In village myths this is a central question. It is interesting to note, for example, that husbands and wives in successive lives are rarely married to other partners even though they reappear in different condition—and occasionally with sex reversals. An example of the outworking of karmic consequences within the dynamics of human groups is the story of the ascetic, the butcher, and the cow.

The Ascetic, the Butcher, and the Cow

There once was an ascetic who lived in the forest in constant meditation. One day a butcher brought a cow to slaughter in the forest. "Ah, you are going to kill me!" thought the cow, so it broke the rope and ran. In its flight, it passed the ascetic. Shortly thereafter the butcher came running. "Have you seen my cow?" he asked. The ascetic, pledged to silence, gestured with his clasped hands and pointed the direction the cow had gone. As a result of this the butcher found the cow, slaughtered it, and sold the meat for profit.

In time both the butcher and the ascetic died and were reborn on this earth, the butcher as a merchant and the ascetic as an ascetic. The cow was reborn a woman. It came to pass that the merchant married the woman, and the couple became known for their hospitality to passing beggars and ascetics. One day the ascetic passed through the village and stopped at their home to eat (so the three were joined together again). After feeding the ascetic and giving him a mat on which to sleep, the wife retired to the next room to join her husband.

In the middle of the night the wife, enamored of the handsome ascetic, stole into his room and asked him to sleep with her. "I am a stranger, an ascetic, and your guest! How can you ask me to commit so heinous a sin?" he asked. "You must!" she insisted. "Your husband is sleeping in the next room and will catch us. Don't force me into this," he replied. "If my sleeping husband bothers you, I will kill him," she said. "No! Don't do it!" he cried, but before he could stop her she had plunged a knife into her husband's heart. Thereupon the ascetic raised a row, and when the neighbors came to investigate he told them what had happened.

The next morning both were taken to the king, who examined the case. "Take the ascetic to the forest, and cut off his hands," he ordered, "and put the woman to death."

On the way to the forest the ascetic prayed and asked God, "What was my fault? Why am I punished when I committed no crime?" God had pity on him and said, "In your previous life you were an ascetic meditating in the forest when a butcher came by seeking his cow. When he asked you, you pointed where it had gone with your clasped hands. This led to the death of the cow. Therefore your hands have been cut off. Had you spoken, you would have lost your head. The cow became the woman who married the butcher and killed him. Now you must repent of your previous sin."

The ascetic repented of his wicked deed, and God restored his hands. The king was astonished at this miracle, and asked the ascetic what had happened. Whereupon the ascetic told him the whole story. The king ordered the woman set free for she was not to blame for killing her husband. Both the ascetic and the butcher suffered on account of their previous sins, but not the woman, who was only gaining revenge when she killed her husband.

A second common theme in village myths has to do with mitigating the evil consequences of one's bad karma. Most Konduru villagers believe that one cannot change one's headwriting.[2] Only God can change it, and only when he is persuaded through vows and sacrifices. But karmic consequences can be altered through magic and medicines and, above all, by preventing the consequences if these can be known. For example, a king who knows through divination that his heir will be killed by a knife before the age of five may banish knives from his kingdom to prevent this from occurring. The following story from the *Neethishastramu* (Lessons on Righteousness) illustrates the dynamics of karma and of human efforts to alter its consequences.

[2] It should be noted here that there are some problems in reconciling the explanation tradition involving karma with that involving headwriting. The former is basically mechanistic and the latter depends upon the conscious decisions of God. Most villagers readily appeal to both. But some of the village philosophers deny the credibility of headwriting and argue, at least in a philosophical context, only in terms of karma when it comes to answering ultimate questions. They cite sources such as the famous Telugu poet Vemana, who says:

> Fate written on the forehead is easily erased,
> Whether this be of gods or common men,
> Simply rub the forehead, and it will come off.

The Careless Mother

There once was a devout man whose barren wife longed for a child. After long penance, they were blessed with a son. One day the father took his son to the graveyard and asked the infant why it had come to earth [within the first year or two of life, infants taken to a graveyard can talk and can reveal the conditions of their previous lives]. "I have come to collect the money you owed me in our previous life," said the son. When the father repaid the debt, the son died. After burying the body, the man returned home. When his wife asked where their son was, he said, "This child was not really our son. He only came to collect a debt we owed him in a previous life. Had he been our son, he would have remained with us after it was repaid."

In time a second son was born, but he lived only a month, leaving when he too had collected a debt from a previous life.

When a third son was born, the father took him to the graveyard and asked the same question. The infant replied, "In your previous life you were a merchant, and I your debtor. I then owed you fifteen thousand rupees. I have come back to repay you."

Determined to keep this son, the father warned his wife never to take any money from their son lest he repay his debt and leave. So they raised their son, saying to each other, "As we raise him, he is even more in our debt. If we marry him and establish him in business, he will owe us yet more. Then he can pay off his debt by supporting us in our old age."

The couple raised their son, arranged his marriage, and set him up in business, all of which put him much more in their debt. The son prospered in his business, but they would not take any money from him.

One day when the father was away, the son said, "Mother, I must go to the city on business. Please give me some food to take along." Mounting his horse with all his money in a sack, he started to leave. Suddenly he stopped and said, "Mother, I have forgotten something in the house. Please hold my money until I get it." Without thinking, the mother took the money as he dismounted. Thereupon the horse kicked him and he died.

When the father returned, the mother told him what had happened. "I told you never to take money from our son," he said. "But I didn't think of this as taking the money. I just wanted to help him," she cried. "It was your karma," he replied.

Now the meaning of the story is this: The son did not die on account of his karma, for he was not sorry to leave the world and its sorrows. Rather, it was his headwriting to return to earth, for God had sent him back to repay his debt. Nor did the son die because of the father's karma, for the father had not taken the money, nor had he craved a son. He was content with whatever happened to him, with having a son or not having a son. The death was due to the mother's karma, for it was she who wanted a son, and who lost him by negligence.

One lesson of this story is that a person can avoid the consequences of his bad karma, but this requires a knowledge of its consequences and persistence in thwarting them. The former can sometimes be known through divination. The latter requires unbroken discipline. But in most people there is a moment of neglect or weakness, and then bad karma comes to fruition.

The main function of these stories is to reaffirm the people's belief that despite the seeming chaos of everyday life the world is indeed orderly and meaningful. Death and suffering bring sorrow, but if they can be explained, life is not meaningless. As Geertz has pointed out, the greatest of human fears is the loss of a sense of meaning (1979:83–85). By fitting all human experience, even the most tragic, into an orderly framework, these myths provide the villagers with a model of the universe that renders it meaningful.

This order-affirming function of karma, and indeed of most Hindu beliefs, can be seen in the rituals in which they find expression. For the most part, Hindu rites and festivals are cyclical. Their timing and

Figure 3

Central Problems Underlying Upper and Middle Level Explanation Traditions

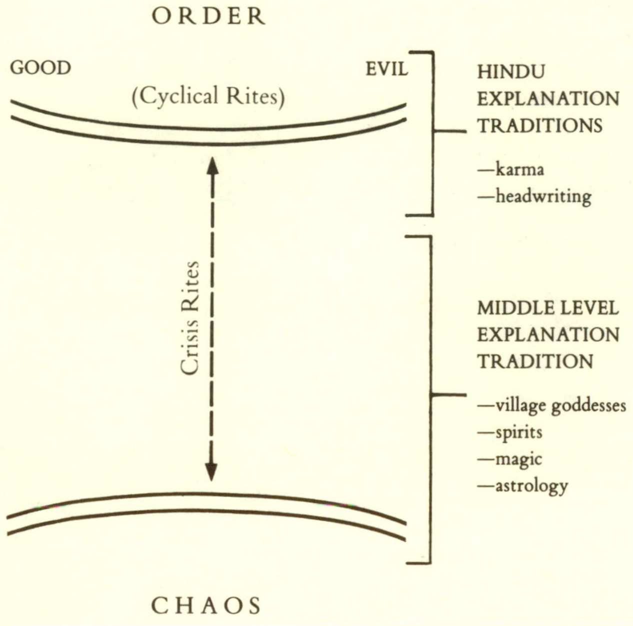

order of ceremonies are highly predictable. The underlying issue in Hindu rites and myths is that of good and evil, but evil in the karmic sense is as much a product of order as is good. Karma therefore provides an answer to the question of theodicy by fitting evil into a greater cosmic order. In contrast to Hindu rituals, those associated with the goddesses and with magic and astrology are crisis rites designed to stave off chaos that renders the world not evil but meaningless (Fig. 3).

Karma provides the people of Konduru not so much with an explanation tradition or model for solving the immediate problems of everyday life, as with an explanation tradition of an orderly universe that brings meaning and purpose to life itself. It is not surprising, then, as Babb quotes Sharma (1973:358) as suggesting, that "while karma is rarely the first explanation a villager might give for misfortune, 'it is generally the last which he will abandon.' "

References Cited

Geertz, Clifford
1979 Religion as a Cultural System. *In* Reader in Comparative Religion: An Anthropological Approach. 4th ed. W. A. Lessa and E. Z. Vogt, eds. New York: Harper and Row.
Laudin, Larry
1977 Progress and Its Problems: Towards a Theory of Scientific Growth. Berkeley: University of California Press.
Muggayya, B.
1978 Oral recount of the story of "The Careless Mother," from *Neethishastramu*, a popular religious text on morality and righteousness.
Rao, Rajarao
1963 Kanthapura. New York: New Directions.

· 5 ·

Astrology and Fate: The Hindu and Muslim Experiences

Judy F. Pugh

Astrology is one of India's richest and most vital traditions. A few sketches from the city of Benares will help to illustrate the flavor and variety of astrological practices in contemporary North Indian life. The calm and sublimely humorous Tiwari ministers to businessmen and politicians; the scholarly Sharma trains a new generation of astrologers in the university; the clairvoyant Mata-ji reads palms amidst a constant crowd of people seeking her advice in a back lane; the vigorous Rishikesh Pandey reads the almanac, prepares horoscopes, and performs rituals in the nearby village of Rajpur; the young and modern J. C. Shastri provides advice in a fashionable office in the orthodox Jain household of his parents; the respected Mohammed Aziz advises Muslims and Hindus in an antechamber of a mosque in which benches are curtained off to maintain *parda* for women clientele; the venerably ancient Abdul Rashid of a small mosque in a busy neighborhood reads almanacs and writes charms for protection against the planets and the evil eye; the clever and programmatic Abdul Alam, former bangle-seller turned astrologer, uses the Arabic system of dice to identify planetary influences and make prognostications for clients on a bustling thoroughfare; the businesslike Mali Ram Gupta skirts the Brahmin hegemony by working the tourist trade and writing astrological advice columns for local newspapers; Lakshman

This essay is based on research conducted in Benares and in a nearby village, from January 1975 to June 1976. I am indebted to the Social Science Research Council for an Overseas Dissertation Fellowship which supported the research. I am also grateful to Brenda Beck and Liz Coville for comments on a draft of the paper.

Upadhyaya, priest of a Saturn temple, eats *bhang* and tells of the greatness of Lord Shani.

The vitality of contemporary astrology which these sketches portray, and the lengthy history of prodigious systematization of heavenly phenomena and their relationship to human action, reflect the significance of fate in Indian culture. The celestial realm is an important part of the South Asian life-world, and fate—karma for Hindus and *qismat* for Muslims—is commonly associated with the heavens. The life-world reflected in astrology is a unitary field in which the reciprocal relatedness of all entities is a fundamental axiom, and the ceaselessly patterned turnings of the heavens image a determinateness of events and conditions in the realm of human action.

For this reason astrological settings provide ideal contexts in which to analyze concepts of fate. Exegeses provided by astrologers, plus observations of their advisory sessions and discussion with a whole range of city residents, provide the main data for the analysis. Ceremonies performed at shrines for planetary deities, and case studies of planetary affliction, add to this emergent picture of fate as it is understood at a popular level.

My use of the term "popular understandings" refers to the knowledge and interests of ordinary North Indians. It is true that popular understandings of karma and *qismat* are not organized with the fineness of detail nor the thoroughness of integration nor yet the generalized abstractness of doctrines of destiny known in "high" Hinduism and Islam. Yet against this kind of characterization of popular or folk culture as a residual dimension of learned knowledge, it is important to present a different perspective, one which demonstrates an essential integrity in popular culture and also describes links between learned tradition and popular belief.

What my analysis suggests is that popular ideas of fate in North Indian society are oriented to a comprehension of everyday life. The speculations of philosophical Hinduism about the detailed mechanisms of karmic process, and the doctrinal interpretations of Islamic theology on the topic of destiny,[1] are transfigured at a popular level by a concern with manifestations of fate in the realm of commonplace life-experience. This experiential, life-contextual orientation provides

[1] Among the many sources on philosophical views of karma, see, for instance, Radhakrishnan and Moore (1964). For perspectives on the topic of destiny in Islamic theology, see Rahman (1968) and MacDonald (1973).

a focal point for an analysis of popular understandings of fate among the Hindus and Muslims of North India.

Text and Context: Astrology as Applied Science

Astrology is fundamentally an applied science which aims to inform the organization and scheduling of important events and to provide practical information and counseling on matters of basic life-activities. The pragmatic orientation of this "science of the heavens" is grounded in astrological texts themselves and their role in astrological practice. Sanskrit astrological traditions date back to the Vedas, the *Vedanga Jyotisha*, and other early texts.[2] Many of these classic texts are still used as standards of instruction in colleges offering programs of study in astrology, and these Sanskrit texts with Hindi translations are commonly used by both Hindu and Jain astrologers. Muslim learned men who practice astrology commonly base their work on Urdu texts, some of which are translations of works in Persian or Arabic.[3] A number of these show borrowings from Sanskrit sources.

These texts present detailed schematizations of the attributes of celestial bodies and their patterns of movement, and they include with these descriptive and classificatory accounts specifications for use or application (*prayojan*, *istamāl*). For instance, Varahamihira's classic *Laghujātakam*, a fifth-century text still widely used and available with Hindi translation, includes explanations of procedures for performing calculations and applying classificatory schemata to practical situations. This emphasis on application continues in textual materials today.

One may suggest that textual directives for practical application have had a lengthy history in the field of astrology. Several astrologers with whom I worked were writing texts, and they stressed that their writings reflected the knowledge they have acquired during the course of interactions and divination sessions in which the problems and beliefs of ordinary people have been the central focus. One may speculate that astrology as an applied science has maintained active

[2] Kane (1974) provides a detailed history of Hindu astrology. He dates the *Vedānga Jyotisha* to the fifth century B.C. (p. 477).

[3] For a history of important developments in Islamic astrology, see Nasr (1964). Alberuni's valuable observations on Hindu astrology and its relation to Islamic astrology in eleventh-century India are found in *Alberuni's India* (Sachau 1964).

channels of reciprocal influence between popular setting and textual rendition throughout its history.[4]

Fate and the Heavens in Popular Hinduism and Islam

In the popular understandings of Hindus, the term *karma* refers to "cause," "effect," and "processes of cause and effect." *Karma* refers to the person's store of moral codings, which are considered both consequences of prior actions, either in this lifetime or in a past lifetime, and causes of future activities or conditions; it also refers to actual events, qualities, and conditions which are considered to have been affected by this store of moral codings.[5]

What is especially important about the nature of karma is that it is a process which is imperceptible and unknowable in the interstices between cause and manifest effect. Hindu astrologers refer to karma in this unmanifest form as "unseen" or "invisible" karma (*adṛṣṭa karma*), and they say that the heavens, when correctly calculated, make this "unseen" karma "visible" (*dṛṣṭa karma*) before it actually manifests itself in event or circumstance. Also, ordinary Hindus from all walks of life say that through astrological consultation they can know their own karma.

Hindus believe that the heavenly bodies—the planets (*graha*), constellations (*rāsi*), and asterisms (*nakṣetra*)—have a natural influence on the earth and on the person. Hindus commonly say that these planetary influences are "the fruit of karma." Hindus consider the planets to be deities who influence earthly life and who may be worshipped and propitiated. Some asterisms are also propitiated, such as the evil-inflicting Mul *nakshatra* (the stars from ϵ to μ Scorpionis which form the stinger of the Scorpion [Allen 1963:370]). Planetary deities are said to "strike" (*lagnā*) people with light and rays; they are also considered to "spin over" (*gardish honā*) or "climb onto" (*caṛhnā*) the person whom they are afflicting. Today Western scientific jargon is becoming common in contemporary expositions of astrological

[4] Cf. Singer's (1972) discussion of media which provide continuities between Sanskritic and popular Hinduism, and Mandelbaum's (1964) reference to astrology as a bridge between the transcendental complex and the pragmatic complex.

[5] For important statements on substance and code in the South Asian setting, see Marriott and Inden (1974) and Inden and Nicholas (1977).

principles: astrologers and lay persons alike say that the celestial bodies operate through radiation, gravity, magnetism, and other physical forces, and they feel that the influences of these forces can be calculated to a very precise point.

These celestial forces begin to influence the person from the time of conception and birth. Hindu astrology offers schematizations of the influence of planets on the developing embryo and stresses the importance of birth-time as the key point through which karma is made visible and hence future actions and circumstances are made knowable. As the embryo develops, each of the planets in successive order regulates one month of the pregnancy and governs the development of particular parts of the body and mind.

The specific quality of this developmental process is a manifestation of the karma of the soul which has taken birth. Hindus believe that the configuration of stars and planets at the time of birth has a pervasive influence on the physical and psychical qualities of the person. It is sometimes said that celestial forces "imprint" a pattern on and within the person, in the manner in which a phonograph record is imprinted. According to this view, the person's fate is formulated as a kind of interior template which guides the unfolding of his life.

Astrologers and lay persons also suggest that birth-time is critical because it is the point at which the person enters celestial cycles, and hence the point from which a future trajectory of planetary influences is established. According to this view, the person's fate is manifested through an exterior celestial template which organizes the effects that the heavens will have on him during the course of his life. In either case, many Hindus feel that birth-time and its associated planetary configurations fulfill the karmic process which links the person's present lifetime to his previous lifetime. A person is born at a particular nexus of time, place, and familial and social position through which planetary configurations and their ongoing permutations intimate and actually effect the unfolding of his karma.

Planetary forces sustain an unfolding of fate throughout the lifetime of the person. Fate is manifested in the general features of the person's physical and psychical constitution and sociofamilial relationships, which together articulate a whole panoply of life-experiences, including, among many others, experiences associated with health and disease, family crises, and economic circumstances.

In assessing beliefs about the relationship between planets and karma, one must also include a discussion of the role of God (*Bhagvān*).[6] It is a common view among Hindus that it is God who acts as judge to decide the just recompense for thoughts and acts in this lifetime, as well as those of other lifetimes of the past. The planets, which are considered deities, are generally believed to be subordinate to the greater power of God, and people frequently say that God controls the planets. Powerful deities such as Śiva and Hanuman are considered particularly capable of controlling the planets, and it is said, for instance, that Hanuman can "catch the planets in his fist."

However, there is also something autonomous and irrevocable about the power and movements of the heavenly bodies, and many Hindus feel that God cannot completely control the planets. Very inauspicious celestial conjunctions are considered to be almost beyond the control of the gods, especially conjunctions involving Saturn. When Saturn afflicts someone, it is felt that prayer and ritual may help alleviate some of the difficulties, but that the affliction as a whole cannot be eliminated until it has run its prescribed course.

Muslims commonly talk about fate (*qismat*) within the context of Islamic belief and practice. Allah, as omnipotent deity, decides the fate or "lot" (*qism*) of each person. Muslims stress as frequently as Hindus their belief that each person gets the consequences of his own actions. One should follow the basic tenets of Islam, and one should also fulfill familial and social responsibilities and act justly and equitably toward one's fellow man. Negligence in religious duties and impropriety in social relations are believed to contribute to unfortunate consequences in one's fate.

It is Allah who judges men's thoughts and actions and metes out the consequences. God decides the *qismat* of each person once every year on the night of Shab-i-barat, the fourteenth night of the Islamic month of Sha'ban. Allah weighs each person's thoughts and acts of the preceding year on that night and makes a decision about their *qismat* for the coming year. Muslims believe that their fulfillment of duties and responsibilities during the past year contributes to a positive decision. It is customary to pray on that night and to give food offerings and prayers for the dead. Although Muslims feel that God deals justly with those who fulfill their responsibilities, they also know

[6] For a discussion of North Indian untouchables' views on the relationship between God and fate, see Kolenda (1964).

that God is not bound by the moral quality of men's acts; rather, God in his omnipotence may act wilfully to influence or alter the course of events in a person's life without regard for the quality of his deeds.

Astrology (*najūm*) has occupied a controversial position in the history of Islam, and today this fact is reflected in North Indian Muslims' views on the question of the validity of astrology and the relationship of the stars to God and to man's destiny. Many Muslims reject astrology as "magic" (*jādū*) and condemn those who practice it or who consult astrologers. They feel that only God plays a role in man's life, and that only God knows what he has decreed for each person. Human efforts to divine the dictates of fate, the word of God, are both futile and blasphemous.[7]

On the other hand, a sizeable number of Muslims consult astrologers, and in Benares there are numerous Muslim practitioners who include astrology in their advisory work. Whereas a Hindu practitioner who specializes in astrology calls himself an astrologer (*jyotishī*), a Muslim practitioner who uses astrology refers to himself as a learned man (*maulvī*) and not as an astrologer. Muslims who use astrology or practice it consider the planets (*sitārā*) and constellations (*burj*) to be part of God's creation. They describe celestial bodies as having natural power (*qudrat*) and strength (*tāqat*), and they believe that stars and planets have an influence (*asar*) on men's actions through light and other rays.

Muslims who use or practice astrology believe that the planets are under the control of Allah, and that the indications and influences which they display are part of God's divine plan. Despite Quranic injunctions against soothsaying, there is such emphasis in the Quran on signs and portents which reveal God's power to men, that believing that the heavens may indicate or manifest a person's *qismat* may seem neither unreasonable nor sacrilegious to many Muslims. Astrological divination, when performed in the name of God, may then be considered to offer the possibility of insight into one's destiny.

Muslim learned men and clients alike are usually careful to emphasize that man is fallible and that procedures which require complicated calculations and interpretations involve a high risk of mistaken predictions. On the whole, then, devices and procedures used by Muslim

[7] Cf. Siegel's (1969) discussion of the emphasis which Atjehnese Muslims of Indonesia give to reason (*'agal*) as a means of comprehending divine decree.

learned men offer less scope for human error in the divination process than those used by Hindu astrologers. A major difference in interpretive technique is that Muslim learned men rarely cast horoscopes, a task which requires complicated calculations. Muslims prefer to use existent horoscopes printed in the Urdu almanacs, which are considered to have been correctly calculated. They also tend to describe short-term trajectories for a client, a reflection of belief in the annual writing of fate on Shab-i-barat, and a reflection, too, of an awareness of the power of God to change a person's fate at will.[8] Muslims make frequent use of "electional" devices, such as dice or dishes of tokens labeled with the names of planets from which clients may make blind selections. A given selection or a particular configuration of dice indicates planetary influences at that point in time.

Let me summarize these popular understandings of karma and *qismat* which are reflected in astrological settings:

1. Both Hindus and Muslims consider themselves part of a greater order of events. Karma and *qismat* are definite components of that order.
2. Both Hindus and Muslims feel that the moral quality of their thoughts and acts influences their fate.
3. Both Hindus and Muslims feel that God plays a role in deciding man's fate.
4. Hindus and a sizeable number of Muslims believe that stars and planets influence man and manifest his karma or *qismat*.
5. Hindus and Muslims who use astrology feel that God controls the planets, but Hindus feel that there are kinds of planetary afflictions which God has little or no power to alter. This points up an area of autonomous, automatically operative fate which is beyond God's control and unamenable to modification. On the other hand, Muslims who use astrology believe that the celestial bodies, as part of God's creation, are completely under the control of Allah.
6. Hindus are oriented toward specification of the unfolding of fate over long spans of time, including horoscope predictions which cover an entire lifetime. Muslims are oriented toward shorter spans of time in astrological assessments of the dictates of fate; this reflects the omnipotence of Allah and gives to man's glimpses of fate an uncertain character.

[8] Harold Gould has suggested to me that the Islamic notion of the millennium may be an additional consideration here.

7. In viewing stars and planets as indications of fate, Hindus accept as legitimate a wider range of methods of prognostication than do Muslims. Muslims state that men who seek knowledge of destiny should be careful not to make undue pretense to powers of prescience which rightfully belong to God.

These understandings form the core of popular views of karma and *qismat*. What I will suggest now is that these understandings are directed by ordinary North Indians to a comprehension of the manifestations of fate in everyday life, and that karma and *qismat* find salience as dimensions of personal experience.

Fate and Experience

North Indian interest in notions of karma and *qismat* is grounded in a concern for the everyday world, and astrology provides an important channel for expressing this practical concern with the routine world and the vicissitudes of personal experience. This orientation is especially evident in astrological advisory sessions, where ordinary people seek advice and remedy for a wide variety of personal circumstances. An analysis of several key concepts reflected in these advisory sessions will serve to outline North Indian understandings about the experiential grounding of karma and *qismat*.

Astrology is widely used because it provides a tangible, visible template for knowing one's fate. The stars and planets are signs whose positions and influences can be determined, and in the advisory session processes of divination, involving horoscopes, palms, dice, and other devices, offer the client an interactional setting in which to objectify his circumstances and locate them within specific temporal trajectories.

Observation of an astrological advisory session for several hours reveals a basic array of kinds of life-experience which clients believe to be implicated in processes that they can neither fully comprehend nor adequately manage. For instance, the problem-situations counseled by Mata-ji, a charismatic back-lane palmist, in the course of a morning include a husband and wife who desire a son; a man whose driver's license has been lost or stolen; a woman whose daughter has seemingly irremediable boils on her legs; a woman whose son has recurrent stomach pain and evident emotional disorders. A sample of problems from a variety of other advisory sessions reveals a similar range of basic personal situations: to Mali Ram Gupta comes a man seeking advice about his dying son; to Sharma, a student who wants advice and prognosis for his examinations; to Tiwari, a politician worried about his thwarted political ambitions and his chances for success; to Abdul Rashid, a man whose tobacco shop has not been doing enough business; to Abdul Alam, a woman whose court case has been stalled for over a year and another woman whose husband has been staying away from home; to Mohammed Aziz, a woman who is afflicted with physical pain, mental distress, and family conflict; to Ayar, a successful professor who wants an assessment of the future course of his career.

What this brief survey of advisory sessions points up is that personal situations constitute the frame within which the workings of fate are manifested. The groundwork of these personal situations lies in four aspects of the person, aspects which are schematized astrologically and which are also commonly used by ordinary North Indians to discuss personal circumstances. These four aspects of the person include the body (*sharīr*, *badan*); the psyche—which includes the intellect (*buddhi*; *dimāg*), the heart-mind (*man*, *dil*), and the soul (*ātmā*, *rūh*); and family (*pārivārik*) and community (*sāmājik*) relationships.[9] These four aspects of the person in their complex interrelationships provide the matrix from which specific experiential situations are organized. And it is in the detailed particularities of these personal circumstances that ordinary North Indians commonly locate the workings of fate.

Divination devices and planetary significations provide an extensive set of categories which serve to reflect and interpret the experiential structure of the situations which clients describe to astrological practitioners. The horoscope (*kuṇḍlī*, *patrī*) and the palm (*hasta rekhā*), the most widely used divination devices, are each partitioned into a number of components or areas which represent basic categories of experience. The horoscope is divided into twelve spaces known as "houses" (*ghar*). They are numbered from one to twelve, and they are termed "first house," "second house," and so on. Each of the twelve houses of the horoscope designates particular areas or aspects of life-experience (Fig. 1).

The horoscope provides a partitioned space within which to locate planets and constellations. Since each planet and constellation is considered to regulate specific qualities, the mapping of planets and constellations in the horoscope provides a means of assessing condi-

[9] Pugh (1981) presents a fuller discussion of these North Indian concepts of the person.

Figure 1

The Horoscope

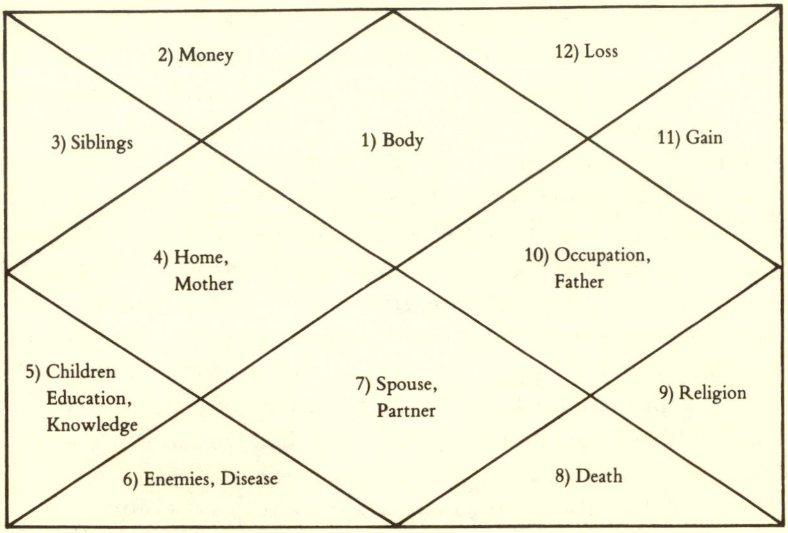

tions which are likely to prevail in particular areas of life at a given point in time.

The planets, to which are attributed special importance in the horoscope, influence the emergence of the following kinds of physical, psychological, and interpersonal qualities:

Sun—fame, success, health
Moon—love, pleasure, fertility
Mars—conflict, persistence
Mercury—intelligence, flexibility
Venus—beauty, passion
Jupiter—wisdom, devoutness
Saturn—sadness, destruction

The planets are believed to promote a susceptibility to or a tendency for the development of these qualities. And these qualities, in their somatic, cognitive, and affective ramifications, express the workings of destiny in the person's sociofamilial world.[10]

[10] Cf. Potter's (1980) description of karmic residues which operate in a new body to influence birth (*jāti*), length of life (*āyu*), and affective tone of experience (*bhoga*).

The categories represented in the horoscope, and the qualities represented by planets and other heavenly bodies, as well as other astrological schematizations, match closely the categories which clients use in describing their situation to the astrologer. If it has indeed been the case that astrology has developed historically as an applied science, articulating theory and technique with the exigencies of human circumstance, then this parallel between the categories that lay persons use to describe their concerns and the categories that are represented in astrological texts and divination devices should occasion no surprise. Clients who have some knowledge of the details of astrological procedures may ask about specific houses of the horoscope, or areas of life-experience, with the intention of obtaining an assessment of particular factors in their present circumstances. Palmistry, as a division of astrology, uses this same general kind of grid: the planets occupy definite portions of the palm, and the mounts, lines, and marks represent areas of life-experience roughly parallel with those in the horoscope and continuous with categories in commonplace usage.

To see personal situations as culturally significant contexts for the manifestation of fate is a first step in understanding popular views of destiny. A second step is to determine exactly what kinds of situations are associated with fate. Are all situations equally and directly linked with fate? Or are there specific kinds of circumstances which are commonly identified as manifestations of the workings of fate? If so, how are these situations to be characterized?

These questions lead to a consideration of the emphasis which North Indians give to fate as a temporally mediated process, an emphasis which again is grounded in an attention to everyday life. North Indians commonly emphasize three kinds of personal situations whose emergence is considered to be especially indicative of the workings of destiny. These categories are distinguished by three modes of change in the person's life: the first category of situations is marked by advancement (*unnati*, *taraqqī*), the second category by obstruction (*vighna*, *bādhā*, *rukāwaṭ*), and the third category by destruction (*nāsh*, *barbādī*) (Fig. 2).

The semantic features which underlie this set of categories include the feature of auspiciousness/inauspiciousness and the feature of simplicity/multiplicity. The feature of auspiciousness/inauspiciousness distinguishes positive from negative situations, that is, situations of advancement from situations of obstruction and destruction. The

Figure 2

Fate and Personal Situations

	Auspicious	Inauspicious
Simple	ADVANCEMENT *(unnati, taraqqī)* "Good planetary condition" *(acchā graha dashā)*	OBSTRUCTION *(wighna, bādhā, rukāwaṭ)* Delay *(der)* Trouble *(kashṭ)* Worry *(pareshānī)* "Bad planetary condition" *(Kharāb graha dashā)* "Planetary turnings" *(Graha cakkar, sitārā gardish)*
Multiple		DESTRUCTION *(nāsh, barbādī)* A lot of trouble *(bahut kashṭ)* "Very bad planetary condition" *(Bahut kharāb graha dashā)* "Saturn condition" *(Shani dashā)* "the seven and a half" *(sāṛhe sātī)*

feature of simplicity/multiplicity distinguishes situations in which change or lack of change, as the case may be, is limited to one or several aspects of the person's life, from situations in which change involves numerous aspects of the person's life. The more auspicious or inauspicious the situation and the more numerous the aspects of life which it involves, the more directly and explicitly is the situation considered a manifestation of planetary influences and the workings of destiny.

These kinds of situations are exemplified by the problems and concerns commonly discussed in astrological advisory sessions: severe family conflict, dire financial setbacks, and death may mark situations of destruction; delay and the failure of interim situations to achieve resolution, as in chronic illness, recurrent occupational difficulty, and stalled litigation, mark situations of obstruction; markedly positive developments in career, family life, economic position, education, and so on, indicate situations of advancement.

Planetary conditions are associated with these situations. At both the popular and the learned level, "good planetary conditions" (*acchā graha dashā*) are linked with situations of advancement; "bad planetary conditions" (*kharāb graha dashā*) and "planetary turnings" or "planetary revolutions" (*graha cakkar*, *sitārā gardish*) are associated with situations of obstruction; and "very bad planetary conditions" (*bahut kharāb graha dashā*) are indicated in situations of destruction. Situations of destruction are closely linked with the planet Saturn (*Śani*, *Zohal*), and accounts of a "Saturn condition" (*Śani dashā*) and the widely salient "seven-and-a-half-year period" (*sāṛhe sātī*) of Saturnian affliction describe situations of devastation.

Astrological counseling helps the client to understand relationships among various factors in his situation, and as part of this process, it provides a temporal framework for developments in his life. The movements of the sun and the moon and the progression of the planets through the constellations of the zodiac are believed to influence changes in life-experience and to provide a complex temporal system through which these changes can be outlined. Temporal systems based on the movements of the heavenly bodies describe units of time, which range from minutes and portions of days to days, months, years, and spans of years. In their analyses of clients' problems, both Hindu and Muslim astrological practitioners provide assessments of the periods of time during which various celestial influences will be present. Hindi and Urdu almanacs contain horoscopes which show planetary positions for each fortnight, lunar month, and solar month, and they also contain tables and charts which provide more detailed information about fluctuations for each day within these longer periods.

Horoscopes cast according to the time and place of birth of the client provide assessments for the entire span of life. Hindu astrology has a unique method, known as the *dashā* system, for focusing on the entire lifetime of the client. The lifetime is divided into nine periods, ranging in length from seven years to twenty years, and each of these periods is ruled by a prescribed planet. Each period in turn is divided into nine subperiods of shorter duration, and each of these is again divided into nine sub-subperiods. This scheme provides a series of nested time periods of various magnitudes which can be utilized in discussing the trajectory of events in the person's life.

The lines of the palm locate points in the lifetime of the client, and a palmist can determine how long certain trends will last. Each of the lines represents a lifetime of approximately seventy to eighty years; curves, cross-lines, and unusual marks at various points on the line indicate the emergence of particular conditions during a specific period of time. The ideograms of the dice system (*ramal*) are associated with general temporal periods framed by the astrologer for a span of weeks, months, or perhaps a year.

Gaining an understanding of the structure of the situation and its temporal patterning is a central achievement for both the astrologer and his client in their advisory interaction. And in keeping with the pragmatic orientation of the system, the advisory session typically concludes with a discussion of remedies (*upāy*, *ilāj*). The most common remedies which astrologers recommend include worshipping in a temple or mosque, wearing charms, wearing gems to absorb planetary rays, following dietary regimens, giving alms, and cultivating patience, honesty, and other ameliorative patterns of behavior. These multifaceted courses of action provide a framework in terms of which the client can work to maximize beneficial trends and minimize harmful ones in a particular set of circumstances.

Conclusion

At the center of these popular orientations toward fate is the commonplace world of the person—his physical and psychological qualities and their implications in his family and community relationships. Recurrently articulated categories describe this culturally organized life-milieu: "father," "mother," "spouse," "children," "health," "happiness," "occupation," "enemies," and many other entities form a web of intersecting relevances in the life of the person. And as an applied science, astrology reflects popular understandings about the manifestations of fate in the experiences of everyday life.

References Cited

Allen, Richard Hinckley
1963 Star Names: Their Lore and Meaning. New York: Dover.
Harper, Edward C.
1964 Religion in South Asia. Seattle: University of Washington Press.
Inden, Ronald B., and Ralph W. Nicholas
1977 Kinship in Bengali Culture. Chicago: University of Chicago Press.
Kane, P. V.
1974 History of Dharmaśāstra. Volume I, Part 1. Poona: Bhandarkar Oriental Research Institute.
Kolenda, Pauline Mahar
1964 Religious Anxiety and Hindu Fate. *In* Religion in South Asia. Edward C. Harper, ed. Seattle: University of Washington Press. Pp. 71–81.
MacDonald, Duncan B.
1973 Development of Muslim Theology, Jurisprudence, and Constitutional Theory. Delhi: Amarko. Orig. 1903.
Mandelbaum, David
1964 Introduction: Structure and Process in South Asian Religion. *In* Religion in South Asia. Edward C. Harper, ed. Seattle: University of Washington Press. Pp. 5–20.
Mariott, McKim, and Ronald B. Inden
1974 Caste Systems. Encyclopaedia Britannica.
Nasr, S. H.
1964 An Introduction to Islamic Cosmological Doctrines. Cambridge: Harvard University Press.
Potter, Karl
1980 The Karma Theory and Its Interpretation in Some Indian Philosophical Systems. *In* Karma and Rebirth in Classical Indian Traditions. Berkeley: University of California Press.
Pugh, Judy F.
1981 Person and Experience: The Astrological System of North India. Ph.D. dissertation, University of Chicago.
Radhakrishnan, Sarvepalli, and Charles A. Moore
1964 A Source Book in Indian Philosophy. Princeton: Princeton University Press.
Rahman, Fazlur
1968 Islam. Garden City, N.Y.: Doubleday.
Sachau, Edward C.
1964 Alberuni's India. Delhi: S. Chand.
Siegel, James T.
1969 The Rope of God. Berkeley: University of California Press.
Singer, Milton B.
1972 When a Great Tradition Modernizes. New York: Praeger.

·6·

Vrats: Transformers of Destiny

Susan S. Wadley

In the popular religion of North India, rituals are not merely a context in which the communication of the sacred takes place; rituals are also powerful transformers of one's life path. Some of the most potent of the life-transforming rituals are *vrats*.[1] *Vrats*, as understood today, are closely allied to *bhakti* devotional practices and constitute a crucial element of many devotional practices. Moreover, *vrats* are performed to gain some end, to transform one's life path. Often they are performed to alleviate present misfortune. And whereas *vrats* aim at bettering one's life, often this betterment requires the eradication of prior sins that have led to present troubles. Hence it is believed that the performance of a *vrat* will alter one's destiny. In particular, past actions (karma) are transformed: the deity worshipped in the *vrat* is believed to destroy the sins that are being endured and causing the present unhappiness. Most important, the classical concept of karma is not denied. Rather, while a traditional view of karma is accepted, additions and transformations are made to it that allow for karma to continue to be a major motivator in modern devotional practices. In

Many individuals and sponsors contributed to the completion of this essay. The initial research into the popular religious literature of North India was undertaken during 1974–1975 on a Faculty Research Grant from the American Institute of Indian Studies. A grant from the National Endowment for the Humanities (Summer Stipend for Younger Humanists 1977) permitted research into the classical *vrata* texts, especially the *nibandhas*. The Joint Committee for the American Council of Learned Societies must be thanked for providing the forum for the initial presentation of this paper. Last, my thanks to Bruce W. Derr, who patiently read drafts and provided the context in which it could be completed.

[1] I am following here accepted practice for transcribing Hindi words. When discussing the Sanskrit texts about *vrats*, I will revert to the proper Sanskrit *vrata*.

the following pages, I attempt to illuminate the additions and transformations of karma that are found in the modern vernacular *vrat* literature of North India.

Vrats

Vrat is most commonly translated as a "religious vow" or "fast." The origins of the word are in dispute, but Kane derives it from the root *vṛ*, "to choose or to will." *Vrata* in Sanskrit, then, means "what is willed" or "will" (Kane 1974:5). The range of meanings of *vrata* is from command or law to any vow, with the modern emphasis on vows associated with a particular pattern of worship. Most authors agree that there is a shift in meaning in *vrata* from an obligatory rite (often to atone for past misdeeds) from Manu to the Purāṇas. Later *vratas* are not for atonement but for gaining something by pleasing the gods (Ganguly 1972:52; Aiyangar 1953). For example, the *Bhavisya Purāṇa* "provides that a man crosses easily the deep ocean of hells by means of the boat of *vratas*, *upavāsas* and *niyamas*" (Kane 1974:43–44), while others promise "heaven and other worldly and spiritual rewards to those who performed *vratas*" (Kane 1974:43).

Through the influence of the Purāṇas and digest writers (*nibandhakāras*), *vratas* were extremely popular by the early medieval period. *Vratas* were among the most frequent topics of the digest writers. For example, Hemadri considered *vrata* one of the fourfold aims of existence, and his description of *vrata* makes up the largest section of his work, and Laksmidhara devoted one volume of his immense *Kṛtyakalpataru* to *vratas*. Through observing *vratas*, one could gain *bhukti* (objects or enjoyment), *mukti* (final release), and the destruction of sins (Mishra 1973:61). Moreover, fasts were open to both sexes and all *varṇas*. Furthermore, the choice of *vratas* as sanctioned by the *nibandhakāras* was immense; Laksmidhara listed over 175 and Hemadri discusses over 700.[2] Moreover, by this time *vratas* were seldom undertaken because they were obligatory or because their performance was inescapable. Of the three kinds of *vrata* recognized in the Sanskrit texts (obligatory, occasional, and optional), optional *vratas* dominate medieval and current practice (Aiyangar 1953:xxiii).

Modern *vratas* imply a willing or a vow to gain some desired end,

[2] The *Vratakośa* (ed. 1929) lists 1622, although Kane considers this list inflated (Kane 1974:47).

undertaken optionally. Often some penance or austerity is required, normally fasting. But a *vrat* is not merely a fast (*upavāsa*) and it is not a festival (*utsava*), although both are often associated with a *vrat*. Some of the popular manuals attempt explanations.

> *Vrat* is also a word with varied meanings. For example, to take a vow, to have an inclination for some good action, for the gain of some merit, to establish some *karma*, or by some special method to gain *puṇya*, or to accumulate merit through gaining superior knowledge—all of these things are implied by *vrat*.
>
> *Vrats* and fasts (*upavāsas*)—The primary difference between these two is that in a *vrat*, food or fruits can be taken. But in fasting one must remain without *any* food. One cannot do each manifestation of each *vrat* according to religious beliefs, for every individual cannot do every *vrat*. Some *vrats* are in the *śāstras* and some in folk practices. Nothing can be found published in the *śāstras* on folk practices. In one category are Pajunonopuno and Asamai *vrats*, and other folk *vrats*. In spite of being non-śāstric, the performance of such folk *vrats* is very common, and Hindus observe them in great numbers. (J:21–22)

Other texts add these thoughts: "And [from doing *vrats*] some inspiration, wisdom, and power (*śakti*)" (K:1); or "That is to say, there is no place equal to the Ganga, there is no guru equal to the mother, there is no god equal to Viṣṇu, and there is no authority equal to fasting (*upavāsa*)" (G:3).

Some type of abstinence from food is not the sole requirement of most *vrats*. Usually a *pūjā* is also enjoined, and the devotee is told to read the *kathā* associated with that *vrat*. The religious manuals examined below concentrate on detailing the rules for food, dress, and behavior of specific *vrats* as well as on giving the correct rules for the associated *pūjā* and the *kathā* that is the primary exegesis of a given *vrat*.

Vrats as practiced by present-day Hindus are part of the *bhakti* tradition. The basic aim of a *vrat* is to influence some deity to come to one's aid as one struggles across the ocean of existence. The austerities associated with the *vrat* are signals to the deity of one's faith and devotion. The assumption is that the deity will reward this faith and service with some kind of boon.

The Texts

This essay is based primarily on a series of popular Hindi language manuals detailing ritual rules and associated myths (*kathās*). These manuals are found in markets, outside of temples, at fairs, on street corners. The language is more likely to be a colloquial dialect than standard Hindi.[3] Although only a few of these texts are used here, they number in the hundreds.[4] They are read in villages and in cities and by women and by men, all seeking advice and instruction on the proper way to perform rituals.

The increasing importance of these texts as purveyors of a modern Hindu dogma cannot be overstated. Most were composed in the last ten years, although a few date from the early 1960s. The output of religious literature from small publishing firms has increased dramatically during this period. While an explanation for this growing popularity cannot be explicitly stated, several factors clearly are important. Increasing literacy allows thousands to use texts where once they had relied solely on oral traditions. A more mobile population separates generations and deprives both men and women of their traditional religious mentors. Finally, texts are valued in Hinduism in part because of their traditional inaccessibility: to many newly literate persons, reading a pamphlet is more authentic and prestigious than reciting the stories of their elders. The stories of the elders had themselves taken the place of the teaching of gurus, to whom people had little access. Currently, then, written texts are replacing the elders and act as a stand-in for the traditions of the guru.

A variety of texts about *vrats* are used in this study. The most popular is the *Śrī Satyanārāyaṇ vrat kathā*. In Karimpūr (a village in the Hindu heartland 150 miles southeast of Delhi), this manual is used by the pandits when asked by clients to perform a *kathā*,[5] usually to alleviate some difficulty, but sometimes to accrue merit. It is also the most popular *vrat kathā* among Hindus in Syracuse, New York. This manual comprises a Sanskrit text and a Hindi translation. Most publishing houses of religious literature have their own version costing under one rupee. The pandit reads the Hindi *kathās* to his clients during his ritual performance.

[3] There is considerable variation, however, in the degree of sophistication in these texts, both in terms of content (e.g., references to major pilgrimage sites or to Sanskrit texts) as well as language and general style (e.g., Sanskrit names for months versus dialect names). Two major orientations have been identified (see Wadley, forthcoming), one with an All-India, urban concern and the other having a rural, family-based orientation.

[4] My personal collection contains over 500 items.

[5] *Kathā* carries two meanings. Most generally and when unmarked, it means a religious story associated with a particular ritual. In a marked sense (when "performed") it means a recitation of a religious story in the context of a specific ritual.

A second text is the *Śukravār vrat kathā*. This manual contains the rules and *kathā* for the performance of a *vrat* in honor of Santōsi Ma, the Contented Mother. This *kathā* is given only in Hindi (or other vernaculars). Along with Santōsi Ma's rapid ascendance as a popular goddess is a proliferation of manuals for her worship. The rules and *kathās* are read by the worshipper herself (or by some literate female such as a daughter or the anthropologist). In Karimpūr priests are not involved in the worship of Santōsi Ma. Moreover, in North India, worship of Santōsi Ma is an exclusively female practice.[6]

Similar to these two manuals is the *Saptvār vrat kathā*. This contains the rules and *kathās* for the *vrats* of the seven days of the week. I have not seen a version with Sanskrit renditions of the rules and *kathās* and would guess that none exists. The *vrat kathās* for the various days of the week can also be obtained individually. Again, most firms have their own versions of these.

These types of manuals are remarkable for their consistency: aside from dialectical differences, they present the same rules and stories, that is, they are almost totally standardized. The other set of texts used here is not standardized (see Wadley, forthcoming). These are manuals containing the rules and stories for the *vrats* and festivals of the twelve months (*Bārah mahīne ke vrat aur tyauhār*). Stories, rules, dates, and so forth, all vary rather dramatically. Costing considerably more than the manuals discussed above, they are less popular, and not every publisher has produced a version, although there is evidence of growing use.

The essential point is that all of these manuals are explicitly instructional and are to be used in the performance of the ritual itself. The introduction to one clarifies this purpose:

> In all countries and among all races, fasts (*vrats*) and festivals have the highest place. From [performing] them the spiritual power of humans blossoms, endeavors are sanctified and many physical ills are allayed. . . .
> All of the fasts and festivals of men and women are described in this book. The language is of an intermediate level so that the barely literate as well as the commonly literate can reasonably profit from it. (H:5–6)[7]

Because the evidence used here is textual, it is not possible to relate

[6] Dr. Neera Desai says that in Gujarat men are now beginning to worship Santōsi Ma.

[7] References to Hindi materials are given by a letter standing for the author and date. Page numbers follow. Unless otherwise noted, all translations are mine. I must thank Barbara D. Miller and William Houska for loaning me their rough drafts of translations of I. Suniti Dutt aided me in completing the translation of A.

these directly to their effects upon behavior. However, as the data will show, the authors clearly intend a causal relationship between concept and behavior, that is, they are prescribing a rationale for ritual practices and expect the basic concepts of this rationale to be accepted. Moreover, as I have shown elsewhere, the *kathās* associated with *vrats* set up a scheme of the world in which ritual behavior is both right and necessary for human well-being (Wadley 1975, chap. 4).

Śrī Satyanārāyaṇ Vrat Kathā

Before proceeding to a discussion of karma, a complete translation of a *vrat kathā* will aid in clarifying the nature of this literature. This example presents two of the five *kathās* in the *Śrī Satyanārāyaṇ vrat kathā* (A:1–14). As was noted earlier, the *Śrī Satyanārāyaṇ vrat kathā* is one of the most popular. Not only is it one of the most widely used *vrat kathās* that deal specifically with the reversal of karma, it is also part of the Sanskritic tradition, unlike the more local vernacular tales used in most of the following examples.

The Story of the Fast of Śrī Satyanārāyaṇ

The First Chapter Begins

[Vyāsjī said,—] Once upon a time in Naimisaranya [a place of pilgrimage], 88,000 sages, such as Sauarvaka and others, asked the wise saint Sutjī about some *vrat*. The sages said, "We want to hear about some *vrat* by which we can achieve the fulfillment of our desires, O Great Saint, please tell us that."

Sutjī replied, "In an earlier time, Nāradjī also asked the same question to the husband of Lakṣmī, Śrī Viṣṇu Bhagvān. Now listen attentively to me: here is how Viṣṇu Bhagvān replied to Nāradjī.

" 'Long ago, in order to help mankind, Nāradjī was wandering in different *lokas* [worlds] and at last he reached *mṛtyu-loka* [the kingdom of death]. There he took birth several times. He saw people suffering in various ways and found them unhappy with their own work. He tried to find out a way by which these people could get rid of their sorrows and unhappiness. Keeping this problem in his mind, Nārad went to *Viṣṇu-loka*, the kingdom of Viṣṇu. After reaching there, he saw Nārāyaṇ, who was fair and bright and was holding a conch shell, a whirling small wheel, a big weapon made of steel or iron, and a lotus in his four hands, and a gorgeous flower garland was hanging around his neck to add to his beauty. Nārad started praying by singing praises to Nārāyaṇ and told him, "O Bhagvān, you are greatly powerful. Neither mind nor vision can reach you; you have neither beginning, middle nor end. Endless virtues and qualities have been assembled within you; you are the creator of the whole universe; you are the one who saves all devotees from their sorrows and agonies. I pay respectful homage to you."

" 'Hearing Nārad's prayer, Bhagvān Viṣṇu stood in front of him and said, "O Muni, you express your desire and ask me whatever you like and I shall give you the good answer."

" 'Nāradjī said, "People living in the kingdom of death are taking birth again and again and are leading a very sorrowful life full of every kind of sinful, unfair works. So, O Swami, if you are kind to me, then please tell me the way by which those unfortunate people can get rid of their sorrows and sufferings."

" 'Śrī Bhagvān replied, "O Putra! [O son] You have asked me a very good question in your desire to help mankind. Now listen to me: I will tell you the way by which people of the world will be able to get rid of their worldly ties or sufferings and sorrows. I love you so much and hence I will tell you about a *vrat* which is rare in the kingdom of god as well as in the kingdom of death and which gives people various types of heavenly pleasure. People can achieve happiness and salvation after death if they sincerely and methodically observe the *vrat* of Satyanārāyaṇ."

" 'After listening to these kind words from Viṣṇu Bhagvān, Nārad said, "O Bhagvān, would you please tell me, what is the good result of the *vrat*, what are the rules of that *vrat* and who has done that *vrat* previously and what are the suitable days for performing this *vrat*? Please clearly tell me the answers to all of these questions."

" 'Śrī Viṣṇu Bhagvān replied, "This *vrat* can pacify sorrows and sufferings: it can increase the amount of wealth and land, it can also give good fortune, children and victory in all spheres of life. And any day when man is filled with devotion and feels like doing the *pūjā* of Satyanārāyaṇ, he can worship him in the evening of that same day. He should do the *pūjā* along with priests, relatives and his friends. He should offer *naivedya* (*prasād*, which must consist of sweets, banana, ghee, milk, brown sugar, and wheat flour). One can use rice flour instead of wheat flour. All these things should be mixed together with devotion to prepare *prasād* for Satyanārāyaṇ. After offering *naivedya* [which is known as *sirini*], he should listen to the *kathā* along with his friends and relatives. Then he should give *prasād* and then *dakṣiṇā* [money as *dān* or gift] to the priest. After that he will eat *prasād* along with his friends and relatives. Then they should start singing and dancing in the *pūjā* place because they are not to sleep at night, which is known as *rātri-jāgaraṇ*. At last, he will go back to his house with the pleasant thought of Satyanārāyaṇ in his mind. Obviously, people can get their desires fulfilled by performing the *vrat* of Satyanārāyaṇ in the way described above. Especially in the *kali-yug*, this is the best and easiest way on the earth for people to get rid of their sorrows and for the fulfillment of their desires." ' "

Now the First Chapter Ends and the Second Chapter Begins

Sutjī said, "O saints! Now I will tell you about persons who did this *vrat* in ancient times. In beautiful Kāshi there lived a poor Brahmin. Being restless from hunger and thirst, he continually wandered the earth. Because of the love of the Brahmin, Bhagvān saw his sorrow.

"Taking the form of an old Brahmin, Bhagvān went to his house where he greeted the poor Brahmin respectfully. 'O wise one. Although you are sad daily, why do you wander the earth? O respected Brahmin, tell me about all this, I want to hear it.'

"The Brahmin replied, 'I am a very poor Brahmin. I go out to beg. O Bhagvān, if you know a remedy for this, have mercy and speak out.'

"The old Brahmin said, 'Satyanārāyaṇ Bhagvān is the giver of the desires of the mind. Therefore, O Brahmin, you do that *pūjā* and *vrat* from whose performance men gain freedom from all sorrows.' Having taken on the form of an old Brahmin and having told the poor Brahmin all the rules of this *vrat*, Satyanārāyaṇ vanished.

"The poor Brahmin could not sleep, having determination to perform the *vrat* told of by the wise Brahmin. Rising in the morning, still determined to perform the *vrat* of Satyanārāyaṇ, the Brahmin went out to beg. On that day, the Brahmin gained a lot of grain from his begging. Using this, he performed the *vrat* of Satyanārāyaṇ along with his friends and relations. From the effect of this *vrat*, being rid of all sorrows, he was joined with every kind of affluence. From that time, the Brahmin did this *vrat* every month. Having done this *vrat* in this way and being rid of all signs, the Brahmin achieved *mokṣa*.

"I told you the same *vrat* that was said to Nārad-muni by Viṣṇu-Nārāyaṇ. O *Vipras*! What would you like me to say now?"

The *ṛṣi* said, "O Muni! Who are the other people who followed that Brahmin in doing Satyanārāyaṇ *vrat*? We have a respectful desire in our minds to listen to these things."

Sutjī responded, "O Munis! I am going to describe those who did that *vrat*, listen to me. One time a Brahmin was bent on doing the *vrat* in conformance with his great wealth, together with his friends and relatives. At this very time, a wood vendor came and placed his wood outside the Brahmin's house. Aching with thirst, the woodseller saw the Brahmin doing his *vrat*. Saying *namaskār* to the Brahmin, he asked, 'What are you doing and from doing this, what kind of dividend is received? Elaborate on this.' The Brahmin replied, 'The Satyanārāyaṇ *vrat* is the maker of all one's desires. From his mercy I have here all sorts of grain and wealth.' The woodseller was very pleased to know from him all the matters relating to his *vrat* and having learned them, left. The thought came into his mind that today with the wealth gained by selling wood, I will perform the *vrat* of Satyanārāyaṇ. Having this thought, he put the wood on his head. He went to a neighborhood where rich people live and that day he doubled the value of his wood. Being pleased, he obtained ripe bananas, ghee, grain, and sugar. Gathering it all together, he went to his home. Calling all his brothers, he did the *vrat* with great ceremony. From its effects, the woodseller was joined with wealth and sons and after enjoying the happiness of the world went away to heaven. The second section of the Satyanārāyaṇ *vrat* is finished." (A:1–14)

The Problem of Karma

In attempting to understand the relationship of *vrat* to karma, we are faced with the problem of just what it is that karma determined, just what circumstances in this life are determined by karma (whether one's own or someone else's). The texts are not explicit, but it is clear that karma is related to the major events of life. And doing a *vrat* can overrule karma. If there is any strong message in any *vrat kathā*, it is that doing a *vrat* destroys past sins and changes the course of one's life.

Now the general rule of karma is that the results of past deeds cannot be gotten rid of except by enjoying or undergoing their consequences. In this purest sense, karma can be described as impersonal and mechanistic—no matter what, you will endure the consequences of past deeds. The *vrat kathā* contain the same basic message: "That seed which a farmer sows in the field, that fruit he cuts. In the same manner in this world, one endures the fruits of one's actions" (E:10). And as past acts are unknown, the future is unknown: "No one knows the results of previous acts." So, as will be shown, even though some *vrats* exist explicitly to counteract karma, the basic tenets of karma underlie the transformation of one's life course that is caused by one's performance of *vrats*.

As others have shown previously (Sharma 1973; O'Flaherty 1976), the issue of karma presents a situation of psychological indeterminacy. Karma is not known, the future is not known. Although karma may present a logical solution to the problem of theodicy (see Sharma 1973 and Obesekeyere 1968), the individual "enduring his or her karma" appears to seek other explanations—or so I read the history of the Hindu search.

One answer to the psychological burden of unknown past deeds is to erase the bad acts. According to *vrat kathās*, this is exactly what happens:

> Because of the mercy of Bṛhaspati Mahārāj, all of his sins are destroyed. (D:54)

> From the mercy of Satyanārāyan, all of his sins are destroyed. (A:34)

But having to endure the consequences of past deeds is only half of the karma message; the future remains unknown. *Vrats* also guarantee the future:

> O Vrikodar! If heaven is dear to you and you desire a guarantee of not going to hell, then you must do the *vrats* of both *ekādaśīs* [elevenths]. (I:39)

> From doing such a good ceremony as the Satyanārāyaṇ *vrat*, living beings quickly endure [eat] happiness and gain *mokṣa*. (A:34)

> The lord said, "Whoever does my *vrat* will be freed of sin [*pāp*] and will gain the abode of the blessed!" (I:38)

> Because of the sadness, the morose Brahmin and his widowed daughter began to keep the *vrat* of *ṛṣi* Pañcamī, and as a result they gained release from continual birth and became dwellers in heaven. (I:75)

That is, *vrats* act within the basic framework of karma; however, because sins are destroyed, one has to endure only one's good past deeds. Likewise, the future is of no concern, as eternal happiness and liberation from the bonds of continual birth are guaranteed. This transformation can be diagrammed thus:

Karma	endures past acts	future unknown
	transformed by performance of *vrat* and deity's reward	
Karma in *vrat* literature	destruction of sins of past, live happily	guarantee happiness, fruits, and *mokṣa*

The Actions of the Deity

Vrats work, of course, only because the deities honored are thought to be capable of imposing their will. Within the limits of their powers, deities are able to reward their devotees. I should note that not all *vrats* gain one eternal happiness or salvation. Others promise only sons, health, wealth, or whatever. But in all cases, the deity is expected to overrule karma and apparently to eliminate those past deeds which have caused the present misfortune.

The list of sins eliminated by various *vrats* is lengthy; a selection is given here: removal of "many bad deeds," the murder of a hundred cows, the murder of a Brahmin, great scandal, unreligious behavior, forgery, deception, gaining freedom from the sins of seven lives, cutting down a pipal tree, and driving a thirsty cow from water.

It is difficult to comment on the exact manipulations by which deities erase the sins of their devotees. Two sets of ideas appear most regularly. First, the deity gives a gift (*dān*, *vardān*) of a son, husband, or whatever. The relationship of such gifts to the karmic legacy of sin is unstated. Second, sins are destroyed. Again, the mechanism is clouded and there appear to be possibilities. One is that the tally in the court of Yama is altered and the sins are removed: the list is recalculated and a new destiny is set. The second is that one gains immediate reward for meritorious acts, just as one gains immediate punishment for sinful ones. That is, my life this instant is based not merely on my actions in past lives but also on those one instant ago, yesterday, and last year. In all of these options, the fact of a destiny written at birth is a contradiction to having one's karma transformed through the results of a *vrat*. This point will reappear later.

The literature on *vrats* states that any sins in this life or past lives can be effectively removed by performing the proper *vrat*. Moreover, the benefits of the *vrat* can be obtained in either this life or the next.

The *vrat kathā* of Arundhatī demonstrates a situation in which the sins of a past life affect the present life, and a happy next life is guaranteed through performance of the *vrat*.

In ancient times a wise Brahmin gave his beautiful young daughter in a marriage of short duration. One day while bathing in the Yamunā river she did the *pūjā* of Śiva and Pārvatī. Luckily, at that very time Śiva and Pārvatī also came there. Pārvatī asked Śiva a question concerning this girl's ritual. Śiva replied, "O Devī, this girl was a man in her previous life. He was born in a Brahmin family. After the marriage this Brahmin left his wife and went to a foreign country. Once there he became detached and forgot about his wife. Because of this sin, in this life he has become a woman with the sorrow of being a childless widow."

Hearing this, Pārvatījī asked, "Is there any scheme for removing this sin?"

Śiva replied, "This girl should die while remembering the pure customs of the special wives like Satī and Arundhatī. In her next life she should remain virtuous—then the full expiation of this sin will be done. Recollect also that those women who are virtuous and who will do the *vrat* of Arundhatī, they will not have to endure the sorrow of being childless."

Hearing this, Pārvatījī told the girl the rules for Arundhatī's *vrat*. From its effect, she was freed of sins, and in her next life she gained a happy family. Since then this *vrat* has become well known in the world. (J:33–34)

In yet another *vrat kathā* we are told of a situation in which a sinful act has immediate effect. In the Plow Sixth (Bhadon 1:5)[8] *vrat kathā*, a woman's child dies immediately after she commits a sin. Here the sin, its effect, its removal, and the removal of its effect all occur in the short space of part of one day. On this day, women worship cows and their calves: in the *kathā* the milkmaid offends the cow, who acts as the unnamed deity in the story.

In current folk stories there is a rumor that in the old days there was a

[8] Bhadon is the month occurring in August–September. This festival occurs on the fourth day of the first (dark) half of the month.

milkmaid who was about to give birth. She was worried both about the pains of childbirth and about selling her cow's milk. She thought that if the child is born, then the milk will be left. Thinking this way, she got up quickly, and putting the pots full of milk and curds on her head, she went off to sell it. A bit later she had an especially sharp pain, so she sat in the shelter of a grove of trees: there a son was born. Leaving the newborn there, the naive milkmaid went off to the nearby villages to sell her milk and curds.

By chance this way was Plow Sixth. Even though the milkmaid's milk was a mixture of cow's milk and water buffalo's milk, she said that it was from buffalo only. She certainly tricked those women!

A farmer was plowing in the field next to the grove where she had left the baby. Suddenly the child was pierced by the point of the plow and died. Seeing this, the farmer was very sad and forlorn. Nevertheless, he took courage and sewed up the stomach of the child with a thorn from the grove and departed. Soon the milkmaid returned from selling her milk. Upon seeing the condition of her child, she thought that it was due to the sin that she had just committed. She thought that this state could only be due to her having lied about the milk for Plow Sixth, thereby destroying the faith of the village women. "I will make atonement by making this clear," she thought. Making up her mind in this way, she went to the village where she had sold her milk. There she wandered from street to street telling that the milk was a mixture of cow's and buffalo's milk. Hearing this, the women blessed her for protecting her faith. Having gotten a blessing from many young women, she went back to the grove. There she found her son alive. From that time on she gave up telling lies, understanding it to be a vile act comparable to killing a Brahmin. (I:61–62)

The *vrat kathās* never deal with situations where the deity is completely powerless to act because of karma. However, there are a few instances where the deity is hindered. But even here, the devotee's will prevails, although longer periods of faith and service are required. If the request is against karma or is too tremendous, the deity overturns karma only after greater demonstrations of devotion from the devotee. In one case, Śiva tells Pārvatī that he cannot give a son to a certain devotee because "there is no son in his fate (*bhāgya*)" (E:10). Eventually, he gives a son who will live only twelve years. This misfortune is again overturned through even more acts of service and the son lives. In a similar example, the actions of the goddess Santōsi Ma are described: "In three months the Mother fulfills the fruits. If someone's stars are not favorable, then the Mother completes the certain action in a year" (Howell 1975:52). Somehow the deities are able to act.

The Transfer of Merit in *Vrats*

Several authors have noted that not only does karma affect the individual acting, but the karma of one individual may affect another (see, especially, Sharma 1973). The *vrat kathās* uphold this evidence, within limits.

All instances of the transfer of merit gained through *vrats* are instances of the transfer of merit between kin. Certain transfers never occur, while others are common. Transfers between parents and children are prevalent. Many women's *vrats*, such as *Putrada Ekādaśī* guarantee a child's life. Children also receive some portion of their destiny from their father: in the *vrat kathā* for the *Āśā-Bagotī vrat*, there is this exchange. Himachal, the father of Pārvatī and Gaurī, asks them, "Whose *bhāgya* (destiny) do you each eat?" Pārvatī said, "I eat my own *bhāgya*." Gaurī replies, "I eat your *bhāgya*." Gaurī's response is correct, and eventually Pārvatī too is convinced that she endures her father's destiny, not merely her own (I:95). But not only do children reap the benefits of their parent's actions; the reverse also occurs. Instances of parents reaping the rewards of their offsprings' behavior are not uncommon. In the *vrat kathā* for Narsinh Jayantī, it is said that Prahlād obtained *mokṣa* for his father through his prayers and devotion to Narsinh (I:37). And the *vrat* of Indirā's Eleventh guarantees that all of one's ancestors will gain heaven (I:99).

Transfers between husband and wife are also prevalent, but in one direction only—from wife to husband. The rules for the *vrat* of *Gugga Pañcamī* state that "from doing this *vrat* the husband will be protected from calamities" (I:60). In the *vrat* of Sāvitrī, Sāvitrī clearly snatches her husband away from his decreed death through her devotion. In the Gangor *vrat* it is said: "Śiva gave Pārvatī a boon. From now on, the husbands of those women who do my *pūjā* and your fast will live a long time and in the end will gain *mokṣa*" (I:8).

I have found only one instance of a transfer between other kin. In the *kathā* for Śarad Purṇimā we find that one sister gains back her dead son because of the merit accrued by the other virtuous sister.

In all of these instances we do not know how or to what extent karma and destiny are altered. But somehow the *vrats* and the concerned deity's actions are efficacious.

Karma Contextualized

It is well known that the concept and term karma, however defined, is not prevalent or widely used in all Hindu communities. In the *vrat* literature, the most common term for destiny or fate is *bhāgya*. In these texts, karma quite clearly refers to actions, with specific attributions of human conditions due to actions. But *bhāgya* is destiny, or fate, as these examples illustrate.

> This *vrat* is done to gain long-lasting good *bhāgya*. (J:32)
>
> This is all the trouble of our *bhāgya*. (D:6)
>
> The queen, being in trouble because of *bhāgya*. . . . (E:29)

Karma refers more specifically to one's past actions, and most critically to one's sins. As sins are removed through the performance of *vrats* and the deity's acknowledgment of that performance in the form of a boon, one's *bhāgya* is altered.

Bhāgya derives from the word share or portion. It is one's share of fortune or misfortune (*nirbhāgya*). While it too can be written,[9] it presents a potentiality of capriciousness and lack of predetermination that contradicts the premises of karma. In a Panjabi folk opera, we find this interpretation:

> Without *bhāgya*, nothing can be obtained in this world,
> but good deeds are never useless. (Temple 1962:127)

Moreover, fortune can contradict karma:

> My share of fortune has been unblemished.
> This has been due to your mercy, guru!
> Otherwise, I would have been a victim of *karam*.[10]
> (Temple 1962:143)

Karma, one's past deeds, can be altered through new deeds. The score, we are told in these devotional texts, is kept up-to-date, for deeds can be immediately effective because of the actions of the gods. Moreover, any individual may have a destiny, a "fate" or fortune that is loosely tied to the classical notion of karma. One's fortune too can change because of ongoing activities. At the same time, fortune may not be allied to karma: in some contexts, *bhāgya* appears to reflect a different system.

[9] "In this world, who can be taken across (saved)? A wretched *bhāg* was written" (Temple 1962:124).

[10] In Punjab, as well as Uttar Pradesh, the typical pronunciation of karma is *karam*, as Temple rightly notes in his text.

Notions of karma are "context-sensitive." The karma of the *vrat* texts is not the karma of the classical sources. Following Ramanujan (1980), I suggest that there are multiple, context-sensitive systems at work. Modern devotionalism requires a break with the total predetermination of some karma doctrines. Human actions must lead to the alteration of life circumstances in this life. Moreover, the concept of *bhāgya*, also context-sensitive, is a counterpoint to the karma doctrine. It presents a potentiality of "luck" or chance or fate (understood as unrelated to past acts) that is not implied by either the classical concepts of karma nor the concept of karma found in the *vrat* literature. Only by attending to the context of a particular utterance or text can we hope to understand it. There are a multiplicity of systems present, and shifts are continually made between them as circumstances change. The system used must fit the situation. Ramanujan quotes William Blake: "One law for the lion and the ox is oppression." He adds, "The Hindu would have approved" (1980:31).

Hindi References Cited

A. Śrī Satyanārāyaṇ vrat kathā pūjan sāmagrī. Delhi: Anand Prakasan, n.d.
B. Śrī Satyanārāyaṇ vrat kathā. Mathura: Bombay Bhusan Press, n.d.
C. Sukravār vrat kathā. Mathura: Sri Krisna Pustakalay, n.d.
D. Bṛhaspati vār vrat kathā bhāsā. Mathura: Thok Pustakalay, n.d.
E. Saptvār vrat kathā. Delhi: Anand Prakasan.
F. Bārah mahīne ke vrat aur tyauhār. Written by Pandit Balmukind "Chaturvedi" Sahitya Ratn. Mathura: Shyamlal Hiralal, n.d.
G. Bārahon mahīne ke vrat aur tyauhār. Written by Roop Kishore Bharatiya. Mathura: Govardhan Pustakalay, n.d.
H. Vars bhar ke vrat aur tyauhār. Written by Ram Krisnadad Agraval "Raski." Delhi: Dehati Pustak Bhandar, n.d.
I. Bārahon mahīne ke sampūrṇ hinduon ke vrat tyauhār. Written by Hiramani Sinh "Sathi." Allahabad: Sri Durga Pustak Bhandar, n.d.
J. Vrat parv aur tyauhār. Written by Rajesh Diksit. Kaṇpur: Dip Prakan Mandir, 1967.
K. Hinduon ke vrat aur tyauhār. Written by Kunvar Kanyaiyaju. New Delhi: Sasta Sahitya Mandal, n.d.

English References Cited

Aiyangar, K. V. Rangaswani, ed.
1953 Kṛtyakalpataru of Bhaṭṭa Laksmidhara. Vratakaṇḍa. Gaekwad's Oriental Series. Baroda. VI(123).

Bharati, A.
1977 Karma: Cognition and Behavior in Contemporary Hindu Society. Mimeo.
Ganguly, Joydev
1972 Dharmaśāstra in Mithila. Calcutta: Calcutta Sanskrit College Research Series. No. 78.
Howell, Catherine Herbert
1975 "Discovering" the Goddess: An Analysis of a *Vrat Kathā*. Master's thesis, Department of Anthropology, University of Virginia.
Kane, P. V.
1974 History of Dharmaśāstra. Poona: Bhandarkar Oriental Research Institute. Vol. 5, Part I.
Kolenda, Pauline Mahar
1964 Religious Anxiety and Hindu Fate. Journal of Asian Studies 23:71–81.
Mishra, Vibhuti Bhushan
1973 Religious Beliefs and Practices of North India During the Early Medieval Period. Leiden: E. J. Brill.
Obeyesekere, Gananath
1968 Theodicy, Sin and Salvation in a Sociology of Buddhism. *In* Dialectic in Practical Religion, Cambridge Papers in Social Anthropology, no. 5. E. R. Leach, ed. Cambridge: Cambridge University Press. Pp. 7–40.
O'Flaherty, Wendy Doniger
1976 The Origins of Evil in Hindu Mythology. Berkeley: University of California Press.
Ramanujan, A. K.
1980 The Relevance of Folklore. Paper presented in the workshop "Models and Metaphors in Indian Folklore." Berkeley, California, February 7–10, 1980.
Sharma, Ursula
1973 Theodicy and the Doctrine of Karma. Man, n.s. 8:348–364.
Temple, Richard Carnac
1962 The Legends of the Punjab. Patiala, Punjab: Language Department (reprint), vol. 1.
Wadley, Susan S.
1967 "Fate" and the Gods in the Punjabi Cult of Gagga: A Structural Semantic Analysis. Master's thesis, Department of Anthropology, University of Chicago.
1975 Shakti: Power in the Conceptual Structure of Karimpur Religion. University of Chicago Studies in Anthropology, Series in Social, Cultural and Linguistic Anthropology, no. 2. Chicago: Department of Anthropology, University of Chicago.
Forthcoming Popular Hinduism and Mass Literature in North India: A Preliminary Analysis. *In* Main Currents in Indian Sociology. G. R. Gupta, ed.

·7·

Destiny and Responsibility: Karma in Popular Hinduism

Lawrence A. Babb

The doctrine of karma has had an odd career in the anthropology of India. In view of its importance in humanistic studies one would expect to find it playing a conspicuous role in anthropological discussions of Hindu culture, especially in those concerned with religion. But this has not been generally so. Rather, karma has tended to be treated as an afterthought in the ethnographic literature. It has usually been given hasty treatment, if any treatment at all, and has often been viewed as something added to, or ancillary to, other patterns of belief and practice that are in some way more fundamental. Few anthropologists have dealt seriously with karma on its own terms, though studies by Kolenda (1964) and Sharma (1973) and essays included in this volume represent obvious exceptions.

This does not mean, however, that the social sciences more generally have ignored karma. Far from it, for the doctrine of karma, together with other associated ideas, has played a central role in another, very different tradition of social scientific inquiry, one that has developed largely in isolation from ethnographic studies. I refer, of course, to discussions of economic development that emphasize what are believed to be the effects of traditional religious ideology on economic behavior. Drawing inspiration from the writings of Max Weber, these theories tend to take a rather dim view of notions like karma. A good example is William Kapp's study (1963), which tries to show that the karma doctrine is associated with a "fatalistic" attitude toward the human condition. This, Kapp argues, leads to passive acceptance of existing social and economic conditions. The same theme is echoed in other writings, including Gunnar Myrdal's widely read and very influential *Asian Drama* (1968).

If nothing else, these theories at least seem to suggest how karma should not be studied. In saying this, my point is not that theories such as Kapp's are necessarily wrong, but that they are really little more than conjectures. It might or might not be true that a belief in karma influences behavior in the ways these theories suggest—or, for that matter, in quite different ways. But what must be stressed is that this is an *empirical* question. A fundamental methodological error accompanies most Weberian or neo-Weberian theories of the influence of concepts such as karma on behavior. Such theories are usually based on an image of Hinduism derived largely from texts, and only some texts at that. Behavorial models are then extrapolated from what are essentially philosophical ideals. The crucial question of what forms ideas such as karma actually take in popular religious culture is effectively bypassed, and thus the question of how existing beliefs and practices might shape behavior can never really be seriously addressed.

The empirical evidence pertaining to these problems is not as rich as one might hope. But on the basis of the available evidence one thing seems clear: whatever the relationship between the karma doctrine and the behavior of most Hindus, it is not simply an acting-out of the worldviews of textual Hinduism. Many other complexities intervene. And if, as the evidence suggests, the karma doctrine is quite widely diffused in popular Hindu culture, it is by no means obvious that the concept is actually applied to human situations in anything like the manner suggested by philosophical texts.

What, then, is actually known of the form taken by the doctrine of karma in popular Hinduism and its influence on behavior? Distressingly little. Still, it seems to me that two points, at least, emerge from what scattered evidence we have. The first is that the doctrine of karma is quite widely and deeply diffused in Hindu culture. That is, just because the doctrine appears in texts does not mean that it is absent from, or unimportant within, the religious life of illiterate villagers. And second, it is also apparent that although the doctrine of karma is deeply entrenched in popular Hinduism, it never functions in isolation. Rather, it always seems to be but one element in a wider blend of religious ideas, some of which apparently collide with or even contradict it. The remainder of this essay will examine each of these points in greater detail, with particular emphasis on the second.

There seems little doubt that the karma doctrine is exceedingly widespread in non-tribal Hindu India. Moreover, the evidence suggests that although the doctrine may be modified in certain ways, the essential idea, that of action determining the subsequent destiny of the actor, is well understood, even by people who have little direct contact with textual religion. Although persons in certain categories, such as Brahmin priests, may be more likely than others to use karmic interpretations of destiny, this does not mean that karmic interpretations are not available to others. My own informants in Chhattisgarh (Babb 1975) were quite conversant with the principle of karma. It is true that they tended not to use the doctrine very frequently in specific situations—of which more later—but they were certainly able to discuss it in general terms. Details vary greatly, but numerous ethnographic studies confirm the same general acquaintance with the doctrine elsewhere: in Gujarat (Pocock 1973), in Malwa (Mathur 1964), in Himachal Pradesh (Sharma 1973), in Uttar Pradesh (Kolenda 1964), in Andhra (Dube 1955), in Karnataka (Beals 1974), in Tamilnadu (Beck, and E.V. and S. Daniel, in this volume), to refer to but a few instances.

There are, of course, exceptions or apparent exceptions. Within a Chamar community of Uttar Pradesh described by Bernard Cohn there appears to be actual ignorance of the entire complex of ideas of which karma is a part (1959:207). I have no doubt that similar instances could be found elsewhere, but I suspect they are relatively few. Other exceptions seem to be matters more of rejection than of ignorance. For example, in his study of a village near Delhi, Oscar Lewis reports that some of his informants were quite skeptical about the traditional theory of rewards and punishments for actions in past lives (1965:253–255). But skepticism is not the same thing as ignorance, and in any case it seems clear that what his informants rejected was not the idea of karma, but rather its conjunction with the theory of transmigration. Most of his informants seemed to accept karmic reasoning about the causes of good and bad fortune, but insisted that the karmic effects of action would be experienced in this life rather than another.

There are also well-known instances of the rejection of karmic rationalizations of caste status. It has been noted many times that the doctrine of karma can lend itself easily to a justification of the hierarchy of castes, the visible hierarchy being viewed as a kind of record of the progression and decline of souls in accord with actions in previous lives, and there seems little doubt that caste status is frequently seen in this light, especially by the higher castes. But as more than one investigator has pointed out, this is by no means a universal view. Kathleen Gough (1960:54) reports that low-caste villagers in Tanjore District view the karmic theory of caste status with skepticism and even amusement. Similar attitudes were expressed to Pauline Kolenda when she questioned North Indian Sweepers about the reasons for their low status (1964:74–76). Her informants would not concede that their low status had anything to do with sinfulness in previous lifetimes. At most, they suggested, karma explains the grossest status distinctions between humans and animals, and, among humans, between those who serve and those who are served. To explain their own situation they resorted to a different kind of theory altogether. They cited origin myths that portrayed the Sweepers as having fallen, as a group, from a formerly high status because they were victimized and tricked by others in the remote past. The same kind of rationale for low status is found among lower castes in many areas of India.

But of course dissent of this kind is not necessarily the same thing as rejection of the doctrine of karma. Rather, I think we must view nonkarmic interpretations of low status as a refusal to employ karmic reasoning in a particular context of potential application. From Kolenda's account it is clear that her informants understood the concept of karma and were quite willing to apply it in some circumstances, though not in others. As we shall see, there is nothing remarkable in this, for it is characteristic of the way the idea of karma is employed more generally in popular Hinduism. There seems to be no human circumstance that *must* be explained in terms of karma, nor does there appear to be any that is not at least *potentially* subject to karmic interpretation. Whether a given situation is viewed karmically or not seems to depend on the kind of point the interpreter really wishes to make, and there is obviously much room for variation in this.

With this we are brought to the second of the points I want to stress, namely that the idea of karma always coexists ethnographically with other, apparently competing concepts. There seems to be general agreement that the ostensible function of the karma doctrine, at least in popular religion, is that of explaining misfortune. It was above all Max Weber who stressed this by characterizing karma as one of only three possible logically pure solutions to the problem of theodicy, the other two being Zoroastrian dualism and the doctrine of predestination (1958:275). Subsequent writers have been uneasy with the characterization of karma as theodicy, mainly because the problem of theodicy, in the strictest sense, arises from a belief in the goodness of an omnipotent god, a belief quite uncharacteristic of South Asian religions (see Obeyesekere 1968; also Sharma 1973). Leaving this issue aside, however, it seems evident that whatever else the doctrine of karma might be, it is a theory of causation that supplies reasons for human fortune, good or bad, and that at least in theory it can provide convincing explanations for human misfortune.

The difficulty, however, arises from the fact that the doctrine of karma is by no means the only way misfortune can be explained in popular Hinduism. On the contrary, there is substantial evidence suggesting that karmic theory is, in fact, resorted to rather infrequently for this purpose, other quite different methods being favored instead. In other words, we cannot say that karma explains the otherwise "inexplicable" twists and turns of fortune, for in popular Hinduism both good and evil fortune are perfectly explicable in other ways. Ursula Sharma, for example, reports that when speaking of misfortune in abstract terms her informants in Himachal Pradesh always utilized the karma doctrine. Concerning specific misfortunes, however, a very different set of ideas come into play: "but perhaps the commonest mode of accounting for misfortune, especially illness or injury, is not in terms of karma, but of the malice of some other person, deity, or personalized agent" (1973:354).

What Sharma describes certainly matches very closely what I found in the Chhattisgarh region of Central India and is typical, I suspect, of most of Hindu India. It is necessary to note first that in Chhattisgarh —and I am sure this is true elsewhere—there is a healthy appreciation of the role of practical activity in the avoidance or alleviation of misfortune. This is a matter not always sufficiently stressed, though Milton Singer has given it considerable attention in his study of urban industrial leaders. He reports that although these men accept the doctrine of karma, they see practical effort as counting heavily in the determination of human welfare (1972, esp. 337–340). The same practical wisdom is characteristic of Chhattisgarhi villagers who display little hesitation in attributing misfortune to laziness or stupidity. There is little evidence, in short, that Hindus are any more inclined than other peoples to ignore the evident proximate causes of human fortune.

But still, practical reason never suffices completely to explain the things that happen. There is always a residuum of occurrences that have no visible or obvious relationship to the intelligence, energy, practical effort, or—to move to another plane—the moral deserts of the persons whom they affect. And here, as elsewhere, the people of Chhattisgarh possess an armory of possible alternative or supplementary explanations. The doctrine of karma is one such, but as in Sharma's village, in fact it is only rarely used, at least in relation to specific misfortunes. The idea that the things that happen to an individual are the "fruits" (*phal*) of past actions was obviously familiar to my informants, but they seemed to regard this as more of a somewhat remote and theoretical possibility than as a convincing or satisfying way of explaining misfortune in any concrete instance.

Far more common were explanations that simply adverted to fate, or that attributed misfortune to angry deities, to ghosts, or to other more immediate agencies. Many misfortunes, especially illnesses of certain kinds, were traced to the anger of unpropitiated deities. Smallpox and diseases similar to smallpox were believed to be caused by the anger of the goddess in one of her various malign forms. Ghosts, who wander about along the boundary between the worlds of the living and the dead, were also believed to be the authors of misfortune, especially sickness. Churalin, a kind of collective ghost of women who have died in childbirth, was seen as particularly dangerous to children. And above all, witchcraft, motivated by the jealousy of the witch for the good fortune of others, was regarded as a potent source of evil occurrences.

In other words, although in the popular traditions of India, karma is indeed one way to explain human fortunes, it is by no means the usual way, or even a very important way, at least as far as certain everyday misfortunes are concerned. It is this fact, I think, that defines for us the essential problem of karma from the standpoint of ethnographic studies. The doctrine of karma appears to be nearly ubiquitous in Hindu culture, but its role in popular religion remains unclear. As Weber pointed out, the doctrine of karma explains misfortune with something approaching logical perfection. But this does not seem to commend it to villagers, who under most circumstances apparently prefer other modes of explanation. Does this mean that the concept of karma is, despite its wide distribution, really unimportant? Possibly, but if this is so, then it becomes difficult to explain the apparent depth of its penetration. On this point, Sharma reports that while karma is rarely the first explanation a villager might give for misfortune, "it is generally the last that he will abandon . . . [he] is more likely to express scepticism towards the cult of the gods or towards the idea of tuna [sorcery] than he is explicitly to reject the doctrine of karma" (1973:358). Karma, then, appears to be both important and unimportant; it has an apparent function, but in its function it seems to be largely preempted by other beliefs and practices. How, then, does karma fit into popular Hinduism, if indeed it fits at all?

One way to approach this problem is to give special emphasis to the historical process by which karma enters local religious ideologies. This approach is best represented by the model of Sanskritization. In this model concepts like karma and *dharma* are viewed as belonging to a pan-Indian tradition that is carried in texts and disseminated by literate priests. These ideas gradually trickle down into popular religion, primarily because of the prestige they carry by virtue of their association with the highest castes. From this standpoint, the doctrine of karma, along with other Sanskritic beliefs and practices, represents essentially a kind of "overlay" on popular religion, deposited by a historical process in which textual elements join, coexist with, and in the end possibly supplant more rustic beliefs and practices. Thus, if Cohn's Chamars are ignorant of karma now, they will probably not always be. With the passage of time their indigenous beliefs and practices will be augmented or displaced by a locally available version of textual Hinduism as they try to rise in status by imitating what they perceive to be the cultural styles of the higher castes (Cohn 1959:210–213).

There is no doubt at all that Sanskritization has been one of the most fundamental historical processes in the evolution of Indian civilization; and in the works of Srinivas, Cohn, and many others we see clear evidence of the outward and downward diffusion of concepts like karma, thus accounting, in historical terms, for the breadth of their distribution. Nevertheless, a troubling aspect of this general approach —at least if it is allowed to stand without qualification—is its tendency to make popular Hinduism seem bifurcated or dualistic in a way that can divert attention from the possibility of a more fundamental unity. From this standpoint the popular religion of a given locality will appear, not as one tradition, but as two in a historically created juxtaposition. And since the juxtaposition is historically fortuitous, the observer is likely to see the relationship between the two as mainly a matter of competition and, ultimately, displacement.

The available evidence, however, suggests that with regard to karma and other kinds of explanation for misfortune, we are dealing not with simple competition but with some more complex kind of coexistence. For example, in Chhattisgarh there are, as everywhere, important religious differences between castes, but there are also broad similarities. The karma doctrine is known to and accepted by all castes, insofar as I can tell. At the same time, most members of the most highly Sanskritized castes do not hesitate to attribute certain kinds of misfortune to non-karmic agencies such as the anger of minor deities, witchcraft, or whatever. What this seems to indicate is that karmic and non-karmic theories of misfortune have somehow found separate functional niches in Chhattisgarhi religion. That is, the evidence suggests that karma is not just a more prestigious way to explain misfortune, but that its contribution is in some way distinct from other theories of destiny. It has become part of the religious culture of all castes, where it seems to exist side by side with other forms of explanation.

It seems very likely, then, that karma and other theories of destiny complement each other in some way. But how? One possibility is suggested by David Mandelbaum's proposal (1966) that two quite distinct complexes of belief and practice coexist in South Asian religions. One of these, the "transcendental complex," is mainly concerned with universal or ultimate problems: the welfare of society as a whole, the passage of individuals through social institutions, the final salvation of the individual. This complex lies in the jurisdiction of priests and centers on deities and concepts derived from texts. The other complex, which Mandelbaum calls "pragmatic," has largely to do with the exigencies of everyday life. It is in the hands of non-priestly specialists and mainly involves the lesser deities of local tradition. These two complexes do not collide or compete, nor are they in mere accidental association. Rather, they complement each other as they are utilized in what are essentially distinct and complementary contexts of application. Each is a response to specific needs that are perennial and ubiquitous in South Asian society.

The appeal of Mandelbaum's scheme as an approach to the problem of karma is its emphasis on complementarity, an emphasis that encourages us to acknowledge the persistence of both complexes and to ask the crucial question, namely, what is it that the karma doctrine does that other theories of destiny do not? It also suggests an answer to this question. From the standpoint of Mandelbaum's scheme, each complex persists because it deals with a different *kind* of human problem. Pragmatic religion has mostly to do with immediate well-being, while the transcendental complex (presumably the natural setting of the karma doctrine) "is concerned with the ultimate purposes of man" (1966:1175).

Yet even this does not quite seem to get at the heart of the issue, at least with respect to karma. The problem is that karmic reasoning can be, and often is, applied to human problems of the most this-worldly sort: health, business success, family, or whatever. Karmic language *can* be the language of ultimate concerns, but it need not always be. It is apparently not, then, simply a matter of karmic and non-karmic interpretations of destiny being reserved for two distinct ranges of human problems. Rather, karma seems to be a point of view that can be brought to bear on any kind of human circumstance.

Some refinement, I think, can be achieved if we follow Sheryl Daniel's lead (this volume) and view karma doctrine as a *frame of reference* that is potentially applicable in any situation that calls for the interpretation of destiny. Misfortunes are what they are, but they may be seen in more than one light. They may be viewed as simply "fated," as caused by witchcraft or ritual omissions of some kind, or they can be interpreted as the karmic consequences of past misdeeds. The same misfortune may be viewed in more than one frame of reference, even by the same individual. If this is so, then the most important question becomes that of why one frame of reference might be adopted rather than another. This is a complex and subtle matter in which the ethnographic literature does not give us much guidance. But it seems reasonably certain that at least part of the answer lies in the different ways in which theories of misfortune deal with the problem of human responsibility.

In popular Hinduism we encounter a highly varied array of explanations for misfortune, and these explanations allocate blame and responsibility differently. This is especially clear in Ursula Sharma's study. She points out that explanations offered by her informants can be arranged on a scale of varying degrees of responsibility imputed to the sufferer or to others (1973:355). When misfortune is viewed as a karmic consequence of actions of the sufferer in his present lifetime, heavy moral responsibility is implied. Great responsibility also attaches to offenses knowingly committed against deities. Some responsibility, though less, attaches to unintentional offenses against the gods. Even less is implied when an individual suffers because of the transmitted karma of someone else or because of misdeeds in a previous life. Sins in past lifetimes were committed by the same self that suffers now, "but it is a rather remote kind of self, differently constituted" (1973:356). Finally, one who suffers because of sorcery is essentially blameless, being the victim of the unprovoked malice of someone else.

Though details differ greatly from the foregoing, the same principle is evident in the materials from Tamilnadu presented by Sheryl and Valentine Daniel in this book. S. Daniel describes two alternative theories of misfortune that coexist in Tamil culture. One of these interprets destiny as the result of the individual's "headwriting"; the other emphasizes the role of karma. The implications for responsibility are opposed and complementary. To refer to headwriting is to establish a frame of reference in which the individual ultimately has no control over his actions and is thus not finally responsible for his destiny. Conversely, to stress karma is to lay the emphasis on willful action, and thus to imply genuine moral responsibility. Which of these frames of reference is chosen depends on the interests and intentions of the chooser. If he wishes to elude blame for some misdeed, or to console himself with the thought of the inevitability of some misfortune, then the fatalistic interpretation will have an obvious appeal. But if he wishes to stress the culpability of the performer of some misdeed, or to encourage himself in the belief that the course of his destiny can be altered for the better, then the karmic frame of reference is the most suitable recourse.

A very similar theme can be seen in the Tamil rituals of flower divination described by E.V. Daniel. Two ideas of destiny mingle in the symbolism of these rites. One places emphasis on fixed potentialities inherent in the moral and physical constitution of the individual, while the other stresses the karmic principle of action as the determinant of destiny. However, though inherent, the fixed factors are not ineluctable. They are only potentialities until realized in activity; and action, even as it embodies these potentialities, can alter them. But of course action itself is determined by the inherent potential of the individual. Are action and potential, then, really the same or different? It is a matter of interpretive choice, for although the distinction between action and potential is logically empty, it is psychologically vital. Whether they are seen as the same or different depends on context. When the distinction is emphasized it becomes possible for the individual to conceive his destiny as within his control. But when identity is stressed, disengagement from responsibility becomes possible.

Leaving specific differences aside, these accounts show that how the problem of misfortune is dealt with in situ has much to do with variables pertaining to the situation, intentions, disposition, and even mood of the interpreter. In part this is obviously related to the position in the social structure of the sufferer and the interpreter, who might or might not be the same person. The friends and relatives of the chicken-thieves described by Sheryl Daniel blame the misdeed on simple fate, thus exonerating the perpetrators. But the victims of the crime, favoring punishment, advance the karmic view with its implications of culpability. And as Sharma points out, to attribute misfortune to witchcraft is to inject it as an issue into conflict situations, especially within the family (1973:354–355). But interpretations of misfortune also seem to respond to factors that lie deep within the inner life of the individual. About these we can say little. It is evident, however, that popular Hinduism provides more than one way for the individual to explain, rationalize, or justify his own situation to himself in a way that is consonant with his feelings of personal efficacy, self-esteem, and psychic stance in the most general sense. At the very least, one important choice lies before him. He may view himself as essentially helpless, unable to deal with his predicament. Such an attitude might or might not be realistic, but in any case its religious expression is found in fatalistic theories of destiny. On the other hand, he might feel actively engaged with his situation, able to alter his lot by means of activity. Theories of misfortune that stress responsibility, of which the karma doctrine is one example, express and sanction this disposition.

With this we are brought to what strikes me as a most important point, the connection between ideas of responsibility and the possibility for palliative activity. Theories of misfortune that posit human responsibility for destiny are concerned, at least implicitly, with the future as well as the present and the past. Any theory of misfortune that relates present experience to choices made or not made, or actions performed or not performed in the past, has implications for how individuals might alter present or future circumstances for the better. On the one hand, such a theory is retrospective, pointing backward in time to events that shaped the present; on the other hand, it looks ahead to a future that can be influenced by actions taken now. Thus, theories of destiny that indicate human responsibility are not just rationalizations of the present; they are recipes for human response to destiny as well.

The degree to which concrete responses are actually suggested, however, varies greatly from one kind of theory to another. Obviously, to attribute misfortune to fate—that is, to avoid implicating human responsibility at all—suggests little in the way of remedy. And just as clearly, karmic reasoning, with its stress on individual responsibility, has potentially more complex implications. The theory of karma certainly implies that a righteous life in the present will be rewarded in the future, and this suggests that present and future difficulties can in some way be ameliorated by means of virtuous action. But I do not recall karmic theory commonly being used in quite this way in Chhattisgarh, and I suspect the same to be true elsewhere.

Rather, in Chhattisgarh the question of how misfortunes might actually be dealt with (leaving aside questions of practical cause and effect) seemed to belong more properly to the sphere of theories that pointed to angry deities, malevolent spirits, or witches as causal agents. Such explanations did not always assign responsibility to the sufferer (or to those close to him) for his misfortune, but when such responsibility was indicated it tended to be some kind of ritual or other precautionary omission, usually inadvertent. Thus, when the question of responsibility arises in connection with these explanations, it seems to be of a different order than that implied by karma, a responsibility that focuses on neglect and inadvertence rather than moral failing in some more general sense. Moreover, in suggesting specific kinds of causes for misfortune, these explanations also pointed to remedies for misfortune that were essentially reflexes of the causes, and thus quite susceptible to corrective action. The source of the problem could be determined by divination, and the difficulty alleviated by any of a variety of means. In fact it might fairly be said that a significant part of the actual content of Chhattisgarhi religion consists of beliefs and practices concerned with the etiology and relief of misfortunes of this sort. For the most part the corrective measures are ritual ones: the propitiation of the offended deity, the exorcism of the possessing spirit, the avoidance of certain places or activities, the wearing of charms and amulets, and so on.

Thus, one apparent difference between explanations of this sort and karmic theory is that they are therapeutic as well as explanatory. There are quite specific measures that can be taken against witches or ghosts, and things that can be done to mollify deities. But this hints, in turn, at a more fundamental difference too, one that seems to have to do with the basic question of the connection between morality and destiny.

Any theory of misfortune that assumes that human beings are responsible for the things that happen to them must inevitably face an awkward dilemma. The source of the dilemma is that feature of misfortune that is really its most intolerable aspect: its sheer intractability. If men are responsible for their destiny, then in some sense they must control it. But in point of fact, they do not. How, then, can individuals truly be responsible for a destiny that is finally out of their control? Writing of Tallensi religion, Meyer Fortes remarks: "What ancestor worship provides is an institutionalized scheme of beliefs and practices by means of which men can accept some kind of responsibility for what happens to them and yet feel free of blame for failure to control the vicissitudes of life" (1959:61). Hindu theories of misfortune manage to do something of the same sort.

The key to how it is done lies in the nature of the causal connections that these theories posit. These connections are at once both determinate and indeterminate. It has been suggested that a distinctive feature of the karma doctrine is its psychological indeterminacy (Obeyesekere 1968:21). This is because it imposes on the individual an unknown and unknowable karmic debt from the past. It seems to me, however, that theories of misfortune that stress the role of omitted ritual precautions or propitiations are equally indeterminate, though for a somewhat different reason. It is because of the essential inscrutability of the supernatural world itself. One can never really be certain that all crucial ritual requirements have been met. Ritual omissions or errors that lead to misfortune are usually discovered in retrospect, and even after the cause of the problem has been determined and corrective measures taken, the sufferer is still not guaranteed immunity from future misfortunes (see also Fortes 1959, esp. pp. 56–59). Indeed, he cannot even know for sure that he has permanently solved his present difficulty, for diviners can err and rituals can be undertaken faithlessly or incorrectly. Even the success of ritual palliatives is known only in retrospect, and never with certainty.

The point is, if a theory of misfortune is to explain convincingly, it must be believable. And to be believable it must in some way acknowledge the unpredictability of destiny. Simple fatalism at least answers this requirement, but in another respect it seems wanting. This is because it does not convey any sense of human responsibility or control. This is the real trick of both karmic and non-karmic theories of misfortune. In a sense each manages to affirm and deny human responsibility at the same time. Karmic theory achieves this paradoxical result by means of the hypothesis of amnesia: human control is absolute, but the present self can never take into account all of the controlling actions of the past. Non-karmic theory achieves the same result by means of the uncertainty of ritual or precautionary obligations: the individual is responsible for his errors and omissions, but he can never really know whether he has propitiated all the appropriate deities in appropriate ways, or whether he has taken all necessary precautions against life's numerous and unpredictable hazards.

But despite the fact that both karmic and non-karmic theories of misfortune acknowledge the unpredictability of destiny, each, in its own way, defines a form of human responsibility, and thus carries implications for human response. The implications, however, are different. In large measure this difference is a matter of specificity, and specificity, in turn, seems to be related to the kind of time frame in which these theories situate misfortunes.

There is a sense in which theories of misfortune are, by indirection, theories of time as well. By this I mean that a theory of misfortune creates a kind of temporal environment of its own by supplying certain kinds of emphasis to past, present, and future. In each case there is a past in which actions taken or not taken influence the present and the future. There is a present in which the legacy of the past can be altered, and there is a future that, while never fully knowable, can be influenced by actions taken in the present. But pasts, presents, and futures need not be given the same relative weights by all theories of destiny.

Comparatively speaking, the temporal perspective of non-karmic explanations of misfortune seems foreshortened. When witchcraft or the malice of deities or spirits are cited as causal agents, what is being stressed is the immediacy and urgency of human problems. This entire complex of thought and action seems present-oriented, and it reaches from the present into a relatively recent past in which the error or omission that led to the misfortune was committed. This mode of dealing with human problems is, above all, specific: it seeks isolable causes, and yields remedies that are tailored to the occasion and are, at least in theory, immediately efficacious. The present looms large, and the relevant past is immediate, while the more distant future receives little if any emphasis at all. It is *this* specific difficulty, occurring *now*, that is the chief consideration.

Karmic reasoning situates human problems in a deeper temporal setting. It must do this because of what is surely its most crucial characteristic: its emphasis on the moral awareness of the individual. Non-karmic theories can, in the end, fall back on the principle of inadvertence in explaining the unpredictability of misfortune: problems arise, and will always arise, because of the inevitability of unwitting mistakes, and in these matters principles of abstract morality can never be a guide. The individual can never know the full implications of what he is doing, has done, or has failed to do, until after the fact, and even in retrospect certainty is not possible. But because of its intimate connection with *dharma*, karmically determined destiny can, at least in principle, be known in prospect. Normative obligations, by their very nature, are knowable, and thus the individual can, in theory, anticipate the consequences of his actions. This being so, it is necessary to allow the karmic origins of present experiences to extend into a past that is hidden, and the karmic consequences of present deeds to be, in some measure, realized in a future that is likewise hidden. As many writers have pointed out, only thus can the misfortunes of the apparently righteous and the good fortune of the apparently villainous be explained. Amnesia is the key to karma.

Within the karmic frame of reference, then, present experiences become the product of the entire moral career of the transmigrating self. The present is authored by a morally aware actor in the past, an actor who now confronts similar choices with similar implications for times to come. From this perspective, specific misfortunes become less isolable as such. They are less the consequences of specific, discoverable, and thus correctable omissions or errors, and more the symptoms of the general moral condition of the experiencing self. And this general condition, in turn, is referred to a past that is mostly hidden, and implies a future that, while obscure, is within the long-term control of the individual.

Of course karmic destiny is also subject to more direct intervention. Karma is action and its consequences, and thus its course can be altered or rechanneled through action. Any action has karmic reverberations, but certain kinds of action seem to have special karmic efficacy, and chief among these are certain ritual acts, especially those involving austerities. As Brenda Beck (in this volume) points out, of all human acts, penance is the one that implies the greatest degree of human control. Here the desires that impel the self into worldly activity are brought into check, and accordingly the practice of austerity becomes the most decisive human intervention into the process by which destiny is created. The same principle seems to me to be evident in the religious vows described by Susan Wadley, though here it is tempered by the values and attitudes of devotional religion. Vows are undertaken in honor of particular deities, who, if the vows are successful, will aid their votaries. A vow usually involves some mild austerity, often a fast, and the effect of the vow is believed to be the destruction of the karmic consequences of past sins and an amplification of the effects of righteous behavior. Penance is evidence of the faith and devotion of the devotee; and devotion, if genuine, will be reciprocated by the deity in the form of transformations of the devotee's destiny.

But even if karmic destiny can be modified, karmic theory seems to have therapeutic disadvantages by comparison with other forms of explanation. This is, again, a matter of specificity. Karmic theory does not appear to lend itself easily to the isolation of specific causes of particular misfortunes. This is the price it must pay for its very convincingness at a more general level. Karmic theory implicates the entire world-career of the self in its present experiences, and in so doing leaves obscure the question of how an individual might specifically respond to a particular problem. But to attribute misfortune to witchcraft or to the anger of a deity is to connect it with a cause with which the affected persons can deal directly. It seems probable that this is one of the reasons Hindu villagers so infrequently allude to the karma doctrine in relation to specific misfortunes. Non-karmic explanations seem to convey a Malinowskian confidence in the immediate efficacy of human actions.

But on the other hand, the very specificity of these explanations limits their role in another respect. Non-karmic explanations of misfortune are not really able to weave discrete occurrences into a more comprehensive interpretation of the human situation and the longer-term destiny of the individual, whereas karmic theory can. It seems to me that there is no question of inconsistency here. Ritual errors or omissions can simply be the occasions for karmically ordained calamities in the same way that structural defects in Zande granaries can be the proximate causes of collapses that are, in a more important sense, the results of witchcraft (Evans-Pritchard 1937:69–70). To apply the karmic frame of reference to life's problems is to relate them to a higher order of moral responsibility. By grounding destiny in the moral awareness of the individual, karmic theory links the experiences of the individual to the general principles of *dharma* and implies that whatever the uncertainties of the present, there is a sense in which long-term destiny is subject to human control, even if there is, in the short run, very little that can be done about it.

Karma may therefore have more to do with futurity than is commonly supposed. I certainly do not wish to suggest that Indian villagers spend much time or energy worrying about the karmic consequences of present actions for the remote future. Sharma observes that villagers in Himachal Pradesh do not "lose much sleep" over this, and the same is surely true elsewhere. What might be most important, however, is not the question of what consequences might flow from specific acts, but a more general feeling that the moral life is, in some way, consequential. In contrast to ritualistic or practical theories of misfortune, the doctrine of karma posits a distinctive connection between moral responsibility and destiny, but does so in a way that preserves the unpredictability of human fortune in the short run. I should like to conjecture—and it is really no more than this—that one of the contributions the karma doctrine makes to the worldview of popular Hinduism is in supplying a sense of the existence of a wider moral order within which the choices people make in acting mean something, even if this meaning can, in principle, never be fully clear. This is a matter not just of "explaining misfortune," but of doing so in a way that affirms something of basic importance about the place of men and women in the world.

At one level Hinduism deals with life's troubles as discrete occurrences with isolable causes. Responses take the form of ad hoc, though stereotyped, interpretations of particular misfortunes that point to specific remedies. Within this frame of reference, problems arise largely from mistakes made in the proximate past. This past is easily redeemable, and if the future cannot be secured, at least the present can be, though never fully. And if the effectiveness of human counteraction is limited to the instance that occasioned it, at least the misfortunes of daily life do not have to bear the weight of the human predicament in the more general sense. But long-term destiny is important too. By giving the remote past a claim in the present, the karma doctrine gives the present a more comprehensive claim on the future. Within this frame of reference, life's troubles are less discrete occurrences and more symptoms of general conditions. And these general conditions are at least potentially subject to a form of control arising from the moral awareness of man, though with the proviso that nothing is ever guaranteed.

The very last thing I want to consider is the suggestion that the karma doctrine expresses a kind of general optimism about the human condition. If anything, the reverse is true. Since the past is unknowable, so is the future, and thus the self (unless radically modified) must wander not only endlessly but blindly through what, given this view of the world, is so often, and so appropriately, characterized as the "ocean" of existence. Yet a world that appalls can be a world that has meaning, even if that meaning is impenetrable to man. Such was Job's discovery, and though very different in its basis and implications, there may be a similar message in karma. If, as one writer has suggested, religion invests human life with distinctive moods (Geertz 1966:11–12), then it may be that one of the contributions of karmic thought is its support for a general disposition to believe that, despite much evidence to the contrary, a moral will counts for something. Whatever else it may do—and I feel certain that there is much else it does do—the doctrine of karma can supply a basis for the conviction that human intentions really do matter, and if the future is beyond our knowledge or understanding, it will still be shaped in some sense by a morally awakened consciousness.

References Cited

Babb, Lawrence A.
1975 The Divine Hierarchy: Popular Hinduism in Central India. New York: Columbia University Press.

Beals, Alan R.
1974 Village Life in South India: Cultural Design and Environmental Variation. Chicago: Aldine.

Cohn, Bernard S.
1959 Changing Traditions of a Low Caste. *In* Traditional India: Structure and Change. M. Singer, ed. Philadelphia: American Folklore Society. Pp. 207–215.

Dube, S. C.
1955 Indian Village. Ithaca, N.Y.: Cornell University Press.

Evans-Pritchard, E. E.
1937 Witchcraft, Oracles and Magic among the Azande. London: Oxford University Press.

Fortes, Meyer
1959 Oedipus and Job in West African Religion. Cambridge: Cambridge University Press.

Geertz, Clifford
1966 Religion as a Cultural System. *In* Anthropological Approaches to the Study of Religion. M. Banton, ed. London: Tavistock. Pp. 1–46.
Gough, E. Kathleen
1960 Caste in a Tanjore Village. *In* Aspects of Caste in South India, Ceylon, and North-West Pakistan. E. R. Leach, ed. Cambridge: Cambridge University Press. Pp. 11–60.
Kapp, William
1963 Hindu Culture, Economic Development and Economic Planning in India. New York: Asia.
Kolenda, Pauline M.
1964 Religious Anxiety and Hindu Fate. Journal of Asian Studies 23:71–81.
Lewis, Oscar
1965 Village Life in Northern India. New York: Random House (Vintage).
Mandelbaum, David
1966 Transcendental and Pragmatic Aspects of Religion. American Anthropologist 68:1174–1191.
Mathur, K. S.
1964 Caste and Ritual in a Malwa Village. Bombay: Asia.
Myrdal, Gunnar
1968 Asian Drama: An Inquiry into the Poverty of Nations. New York: Pantheon.
Obeyesekere, Gananath
1968 Theodicy, Sin and Salvation in a Sociology of Buddhism. *In* Dialectic in Practical Religion. E. R. Leach, ed. Cambridge: Cambridge University Press.
Pocock, D. F.
1973 Mind, Body and Wealth: A Study of Belief and Practice in an Indian Village. Totowa, N.J.: Rowman and Littlefield.
Sharma, Ursula
1973 Theodicy and the Doctrine of Karma. Man 8:347–364.
Singer, Milton
1972 When a Great Tradition Modernizes. New York: Praeger.
Weber, Max
1958 The Social Psychology of the World Religions. *In* From Max Weber: Essays in Sociology. H.H. Gerth and C. Wright Mills, eds. and trans. New York: Oxford University Press. Pp. 267–301.

· Part Two ·

TIBET AND SOUTHEAST ASIA

·8·

Incest Recaptured: Some Contraries of Karma in Balinese Symbology

James A. Boon

> No true Hindu doctrine knows of a "last day." Widely diffused doctrines maintain that there are epochs in which the world, like the Germanic *Götterdämmerung*, returns to chaos, but only to begin another cycle. The gods are as little immortal as men. . . . An especially virtuous man may, indeed, be reborn as a god. . . . The fact that the devout individual Hindu usually did not realize the grandiose presuppositions of karma doctrine as a whole is irrelevant for their practical effect which is our concern. (Weber 1958:121)

In his comparative sociology of religions, Max Weber situates karma somewhere between two fundamental types of civilizational values: (1) the traditional, cosmological, and ritualistic versus (2) the reformist, ethical, and world-disparaging. Unlike ultimate Indic ideals of renunciation, karma doctrine seems to blend a partial world-rejection with continued celebration of opposed and complementary deities, rites, occupations, and *varṇas*. Modified ideals of social resignation and qualified benefits of metempsychosis keep the traditional panoply of categories whirling.

Weber isolated Indic karma concepts with characteristic boldness. Hinduism's sole dogmatism is, he insisted, "the *samsara* belief in the transmigration of souls and the related *karman* doctrine of compensation" (1958:118). Moreover, in karma doctrine,

This essay forms part of a book in preparation for Cambridge University Press titled *Other Tribes, Other Scribes*. Preliminary versions were presented at the S.S.R.C. conference on Southeast Asian Aesthetics chaired by Alton Becker and Ben Anderson, 1977–1978, and in a lecture at McGill University organized by Lee Drummond. Immediate thanks are due Cornell's Department of Anthropology, Southeast Asia Program, and Society for the Humanities for support. Thanks also to David Holmberg and John Eidson and more recently to Oliver Wolters for continuing discussions; to John Pemberton and Nancy Florida for helpful comments; and to Olivian Boon.

> the idea of compensation was linked to the individual's social fate in the societal organization and thereby to the caste order. All (ritual or ethical) merits and faults of the individual formed a sort of ledger of accounts; the balance irrefutably determined the fate of the soul at rebirth. (P. 119)

For Weber, then, karma partly rationalized the cosmos, but not the economy, hence its spectral aspect:

> *Karma* doctrine transformed the world into a strictly rational, ethically-determined cosmos; it represents the most consistent theodicy ever produced by history. The devout Hindu was accursed to remain in a structure which made sense only in this intellectual context; its consequences burdened his conduct. (P. 121)

While karma provided Weber a key to India's socioeconomic stagnation, he never reduced the whole of Hindu religion to this single dimension. Indeed, earlier he stressed that

> if we look beyond the ritualistic prescriptions to the structured core of Hindu ideas, we fail to discover in the Vedas a single trace of such fundamental conceptions as the transmigration of souls and the derived *karma*-doctrine (of compensation). These ideas can only be interpretively read into some ambiguous and undatable passages of the Vedas. (P. 28)

Subsequent scholars have argued that the "structured core" of Vedic rites contained seeds of karma in values of the transfer of merit through sacrifice. Moreover, W. O'Flaherty (1973, 1980) suggests that the "pre-rebirth, Vedic model of birth"—transformed and indirectly perpetuated in myth—posed a complementarity of extremes: both sacrifice and *soma*, both asceticism and eroticism. In this light, ethical karma doctrine would appear less spectre than compromise, blurring the vivid polarities of Hindu mythology. For Weber as well, the eventual karma-samsara doctrines represented a reformed, rationalized, diluted, traditional cosmology, more compromised than the Buddhist Middle Path even, which still accentuated extreme renunciation embodied in the various ascetic orders implementing the example of the Buddha.

Enter Bali. Extending this comparative typology to Balinese variations of Hindu-Buddhism, we find a contemporary *culture* that in certain respects recalls the structure of *mythic* transformations of Vedic traditions based on a complementarity of extremes. Balinese symbology, ritual, and social organization exaggerate two opposed factors: (1) the rampant, sexual-demonic *and* (2) the controlled, incest-like near-spouse. Balancing this double extreme, prospering groups ensure ancestral benefits by displaying a full array of social categories, ritual devices, and dramatic-literary performances. I shall argue that Balinese Hindu-Buddhism is incompatible with a full-fledged ethical karma-samsara doctrine because of the force of an Indonesia-style ancestor cult with its hierarchy of rites, vocabularies, social structures, and in particular, marriage types. Balinese culture has long been exposed to karma theories, but they have never become central. Bali thus provides evidence of religious, ritual, and social possibilities that are suppressed where karma values become encompassing. And the comparative study of karma requires a sense of both what it establishes and what it precludes. In ideals and practices of karma, Bali represents something of a limiting case.

Like the erotic/ascetic complements of Tantric mythology (cf. O'Flaherty 1973), Balinese traditions conjoin polarities—in this case *kāma* (lust, desire), on the one hand, and *dharma-artha* (ancestral duty–political prowess), on the other. The related symbology envisions little compromise-ethic of compensation that would imply a universalistic consequence of deeds next-time-round. Indeed, any cyclic returns—whether future births or rebirths, or future consequences of present action—are presumed to remain within an ancestral division attached to an origin point (*kawitan*). Thus, ethical karma-samsara doctrine has been hemmed in by Balinese culture. In religious action Balinese karma suggests Vedic ideas of "parental karma" or perhaps Smarta Brahmin beliefs "that children are incarnations of dead grandparents" (O'Flaherty 1980). How are doctrines like karma "localized" in places like Indonesia? What enables them to be borrowed without being embraced?[1]

The above remarks would be disputed by one sector of Balinese literati. Religious functionaries attuned to Indonesian national policies now emphasize ethical karma in manuals that reform Bali-Hinduism into a moral creed to be propagated beyond Bali's cultural context. Here for example, in an influential Indonesian-language manual, *Upadeca*, Rsi Dharma Kerti instructs his naive interrogator on *hukum karma phala*, the law of karma:

[1] See C. Geertz (1966); Boon (1977, chap. 4, p. 224). The field work on which portions of my essay are based was sponsored by Lembaga Ilmu Pengetahuan Indonesia and funded by a N.I.M.H. Combination Research Fellowship (1972–1973). "Localization" is a theme of current work by O. Wolters.

So the meaning of *karmaphala* is the harvest from human deeds [*hasil dari perbuatan seorang*]. We believe that good deeds produce good results and bad deeds bad results. In other words, fast or slow, in this life or a future one, all the rewards from those deeds are definitely received. . . . And so my child, the law of *karmaphala* does not cause hopelessness [*putus asa*] and surrender to fate, rather it is positive and dynamic. (Upadeca 1968:31–33; my translation)

Nor is *Upadeca* the most reform-minded publication of *Parisada Hindu Dharma*, the primary agency of Bali's religious rationalization.[2] For example, while *Upadeca* still glosses the key term of Bali-Hinduism (*agama*) as "motionless, precisely in-place, eternal" (*tidak pergi, tetap ditempat, langgeng*), the more scholarly *Pancha Cradha* abruptly glosses *agama* as "arrival" (*kedatangan*; pp. 15–16)! Moreover, the *Pancha Cradha* construes Balinese ancestor obligations in terms of ethical karma rather than ritualistically:

The law of karma which influences anyone will not be received by himself alone but will also be inherited by his children and grandchildren [*anak tjutju*] or by his descendants as well. We see many examples in this world in which, for example, someone leads a life of luxury because he obtains great wealth by illegitimate or evil means—through theft, lying to others, or exploiting others. Yet after such a man dies and his wealth is inherited by his children and grandchildren, often they have bad characters or unhealthy dispositions. For example, one may be mad, or arbitrarily throw away the wealth until the inheritance is depleted and the inheritors impoverished, along with all the inward sufferings. This is caused by the influence of karma from ancestors [*leluhur*] who can directly influence their descendants [*keturunannja*]. (Punyatamadja 1970:60; my translation)

Similar views of karma in Indonesian textbooks on Hindu sociology published by the national department of religion (Gde Pudja 1963:22ff.) follow philological precedents in equating Balinese religi-

[2] Aspects of religious rationalization in certain sectors of Bali are discussed in Geertz (1973, chap. 7) and in Boon (1977, Part II). In areas of religious change, subsistence control, leadership, etc., Bali embeds principles of legitimacy in cyclic, ritual formulation. It is thus disconcerting to see Bali used to resurrect the old notion of "linear time" with a stress on individuals versus detemporalized "ritual communication" in M. Bloch (1977). Oddly, Bloch uses Geertz (1973, chap. 14) to illustrate an example of cultural anthropology overlooking everyday practical affairs. He calls on us to move past concern with esoteric, ritual "idioms" and get on with serious study of hard facts, like entrepreneurship, overlooking that Geertz's first extensive publication on Bali (1963) treated, precisely, post-colonial entrepreneurship. Geertz showed how cyclic, ritual formulations in courtly traditions are intimately involved in influencing others, organizing any activity, and transforming praxis. To call "ritual communication" in Bali an *idiom* is to miss much of the power and subtlety of a general ritual system.

osity with themes in cosmological texts and related traditions of the palace.[3]

I cite this sample of sources to suggest the availability of ethical karma-samsara doctrine to interested Balinese, Indonesians, and diverse outsiders. But my argument remains that for ethical (versus parental?) karma to penetrate Balinese ideals and actions, radical transformation, or really reformation, of the culture's symbology would be necessary, especially where it articulates ritual, myth, and marriage. In these domains Balinese traditions conform to principles more tantric than karmic.

But Her Vagina's in Her Foot

> Myths stick together because of cultural forces impelling them to do so: these forces are not primarily literary, and mythologies are mainly accepted as structures of belief or social concern rather than imagination. But it is the structure of myths that makes the process possible, and since folktales possess the same kind of structure they can stick together too. (Frye 1976:12)

Again, we stretch to Bali from India. In his Durkheimian study of Indian caste and culture, Louis Dumont reserves a special place for marriage. Dumont's emphasis on Brahmanic and royal idealizations of marriage enable him to relate the pattern to Dravidian terminology, cross-cousin alliances, and other South Indian principles of organic solidarity that perpetually join opposed categories. Whether for methodological or intrinsic reasons, or both, Dumont stresses the absence of symbols of impurity in marriage rites:

[3] Of particular note regarding *saṃsāra* is the Bhima cult in Java. See, for example, the interesting analysis by A. Johns (1970) of *Bhimasuci* with its ascetic and Tantric components. Johns emphasizes the "radical monism" of Bhima's enlightenment in which everything "is the product of the One Mind, the microcosmos is the macrocosmos, Nirvana is Samsara, there is no duality" (p. 146). Below I try to refute an oversimplified dualistic analysis of Balinese materials, not, however, to champion monism. I find the monism/dualism distinction (itself dualistic?) oversimplified. Johns allusively rejects the "shade of Durkheim" (and by implication, I suppose, Rassers); perhaps this is appropriate for materials from the Javanese *kraton*. Yet in Balinese symbology distinctions are not collapsed into any ultimate rarefication; this maintaining of distinctions strikes me as more compatible with the "dualism" of Durkheim's *L'Année sociologique* than with any monism. For a fuller sense of Durkheim's dualism (implying organic solidarity) with reference to Indic traditions, see Dumont (1970) and Boon (1979). An elaborate debate over India between "monists" and "dualists" has been waged recently in the *Journal of Asian Studies*; see Richards et al. (1976); Marriott (1976); Barnett et al. (1977). Other karma symbols of the Javanese palace are reviewed in Gonda (1970); see also Gonda (1975).

> Thus one can observe a parallelism between the states which accompany the ceremonies of the ages of life, and even the main actions of everyday life, and caste ranking. A mourner not following the precepts and lacking the help of specialists would remain more or less untouchable. A menstruating woman may not cook for her family. Marriage on the contrary, the only *rite de passage*, it may be noted, which is not accompanied by any impurity, gives the impression, by the prestige which it radiates and many other traits, that in it the Hindu finds himself symbolically and temporarily raised from the condition and assimilated to the highest, that of prince or Brahman for a non-Brahman, that of god for a Brahman. (Dumont 1970:53)

Even allowing for Dumont's aim to encompass North and South India in a single interpretation, his comment leaves one wondering if the complementary impurity has been reformed away. I raise the question not to answer it, but to contrast Bali.

Although India is the source of much Bali-Hindu marriage symbology, Bali displays more totalized hierarchy here than Dumont admits in India itself. The impure, the licentious, the demonic-*rākṣasa* side of marriage is less sublimated in Balinese culture. Myth-like, Balinese marriage requires a coexistence of opposite extremes: the capture-like and the incest-like, both necessary to the complete hierarchical order.

Balinese marriage revolves around three basic options. Any ambitious ancestor-group, whatever its caste-title, may enhance itself by accentuating first-son rights and obligations and by (1) making ancestor group-endogamous marriages (some degree of patrilateral parallel cousin or father's brother's child), (2) facilitating favorable prearranged outside marriage alliances, and (3) allowing not unfavorable mock-capture marriages with individuals. I shall here outline this hierarchical system with notes on relevant symbolic correspondences (recalling that in a hierarchy the bottom is as essential as the top, and the middle is by no means the average).

1. Endogamous marriage. In cosmology: unions of gods, as in the Hindu consort motif, sun-moon spouses, hermaphroditic attributes, and so forth; in short, the conjunction of two differences that are halves of the same whole. In social action: unions of patriparallel cousins; second patriparallel cousins (grandchildren of brothers, *mindon*) are considered a diminished version of first patriparallel cousins (children of brothers, *misan*); the latter are in turn a diminished version of siblings, and siblings are a diminished version of opposite-sex twins. (One might call patriparallel

cousins "genealogical gods" of social groups.) These versions of actual or ideal spouses can symbolize different levels of the cosmos (divine, earthly, demonic), of social *warnas* (Brahmanas and Satrias, Wesias, Sudras), and even of ancestor groups (as when elder sons by a father's higher wife are deemed most suitable to make first-cousin marriages). Symbols of endogamy, most elaborate for the higher sectors of society, are complemented by principles of hypergamy (daughters may not wed inferiors). Rituals surrounding endogamous unions center on a group's ancestors, whatever its title-caste. If one correlated Balinese marriage types with G. Dumezil's formulation of tripartite Indo-European ideology, endogamous unions would represent the *dharma* component; since duty in Bali is ancestor-oriented, and patriparallel cousin marriages, if properly executed by auspicious members of the group and fertile, intensify ancestral essence in descendants.[4]

2. Exogamous marriage alliance. In cosmology: unions of god with god-in-earthly-guise, thus connecting two separate spheres; hypergamy would require the divine component to be male, the earthly, female. In social action: unions between separate houses (ancestor groups) with elaborate arrangements concerning dowry, reciprocal title acknowledgments, mutual temple attendance, and so on. Symbols of alliance are highlighted in the Satria palaces (*puri*) and those sectors of the title-caste system (*Dewa* or *Gusti*, depending on the kingdom) most involved in the traditional state. Rituals emphasize the joint role of two separate groups, the power-alliance of prestigious houses, and so on. In Dumezil's formulations, alliance unions would correlate with Indic *artha*: force, worldly power.
3. Capture marriage. In cosmology: abductions by demonic *rākṣasas* (see below). In social action: mock abduction, the ordinary marriage of commoners and auxiliary marriages of rajas or anyone else who is smitten; blurs with concubinage at upper social levels.

[4]Tripartite Indo-European ideology as developed by Dumezil (1966) links three "functions": sovereignty (cosmic and juridical order); prowess; life-maintenance. See also Littleton (1973). On transposing the flexible scheme to Bali, see Boon (1977:238–240).

Incest has many symbolic complexities in Bali (Boon 1977, chaps. 6, 9). Sibling incest has positive connotations if associated with godly marriage. Claimed by or attributed to a ruling group, it apparently could be used to argue their divinity if all other signs confirmed it, or their criminality if not. Of course, opposed parties would differ. These cultural aspects of incest values are crucial, if one is to make sense out of traditions such as the records and chronicles of rival ruling houses recently reviewed, for example, in Hanna (1976, chaps. 5 ff.).

> Symbols and rituals revolve around the furtive escapade of two lovers, romantic allure, love potions, auspicious signs that stress the essential intrusion of passion in the total marriage scheme. Romantic attraction is an elaborate theme in Balinese literature as well. In Dumezil's formulation, marriage by capture would correlate with Indic *kāma*, sexual desire.

In a previous work (Boon 1977, chaps. 4, 6, 8–9) I related this set of marriage options to Balinese social change, political action, and title-caste dynamics. I also traced symbols of provisionally separated, incestuous twins and the sun-moon imagery of Panji tales—all pertaining mainly to endogamy and marriage alliances (1 and 2 above). Here we shall peruse texts underscoring the fundamental place of capture values in Bali's marriage hierarchy.

One example is *Windu Sara*, a romance that commences by distinguishing (1) sexual abstinence, (2) cousin marriage, (3) auspicious prearranged alliances, and (4) passionate allure that, in this case, eventuates in adultery. As in all Balinese romances, matters become very convoluted; but a summary of even the tale's first parts suggests the catalog of marriage motifs emerging:

> Windu Sara only cared about flowers and books, and took no interest in women. His mother was always urging him to marry, and one day she told him that she had chosen for his wife a cousin of his, named Mertadjadnya. He still protested that he had no wish to marry, and besides the girl in question had a dimple on her shoulder, a sure sign that she would be fatal to men. His mother replied: "If she is not to your taste, I have another choice for you: Navartna, a sister of Djagasatru who is also of royal blood." But he explained that she was *ngelangkargunung*, i.e., her birthday was in an unlucky relation to his own; there was [*sic*] only two days difference between them. "Who then would you like to marry? You have only to say the word and I will get her for you, from wherever it may be." But Windu Sara said that he could see no reason for marrying any one; he did not want a wife.
>
> His friend Djagasatru meanwhile married Mertadjadnya, and begged Windu Sara to come and help him to entertain the wedding-guests. The wedding-day came. Mertadjadnya was fetched in a litter; there was a great banquet and Windu Sara entertained the guests. Mertadjadnya was marvellously dressed, and as Windu Sara was helping her to descend from her litter he was so overwhelmed by her beauty that he fainted. And Mertadjadnya gave him medicine to revive him. But he left the feast and went home; and the wedding went on without him. When he got home he would eat nothing and his mother asked him what was wrong. At first he would not reply, but after long asking he confessed that he had fallen passionately in love with his

friend's wife, and that he would die unless he got her for himself. His mother was angry, and reproached him for his former obstinacy. Now it was too late; but she promised to try and get him a *vidyadhari* in place of the wife he could not have. (DeZoete and Spies 1939:314)

As episodes unfold all the forces of nature and society insure that a full range of marriage possibilities will come into play, set in relief against the possibility of celibacy.

Traditions with still richer implications for the capture side of Bali's marriage system surround the well-known tale of Lady Uma. A written Balinese-Javanese form dates from 1500, and its episodes and themes recur throughout Balinese oral traditions to this day. Here is a summary of the story, by J. Hooykaas, whose ear for popular Balinese traditions may have helped determine how she condensed and translated Th. Pigeaud's Dutch translation of the courtly text *De Tantu Panggelaran*:

The mahasuras and kalas had been subdued and were afraid of the five gods. The five gods then waited upon the Lord Guru to ask for teaching. The Lord would not allow the Lady Uma to listen to the teaching. He, therefore, sent Her away, telling Her to fetch the milk of a virginal black cow. The Lady Uma obeyed and went on Her way. Peaceful was the teaching by the Lord Guru to the five gods. . . .

Meanwhile, the Lady Uma wandered through the Heavens in search of milk of a virginal black cow: She went to the Underworld, but She did not find milk of a virginal black cow. Then She wandered on Earth and happened to bump Her foot against a rock. And the big toe of Her left foot was split and She had to walk with a stick.

The Lord Guru wished to test Her and to try Her faithfulness. He, therefore, became Kumara Gopala, an extremely handsome young cowherd. His vehicle the white bull He turned into a virginal black cow when Uma came upon Him.

"Cowherd," She said to Him, "I want to ask you for some milk."

"I will not give it to you."

"Well, if you will not give it, I will buy it for gold and jewels."

"Well, I will not give it. What is the use of gold and jewels to me?" So He spoke.

In the end Kumara Gopala asked for union with Her. The Lady Uma felt ashamed, which was the expression of Her faithfulness. . . . However, She desired the milk of the virginal black cow, so She had union with Kumara Gopala. Nevertheless, She remained faithful to the Lord Guru, for She had not united in Her vagina, but between her thighs, which She bent so that they became like Her vagina. . . . The semen flowed on the earth. . . . It dripped into the Lady's split toe which then swelled up.

Kumara Gopola gave the lady the milk of the virginal black cow and then He flew away, and became the Lord Guru again. The bull also flew away at the same time. (J. Hooykaas 1960:267–268)

It takes little stretch of the imagination to diagnose the split big toe of Lady Uma's (inferior) left foot that swells up when Gopala's semen drips in. Who would dispute that three levels of vagina are implied: the actual vagina and two surrogates—the thighs explicitly "like her vagina" and, here inexplicitly, the split toe? This bizarre anatomy materializes amidst Heaven/Earth/Underworld where opposed categories manifest in virginal-black-cows-giving-milk *versus* rutty-white-bulls-ejaculating (Śiva-Pārvatī's mount, transformed into a virginal-black-cow by the Lord Guru) play out the familiar Indo-Javanese-Balinese cosmography.

In this article and elsewhere, J. Hooykaas noted the pervasive influence of Tantrism in Balinese cosmology:

The religion which found its way from India to Java was a Siwaistic Tantrism.... In this religion the sexual union of the Upper God Siva and His spouse plays a prominent part. It is believed that a *yogin* who is able to effect in his body the intercourse of these two gods achieves liberation. In Java several images of the divine figure have been found in which is expressed this complete blending of male and female. They are called *Ardhanareswari* and have one male and one female breast. In Bali nowadays, when the Brahmin priest, to prepare the holy water, achieves this mystic union in his body, he mentions the divine couple (*dampati*) in his chant.... The influence of Tantric thought has played an important role in both Java and Bali. In a bride and groom the god and goddess of love are regarded as having entered. Even in Muslim Java bride and groom are still worshipped on their wedding day as if they were gods.... We [find the literary expression of this Tantric belief] again in the introduction to "Tantri Kamandaka" [a version of the Indian *Panchatantra*]. Here the King decides to take a new bride every night; he justifies his desire with the words:

"At the exact moment of the consummation of the marriage, the God Iswara and His spouse Ardhanari incarnate themselves in the bridal couple when they are on their couch. Batara Wisnu and His spouse, Batari Sri—all the gods are there. This is the result of marriage: the daily worship to all the gods. Do not forget that. What is the result? The whole country is prosperous, the rainy seasons are long, all plants grow lusciously on earth and so there is plenty of food. That is why I want to marry daily." (J. Hooykaas 1957:276–277; De Zoete and Spies 1939:97, 273; Boon 1977, chaps. 4, 6, 9)

We should note that in these Javanese-Balinese versions of Indic themes, Uma, Wisnu's spouse, tends to merge into Sri, Siwa's spouse, yielding an arch-couple, like Gopa and Gopi.

But important components of "Tantrism"—the very ones perhaps least sublimated by priestly formulations—go unmentioned in J. Hooykaas' observations on Lady Uma. Hooykaas clarified neither Uma's swollen toe nor her vagina-thighs nor the concrete specifics. Instead, she followed precedents of reducing sexual imagery to vague fertility beliefs and a pan-Malayan-Indonesian harmony, static and archaic, between casually dualistic conceptions of Father Sky and Mother Earth evidenced in the rice-goddess cult of Dewi Sri. Was it for cultural and historical reasons that many Western interpretations of an earlier day—ethical, moralistic, and reformist in their own right—skirted the issue?

In interpretations, no less culturally and historically determined, of our day (my own interpretation included), it would be unthinkable to play down "the semen... dripped into the Lady's split toe which swelled up"—unless one were tending to mold Balinese traditions into conformity with karma-samsara or some other ethical doctrine. Recent less reformist philological work restores the emphasis on *kama salah* in translations and summaries of texts on Lady Uma (who eventually is transformed into the evil, corpse-stealing Durga, as J. Hooykaas stressed). For example, C. Hooykaas has consolidated all the priestly texts at his disposal that bear on *kāma/kāla* (love/evil), which some Balinese exegetes consider to be the essence of *wayang* shadow-puppet performances. He concludes in his account of texts on Lady Uma:

> The sperm does spill (*kama salah*) onto the ground but some of it finds its way into the split in her left big toe. As a consequence she bears male triplets. (C. Hooykaas 1973:307)

While today's philology is, in matters of *kāma*, less reformist than yesterday's, it still does not penetrate the dimensions of Tantrism that concern us here. We are after not what lies in these texts but what lies between them and historical change, social action, and complexities of rank, capture-marriage, and so on. Hence the preference, standard in anthropological structural-functional and structuralist accounts, for folk "oral" versions over literati "textual" versions even in a highly literate society. I suggest that the seamier side of traditions surrounding Uma-Sri, viewed in light of the system of social marriage options outlined above, may further our understanding of Balinese "Tantrism" at all levels of society and "cultural performance" (cf. M. Singer 1972). Uma's thrice-located vagina, epitomized in the vagina–

foot extremity, could again allude to the total marriage system—which we might now consider a sort of "primitive classification" (Durkheim and Mauss 1963), here, however, purged of any archaic overtones, or as a sort of "cryptotype" (B. Whorf 1964) embedded in marriage symbology.[5]

If a vagina-part (metonymy) implies the hierarchical whole (metaphor), the institution of marriage reveals covert extremes. It becomes, like coitus, symbolically threefold. Heavenly marriage, explicitly coded as incest mythically, becomes vagina-located-in-the-vagina in anatomical symbols. In a sense the vagina situated naturally symbolizes "unnatural" (incestuous) intercourse. Underworldly marriage, coded as *rākṣasa* capture in myth, drama, and ritual, becomes vagina-footedness in anatomical symbols. Finally, the anatomical symbol for earthly marriage is vagina-thighs. Earthly marriage, then, is not an average of the two other types: it implies a complementarity of extremes.

Earthly marriage does, however, point toward the "socio-anagogic" (K. Burke 1966:108) dimension of this symbology: namely, that ambitious houses aspiring to prominence would most fully embody all three marriage types, with the accent on political alliance. Earthly marriage as well conjoins the three types: incest-like cousin marriage and romantic capture (partly illicit) with political alliance. Indeed, as the story of Lady Uma itself stipulates, "the milk of the virginal black cow was to be found neither in Heaven, nor in the Underworld, but on Earth" (J. Hooykaas 1960:276).

In these respects Balinese marriage diverges from Indic Laws of Manu which assign capture marriage (one of eight varieties) to the

[5] This part of my argument attempts to add specifics and systematics to another comment by J. Hooykaas, in fact a parenthetical one:

> In the "Tantu Panggelaran" Siwa mostly appears as Batara Guru, the Divine Teacher. The whole book is principally concerned with the teaching of the Saiwa religion in Java. It deals with the founding of *maṇḍalas* on the slopes of Java's mountains, which were places for religious concentration as well as for teaching. Many stories have been woven through this main Saiwite thread. One motif which keeps returning time and again in these stories is that of gods in their anger turning into demons, and what is done to placate their wrath. (A student of Balinese religion finds much in present-day Bali which calls to mind the "Tantu Panggelaran." The Balinese too are constantly preoccupied with gods who can become or might have become demons; this belief consequently necessitates continual rites of exorcism). (1960:269)

A parallel I would emphasize in ritual and symbolic action is this: high-level marriage alleviates threats that the bride will be stolen, just as cremation alleviates threats that the corpse will be stolen. Parallels, perhaps even identities, between aspects of death and aspects of marriage demand concerted study in Balinese symbolic action, popular as well as courtly.

military sector of society. Balinese capture rites, as would be expected in a partly Pacific culture, characterize both the general populace and rajas and other polygynists whose spouses run the gamut. Yet, as the arch political category, rajas and nobles (*Dewa* or *Gusti*) are epitomized by alliance, just as priestly Brāhmaṇas are epitomized by endogamy. Lady Uma helps expose the partialness of these two types emphasized in courtly traditions. She underscores how thrusting sexual escapades—the domain of *rākṣasas* and of capture rites—complement the political and endogamous dimensions.

Lady Uma's anatomy recalls the familiar equivalence of microcosm (body) and macrocosm (cosmology) basic in many Indic, Pacific, and other symbolisms. But the dislocation of her vagina reveals dialectical complexities often underestimated in standard microcosm/macrocosm analysis, and always overlooked in sociologistic reductions of symbol systems. What appears bodily most "normal" and human—the vagina where it naturally occurs—is associated with the divine-incestuous level of cosmography, leaving one abnormal vagina (in the foot) to the demonic-capture realm and another abnormal vagina (in the thighs) to the "ordinary" human realm. *Nowhere in such symbolic conventions is a naturalistic gloss appropriate.* All the realms—including the human political arena—are mutual extremes. This relational and shifting symbolism, dynamic and hierarchical, contrasts vividly with a stratificational symbolism—for example, head-Brahmin, shoulders-Satria, feet-Wesia—often assumed to exhaust macrocosm/microcosm equivalences. I suspect that the hierarchical-dialectical is compatible with Tantrism, while the stratificational-reflectionist already implies a tendency toward reformism.[6]

The complete marriage scheme is simultaneously Divine/Human/Demonic and ancestral/political/romantic at the levels of cosmology, society, and actor motivation (Boon 1974). It helps expand another surmise by J. Hooykaas, once Uma and the Lord Guru appear as analogous to Dewi Sri and Siwa, ultimately returning to heaven astride their white bull:

> So one may surmise that when the gods performed a *wayang* play as a means of exorcism, which showed "the true nature of the Lord and the Lady on earth," it was the kind of story as told above.

[6] For insights into body symbols which remain, however, somewhat "architectonic," see Douglas (1970). A compendium of standard microcosm/macrocosm views in Bali runs through Covarrubias (1937). For other sources, particularly Dutch ones, see Boon (1977).

> In conclusion: first I have compared the myth with ancient conceptions of the union of Father Sky and Mother Earth. This concept was widespread in pre-Hindu Indonesia. The XVth century form of it might have been modernized to suit the ideas of that period, which were dominated by Tantric thought with the union of Siwa and Uma as its kernel. The union described in the myth was probably thought of as an initiation, a parallel to that of the Half-One. The fertility myth in its new form brought in its train stories that were exorcistic in character, with the young cowherd and the little girl on the bull being victorious over the demon. The true nature of the gods was the very old one: that of fertility. (J. Hooykaas 1960:278)

A counter-surmise would be that the fertility involved entails not just an archaic-abstract union of Father Sky and Mother Earth but a conjoining of all marriage aspects, particularly the demonic-sexual. How else might one solve the riddle unanswered by the demon Kāla elsewhere in these traditions:

> There is a being with three heads, two horns, one female part and two male ones, one tail etc. (J. Hooykaas 1960:277)[7]

One possible solution, as certain texts confirm, is the united couple astride their bull: three heads (Siwa, Sri, bull), two horns (bull), two male parts (Siwa, bull), one tail (bull). The double male parts imply that Siwa's divine *liṅgam* is complemented by the bull's lusty one. Hence in a modern drawing depicting the riddle (J. Hooykaas 1960), the demon-giant Kāla's arm penetrates the *galungan*, fundamental symbol of a balanced cosmos inevitably displaced from the screen by *wayang* episodes. Nothing could be more suggestive of *kāma*'s thrust into incomplete *dharma-artha* (ancestral duty cum political prowess) essential in dramatic narrative.

[7]For variants of the riddle (one with an answer) in different esoteric texts, see C. Hooykaas (1973:167, 247, 257). Again, J. Hooykaas's rendition and her relating Lady Uma's themes to tales of the Half-One and other folk traditions points toward the locus proper for anthropological concerns with how symbolic schemes mediate actions and texts.

Compare also themes discussed by Sweeney in his important study of *The Ramayana and the Malay Shadow Play*, in particular its ritual aspects:

> This drama is parallel to, and clearly a version of the Javanese exorcistic lakon Murwakala/Purwakala, of which versions also exist in Bali. Kelantan has, in common with several Javanese/Balinese versions, the following major features: (1) Kala's hunger, (2) his taste for blood, (3) his right to eat certain persons, (4) a riddle which prevents his eating his father, (5) his chasing a victim, (6) a wayang within a wayang, (7) the victim is saved by the wayang. (1972:282–283)

Finally, we now know from Lady Uma that the "one female part" of the riddle (Sri's) is implicitly three, again completing the picture by confirming the tripartite values of marriage: not an ethical compromise but an interrelation of extremes behind Balinese life and imagery. Or in terms to be adopted below: not a solution but a suspension. I submit that where such extremes remain hierarchically interrelated, ethical karma doctrine remains culturally "shallow."[8]

Hypergrammatical Love

> The myth is certainly related to given (empirical) facts, but not as a *re-presentation* of them. The relationship is of a dialectic kind, and the institutions described in the myths can be the very opposite of the real institutions. This will in fact always be the case when the myth is trying to express a negative truth. (Lévi-Strauss 1967:29)

Balinese culture enables me to put my argument otherwise, to elicit convergent data from different symbols. That karma-samsara has not become a central theme in Bali may in part be explained by the fact that incest remains, indirectly, exemplary. Balinese incest symbolizes the mutual desirability of extremes. Again, in Bali patriparallel cousin marriages appear as diminished equivalents of sibling marriages, which are diminished equivalents of twin marriages. We should note that the separation between each simile in the sequence—second cousins, first cousins, siblings, twins—is itself a factor ultimately represented by "capture" as a bridging of distance between suitable spouses. Ethical karma doctrines, like any reformism, would modify such extremes; incest imagery glorifies them and thus converges with Lady Uma and related traditions.

To gain perspective on this aspect of Balinese symbology, we shall stretch now toward, not India, but Oceania, in light of D.M. Schneider's argument that incest is a cultural code regardless of any naturalistic basis. Schneider's general thesis is confirmed by Bali, although its finer points require a profound twist. He summarizes:

> "Incest" is symbolic of the special way in which the pattern of social relationships, as they are normatively defined, can be broken. "Incest" stands for the transgression of certain major cultural values, the values of a particular pattern of relations among persons. For those who should be respectful

[8] For criteria of "deep" versus "shallow" cultural forms, see Geertz (1973, chap. 15).

> "incest" signals the lack of respect. For those who should have responsibility and authority it is a sign that responsibility has been abrogated and authority misused or broken down entirely. "Incest" means the wrong way to act in a relationship: as father-son, as father-daughter, as mother-son, as mother-daughter, as brother-sister, as cousins, as kinsmen. . . . To act not merely wrong, but to act in a manner opposite to that which is proper. It is to "desecrate" relationships. It is to act "ungrammatically." And each particular definition of "incest"—as "cannibalism," as "animal," as "eating blood"—gives the special meaning of the "desecration," the meaning that is special to that particular system of symbols and meanings, the culture, that is, in which it is embedded. . . . The meaning of "incest" as it appears in known societies where it is disapproved (without qualification, without ambiguity), is that it is a "desecration," it constitutes "cannibalism." (Schneider 1976:166–167)

In contrast to these Oceanic societies, Bali's incest prohibition is *not* unqualified; that is, the prohibition is qualified. One might even playfully deem Balinese "incest" not "ungrammatical love" but "hypergrammatical love." The grammar-analogy collapses: we must shift from a linguistic metaphor of competence to one of poetics. Balinese incest represents the too-grammatical, in a way that recalls K. Burke's principle of "perfectibility" in systems of rhetoric/poetics, systems ordered like some cultures themselves. Incest in Bali is like three perfect statements simultaneously, or better, like a triadic chord whose harmonics are more than the sum of its individual notes. Incest implies a superabundance of attributes: more in the marriage-gamut than any given marriage may contain; yet the full-gamut remains the cultural desideratum. Incest thus plays a double role symbolically. It epitomizes endogamy itself (stepped back to cousins in actual practice). And it symbolizes the conjunction of all three marriage types. The sister-spouse (most extremely a twin) conceals three dimensions: like actual cousin spouses, she is endogamous; like alliances, she joins houses (in narratives twins are separated into different kingdoms; also, cousin spouses rejoin collateral lines); and like captured lovers, she is desired and desires, to the point of self-immolation (see below). Note as well that in Bali captured outsiders are eventually cremated and elevated into ancestresses of their children's and the husband's group. The triple ideal symbolized in incest is in any given instance or at a given level unachievable; it is truly an ideal: cultural hyperbole. *Only the culture as a whole through time and throughout its differentiations, achieves the implications of incest.*[9]

[9] Additional implications of Balinese kinship as a cultural system are discussed in H. and C. Geertz (1975) and Boon (1974, 1978).

Yet hypergrammatical love, like the Oceanic ungrammatical love Schneider discusses, relates incest to other cultural domains. Consider, for example, cremation, the ultimate ritual and religious concern of Bali, derived from India, yet markedly different from South Asian practices. I am one of the quickest to acknowledge the risks of interpreting Balinese traditions using South Asian texts or contexts (Boon 1977, chap. 9). But I want at least to raise the possibility in the matter of Balinese incest and cremation. In particular, one secret of the Balinese variety of Indic *satī*, or widow immolation (in Bali, called *satia* and practiced at least into the second decade of our century) emerges in *Śiva Purāṇa* myths from India on the birth of Pippalāda. In an analysis of Tantric components of Hindu myths, O'Flaherty summarizes certain variants as follows:

> One text offers as a specific parallel to the myth of Śiva and Pārvatī the story of Pippalāda and Padmā, who are considered to be incarnations of the god and his wife. Pippalāda was born when a pregnant woman mounted her husband's funeral pyre; another version states that he was born when a woman wearing the loincloth of her brother, stained with his seed, bathed and became pregnant, whereupon, in fear of her husband, she deposited the child at the foot of a fig tree (pippala), whence his name. (O'Flaherty 1973:62)

We find here a striking case of mythic "multiforms." In the Pippalāda birth stories the husband's cremation implies the brother's semen. Whether these multiforms existed as texts or even oral versions in traditional Bali is beside the point; they could have been implicit in ritual forms just as well as textual ones. I want merely to suggest that a code could not be better suited for Balinese ancestor ideology, in which brother and sister may symbolize ideal spouses for perpetuating houses. An equation between husband's cremation and brother's semen might even clarify the sensational *satia* at the end of a raja's reign, when his consorts could follow his corpse into the flames. Did the fires of *satia* ritually realize the full marriage ideal by converting all spouses into immolated widows, equivalents of incestuous wives whose progeny, as products of the highest union, would enhance the realm's future? Judging from Pippalāda, perhaps.

If, following Schneider, we interpret incest and kinship culturally, incest does not necessarily represent the horrifying or the psychologically ambivalent, such as sons' hearts murmuring subconsciously for their mothers or sisters, and vice versa. Nor, I would add, need incest exactly represent the ungrammatical. Rather, in Balinese symbology, incest implies the more-than-can-actually-happen and the complementarity of conflicting ideals: always oxymoron. "Incest," perhaps traditionally reiterated in *satia* or *satī*, means all the advantageous attributes of marriage at once: sister-cousin, political spouse, lover. So enhanced, the cosmos is complete, kingdoms would be perfect, and an ancestor group's ambitions could be achieved. Finally, stylized, sublimated Balinese *satia* is a far cry from the lusty details of Lady Uma —all semen, vaginas, mis-ejaculations, and mixed-up categories. Yet both symbols run counter to ethical reformism. In Bali *satia* and Uma appear to have become variations on the same ritual symbology: as imaginary as copulating twins, and as real as a widow's suicide.

Rāma Redux

> During an important temple-feast, a *Wajang Wong* festival may last for a week, different episodes of the story following each other on successive days without regard to their sequence. We may have, as it were, *Das Rheingold* interposed after *Siegfried* or even after *Götterdämmerung*; in terms of *Wajang Wong* the episode which led to the rape of Sita and the subsequent mobilization of the monkeys, on the last day of the festival instead of on the first, as epilogue instead of prelude. Ritual requirements are satisfied by the performance of scenes from the *Ramayana*, from which every episode in *Wajang Wong* is drawn. (De Zoete and Spies 1939:152)

The types of religious reformism implying world rejection include renunciation, monastic celibacy, and various strains of rationalism, such as karma doctrine. Whether in Hindu, Buddhist, or Islamic traditions, reformism, accompanied by moralistic values of education and literacy, requires that *kāma* either decline or be sublimated (as in *bhakti* communal devotionalism). On the other hand, the Indo-Pacific culture of Bali (perhaps like Tantrism) gives *kāma*, embodied in *rākṣasas* and capture-marriage escapades, co-primacy with *dharma* and *artha*. Dramatic narratives envision a recurrent, complementary standoff among all three. Again, the generalized symbology of love and marriage in Bali calls to mind Hindu mythology more than karma doctrine, particularly insofar as mythology is "solutionless":

> These fleeting moments of balance provide no "solution" to the paradox of the myth, for indeed, Hindu mythology does not seek any true synthesis. Where Western thought [most of it anyway] insists on forcing a compromise or synthesis of opposites, Hinduism [that is, its mythology] is content to keep each as it is; in chemical terms, one might say that the conflicting elements are resolved into a suspension rather than a solution. (O'Flaherty 1973:317–318)

Similarly, extremes of incest/alliance/capture are suspended in the symbology implicit in Balinese ideals and action.

To reiterate the fundamental significance of Lady Uma's nethermost vagina, we can turn to the ultimate text of the capturing *rākṣasa*, the *Rāmāyaṇa*. Just as in its own texts, the Indic *Rāmāyaṇa* never really concludes (consider the so-called "supplemental episodes"), so in Balinese culture the *Rāmāyaṇa* never exactly commences, but always "already commenced" (consider the *Ragu* tales of *Arja* performances which treat Rāma's Śūdra ancestor). I hope to show that in a more profound sense still, the implicit order of the *Rāmāyaṇa* in Bali is fundamentally recurrent.

As a preliminary we should note that *rākṣasas* figured in the original anthropological view of "capturing wives" as the foundation of exogamous marriage. In 1865, McLennan's *Primitive Marriage* cited Sir William Jones's 1863 translation of the *Institutes of Manu* to place India among the many areas revealing customs of capture:

> In the *Institutes of Manu* we have marriage by capture enumerated among "the eight forms of the nuptial ceremony used by the four classes." It is the marriage called Racshasa, and is thus defined: —"The seizure of a maiden by force from her house while she weeps and calls for assistance, after her kinsmen and friends have been slain in battle or wounded, and their houses broken open, is the marriage called Racshasa." Elsewhere in the code it is mentioned as appropriated to the military class. (McLennan 1970:34)

Before veering into comparative folklore, McLennan's inventive appendix on the *Probable Origin of the Name Racshasa* pondered the curious association of a high-caste martial-style marriage with a race of demons:

> The story of the Ramayana may be said to be that of the carrying off of Rama's wife, Sita, by the Racshasa, Ravana, and of the consequent war carried on by Rama against the Racshasas, ending in their defeat and the recovery of Sita [cites sources].... Wilson... speaks of the Racshasas as "a people, often alluded to, from whom the Aryas suffered much, and who, by their descendants, were transferred in idea to the most distant south, and treated by them as a race of mythical giants."... Lassen takes the same view. "The *Ramayana* ... contains the narrative of the first attempt of the Aryans to extend themselves to the south by conquest; but it presupposes the peaceable extension of Brahmanical missions in the same direction as having taken place still earlier.... The Racshasas, who are represented as disturbing the sacrifices and devouring the priests, signify here, as often elsewhere, merely the savage tribes which placed themselves in hostile opposition to the

Brahmanical institutions. The only other actors who appear in the legend, in addition to these inhabitants, are the monkeys, which ally themselves to Rama and render him assistance. This can only mean that, when the Arian Kshatriyas first made hostile incursions into the south, they were aided by another portion of the indigenous tribes." Dr. Muir can find no authority for saying that the word Racshasa was originally the name of a tribe. At the same time... he inclines to hold the descriptions we have of them as having more probably originated in hostile contact with the savages of the south, than as the simple offspring of the poet's imagination.... He quotes from the Ramayana a passage which represents them as cannibals—feeding on blood, men-devouring, changing their shapes, etc., and another, in which they are described as "of fearful swiftness and unyielding in battle"; while Ravana, the most terrible of all the Racshasas, is stigmatised as a "destroyer of religious duties, and ravisher of the wives of others." Dr. Muir adds, that the description of the Racshasas in the *Ramayana* "corresponds in many respects with the epithets applied to the same class of beings (whether we take them for men or for demons) who are so often alluded to in the *Rigveda*," and that it is quite possible that the author of the *Ramayana* may have borrowed therefrom many of the traits which he ascribes to the Racshasas.

But how came the name of a legal mode of marriage to be that of such a race of beings? The only answer that we can make is a surmise—viz., that while the system of capture had not as yet died out among the Kshatriyas, or warrior caste of the Aryans, it was perfect among the races to which the name Racshasas was applied; and that what was their system gave its designation to the exceptional, although permitted, marriage by capture among the Kshatriyas. This is the more probable, since, so far as we can ascertain, there is nothing in the name—Racshasa—itself, descriptive of the mode of marriage.

From another point of view, it may be observed that the Racshasas hold nearly the same place in Hindu tradition that giants, ogres, and trolls occupy in Scandinavian and Celtic legends. They are supernatural beings—robbers and plunderers of human habitations—men-devourers and women-stealers. The giants and ogres of the north share the characteristics of Ravana. The cruel monsters are always carrying off kings' daughters. As Rama's exploits culminate in the recovery of Sita, so the northern giant-slayer is crowned with the greatest glory when he has rescued the captive princesses and restored them in safety to the king's—their father's—palace. (McLennan 1970:123–124)

One could almost say that Balinese formulations of their own marriage system and Western formulations of exotic marriage systems are cognate. Both descend (although through dialectics of cross-breeding rather than unilineally) from distant understandings of the *Rāmāyaṇa*: Bali's on the one hand, McLennan's on the other. If nothing else legitimated a comparative study like the present one, the common reference point of Balinese and anthropological typologies would.

McLennan's suspicions about *rākṣasas* and giants, expressed in an evolutionary framework, echoed a Sanskrit-German connection mentioned by Romantic philologist F. von Schlegel two generations earlier:

> The lower German is generally of importance in regard to the etymology, the old form being often exactly retained. *Roksho* and *rakshoso* may be the ancient *recke* [giant]. (Schlegel 1860 trans.:430–431)[10]

Finally, McLennan's concluding speculations illustrate the inevitable difficulties with historicist interpretations of the *Rāmāyaṇa* and texts like it, even in our own day:

> Are we to hold all such beings—giants, ogres, trolls, etc.—wherever they occur, as representing savage races, between whom and the peoples in whose legends they appear as supernatural beings, there was chronic hostility? (1970:124)

That the *Rāmāyaṇa* itself cannot be so construed is underscored by its central place in traditions far from South Asian history. In fact, what the *Rāmāyaṇa* "becomes" in export enables us to modify speculations about what the *Rāmāyaṇa* "was" in situ. (It is possible that such texts are in a way "always exported," not susceptible of definitive editions, not centralized, not canonical.) In Bali the *Rāmāyaṇa* stands first among epic, mythic, and dramatic traditions (cf. Robson 1972:316). Yet the events of Balinese "history" afford no program that, so to speak, explains the *Rāmāyaṇa*'s meaning as their allegory. Nevertheless, Balinese culture's *reception* of the *Rāmāyaṇa* confirms the significance of Rāma-Sītā consorts and *rākṣasa*-capture—not as McLennan's evolutionary source-custom eventually yielding in turn matriliny and patriliny, but as components in a total Indo-Pacific marriage system.

In order to suggest how an Indic literary tradition penetrates the Balinese context, let me venture a provisional reading *between* India's *Rāmāyaṇa* and Bali's culture.[11] The *Rāmāyaṇa* opens with Daśaratha's

[10] On the response by early Romantics to Indic literary and institutional forms, see Boon (1979).

[11] In this suggestive reading I try to remain between many variants of the *Rāmāyaṇa*, including Valmiki's translated texts, outright sentimentalizations (e.g., Dutt) and related lore. The process extends in Bali not just to variants within a code (the textual) but to variants of the codes themselves (texts, rites, dance, illustrations, social regulations, etc.). Here interest in the *Rāmāyaṇa* centers on what it can *become* in translation, transposition, and transformation—an important issue in pursuits as different as structuralist analysis and *Rezeptionssociologie*.

"political" infertility, his lack of male progeny. The solution promises conflict as four sons (avatārs of Viṣṇu) are born of three wives whose fertility was enhanced by different amounts of divine aphrodisiac; as I work it out:

Rāma, son by first wife Kauśalyā (1/2 of beverage);
Bharata, by third wife, Kaikeyī (1/8 of beverage);
Lakṣmaṇa and Śatrughna, twins, by middle wife,
Sumitrā (1/4 + 1/8 of beverage; 3/16 per son?).

Accordingly, the two sons with highest factors of seniority, mother's seniority, and beverage, Rāma and Lakṣmaṇa, perform with the sage the initial demon-killing. Bharata, through the devices of his mother, assumes the throne; the impropriety of this event is underscored by the implicit but unstressed rival, Śatrughna. Obviously *artha* is out of gear; only *kāma* will restore the balance, but never permanently, never uncompromisingly.

Back to the story. Heirless Kośala is echoed in heirless Videha. King Janaka's only potential alliance-credit is the adopted Sītā (her obscure origins enable the events of the narrative to reveal her ultimate nature: Rāma's cosmologically perfect spouse). A political alliance between the houses is arranged, but excessively, as many Kośala men prepare to marry Videha women. The uxorilocal setting of the marriage festivities counters regular Balinese marriage; in fact the entire episode suggests a *sentana,* "borrowed son-in-law," pattern in Balinese practice. But the multiple marriages complicate this *sentana*-like arrangement even more (in fact Balinese rules preclude one-way exchange relations repeated between lines or houses—see Boon 1977, chap. 6). From the outset everything is fraught with imbalance and excess: four sons and four daughters are expended on the same alliance, a *nyentana*-like ceremony (a real option, polygyny, is never entertained). The precise ranks of the sons cannot perfectly mesh with respective ranks of the daughters, who include no explicit twins, although Urmilā is Sītā's sister. But Urmilā marries Lakṣmaṇa. Thus, we have sisters (Sītā and Urmilā) divided between half-brothers (Rāma and Lakṣmaṇa), and whole brothers (the twins) divided between non-sisters (Urmilā and Śrutakīrti). And the ambiguous Bharata marries Janaka's brother's daughter, underscoring his secondariness. The *Rāmāyaṇa* thus poses excessive marriage-alliance (type 2) which will have to be counterbalanced by excessive passionate capture (type 3) that in turn reveals the arch spouses Rāma-Sītā as, more than just an alliance match, cosmological complements: like incestuous twins (type 1).

The values of alliance fracture at once. Rāma is not eager to rule; in the idiom of romance, he requires experience. Then Rāma and Sītā appear as a prematurely complete couple in *tapas* rather than producers of progeny or centers of a Kingdom. And intrigue: Kaikeyī's ambition for Bharata; the background of the boons promised her by the king which place Bharata on the throne and banish Rāma to a hermit's life, uncomplaining. Subsequent scenes portray Rāma and Sītā in truncated, complacent love in their *ashram,* free of social or cosmological consequence. This is the false solution, the love-couple:

> Years will pass in happy union—happiest lot to woman given—
> Sita seeks not throne or empire, nor the brighter joys of heaven,
> Heaven conceals not brighter mansions in the sunny fields of pride,
> Where without her lord and husband faithful Sita would reside!
> Therefore let me seek the jungle where the jungle-rangers rove,
> Dearer than the royal palace, where I share my husband's love,
> And my heart in sweet communion shall my Rama's wishes share,
> And my wifely toil shall lighten Rama's load of woe and care!
> (R. Dutt, trans. 1910)

The false, partial solution (like a cosmological metonymy) fails to convey the ideal, totalized *suspension*.

Upon Daśaratha's death Bharata himself tries to restore Rāma to his throne, but Rāma remains in exile to fulfill his father's vow. Into this false solution—Rāma, Sītā, and Lakṣmaṇa tranquil and complete in their Pañcavaṭī retreat, with home and society mere memories—the *rākṣasas* intrude.

Śūrpanakhā, sister of Rāvaṇa, king of the *rākṣasas*, is smitten by Rāma. Rāma's joke again contradicts birth-order, when he suggests that she (a king's sister) should consider not himself but his younger brother. Her wrath then provokes Lakṣmaṇa's dismembering of her nose and ears. The fundamentally incomplete harmony of the love retreat is obliterated by the great slaughter of *rākṣasas* at Pañcavaṭī.

We need not follow the *Rāmāyaṇa*'s episodes step by step to their conclusion or supplements. Once the *rākṣasas* and in particular the monkey-warriors enter the scene, the full conjunction of extremes becomes patent. It is the capture of Sītā, the monkey-antics, and Sītā's ordeal that dominate Balinese performances, especially masked dance-dramas (*wayang wong*). From the point we have reached, typical Balinese versions of *Rāmāyaṇa* themes proceed selectively as follows:

To avenge [Śūrpanakhā] Ravana sent the rākshasa Marica in the semblance of a deer, to lure away the hunter Rama, thus leaving Sita unprotected. Sita fell into the trap; she was so captivated by the delicate mottled coat and "variegated countenance" of the deer that she implored Rama to go and catch it for her as a playmate. He leaves her in the care of his brother and goes off into the forest. But Sita becomes anxious at his long absence and imagines she hears his voice crying for help. Nothing will satisfy her but Lakshmana must go after him, and while she remains alone Ravana gets admission to the house in the disguise of a mendicant and carries her off to his kingdom of Lanka (Ceylon). The bird Jatayu, which owed its life to Rama, is mortally wounded in an attempt to win her back, but survives to deliver Sita's ring to Rama, and tell him what has happened. Rama, despairing in the forest, meets the monkey-king Sugriva, who promises the help of all his monkey host if Rama will destroy his twin brother Subali, who has taken his wife and kingdom from him. Subali is killed and the monkeys, led by Hanuman, build a bridge across the sea to Lanka, and after a long and terrible war defeat and kill Ravana. Sita, on suspicion of infidelity during her long captivity, undergoes the ordeal by fire. She emerges victorious and accompanies Rama to his Kingdom of Ayodhya, but again the people begin to murmur and again Rama listens, and banishes her to the Ganges, where in the hermitage of the sage Valmiki (author of the *Ramayana*) she gives birth to two sons. They are brought up by Valmiki and are only recognized by their father on the occasion of a great horse sacrifice, when they visit the court and recite the epic made in his honour. But just as he seems about to win back Sita, cleared of suspicion by the solemn oath of Valmiki, she calls on the earth to take her and vanishes from his sight. Rama eventually resumed his godlike being, and rejoined her in Svarga. (De Zoete and Spies 1939:153)

If we zoom in on a segment of an actual performance, the emphasis on *rākṣasa* thrusts and monkey antic-reactions is conspicuous:

There are now two groups, Jatayu and his passive ladies, Ravana crouching in loud despair between [his clown-servants] Delem and Sangut. At last he draws his kris, and advancing in huge swirls of movement beats down the fluttering bird, round whom all circle with loud cries. Jatayu, mortally wounded, drags his limp feathers without aim over the ground like a wounded fighting-cock with trailing wing or severed leg. Sita, still passive, is seized by Ravana and led off, of course through the air. Rama and Lakshmana re-enter solemnly singing, and wind up the stage, while the bird flaps madly round and round, beating the earth with its wings. They close round it as it sinks into a lovely crouching posture, and in a high wounded voice tells its tale to Rama, while Twalen interprets. This scene was again without [gamelan] music. The death of the bird, swaying strangely before its final passionate fall, was very moving. It rose and was led off. The music again grows wild. Rama dances, then stands long motionless. A host of monkeys troop in in two files led by Sugriva and Hanuman, the latter recognizable by his white tail. They address each other with monkey cries, changing restlessly from knee to knee, moving about continually with queer fastidious steps. The monkeys,... are in style quite carefully differentiated, as well as by their distinctive masks. Sugriva now approaches with majestic but uneasy gestures, never still, punctuating his gliding, darting steps with swift accents. He is joined by Hanuman and the three so-called alus [refined] monkeys.... Subali, identical with Sugriva in mask and voice, now whirls up the stage, the wings of his dress held wide, a thin sash to toy with in his hand. They threaten each other with the familiar gesture of two pointing fingers sharply withdrawn. They fight with curious square poses and jagged cries, watched by the immobile Rama and commenting Twalen. Sugriva is the first to fall, for Subali is invincible so long as he has only a brother monkey to deal with. It is not until a flower or string is tied to him to distinguish him from his twin, that Rama dares to shoot his arrow. (De Zoete and Spies 1939:159)

The significance of Hanuman and Sugrīva/Subali as mediators in Balinese symbology cannot be overestimated. They obviously conjoin different spheres: animals categorized like gods/men (demonic Subali, like Rāvaṇa; princely Sugrīva, like Rāma; refined yet spritely Hanuman). Moreover, in Balinese *wayang wong* the uncompromising comic "multivocality" generally associated with clowns (*parekan*)—placing them, like Sancho Panza, in contact with all levels of society and cosmos—extends to monkeys. As De Zoete and Spies remind us:

In *Wajang Wong* the role of Twalen and Merdah is much more restricted than in *Wajang Koelit*, where they mix themselves in the divine battles and are obstreperously comic. Everything is allowed to them as to old-fashioned and trusty servants, but their chief purpose in *Wajang Wong* is to advise their master, and to translate into Balinese the unintelligible Kawi of the main characters.... They trot clumsily after their master in a dance style peculiar to themselves, progressing with awkward, inept movements, their arms bent and jerking like pump handles to and fro, their hands folded in a styleless, inconclusive manner, in striking contrast with the highly stylized movements of the hero. (1939:156)

We might contrast *wayang kulit* and *wayang wong* in this way: *wayang kulit*'s primacy of joking clowns—who must, like the *dalang* (puppeteer) himself display all levels and modes of voice or speech (antic is secondary in puppets)—is transformed into *wayang wong*'s co-primacy of clowns and monkeys, the latter displaying all levels and modes of antic and gesture. It would seem that *wayang kulit*'s singular, intensive source of codes, the *dalang*, is epitomized in the generalized mediating of clowns, bridging all languages, voices, motions, gestures (the latter, however, restricted by the genre). *Wayang wong*'s more diffuse source of codes—multiple performers with varied skills—is epitomized in the differentiated mediation of clowns (translators) and monkeys (acrobats), the one bridging language codes, the other bridging gesture codes that gain new prominence in dance. Regardless, like the clowns themselves but in a different register, Hanuman et al., implicated in all the forces at odds in *wayang* episodes, perform a dramatic conjunction of extremes: both refined and animal, both controlled and capturing, both/and. . . .

The dynamics and dialectics we detected above in microcosm-macrocosm body symbols reappear in the realm of monkeys and *parekan*. This fact is suggested by iconographic conventions:

> [*Parekan*] are among the most popular characters in the *wayang kulit* where their functions somewhat resemble those of jesters, or wise fools, in the pastoral idiom of Western art. Whereas Twalen and Merdah serve causes of righteousness, their counterparts, Delam and Sangut, function as the *parekan* of evil and demonic personages. . . . Although all four possess certain traits of the *kras* or *kasar* [rough] type, only Delam and Sangut have round, bulging eyes [versus the narrow-refined eyes of Twalen and Merdah]. (Gralapp 1967:257)

Thus, the arch-*kasar* itself subdivides into rough/refined (see Peacock 1968). Such contrasts are relational and shifting. And more subtly, as one moves across Balinese "genres" of ritual, art, and social structure, a particular set of symbolic "functions" subdivides for redistribution. Again, the clowns of *wayang kulit* are full mediators of all idioms and styles across disparate realms: Heaven/Earth/Underworld in both refined/rough aspects of all three. In *wayang wong* clowns specialize in speech—mediating (translating) Kawi, different levels of Balinese, and occasionally nowadays Indonesian—while physical mediation—exaggerated refined manners (parody), exaggerated clumsiness (pratfalls)—is assumed partly by monkeys. Yet in both varieties of *wayang* mediation occurs through the mutual exaggeration of extremes and the juxtaposition of all codes.[12]

[12] Many complexities and paradoxes of hierarchical vocabularies and speech styles enter into such considerations. To develop these issues would require a focus on performance rather than, as here, typology. I would also stress *transmission* of codes through the generations. It is worth rethinking recent work on Balinese rites and symbols along more dialectical lines. On Javanese *wayang kulit* and its epistemologies plus performance, see in particular Becker (1979). For some suggestions about Javanese *wayang beber*, see Anderson (1974).

It is not only dancing monkeys and bawdy clowns that enable Bali's *Rāmāyaṇa* to underscore the adventuresome, demonic, and dislocating side of marriage. Indeed, Sītā herself, at the victorious moment of proving her purity, alludes to the *kāma*-capture complement of marriage symbols. Sītā's ordeal is a major subject of traditional Balinese painting, a third genre or vehicle for the appearance of the forces of the *Rāmāyaṇa*, this time as immobile figures. One typical version of the episode transposed into court painting stresses spiritual elevation (see, for example, Gralapp 1967, fig. 14). Conventional divine aureoles predominate. Sītā herself, preserved in the flames, inclines toward the right, relatively sacred side. Twalen and Merdah are both rightward, at a respectful distance from Sītā's female attendant. Hanuman is elevated; no monkey intrudes raucously into Sītā's sphere of repose. Even Wilmana, demonic bird-vehicle of *rākṣasa* king Rāvaṇa, is restrained beneath an aureole. All is symmetry and hierarchy, ordered to the verge of sublimity. The entire scene, likened in Balinese conventions to a cremation (Sītā leaps from a cremation tower or *bade*), is in this case more precisely a *mukur*: "The imagery above the cremation tower recalls the Balinese custom of placing effigies of a bird and a lamp near the *mukur* tower for the guidance of the soul on its journey to heaven" (Gralapp 1967:266). Now, a *mukur* is a cremation of a cremation: reburning the body forty-two days later, without the body. The iconography could hardly be more explicit.

Set in the ritual register of *mukur*, Sītā's ordeal appears sublime. This particular Balinese version could almost be set to a patently sentimentalized translation of the *Rāmāyaṇa*, which suggests that pure-Sītā, restored blameless to Rāma, is a *solution*:

> Slow the red flames rolled asunder, God of Fire incarnate came,
> Holding in his radiant bosom fair Videha's sinless dame,
> Not a curl upon her tresses, not a blossom on her brow,
> Not a fiber of her mantle did with tarnished luster glow!
> Witness of our sins and virtues, God of Fire incarnate spake,
> Bade the sorrow-stricken Rama back his sinless wife to take.
> Rama's forehead was unclouded and a radiance lit his eye,
> And his bosom heaved in gladness as he spoke in accents high:
> "Never from the time I saw her in her maiden days of youth,
> Have I doubted Sita's virtue, Sita's fixed and changeless truth.
> I have known her ever sinless—let the world her virtue know,
> For the God of Fire is witness to her true and changeless vow!"
> (R. Dutt 1910)

But this sort of reading of the *Rāmāyaṇa* as depicted in Balinese painting would fail to explain why pictures of Sītā's ordeal *vary*. If my suggestions about Balinese symbo-logics are accurate, we would expect the register of divine-sublimation (in death-ritual terms, *mukur*) to be complemented by a register that suggests demonic agitation. And such is the case. Another version of the episode (see, for example, Grallap 1967, fig. 13) at first glance looks similar, but in detail it is a polar extreme. No *mukur* ritual items enhance the scene. The ritual register is rather cremation itself (*ngaben*), body and all. Sītā inclines toward demonic-left. The flames around her have not been decoratively conventionalized into an aureole motif; Wilmana too is unconstrained by the visual code of divine influence. Hanuman remains next to Sugrīva; symmetry is unsettled, the bottom of the hierarchy accentuated. Twalen himself is situated demonic-left. Most conspicuously:

> At bottom center, with the assistance of Merdah, Twalen, in a typical note of erotic comedy, parodies the central event by testing the chastity of Sita's servant, Pengeruan. A further comic touch is furnished by the monkeys who impudently, if rather apprehensive [?], climb on the lotus throne and the ramp of the *bade*. (Gralapp 1967:266)

The painting is actually even bawdier than Gralapp suggests. Twalen's hand extends under Pengeruan's skirt, a standard gesture in Bali-Hindu iconography. And clinging to Sītā's fiery sphere is a large monkey with a netherly orifice (because of the blending of front, profile, and rear views in Balinese painting, it is hard to tell which one) exposed just above Pengeruan's head.

Gralapp's informative reading of assorted Balinese paintings mentions that the other refined version "has the effect of minimizing the human drama of the event while giving greater emphasis to its hieratic and doctrinal significance" (p. 266). But he suggests no thoroughgoing contrasts such as *ngaben/mukur*. Moreover, it is crucial to note that the "human drama" neglected in a *mukur* variant is more precisely the demonic, lusty, sensual realm of capture and *kāma*. Thus in Balinese cremation as well, symbology is relational and shifting; and every variant alludes to the total scheme. While *ngaben* following exhumation is at one level the purer rite, contrasted to prior burial, it appears relatively demonic beside elevated *mukur*. (Just as, in reverse, the burial of an upper-title corpse is less demon-threatened than the burial of an inferior.)

Thus, by moving across Bali's dramatic genres and institutions, we discover a premise of their symbology: Balinese variations on the *Rāmāyaṇa* never forget that pure Sītā enflamed and sullied Sītā abducted are two Sītās in the same. In fact, three. By spanning convergent meanings in Balinese ideals, we can now read Sītā herself as a triad of extremes: the essence of capture (abducted by Rāvaṇa and returned, thanks to Hanuman); the essence of political alliance (Kośala cum Videha); and the essence of incest (divine consort of Rāma)—like an immolated sister-spouse with a vagina in her foot.

The Monastery's Antithesis

Typologically and comparatively, Balinese symbology contrasts with aspects of religious development that A. M. Hocart deemed "the Good," which recalls Weber's notions of world-rejecting reformism:

> By 500 B.C. a great change had come over religious thought: worldly welfare was considered an unworthy aim; spiritual elevation became the goal of the religious leaders. The objective of the preachers is still welfare, but welfare is differently conceived: it is to a large extent identified with goodness. It is better to be good than to be healthy and wealthy, and so a ritual which leads to goodness takes the place of a ritual that only gives material prosperity.
>
> India has not been unique in undergoing this transformation. A tendency to cast the sober hue of morals over all seems a recurring phenomenon in the life of civilizations. As they get older, they exalt the spirit higher and higher above the flesh, till at last the flesh becomes a thing to be ashamed of, bodily wants are tolerated as an unfortunate necessity, not enjoyed. Ritual has either to conform to the fashion or perish. At first, ritual falls into discredit, because the moralists, being intellectuals and individualists, are hostile to a materialistic and intensely social ritual. In the end, however, the ritual saves itself by adopting the new moral tone.
>
> The causes of these ethical movements are not known. They have generally been accepted without question as stages in the evolution from low to high. As a matter of fact they seem to herald the fall of civilizations. The more decadent a people, the higher the moral tone.... We have to accept [these ethical movements] as *facts* which go under the name of Buddhism, Christianity, Islam, philosophical Hinduism, Confucianism, and the rest. The rituals we may label "ethical rituals." (Hocart 1970:72)

With a unique combination of ethnological and philological insight, Hocart suggested that the rituals of "life" (renewing a diversified social organism), rather than ceremonies of moral betterment, prevail in Fiji; he surmised that similar conditions characterized South Asia's Vedic period. I have argued that such a ritual basis—similar both to Pacific social forms (see Sahlins 1976:42–46) and to certain Indic traditions—underlies Balinese resistance to ethical aspects of Hinduism, Buddhism, and, of course, Islam—this resistance qualifies Balinese variations on renunciation, monasticism, literalism, and legalistic rationalism, and karma doctrine as well.

Balinese culture contains many traces of "ethical rituals" (and even a dash of devotionalism), but the "new moral tone" has never pervaded the whole. While Indic renunciation may imply a total social antithesis (see Dumont 1970b and Tambiah 1970), the Balinese renouncer tends rather to reinforce social bonds of kinsmen who intensify their ancestor rituals in light of his example. Even in the Brāhmaṇa sector, *saṃnyāsin* ideals are embedded in kinship and the related state mode of organization, which accentuate fertility and descendants. Similarly, Tantric *tapas*, the "heat of asceticism," appears in Balinese texts and life-stages based on the South Asian paradox of fertility/release; for example:

> Throughout [South Asian] mythology, whether or not *tapas* is accepted as a valid means of creation, it is practiced for another goal: immortality, freedom from rebirth. In the Vedas, *tapas* is able to accomplish the chief desideratum, fertility; in the Upanishads, *tapas* is the means to the new goal, Release. Both are forms of immortality, both promising continuation of the soul without the body—Release giving complete freedom of the soul (or absorption into the Godhead), progeny giving a continuation of the soul's life in the bodies of one's children. (O'Flaherty 1973:76)

In this particular domain Balinese culture as a whole is less co-extremist than textual Tantrism: given the progeny/release dichotomy, Bali privileges progeny; fertility encompasses release. I suspect that any bifurcation of *tapas*-Release (Upaniṣads) and *tapas*-fertility (Vedas) into distinct alternatives would run counter to Bali's Indonesia-style ancestor cult and ideology (Boon 1977, chap. 4).

Yet Bali's failure to accentuate equally the fertility/release polarities of mythology and Tantrism hardly implies reformism. This localization of religious tenets slants not toward ethics (the social equivalent of *tapas*-release minus the social equivalent of *tapas*-fertility) but toward progeny: what Hocart called "life."

Indeed, wherever the progeny/asceticism contrasts appear in

Balinese traditions, emphasis finally falls on immortality through "the bodies of one's children." For example, in Indic traditions:

> According to the *Rāmāyaṇa* and *Padma Purāṇa*, however, (the sage) remains with Santa and does not return to the forest, while the *Mahābhārata* suggests a compromise of considerable significance in the context of the Indian ascetic paradox: Ṛṣyaśṛṅga returns to the forest, but with his wife. (O'Flaherty 1973:49)

Again Balinese culture echoes the *Rāmāyaṇa*, perhaps contrasting with Java's emphasis on the *Mahābhārata* (see Geertz 1960:263). Like the *Rāmāyaṇa* itself, Balinese culture (a "text" in its own right, when read comparatively), while admitting the co-*ritualism* of *pedanda* (male priests) and *istri pedanda* (female priests), rejects the compromised co-asceticism of the hermitage-couple. Bali's dramatic and institutional forms alike point to the full cosmological and social order: ancestral and descendant.

In the more specifically Southeast Asian context, Bali and other Indonesian cultures conspicuously have resisted monastic ideals, that is, institutions organized around chastity or celibacy, mediation, group and residence, and literacy-writing-reciting-chanting. In Bali some of these functions fall to casual reading clubs, or *sekaha bebasan*. In the historic Hindu-Buddhist states of Indonesia, priestly functions were associated with the courts; scribes complemented the legal, textual, calendrical, and temple dimensions of state ritual in kings' spheres of influence. In Bali no monastic institution or ethical path emerged as a total alternative to ancestor groups and related temple networks or religious and political organization. Any ethical components remained diffused and suspended in Bali's ideas, action, institutions, and texts. Or in Weber's terms, monasticism never became the "single dominating confession."

If we compare religious symbol systems at the broadest level of ideal-types, Hocart's sense of "the Good" (versus "life-maintenance") illuminates dilemmas inherent in monasticism as a social value. Non-monastic traditional systems (including, I would argue, both tribes and Tantrism) are *generalized*. Tantrism can contain monastic and ethical elements, but they do not symbolize the whole. In a generalized order each smaller division—two exogamous clans, say, or some other type of alliance partners—replicates the full degree of differentiation recognized; small-scale wholes engage in rituals of the total whole. Compared with such systems monasticism appears revolutionary, or at least antithetical: celibacy, which must remain ambivalent or even deviant in tribal (or Tantric?) systems, becomes institutionalized in monasticism. "A-sociality" is legitimated as an alternative to "society." From the vantage of society and its perpetuation, the monastery epitomizes incompleteness: not self-regenerating, often not self-sustaining. Yet while the monastery can survive only through recruitment, it presumes to represent the entire cosmos, society included. Hence, from the vantage of "life," there is a fundamental discrepancy: the cosmic whole is lodged in a social part (*ceremonies* of monks), not in the social whole (*rituals* of procreative clans or ancestor groups).[13]

If one assumes with believers that religious merit is vital to society's perpetuation as well as to ultimate release, then monasticism achieves what Durkheim called "organic solidarity" with an incremental level of differentiation: reciprocity between two specialist sectors or categories, one producing merit and release, the other producing successors and subsistence. Neither lay nor monk alone can reproduce the socioreligious totality. When opposed to the extreme monastic alternative, the lay sector appears relatively homogeneous; the monk/lay distinction overshadows all others. The nearest tribal equivalent to this lay/monk distinction is male/female; in other words, the only ideal tribal division that is not self-reproducing is one-sex or, analogously, one exogamous clan. In tribal systems (and I think indirectly in Tantric ones as well), the whole is implied in society's sexuality, in coitus itself. (Tantric forms suggest a sort of nostalgia for this symbolic basis of solidarity in radically divided social orders like caste systems.) In contrast, monastic systems totalized around celibacy rather than sexuality replace coitus and ritual with *lettres* and ceremony as their primary symbolic media. In the "primitive classification" of generalized tribal kinship, ideally every marriage and ritual exchange conjoins representatives of the extremes of social and cosmic divisions. In contrast, monasticism totalizes cosmic order through the organizing power of specialized writing, chanting, and liturgical canons: all these alternatives to fertility, all these ingredients of "historical society" and of the idea of "history" itself.

[13] For examples of relevant comparative studies of various Buddhist cultures, see Kirsch (1977), Holmberg (1980).

I broach such immense issues—at once Weberian, Hocartian, Durkheimian, and structuralist—both to accentuate Bali and to allow Bali to illuminate comparative studies. Balinese symbology, which I have tried to show is broadly more Tantric than reformist, reveals specialized institutions of writing, reading (*sekaha bebasan*), and text-based performances; this differentiation parallels monastic systems. But like tribal cultures, any symbolic totality in Bali obtains from a fertility of variant extremes. Thus, a problem in interpretive method arises. Standard approaches to literate cultures proceed as if aspects of monasticism necessarily underlie textual values, and as if history moves such cultures progressively either away from the perfections imagined in texts (golden ages of prior kingdoms) or toward such perfections (revolutionary utopias, religious release). Western analysis of literate cultures often aims for singular, literal translations and canonical interpretation. Rationalized analysis assumes, indeed often imposes, centralized, uniform literate standards. One might say that philological and historical approaches to literate cultures are themselves "monastic." I have suggested that applying such reformist assumptions to a generalized, "unethicalized" symbology like Bali's can obscure a recurrent tripartism, an emphasis on complementary sexuality, and a pervasive dynamic variation stretching well beyond the courtly and priestly sectors.

Yet, that Balinese culture and symbology is less reformist than many historical societies should imply neither stagnation nor archaic "traditionalism" (a concept sustained in part by analyzing exotic civilizations from documentary evidence such as courtly chronicles). Traditionally, Bali contains elaborate regulations: legal spheres (*adat*), rules for hamlet and irrigation control (*awig-awig*), and so forth. Yet even neighboring locales reveal elaborate variations in their rules (see Korn 1932). And their complex dynamics have not moved irrevocably toward the sort of centralized, uniform code we associate with bureaucratic rationalization.

The traditional Balinese state itself perhaps never tended toward a centralized status quo (see Geertz 1973, chap. 12; 1980). Yet the Sanskrit-oriented scholarship on Balinese royal courts long emphasized the idealization of Majapahit Java, the alliance of Siwaic Brāhmaṇa and raja-enthroned (recalling the Mitra/Varuṇa duality in Indic sovereignty—see Dumezil 1966), the state temples, royal chronicles and cremation, and the legal, priestly, and literary texts of the courts. Less attention was paid to the plentiful institutions, rituals, and *lettres* that counterbalanced any centralization by dislocating, shifting, and renewing the center from the periphery. Bali's refined, Brāhmaṇa-backed courts have been regularly qualified in social action by rival ancestor groups, trance practices, local temple lore, the demonic register of rituals, and, of course, the conspicuous clowns of dramatic performance. A centrist status quo—whether royalist, colonialist, or now nationalist—has remained in Bali an unattainable, Dulcinea-like ideal, continually and essentially fractured by the Panza-like play inherent in ideas and actions (Boon 1977, Part I).

Balinese symbology confirms the point. It operates less through symbolic partials implying a solution, than through symbolic multiples implying a suspension. Not monks, but clowns and monkeys. As a pure, ideal type of mediation and totalization, monks convert variant codes into a conformist code that promises ultimate, radical, rarefied release. In contrast, clowns exaggerate variant codes, never converting and consolidating them but juxtaposing them incongruously. Comparative anthropology invites us to take clowns seriously and monks playfully, to help them complement each other. Of course, no actual culture is a pure type; even Theravāda cultures are not thoroughly monastic; even Balinese Tantrism is not thoroughly "ludic." There is a bit of the monk in the latter and a bit of the clown in the former.

The heady brew of social and textual forms in Balinese culture—marriage and politics, religion and ritual, myth and narrative, dance and drama—reflects no monolithic substantive theme, no deep religiosity, no exploitative power. Rather, the forms act as complex commentaries on each other (see Geertz 1973, chap. 15). Moreover, they act as figurations of something relatively lacking in Balinese culture: ethical ideals such as monasticism, karma, and the like. At the fullest comparative level, we must interpret Balinese meanings in terms of both their multifarious presences and this pervasive absence. By the same token those South and Southeast cultures most pervaded by the "sober hues" of karma can be expected to conceal a muted dialectic with extremist rituals of "life."

Tantric cultures (to coin a type) revolve around a generalized *ritual* symbology; this fact recalls principles of tribal cultures themselves. In Balinese culture even ultimate Release is thought to be embodied in the ashes of the cremated corpse (see Soebadio 1971:52–53), ashes that result from rituals performed by the deceased's descendants, who will in their turn, particularly if fertile, gain Release. In Bali final liberation is dramatic, episodic, recurrent, and procreative. This fact is nowhere more evident than in symbols of incest, alliance, and capture, all conjoined in—to chant the mantra one last time—a systematic suspension of complementary extremes.

References Cited

Anderson, Benedict
1974 The Last Picture Show: Wayang Beber. Proceedings of the Conference on Modern Indonesian Literature. Center for Southeast Asian Studies, University of Wisconsin, Madison.
Barnett, Steve, L. M. Fruzzetti, A. Östör
1977 On a Comparative Sociology of India: A Reply to Marriott. Journal of Asian Studies 36(3):599–600.
Becker, A. L.
1979 Text-Building, Epistemology, and Aesthetics in Javanese Shadow Theatre. *In* The Imagination of Reality. A. L. Becker and Aram Yengoyan, eds. Norwood, N.J.: Ablex. Pp. 211–243.
Bloch, Maurice
1977 The Past and the Present in the Present. Man 12(2):280–291.
Boon, James A.
1974 The Balinese Marriage Predicament: Individual, Strategical, Cultural. American Ethnologist 3(2):191–214.
1977 The Anthropological Romance of Bali, 1597–1972: Dynamic Perspectives in Marriage and Caste, Politics and Religion. New York: Cambridge University Press.
1978 The Shift to Meaning. American Ethnologist 5(2):361–367.
1979 An Endogamy of Poets and Vice Versa: Exotic Ideals in Romanticism/Structuralism. Studies in Romanticism 18:333–361.
Burke, Kenneth
1966 Language as Symbolic Action. Berkeley: University of California Press.
Covarrubias, Miguel
1937 Island of Bali. New York: Alfred A. Knopf.
De Zoete, Beryl, and Walter Spies
1939 Dance and Drama in Bali. New York: Harper's Magazine Press.
Douglas, Mary
1970 Natural Symbols. New York: Vintage Books.
Dumezil, Georges
1966 Mythe et épopée, Vol. I: L'Idéologie des trois fonctions. Paris: Gallimard.
Dumont, Louis
1970a Homo Hierarchicus: An Essay on the Caste System. Mark Sainsbury, trans. Chicago: University of Chicago Press.
1970b Religion/Politics and History in India. Paris: Mouton.

Durkheim, Emile, and Marcel Mauss
1963 Primitive Classification. Rodney Needham, trans. Chicago: University of Chicago Press.
Dutt, Romesh C., trans.
1910 The Ramayana and the Mahabharata: Condensed into English Verse. New York: E. P. Dutton.
Friederich, R.
1959 The Civilization and Culture of Bali. Calcutta: Susil Gupta.
Frye, Northrop
1976 The Secular Scripture. Cambridge: Harvard University Press.
Geertz, Clifford
1960 The Religion of Java. New York: Free Press.
1963 Peddlers and Princes. Chicago: University of Chicago Press.
1973 The Interpretation of Culture. New York: Basic Books.
1977 Found in Translation: On the Social History of the Moral Imagination. Georgia Review 31(4):788–810.
1980 Negara: The Theater State in Bali. Princeton: Princeton University Press.
Geertz, Hildred, and Clifford Geertz
1975 Kinship in Bali. Chicago: University of Chicago Press.
Gonda, J.
1970 Karman and Retributive Justice in Ancient Java. *In* R. C. Majumdar Felicitation Volume. H. B. Sarkar, ed. Calcutta: K. L. Mukhopadhyay.
1975 The Indian Religions in Pre-Islamic Indonesia and Their Survival in Bali. Handbuch der Orientalistik, III. Leiden/Cologne.
Gralapp, Leland W.
1967 Balinese Painting and the Wayang Tradition. Artibus Asiae 29(2–3):239–266.
Hanna, Willard A.
1976 Bali Profile. New York: American Universities Field Staff.
Hinzler, H. I. R.
1975 Wayang op Bali. Nedelandse Vereniging voor het Poppenspel.
Hocart, A. M.
1952 The Life Giving Myth. London: Methuen.
1970 Kings and Councillors. Introduction by Rodney Needham. Chicago: University of Chicago Press.
Holmberg, David H.
1980 Lama, Shaman, and Lambu in Tamang Religious Practice. Ph.D. dissertation, Cornell University.
Hooykaas, C.
1973 Kama and Kala: Materials for the Study of Shadow Theatre in Bali. Amsterdam: Verhandelingen der Koninklijke Nederlandse Akademie van Wetenschappen, afd. Letterkunde. Nieuwe Reeks, Deel 79.
Hooykaas, Jocoba
1957 De Godsdienstige Ondergrond van het Praemuslimse Huwelijk op Java en Bali. Indonesie 10(2):109–136.

1960 The Myth of the Young Cowherd and the Little Girl. Bijdragen tot der Land-, Taal- en Volkenkunde 117. 2e Aflevering.

Johns, A.
1970 The Enlightenment of Bhima. *In* R. C. Majumdar Felicitation Volume. Himansu Bhusan Sarkar, ed. Calcutta: K. L. Mukhopadhyay.

Kirsch, A. Thomas
1977 Complexity in the Thai Religious System: An Interpretation. Journal of Asian Studies 36(2):241–266.

Korn, V. E.
1932 Het Adatrecht van Bali. 2nd ed. The Hague.

Lévi-Strauss, Claude
1967 The Story of Asdiwal. *In* The Structural Study of Myth and Totemism. Edmund Leach, ed. London: Tavistock.

Littleton, C. Scott
1973 The New Comparative Mythology: An Anthropological Assessment of the Theories of Georges Dumezil. Berkeley: University of California Press.

Marriott, McKim
1976 Interpreting Indian Society: A Monistic Alternative to Dumont's Dualism. Journal of Asian Studies 36(1):189–195.

McLennan, John F.
1970 Primitive Marriage: An Inquiry into the Origin of the Form of Capture in Marriage Ceremonies. Peter Riviere, ed. Chicago: University of Chicago Press.

O'Flaherty, Wendy Doniger
1973 Asceticism and Eroticism in the Mythology of Śiva. London: Oxford University Press.
1980 Karma and Rebirth in the Vedas and Purāṇas. *In* Karma and Rebirth in Classical Indian Traditions. Wendy O'Flaherty, ed. Berkeley: University of California Press. Pp. 3–37.

Peacock, James L.
1968 Rites of Modernization. Chicago: University of Chicago Press.

Pudja, Gde
1963 Sosiologi Hindu Dharma. Djakarta: Jajasan Pembangunan Pura Pita Maha.

Punyatmadja, I. B. Oka
1970 Pancha Cradha. Den Pasar: Parisada Hindu Dharma Pusat.

Richards, J. F., et al.
1976 Symposium: The Contributions of Louis Dumont. Journal of Asian Studies 35(4):579–650.

Robson, S. O.
1972 The Kawi Classics in Bali. Bijdragen tot de Land-, Taal- en Volkenkunde 128(2–3):307–329.

Sahlins, Marshall
1976 Culture and Practical Reason. Chicago: University of Chicago Press.

Schlegel, Frederick von
1869 The Aesthetic and Miscellaneous Works. E. J. Millington, trans. London: Henry G. Bohn.
Schneider, David M.
1976 The Meaning of Incest. Journal of the Polynesian Society 85(2):149–169.
Singer, Milton
1972 When a Great Tradition Modernizes: An Anthropological Approach to Indian Civilization. New York: Praeger.
Soebadio, Haryati, ed. and trans.
1971 Jnanasiddhanta. Bibliotheca Indonesica. The Hague: Martinus Nijhoff.
Sweeney, F. I. Amin
1972 The Ramayana and the Malay Shadow-Play. Kuala Lumpur: Penerbit Universiti Kebangsaan Malaysia.
Tambiah, Stanley J.
1970 Buddhism and the Spirit Cults of Northeast Thailand. Cambridge: Cambridge University Press.
Upadeca
1968 Upadeca: tentang Ajaran-ajaran Agama Hindu. Den Pasar: Parisada Hindu Dharma.
Weber, Max
1958 The Religion of India. H. Gerth and D. Martindale, trans. New York: Free Press.
Whorf, Benjamin
1964 A Linguistic Consideration of Thinking in Primitive Communities. *In* Language in Culture and Society. Dell Hymes, ed. New York: Harper and Row.

·9·

Irony in Tibetan Notions of the Good Life

David Lichter
Lawrence Epstein

Our subjects are happiness, unhappiness, and their causes in Tibetan Buddhism. While consideration of karma is central to any approach to these subjects, it is neither exhaustive nor even the most fundamental consideration. Our contention is that in all Tibetan Buddhist thought and sentiment about ethical causation, unhappiness is the touchstone. Since the Buddha himself revealed this as the First Noble Truth in founding Buddhism, it may seem an unremarkable observation to make at this late date. Yet in anthropological studies unhappiness tends to be dismissed as an academic Buddhist's concern which has little concrete importance in Buddhist village life. Considering how anthropologists like to approach things, it is no surprise that they have concentrated on ameliorative ritual and merit-making without investigating ethnographically those concepts of the good life and happiness which allegedly motivate such activities. As a practical matter, Buddhist societies often seem to leave the niceties of doctrine to specialists and to go about their normal business secure in the belief that they are Buddhist anyway. The "real" Buddhism, then, is a matter of institutions and hallowed eccentrics. To learn the local orthodoxy, one consults monastics and recluses, because lay people's

This essay is based on data collected in Tsum in northern Nepal (Lichter) and from Tibetan refugees in India (Epstein). Previous versions were presented as a paper at the annual meetings of the American Anthropological Association, Houston, 1977, and the Association for Asian Studies, New York, 1977.

We gratefully acknowledge the assistance and suggestions of our friends and colleagues, too many to name here individually, who patiently listened to and commented upon various drafts.

Buddhist concerns are circumscribed by worldly goals. Their pious hopes revolve around ideas of heaven and improved worldly status. Anthropological suspicions are even further aroused when these purported Buddhists are discovered placating an abundant pantheon of gods and demons and generally attempting to cheat their karma in every way possible.

Many Tibetans would accept this cartoon as a reasonable picture of the Tibetan Buddhist scene. The vocabulary accommodates the distinction between the laity's Buddhism and the clergy's — *'jigs-rten-pa'i chos* and *chos-pa'i chos*, respectively. The distinction hinges on the clergy's supposed soteriological interests as opposed to the laity's occupation with more mundane goals, which include those attainable in the short term by karmic striving. In opposition to this-worldly ends, even those of the very next world take on a devout color, and the whole emphasis of religious education is placed on the importance of next-worldly concerns as an improvement over this-worldly ones. Transcendent goals such as liberation are thought to be too distant to understand, much less to aim at, even for most of the clergy. A *geshe*[1] living in the community of Tsum in northern Nepal once told Lichter that for the monks and nuns there even simple philosophy would be too abstruse, and aside from ritual the best they might do would be to learn ethics: by which he meant karma and how to tell virtue (*dge-ba*) from sin (*sdig-pa*). This *geshe* was the man principally in charge of the education of the whole community of monks in Tsum.

Together with this scholar's insistence that karmic ethics is the proper philosophy for common folk is the commonly held and very pious assertion that karma is the most general overarching system of ethical causation. One may often hear preaching on this point and observe the audience's pious amens. This assent often has a peculiar manner to it, a tone of awe or an intimation of being in the presence of a great mystery. Why should this be a mystery rather than the most obvious of platitudes? Evidently this is far from ordinary or straightforward thinking for people who, like Tibetans, customarily populate their worlds with all manner of ethically unaccountable supernaturals. One result of our ethnographic investigations is the finding that these supernaturals are involved in their own proper system of causation. This system gives supernaturalism a Buddhist form by making its

[1]The degree and title of *geshe* (*dge-bshes*) is awarded to clergy who have completed higher monastic studies and passed an oral examination in logic.

categories neatly analogous to karmic categories, and this systematic analogy is much more important in the wide cultural scene than the academic response to it. The latter is an attempt to incorporate it directly into a subservient role in the accepted hierarchy of ethical cosmography.[2] Where Tibetan Buddhist academics, and often Western academics as well, see a failure to take a Buddhist approach to things, we see a Buddhist approach of an unanticipated sort. Anthropologists often seem to be most vexed by their difficulty in reconciling supernaturalism with karma. While this may be a problem in the Tibetan case also, we find it already solved for us by the Tibetans. The Tibetan laity's commitment to Buddhism goes deeper than this reconciliation, however.

We find the core of Tibetan analogical Buddhism in the acceptance of the First Noble Truth, that all is suffering. In accepting the doctrine of karma, Tibetans accept both an idea of human happiness and certain means of striving for it. Yet they believe that the goods of the world are impermanent, that the impermanence of happiness is not only its limit but its negation, and that it is their need for the world that causes their unhappiness. We can support this contention empirically, by fine study of the concept of happiness and its pitfalls. We are not the first investigators to establish assent to the Four Noble Truths as a criterion of sorts for full-fledged Buddhist credentials. The question we wish to emphasize is this: how can one observe, empirically, acceptance of the Four Noble Truths in lay Buddhist culture? In *Buddhism and Society*, Spiro dealt with people who actually expressed these tenets to him, and yet he concluded that they in fact reject them (1976:36–38, and especially 73–76). We deal with people who might not even know much less understand the tenets, and yet we conclude that they accept them. Spiro based his conclusion on the observation that the people were actually interested in promoting their own worldly happiness in every way possible. We find this also, but then no Buddhist seems to suggest that this is out of order. The observation that lay people lead normal lives is sufficient evidence only for the conclusion that they are lay people. Even monastics live in the world and under its conditions, so of course they try to make the best of it. Lay people express themselves about the world in many ways which we ignore at the risk of serious distortion and oversimplification of

[2] Tibetan scholarship has produced a great number of schemes attempting to organize a pantheon. For a general overview, see Nebesky-Wojkowitz 1975.

their views. We hold that Tibetans reflect on their happiness from a certain ironic distance, which we detect by observing the many ways in which they say that suffering arises from aspects or causes of happiness itself. Our data derive mainly from the subtleties and nuances of the Tibetan world view, which we find in texts, rituals, conversations, quarrels, complaints, jokes, and so on. We find justification for our position in the things people do by choice rather than by necessity.

First, we will discuss happiness and unhappiness. To establish a sort of ideal Tibetan type of unhappiness, we cite certain classic texts. The notions of happiness we contrast with those that are ethnographically derived. Once having established these goals of action, we outline the meaning of karma by dealing with its operational categories, such as sin, virtue, and so forth. We intend to establish the commonplaces about karma which any Tibetan could recognize and accept. From karma we proceed to supernaturalism, establish it as a causal system in its own right, and discuss its relationships with karma. In examining the effects of supernatural causation and karma on happiness, we are led to consider a third Tibetan concept of causation called *la-yogs*. In explaining *la-yogs*, we bring our argument full circle to direct confrontation with the idea of striving for happiness. There we find the most compelling evidence for our conclusion that these Tibetans have taken the Four Noble Truths to heart after all.

Happiness and Unhappiness

Of the Buddha's Four Noble Truths, the first is *sdug-bsngal* (Sanskrit *duḥkha*), usually glossed in English as misery or suffering.[3] Buddhist texts recognize three "root" sufferings: the Suffering of Suffering, the Suffering of Change, and Conditioned Suffering.[4]

The Suffering of Suffering designates the reiterative nature of suffering; your house burns down just after thieves have rustled your cattle, or your father dies just after your mother has died.

[3] As Gombrich observes (1971:69), these glosses hardly do justice to the term in its most general or technical meanings.

[4] Respectively, *sdug-bsngal-gyi sdug-bsngal* (*duḥkha-duḥkhatā*), *'gyur-ba'i sdug-bsngal* (*vipariṇāma -d.*), and *'du-byed-kyi sdug-bsngal* (*saṁskāra-d.*). An excellent exposition of suffering is given in Yon-tan-rgya-mtsho 1969:108ff. and 137ff. The three root sufferings (*rtsa-ba'i sdug-bsngal*) are, of course, based on the Buddha's first sermon, along with the eight branch sufferings (*sdug-bsngal yan-lag brgyad*).

Dpal-sprul Rinpoche,[5] one of Tibet's greatest modern exegetes, writes the following to show the Suffering of Change:

No sooner do you find some happiness than you are miserable. Having eaten food that is beneficial to the body, you feel satisfied and full. But as you are feeling contented, you get a cramp in your stomach and suddenly you suffer a terrible case of indigestion. Here you are enjoying life, when all of a sudden your enemies rustle your cattle, a fire burns your house to the ground, you catch a terrible disease, you hear scandalous talk about you everywhere, and such things cause you suffering.

Generally speaking, the state of *saṁsāra* appears as if it were comfortable, happy and pleasant. But lacking even a hair's worth of permanence and solidity, in the final outcome *saṁsāra* does not transcend pure suffering, and so it produces despair. (Dpal-sprul 1971:116)

Conditioned Suffering is more abstract than these commonplace intuitive versions of suffering. We have been talking about things which anyone would recognize as suffering, but Buddhism involves the idea that even what seems to be happiness is unhappiness. Fundamentally, this is the Buddhist principle that everything which is, is impermanent, and impermanence is suffering. It is as though the commonplace observation that all things pass were elevated to the status of an a priori principle. To communicate the message that the very stuff of our happiness is unhappiness, Dpal-sprul Rinpoche provides us with the passage that follows.

Tea is a plant sown in China. When the seeds are planted and the leaves are cut, the insects that are killed are beyond counting. When bearers come carrying the tea down from Dartsendo, each man carries a load of sixty-two sections. Since they carry it by supporting the whole load with tumplines around their heads, the skin on their foreheads is worn away, and one can see the grey of the bone. Yet still they carry. When they reach Dotok, they load the tea on *mdzo*, yaks, mules and so on. When they travel on, all those animals are made to undergo the inconceivable sufferings of being made to serve with saddle sores on their backs and cinch sores from the braided ropes underneath. Also, when the tea is traded, it is sold only by deception and barter which take into account neither honesty nor modesty.

[5] Dpal-sprul O-rgyan-'jigs-med-chos-kyi-dbang-po (b. 1808) was a leading exponent of the Ris-med (Universalist) Movement (see Smith 1970). (The word Rinpoche is a title.) All the quotations below are taken from his brilliant masterpiece, the (*Rdzogs pa chen po klong chen snying thig gi sngon 'gro khrid yig*) *Kun bzang bla ma'i zhal lung* (Dpal-sprul 1971). In our opinion, and in the opinion of many Tibetan and Western scholars, this work is the finest, and certainly the most delightful, modern introduction to Tibetan Buddhism. See also Smith 1969:13–15. Probably, the best concise technical description of these subjects may be found in Kong-sprul's encyclopaedia, the *Shes bya kun khyab*, 1970:129ff.

The tea is traded for merchandise, usually for things like sheeps' wool and lambskins. In the summertime, the wool consists of an uncountable quantity of single strands of hair and bugs such as sheep lice and other little things. Usually when the wool is shorn with a knife, their heads are cut off or they are cut in two. The ones inside the wool come out and are killed. The ones that do not die in this way get twisted up in the wool and suffer a bad death by strangulation. Regarding lambskins, as soon as a lamb is born, it has all its senses. It can feel pleasure and pain, and it looks after itself. At the beginning of its life, a time when it is happiest, it is killed straightway. Though it be but an ignorant animal, it rejoices in being alive, and it experiences the suffering of being killed. If one also were to regard the suffering of the ewe whose offspring has been killed, it should be seen as that of a mother whose only son has died. (Dpal-sprul 1971:117–118)

Although we do not intend to lean on the distinctions between types of unhappiness, we hope the reader will note this aspect of it: even what we enjoy is unhappiness, because it passes away and because in the final analysis it is made of impermanence, which is to say unhappiness. Unhappiness is not just something specific—it is everything.

Even though the things we enjoy may be unhappiness, nevertheless we enjoy them. Tibetans not only enjoy life, they have definite ideas about what happiness is. A human life is thought of as the greatest reward available, more desirable than heaven. Even enlightenment is commonly thought to result in reincarnation as a lama rather than in extinction. In terms of ordinary ambitions, Tibetans seem to concern themselves with avoiding present suffering, hell, and rebirth as an animal rather than with attaining heaven, and they identify human rebirth as the ideal reward more or less by a process of elimination. All of this places a great burden of significance on any ideas of human happiness which we may discover. These ideas of the good life, while clear and affirmative enough, also carry nuances which can get us closer to a Tibetan understanding of the Four Noble Truths.

The general term for pleasure, enjoyment, and happiness is *skyid-po*. Abstractly defined, it is merely the negation of *sdug-bsngal*, or unhappiness: "If you have no great unhappiness, then you are happy," as one Tsumba (a person from Tsum) put it. Tibetans do not show inordinate ambition for happiness, whatever that might be. If they say what it is, they recite a modest list of requirements: to have enough to wear and eat without having to beg, borrow, hustle, or worry all the time; not to have ill health; and to be able to sit with friends, eating and talking together.

About health as a good, there is little to discuss. Obviously, people are concerned about their health. This may be especially true in a place like Tsum, where medical care is unobtainable and every incident of serious injury or illness involves direct confrontation with the possibility of really drastic consequences. Even so, the refugees in India, who are fairly secure with competent clinics close by, complain frequently about risks to their health. Therefore, it seems to be the enjoyment of good health rather than the security of good medicine which Tibetans value.

The way wealth is regarded as a good is remarkable mainly because of its restraint and ethical qualifications. First, the emphasis is on sufficiency rather than superabundance. Second, the way the stuff is gotten turns out to be important. Extreme, hectic busyness is not thought to be a good thing, no matter how productive, because it distracts from more important occupations. Plain, exhausting toil that makes you stiff and sore is disliked on other grounds, just because it is tiresome and painful. Yet Tibetans have their version of a Puritan ethic, which insists that real gratification can only be got from earnest effort, and undeserved gains can never be as good. Greed is a sin, and extraordinary casuistry is to be enjoyed in showing how a fair profit can be turned in dubiously sharp dealings. Stinginess is also a serious fault, magnanimity being both socially popular and morally rewarding. "Even though you have uncountable wealth, you have no power to take it with you," observes Dpal-sprul Rinpoche (1971:127), in chorus with many other Tibetans.

Among the goods which Tibetans reckon as happiness, love and friendship stand out as a special blessing (no distinction is made between them). You cannot take your wealth with you when you die, or your body, but the best of lifelong friends can go to hell together. This touching privilege is reserved strictly for steadfastly faithful friends and withheld even from spouses and the closest kin. Friendship is more a process than a station, progressing encounter by encounter and transaction by transaction, becoming more useful, binding, enjoyable, and sentimentally laden from first acquaintance to the ends of the friends' lives.

When Tibetans talk about the goodness of friendship, in addition to emphasizing the relationship's utility they point out the pleasures of conversation and commensality. These are the basics that make human life as special as it is, preferable not only to that of the beasts but to that of the gods as well. Animals are miserable, mainly because of their dumbness.[6] In the case of domestic beasts they can neither complain nor be reasoned with, and consequently they are ruled by force. The Tibetan attitude toward animals—whether sympathy, fear, or contempt—is based on the idea that dumb creatures have no choice about what they do. They do not control their own lives, nor do they enjoy the human opportunity for self-improvement. Gods also lack this opportunity because they have all they require to sustain themselves in high style without effort or action. Hence they do not make the moral decisions which earn merit for liberation. They dwell in luxury for enormously long times, surrounded by sweet smells, quaffing nectar and supping on ambrosia. They are peculiarly lacking in sexual organs (see, e.g., Chandra 1969:105). Being self-contained and automatically replete with good things, gods are sterile and inert. As they are removed from moral action, they are removed from the social intercourse that makes human life dear. Finally, having exhausted the store of merit which earned them heaven in the first place, they see their auras grow dim, they smell their own sweat, and they experience the horrid anticipation of their own imminent fall. The transitory bliss of gods stands alongside the wretchedness of animals as an object lesson to humans concerning the value of their own happiness.

On ethnographic grounds, we have identified health, wealth, and love as the requisites of human happiness. Significantly, Dpal-sprul Rinpoche, writing in the nineteenth century, chose to emphasize these same topics in illuminating his own lecture on the meaning of unhappiness. Thereby he demonstrates to us the persistent salience of these desiderata, while remonstrating with his Tibetan audience about their evanescence. In doing so, he quotes three poems from the twelfth section of the *Mgur 'bum* by Mi-la-ras-pa, Tibet's poet-saint of the eleventh century (Dpal-sprul 1971:123–124; 129; 132–133). In the first poem, Mi-la presents the infirmities of old age in the pitiable guise of a wrinkled crone—haggard, gaunt, senile, and debilitated, who has no choice but to cope with a life that is all but over. The other poems dispose of wealth and love.

On Wealth

First, you enjoy your wealth and others wish to be like you;
But however much you have, you never know contentment.

[6] The word for dumbness (*lkug-pa* or *glen-pa* in some dialects) has the same connotation as in English: mute and stupid.

Next, you are bound by the knot of avarice;
Being unable to give away wealth for virtue's sake
Is a signal to enemies and ghosts,
And others enjoy what you have accumulated.
Finally, your wealth becomes a murderous devil;
Looking after your enemies' wealth pains your mind.
I have given up the deceits of the world;
I do not wish the cheating of devils.

On Love

First, your son is an attractive *devaputra*;
Your loving mind cannot bear but to do everything for him.
Second, he is a persistent collector of debts;
Though you give him everything, he is never pleased.
He installs another man's daughter at home,
And expels his kindly parents.
The father calls, but he does not answer.
The mother calls, but he never heeds her.
Finally, he is ruined, because he believes
The estranged neighbors' lies.
The enemy you have borne pains your mind.
I have given up the hindering fetters of *saṁsāra*;
I do not desire worldly progeny.

First, your daughter is a smiling divine child,
With great power to take what wealth and profit you have.
Second, she is an endless series of debts for you;
She openly makes off with her father's things,
And secretly pilfers from her mother.
She never appreciates the things that are given her,
And it makes her kind parents heartsick,
Finally, she is a red-faced ogress;
If she is good, she brings others joy,
If she is bad, she is your own collection of calamity.
The ogress that brings ruin pains your mind.
I have given up the impure world;
I do not desire daughters, the foundation of decay.

First, you are glad to meet your friends and smile when you see them;
Everyone's speech is full of "Please come here" and "Please sit here."
Second, you exchange food and drink with them;
In return for giving them something, they give something back to you.
Finally, they are the ones with whom you jealously argue;
The bones of contention with your false friends pain your mind.
I have given up good-time eating companions;
I do not wish for worldly kin.

Karma

It is very difficult to discuss happiness and unhappiness with Tibetans without discussing karma. Even Dpal-sprul Rinpoche, whom we quoted on unhappiness, used that discussion to introduce the subject of karma. Ethnographically, our discussion of beasts and gods is gleaned from Tibetans' comments on merit, sin, and rebirth. Happiness after all is the goal of virtue, and for Tibetans the golden rule is something like a natural law. Karma produces happiness from good actions and unhappiness from bad ones.

Tibetans usually call karma *las*, *las-'bras*, or *rgyu-'bras*. *Las* means work or action and glosses Sanskrit karma. The other two are short for *las rgyu-'bras*, signifying the causes and effects (literally "fruits") of actions. In colloquial usage, any difference between these terms for karma is strictly a matter of idiom or style.

It is essential to realize that for rank-and-file Tibetans karma is not so much an abstract theory pursued to logical extremes as it is a certain sort of hypothetical story with a moral. The story of karma is that if we do good things now, then later good things will happen to us. If we do bad things now, then later bad things will happen to us. For instance, a man who is violent and dangerous in his prime may be a palsied wretch in his old age. Like the Tsumba who recalled this example, everyone can point to cases in which such contingencies are to be observed. If the consequence is not apparent in this life, as when the wicked prosper, it is sure to follow in the next. One may spin out the whole congeries of beliefs in the migrations of the soul, heaven and hell, and so on, from this simple premise.

Actions which are karmically significant can be divided into two types: *dge-ba*, "virtue," and *sdig-pa*, "sin." Those which lead to happiness for the actor are *dge-ba* and those that lead to unhappiness are *sdig-pa*. As far as the contents of the categories are concerned, the sins most prominently mentioned are killing, stealing, and lying. These are the most practically important of the ten classical vices (*mi-dge-ba bcu*) common to all Buddhist traditions. More generally, it is sinful to cause suffering to other beings. Any catalog of virtues includes abstinence from sin, but also such actions as counting beads, circumambulation of holy sites, prostrations, spinning prayer wheels, erecting prayer flags, obtaining blessings, muttering prayers and sacred formulae, sponsoring ceremonies, dispensing charity and alms, and venerating Buddha, Dharma, and Saṅgha.

The difference between these lists, one so concise and practical and the other so full of formalities, can be understood if one realizes how Tibetans believe that the very conditions of existence require innumerable unavoidable sins. Dpal-sprul Rinpoche's text on tea, quoted above, is a good example. In the same section of text, one finds the following:

> We may think that we have never committed the sin of killing, but there is no one who has not committed many times the sin of killing small living things underfoot. Especially in the case of monks and lamas, when they go to the homes of their patrons, the latter kill animals and give the clergy flesh and blood. . . . Since both are desirous of tasting flesh and blood . . . both monk and patron get the sin of killing without distinction.
>
> . . . Herds of cattle, when they go to summer pastures, crush bugs and vermin with their hooves. . . . These sins come to the owner.
>
> When maidens are married . . . as when they are endowered, sent to their husbands or fetched home, countless sheep are slaughtered. Afterwards, the multitudes of people that come to the new couple's home are fed with at least one sheep that is slaughtered for the occasion. When friends and relatives are invited, we believe that they prefer no other kind of food than meat, and they consume it like cannibal-demons, [their mouths stuffed so full] they cannot move their jaws. Having killed some sheep, one prepares the ribs and intestines [for sausage]—whichever cut is best. Having invited the red-faced ogres to sit, they take up their small knives and suck away at the strands of meat. The next day they load up carcasses of meat, like hunters heading home from the kill. . . . We humans are like cannibal-demons, spending all our time in the act of killing. . . . Having killed the female yak, which, having nurtured us with milk that we have gratefully drunk, is like our parents, we now think of using its flesh and blood. Nay, we are even worse than cannibal-demons. (Dpal-sprul 1971:152–154 passim)

The same argument in more restrained form is often offered by ordinary villagers, who are especially impressed with the destruction of life in cultivating the soil, the suffering of domestic animals at their owners' hands, and the sins of the trading arena. These minor or unavoidable sins are compensated for by means of ostensible and routine virtues, which account for the lopsidedness of the list of virtues.

In addition to being unavoidable, many sins are unintentional. There is a gradation of sins, unintentional ones being relatively light. Moreover, Tibetans believe a sin enjoyed is greater than a sin regretted. Even so, ordinarily a sin is a sin regardless of how much one regrets it or how little one intends to commit it. Only Buddhas have omniscience and perfect temper, and karma operates for everyone else.

As to how or when actions will bear fruits, one lives in ignorance. A popular parable is that of the shadow. When a man walks along, he can see his shadow. When a bird flies high, it casts a shadow that cannot be seen, but when it descends its shadow appears on the ground below and looms ever larger.[7] Karma is like the bird's shadow, always there but not always apparent. In the same vein, Dpal-sprul Rinpoche cites the ironic tale of the Buddhist saint, Kaṭyāna.

> Once Saint Kaṭyāna went begging alms and saw a householder, holding a boy in his lap, eat a tasty-looking fish and throw a stone at a bitch who was gnawing at the fish bones. Having clairvoyance, Kaṭyāna saw the fish was a rebirth of the man's father. The bitch was his mother's rebirth, and an enemy whom he had killed in a former life, and who now wished revenge, had been reborn as his son. Kaṭyāna said, "He eats his father's flesh and throws stones at his mother. In his lap he holds an enemy that will kill him. The wife gnaws at the husband's bones. I feel like laughing at the 'realities' of life." (Dpal-sprul 1971:69)

Tibetans seem to speculate more about karmic prospects than they do about retrospects. These they imagine in terms of the Wheel of Life (*srid-pa'i 'khor-lo*). This familiar symbol unites in a single image the realms of rebirth, surrounded by the twelve scenes depicting the causal nexus of dependent origination (*rten-'brel bcu-gnyis*), all around a hub depicting the three cardinal modes of sin. These three are in the forms of animals—a cock for lust, a pig for ignorance, and a snake for anger—each with its tail in the next one's mouth. No one seems to pay much attention to the causal nexus. The upper semicircle of the realms of being consists of attractive representations of good rebirths (*bde-'gro* or *mtho-ris*), and the lower of repulsive representations of bad ones (*ngan-song*). Of the realms, those which seem to dominate the imaginations of Tibetans are heaven and human life as good rebirths, hell and animal life as bad ones. We have already discussed the prevailing views of human, heavenly, and animal existences. Hell is what really impresses people. In the picture we view the gory and

[7] Yon-tan-rgya-mtsho 1969:63. The metaphor also turns up in many popular didactic texts (*dpe-chos*); see, e.g., Lce Sgom-pa 1975: 106.

ingenious tortures of hot and cold hells, where fiendish climates are improved upon by the industry of ghastly demons. They pierce, hew, hack, chop, cleave, disembowel, excoriate, squash, burn, freeze, and boil the hapless sinners. Many people seem to regard hell as an inevitable way station en route to any other rebirth, perhaps because (as in the picture) the Dharmarāja, lord of the dead, holds court there. Before the fearsome judge, a demon holds the scales on which are weighed the sins and virtues of each new arrival. These are envisaged as a pile of white stones for virtues and another of black stones for sins, which are in charge of the god who sits on each person's right shoulder and the demon on the left. These are the advocates who debate each person's merits, recounting each deed.

Beyond this story, exactly how karma carries on from action to fruit of action is not an interesting question to most Tibetans. In large part, act and consequence are referred to in one breath: either *dge-ba* or *sdig-pa* may refer as well to a deed, to its worth or merit, or to its consequence. *Dge-ba* may be contrasted with *bsod-nams* or *bsod-bde*, which would be somehow the credit accrued for good actions. It may also be contrasted with *phan-yon*, which would be the reward or payoff for good actions. Yet all may be synonymous, being freely interchangeable in use and each defining the other. It is the same way when Tsumbas will refer to a whole field of wheat as *rtsam-pa*; or call the grain *rtsam-pa* as distinct from the rest of the plant; or distinguish between the edible part of the grain as *rtsam-pa* and the hull, which is not *rtsam-pa*; or finally and most properly distinguish the unground grain from *rtsam-pa*, which is flour. The essence of karma is the whole causal contingency, not any particular part of it.

Tibetan Buddhism teaches that any given moral act (*las*) is a cause (*rgyu*) of multiple results (*'bras*). Some, mainly scholastics, maintain that all events are, in the strictest sense, karmically determined; "every color of the peacock's tail is determined by its own karma," as one *geshe* put it. Another monk, watching a child trip over a rock and fall down, reflected that there was an example of her karma. Somehow she had earned her fall; therefore the rock tripped her. Others, while perhaps ready to assent to such statements, seem to us to be less emotionally committed to so sweeping a perspective. This has a basis in doctrine; where the exigencies, the little joys and sorrows, of simply living leave off and where karma begins is open to interpretation.

Rgyu is a sort of necessary substantive cause. In an academic metaphor, when a pot is shaped the clay is its *rgyu*. Colloquially, *rgyu* is material wealth or warp in weaving. *Rgyu-ba*, the verb form, means to string together like beads or to wander circuitously. One can imagine a unified meaning in all this, which moreover relates to karma. A household's wealth is its stuff, that without which there is no household. A fabric's warp is that which holds it together. Thread holds beads as a unified object, and the wanderer, whether an itinerant monk or a stream of water, links separate places in a single course. In karma, actions do this by providing the identity of each stream of cause and effect, which within a lifetime is an individual and across lifetimes allows people to identify with the supposed fates of their souls in other existences.

People have the idea that karma is essentially just, or that actions produce appropriate results. For instance, *smyung-gnas* is a ritual observance of fasting, silence, and abstinence in general, the object of which is the transference of merit. By transferring merit to the sinful, participants in *smyung-gnas* hope for specific results appropriate to their vows: a Tathāgata's silver tongue in exchange for the vow of silence, and so on (see Epstein 1977, pp. 170 ff.). In Tsum, one young man explained *smyung-gnas* as merit for the *yi-dwags* (*pretas*). *Yi-dwags* are occupants of one of the unfortunate realms of rebirth, who because of an excess of appetite are condemned to eons of tantalization. In iconography, they appear as huge-bellied, haggard wretches with long reedy necks too small for food to traverse. Any food they touch turns to ashes, and any water they drink bursts into flame. Oddly enough, this Tsumba happened not to know what *yi-dwags* were, but thought that in *smyung-gnas* the silence was insurance against rebirth as dumb animals and the fasting was insurance against rebirth as flies, which instead of eating live on odors.

In hell, it is said, the essential justice of karma is even more readily appreciated, and punishment fits the crime with an unmistakable elegance.

> In the midst of heaps of crackling, glowing iron, upon a flaming iron floor, innumerable people were being burnt. Each person had a tongue like a vast plain. One hundred yokes of iron elephants plowed their tongues... with flaming iron ritual daggers. They were cut and burnt wherever the flaming iron plows dug in.... The Dharmarāja said, "When they were in the human realm, they blasphemed against the clergy, bragged about themselves and abused others. They caused calumny against teachers and said the Holy

Dharma and the law of karma were untrue. . . . This is the punishment for harming others through speech."[8]

There are innumerable such visions, beliefs, legends, and parables about reaping as you sow. This aspect of the fruits of action is called *rnam-smin*, or the full ripening of an act according to its nature. This organic turn of thought, the ripening of fruit, is very characteristic of Tibetans' view of karma and the sort of determinism it involves. A constant theme of discussion is that tall oaks from little acorns grow, or rather *aśvattha* trees a league across from mustard-sized seeds.[9] The moral of such an aphorism might be that great consequences can arise from modest deeds (*las che 'phel-ba*), but still Tibetans are canny enough to realize that simply planting a seed is insufficient to guarantee the fruit. The whole large and complicated plant may be potential in the seed, but it needs rain, sun, and many special conditions in order to grow and bear just such a fruit. This organic metaphor for causation is less conducive than our mechanistic version to imagining that (given karma) every little collision in a person's trajectory through life must be well arranged long in advance. They think that each event of a person's life has its whole complex history and that any little thing could have changed it. Both in prospect and retrospect, such considerations are important.

First, there is the notorious human inability to see the future. Complacency regarding one's prospects is never in order, because however well things may be going at the moment, karma is inscrutable and may have all sorts of horrible surprises secretly in reserve. Interpreting the weighing of deeds at hell's portals purely mechanically, one might suppose that one heap of stones would simply cancel the other, leaving a balance of strictly good or bad karma to be worked out. This is not the case. Instead, good deeds might outweigh bad ones sufficiently to produce a human rebirth, but the bad ones would remain to be worked out in human suffering, in a later sojourn in hell, or whatever.

One must also recall that acts are the stuff of which their results are

[8] Epstein, MS. This quotation is from the biography of a *'das-log* (O-rgyan-rdo-rje 1975:213–214), a person who supposedly journeys to hell, where he witnesses such goings-on.

[9] The *aśvattha* (*Ficus religiosa*) is, like the flying bird, a popular metaphor for an aspect of karma. See, e.g., Lce Sgom-pa 1975:110.

made, as though the acts were clay and the results a pot. But the clay itself could never turn into a pot, and the potter's hands and tools are necessary causes of the pot, just as irrigation and fertilization are necessary causes of the fruit. Again, whether or not these cooperating causes are accepted as part of karma is a matter of opinion. Academically, as we have pointed out before, they are most emphatically included. Nevertheless, the population of Tibetans is far from exhausted by those who espouse such a view. There was, for instance, the man who said that when we are attacked by witches, that is not our karma, because witches attack just for the hell of it. It is easy for these people to suppose that events could occur in a person's life which were not purely the results of their own deeds in this or any other existence. We have mentioned that karma can be recognized as a particular sort of story. The story of karma is not the only sort of story, however. Most notably, there are stories in which bad things happen to people who did not sin to cause them. In other words, the woes of the world are not to be explained entirely by fatalistically invoking karma.

Supernaturalism

The Tibetan word for cooperating causes such as we have been discussing is *rkyen*, which glosses Sanskrit *pratyāya*. If we were to select an Aristotelian gloss for *rkyen*, we would call it the "efficient cause." Jäschke observes that "by a mistake of [Csoma de Körös], the totally erroneous sense of 'effect, consequence' has become current among philologists" (1958:17–18). Yet Jäschke, quite correctly, offers as his third definition of *rkyen*, "misfortune, ill luck, calamity"; these would appear at first blush to be effects of a sort. Ethnographically, we can see how intelligibly the idea of *rkyen* as unfortunate circumstance (or effect) is related to the general idea of *rkyen* as efficient or cooperating cause.

In one breath, Tibetans will assert that almost any bad thing that can happen to a person is *rkyen*. In the next, they will restrict *rkyen* to supernatural causation (*gnod-pa*). One of the most striking aspects of their treatment is that they firmly exclude all happy circumstances (*mthun-rkyen*) from *rkyen*, although formally there is no reason why they should. This is also a feature of their usage of *las-'bras*, when for instance they say that if one is very good karma will not circle (*'khor-ba*), to mean that one will not have to go to hell and so on. What is the basic story of *rkyen*? One is going along happily in good health and prosperity when all of a sudden one gets sick, one's cattle die, and so on. This, then, one says is *rkyen*.

Academic exegesis of such a story always revolves around the roles of *rgyu* and *rkyen* in the stream of ethical causation—the point being that the immediate circumstances of an accident are only the cooperating causes giving shape to events materially formed by the victim's own previous actions (*rgyu*). A *geshe* stated:

> People [laymen] do not realize that [*rkyen*] is a function of karma, and they attribute to it an independent existence, generally calling it harm by spirits [*gdon*]. However, this really means that both the demon and the human who is affected had some relationship in a past existence, and this now becomes manifest. (Epstein 1977, p. 88)

We have already mentioned that explanations of this sort are readily forthcoming to reconcile karma and supernaturalism by co-opting the gods and demons to be the tools of karma, so to speak. But the very abundance of such arguments testifies to the ubiquity of supernatural causation in the Tibetan world view. Tipped off by the distinctiveness of the stories told to define *rkyen* versus karma, we may explore the question whether *rkyen* (as a *distinct* story) involves the actor's deeds as causes (*rgyu*) differently than in karma.

The whole point of karma is that your acts (or those of some previous you) have consequences, if not for you, then for some later you. For karma to make sense at all, it is necessary to view this causal process as extending across lifetimes while maintaining its individuality within each lifetime. With *rkyen* the situation is altogether otherwise. While you may be the cause of your own misfortune, by offending some god or demon, the prospect of this misfortune is limited entirely to this lifetime. Within a lifetime, *rkyen* that you cause may not directly affect you yourself as victim at all, but may instead involve another member of your household or other people by links with whom your (this-) worldly interests are established. For instance, if a man off on a business trip commits adultery, where karma is concerned this is a sin and will have evil consequences for the man himself or one of his later rebirths. Where *rkyen* is concerned, whether or not this adultery is a sin, the adulterer's household god will not like it. As a result, some *other* person at home (say, a daughter) may get sick, the cattle at home may die, and so on. If one were to use the stock explanation of how supernatural causation is really a function of karma, at this point one would have to say that the daughter's supernaturally caused illness was a result of *her* own sins. The stock explanation accounts well for the event, but *not* for the story.

Investigation of such stories produces a new system of causal concepts quite apart from the karmic ones. As we have pointed out, this system is systematically analogous to the karmic one. Where *bsod-nams* is the stored-up karmic merit of a soul's career, *rlung-rta* is the state of a person's worldly luck. Where *bsod-nams* is increased by *dge-ba*, *rlung-rta* is raised by *sku-rim*. Where karma involves the vicissitudes of the soul or consciousness (*rnam-shes*), *rkyen* involves the status of the *bla*, a sort of personal life force. Where *chos-pa'i chos* is supposedly aimed at soteriological goals, *'jigs-rten-pa'i chos* is a matter of averting earthly disasters. Where faith in and prayer to an abstract sort of god (*dkon-mchog*) has effect in the karmic system, in *rkyen* all manner of spooks, demons, and chthonic monsters have a hand.

Rlung-rta is said to be either high or low, unlike *bsod-nams*, which can accumulate (*bsags*) or be exhausted (*skam-pa*, literally "dry up"). This idiom for *rlung-rta* is no doubt related to the physical forms the thing takes, such as small flags or scraps of paper imprinted with prayers and mystical formulae set to fly high above the settlements or cast upon the mountain breezes in hopes that they will be carried as high as possible—thereby elevating one's luck. Originally an astrological concept (see Schlagintweit 1968:253–256; Waddell 1967:408ff.; Epstein 1975), *rlung-rta* can be forecast year by year and can undergo cyclic alterations, unlike *bsod-nams*, which is linear and cumulative. Like *bsod-nams*, it summarizes all the events and prospects of a particular career at a particular time. Very often the difference between *bsod-nams* and *rlung-rta* can be and is ignored, but at other times it can be quite important. As usual, such occasions generally involve some serious misfortune, such as death. When a person dies, the question arises whether it was a result of low *rlung-rta* or simply a timely function of the deceased person's karma. If the former, then the survivors are in jeopardy because causes are afoot that can affect them as well as the deceased. If divination reveals that the victim's karma had simply been used up, then that is a matter of each person's own soul, and normal funerary observances are equal to the situation.

A *rlung-rta* ceremony, in which prints of the "wind-horse" are made and solemnly raised on poles or cast upon the winds, is an example of a *sku-rim*. In a general way, all *sku-rim* are ceremonies aimed at improving the sponsor's luck by propitiation of dangerous supernaturals, but most are used in crisis intervention and are tailored to the particular type of agent divined to be causing the trouble (see Ortner 1978:179, nn. 1, 2). The *rlung-rta* itself and certain other ceremonies are used for general prevention and are performed cyclically, for instance, at the New Year, or at the inception of some new enterprise such as a marriage or a business trip. The contrast between *sku-rim* and *dge-ba*, like that between *rlung-rta* and *bsod-nams*, is often easily overlooked. Both sorts of thing are done to improve one's lot, and, in fact, each *sku-rim* has an aspect of *dge-ba*, if only by virtue of the fact that Buddhist functionaries and sacra are involved. However, the purpose of *dge-ba* is to improve one's karma, whereas the purpose of *sku-rim* is to avert *rkyen*.

A clear illustration of the difference is available in the contrast between two types of ceremony involving souls. One is a *sku-rim* in which the *bla* is recovered. The *bla* is a sort of personal life-force, not involved in karmic transmigrations but subject to loss to demons, which is potentially fatal. Symptoms of such loss include depression and general decline of worldly gumption and success. The remedy is a *sku-rim*, in which a ransom is substituted for the victim—a frequent feature of *sku-rim*. The ceremony also emphasizes the victim's luck; in its closing stages, prognosis is made by means of a lot-like drawing of stones, and the victim rolls dice to symbolize winning back the *bla* from the demon. In contrast to this is a form of funerary *dge-ba*, in which the *rnam-shes* of the victim is conducted away toward reincarnation with all manner of salutary advice, contributions, and admonitions to sever its worldly ties to the life it has left. In addition to the vast differences between the rites themselves, the contrast between the *bla* and the *rnam-shes* is instructive. *Rnam-shes* is what connects successive existences in the train of karma, whereas *bla* is one person's property, connects a person to actual this-worldly phenomena, like soul-trees (*bla-shing*) and soul-lakes (*bla-mtsho*), and is involved in *rlung-rta* (see Epstein 1977, p. 237).

It must be recalled, of course, that the results of good karma and the results of high *rlung-rta* look the same in the world. Actually, since *rkyen* is an aspect of karma also, it seems clear that a person with very high *rlung-rta* can succeed in stalling the consequences of bad karma until some other life and never see them in person at all. The attractiveness of this course is the basis of a difference between *'jigs-rten-pa'i chos*, or lay people's religion, with its emphasis on *sku-rim* and short-term payoff, and *chos-pa'i chos*, or religious people's religion, with its emphasis on soul-saving. This distinction is *never* overlooked by Tibetans and is used in open derision by the clergy.

In general, quite different modes of worship are involved in the realms of *rkyen* and karma. To avert *rkyen*, it is essential to propitiate and to avoid offending all sorts of supernaturals, which, for the most part, are pretty small potatoes on the cosmic scale. This sort of activity has no (or only coincidental) salutary effect on karmic merit. Merit is obtainable through faith and prayer as well as from works, but not from petty supernaturals. Such devotion is due to *bodhisattvas* and to *dkon-mchog gsum*, who have saving grace at their disposal. We say "who" advisedly, because although *dkon-mchog gsum* really refers to Buddha, Dharma, and Saṁgha, it also means "God" to Tibetans (see Ortner 1978:176, n. 31).

Merit gained by faith may seem an odd intrusion in a system so thoroughly ethicized as Buddhism, but in fact the karmic value of an act depends largely upon the actor's intentions (*bsam-pa*, Sanskrit *cetanā*)—as does merit gained by faith, which need not be viewed as something produced by a benevolent deity, although that is often the popular conception of it.[10] Intentions, which are very important in karma, are irrelevant to *rkyen*, where the emphasis is all on accident (*bar-chad*). Likewise, remorse (*'gyod-sems*), which ameliorates sins, is irrelevant to *rkyen*, where only expiation counts.

Interestingly enough, there seems to be no analogue for sin (*sdig-pa*) in the *rkyen* system, where prominence is awarded not to sin or anything like it but to pollution (*grib*). The word is related etymologically to others meaning shade or shadow (*grib-ma*), or shady side, as of a mountain (*srib*), and so forth. Ethnographically, pollution is usually explained as uncleanness, which results in such disorders as eye ailments (pain or rheum in the eye), hoarseness, colds, dull wits, and in extreme cases dumbness or even death. Things which are unclean enough to cause this pollution are legion: feces and urine (*rtsog-grib*), unclean food or food taken in an unclean place or vessel (*zas-grib*), blood or any animal product which falls in a fire (*dmar-grib*), corpses (*ro-grib*), childbirth (*pang-grib*), fights (*'khon-grib*), broken vows (*dam nyams-pa'i grib*), and so forth.

[10] A story known to many Tibetans (*rgan-mo khyi-so sangs-rgyas*) tells of an old woman who begs her son, a trader, to bring from India a Buddha-relic in which she may place her faith. After he forgets to do so several times, she threatens to commit suicide. He forgets once more, but remembers her plea just as he arrives home. Frantically, he looks about and finds a dog's tooth, which he gives his mother, telling her it is a genuine relic. As a result of the old woman's faith in this spurious article, she attains salvation. Many amusing tales affirming the power of simple, albeit well-intended, faith are told. See Epstein 1977, pp. 68–70.

Grib is best understood in relation to supernatural harm (*gnod-pa*). Are they contrasting, independent, coextensive, or does one include the other? *Grib* can be classified along with many other aspects of *rkyen* into high, middle, and low.[11] This is a clue to its connection with supernatural danger, for such a classification is characteristic of the chthonic type of supernaturals (*lha*, *klu*, *gzhi-bdag*). Pollution is the type of offense which antagonizes them, and can be reasonably regarded as coextensive with the harm they do. At first glance, this does not appear to be the case. Simple, direct definitions of *grib* say simply that it means contact with, including sight of, uncleanness (especially feces, urine, blood, childbirth, death, and certain unclean types of people if they enter one's house or give one food), and that it results in such problems as eye ailments, colds, dull wits, and rashes. Pollution then seems almost to be a disease category: a lapse of personal hygiene results in certain definite symptoms. This is the most salient meaning of pollution. But gods and demons can also be polluted, and then, too, people get sick—not the gods or demons. Actually, each household has its own proper gods (strongly associated with the hearth), and as we have mentioned, each person has a god and a demon on his or her shoulders. Personal and household pollution is actually pollution of gods and demons, and all pollution is essentially one sort of thing. Furthermore, some people will attest that any disease can be caused by pollution.

To see how the two views of pollution differ, one can consider a two-dimensional paradigm (see chart on next page). Across the top are things one can do to demons (*rgyu*) and down the side are things demons can do back (*rkyen*). Each of these is divided into *grib*, those things which are obviously pollution (those listed in the previous paragraph); and *gnod*, those things which are not so obviously pollution. If one chooses salience, *grib* is defined solely by square (i): both provocation and retaliation are obviously pollution. If one chooses system, *grib* is defined by the whole paradigm, and the distinction erected here between *grib* and *gnod* fades from significance.

In order to defend the exclusion of some part of this from the category of *grib*, it is necessary to distinguish in terms of causes, effects, or both—and therefore to admit *grib*-like causes with effects that are not *grib*, or both. Even Tibetans with a firm idea that the central meaning of *grib* lies in square(i) do not seem to do this. One does not hear, for instance, discussions in which a whole complex

[11] *Steng-grib* or *gza'-grib*, *btsan-grib*, and *klu-grib*.

mess of demonic disasters are sorted out according to which particular effects are *grib* and which are not. Instead, the fact that all sorts of troubles are piling up is taken to mean that some serious pollution has occurred. Furthermore, much of pollution is neither "obviously" polluting on the grounds of immediate visceral reaction nor included by inference from its connection with supernatural danger. Such things as broken monastic vows or the punishment of a thief are

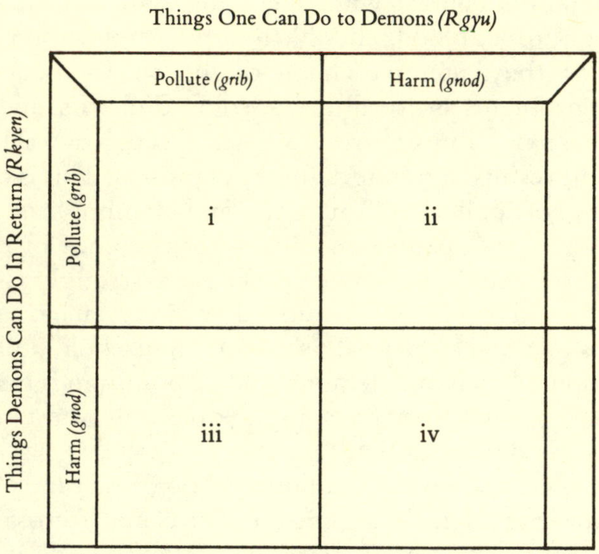
Things One Can Do to Demons (Rgyu)
Pollute (grib)
Harm (gnod)
Things Demons Can Do In Return (Rkyen)
Pollute (grib)
Harm (gnod)
i
ii
iii
iv

i. This is the square which contains *grib* of the sort most often mentioned in brief, off-the-cuff definitions of *grib*—e.g., a person attends at a childbirth or unwittingly lies down on some feces, and as a result feels sluggish and has problems with rheum in the eyes.

ii. This square is less obvious, because the provocation is less obviously dirty, even to Tibetans: a person chops down a tree, and as a result a neighbor breaks out in a rash.

iii. Here there are many events such that the provocation is obviously polluting, but the result is less simply associated with pollution. For example, a person urinates on a bush behind the house, or allows a blacksmith or a woman pregnant with a bastard to come in. As a result, people in the family become ill, household property is lost, stolen, or ruined, business suffers reverses, and so forth.

iv. Here the connection with pollution is essentially theoretical. For example, a person chops down a tree or stirs up a spring, with results as in iii.

extremely difficult to relate to the arbitrary distinction in our paradigm between *grib* and *gnod*. Yet they have their own named types of pollution.[12]

As both causes and effects show, pollution ranges from the trivial to the boggling. Sometimes the whole phenomenon is not worth crossing the street to avoid, and at other times it involves the whole community in desperate crises and communal ceremony. For instance, crowds are polluting (*khrom-grib*) because one never knows what unclean persons may be lurking there, but this deters no one from enjoying crowd scenes. If pollution does occur, its results seem to be no more serious than sore throats, colds, and lethargy. On the other hand, a serious outbreak of big-game hunting can cause massive *dmar-grib*, hold back the rains, and bring about a famine.[13]

The degree of seriousness of a pollutant can be modified over time. Given some typical cause of pollution, an instance of it can become gradually less threatening. For example, a murderer may be admitted to people's houses, with the explanation that his pollution has cleared up (*sangs*). Yet the next murderer would still be polluting. It is also possible that murderers would cease to be polluting altogether if people became sufficiently accustomed to the idea. Examples of this type of change often accompany changes in diet or social structure as previously unacceptable viands or marriages become more routine. People say that pollution is a matter of what one is used to, so that if something ceases to arouse the suspicion that it will make one sick, then it ceases to make one sick.

The word for such suspicions is *rnam-rtog*. Colloquially, *rnam-rtog* means both suspicion (as of a thief) and distaste (as of a dirty teacup). Tibetans will declare straightforwardly that pollution is a function of distaste and hence its causes can be modified by changes in taste. Philosophically, the term refers to discrimination in general, a cognitive function which according to Tibetan Buddhism is an obstacle to enlightenment. A bodhisattva or a saint must overcome all distinc-

[12] There also seems to be a difference between incurring pollution (*grib 'khar*) and suffering its effects (*grib phog*). As soon as it is known that pollution has been incurred, it can be averted by laving with special water (*khrus-gsol*) and sniffing incense (*bsangs*). This is part of the routine, for instance, after handling a corpse or participating at a childbirth (mother and child do it too). Once the effects make themselves felt, then stronger measures are required in the shape of whatever *sku-rim* is divined to be appropriate.

[13] For an analysis of pollution beliefs among the Sherpas, one which differs substantially from our own, see Ortner 1973.

tions between opposites, even good and evil. Through these meanings of *rnam-rtog* one can arrive at an understanding of the relationship between *grib* and its analogue, which we said is not sin but the concept of defilement (*sgrib*) in Buddhist soteriology. Both etymologically and semantically related to pollution (*grib*), this term refers to the cognitive (*shes-bya'i*) and emotional (*nyon-mongs-kyi*) obscurations upon the path toward enlightenment. Discrimination (*rnam-rtog*) plays a role in cognitive obscuration (*shes-bya'i sgrib*) analogous to that played in pollution (*grib*) by scruples (*rnam-rtog*).[14]

Karma, *Rkyen*, and Suffering

Originally, we proposed to reconcile Tibetan supernaturalism with belief in karma by exposing the systematic analogy between the two systems of causation. This, we said, was a step in the direction of elucidating the nature of Tibetan Buddhism. But we also said that there was more to ordinary Tibetans' Buddhism than commitment to belief in karma and this reconciliation of supernaturalism with it. Somehow, the very meaning to Tibetans of happiness and unhappiness reveals their Buddhist premises. In a way, any discussion of *rkyen* with Tibetans is a discussion of unhappiness, for any misfortune may be labeled *rkyen*. In showing, then, that *rkyen* as a causal system is not reduceable to karma, we have established that the causes of happiness and unhappiness cannot be fully explained in karmic terms. In showing that the two systems are analogous to the point of frequent interchangeability, we have shown how supernaturalism retains (or acquires) its Buddhist character. Now, with these means at our disposal, we propose to consider how Tibetans often regard unhappiness as a stage, aspect, or excess of happiness, rather than its mere opposite. In effect, Tibetans seem to hold their own happiness as an object of *rnam-rtog*.

Tibetan culture excels in lessons upon the ironies created by the operation of *rkyen* in the karmic world. In literature, these lessons are improved upon by the obligatory karmic moral. The first example we will cite is a myth taken from a twelfth-century Bon-po redaction of

[14] See, e.g., Lce Sgom-pa 1971:247. According to this source, cognitive obscuration arises from attachment to the faulty discriminations of subject (*'dzin-pa'i sems*) and object (*gzung-pa'i yul*).

the *Gzungs mdo*, a compendium of semicanonical and ritual texts, versions of which are employed by all Tibetan Buddhist sects.[15]

While in her incarnation as a queen, a Bon-po goddess discovers a beautiful land and decides to build her palace there. However, she learns that the land is inhabited by chthonic demons and hence is unsuitable for human habitation. Nonetheless, she ignores the admonitions of her parents and advisers and proceeds apace with her plans. Upon completion of the palace, her parents and those engaged in the construction work die. The queen then erects 108 temples to commemorate her parents and raise their merit, whereupon the queen herself contracts a hideous disease. Despite the best efforts of doctors, diviners, and shamans, the queen's condition does not improve. Finally, an adviser tells her to invite the miracle-working teacher Gshen-rab-mi-bo, the Bon "Buddha," and to him she asks the quintessential question:

> Is this disease with which I am stricken the power of my former karma? Because I built a palace in this... place, am I oppressed by demons? Can it be that one builds temples, yet incidentally acquires the sin of a murderer? Is there no merit in burying the parents that bore one, and building temples with a faithful mind?

The teacher answers, telling her:

> The material cause [*rgyu*] of your disease is the power of your karma. The efficient cause [*rkyen*] is building a palace [in a demon-inhabited place]. It is the retribution for intruding upon the demons.... Some jumped upon you and gave you the disease. As for the beings you conscripted to build the temples [and who died in the effort], your karma will not always be heavy, and your sins and defilements will become cleansed. The sins and defilements of those that were injured or died in building the temples are expiated, and for them the gate to the three evil births is shut. They will be reborn in Paradise. As for the merit of commemorating your parents and building temples out of faith... you will eventually become a Buddha.

It is in the light of the Buddhist equivalence of intention and action that the irony of this tale must be considered. The conversation

[15] This compilation of texts is variously known as the *Gzungs mdo*, the *Mdo mang*, and the *Bka' 'dus*. The translation below is a paraphrase of two versions of this myth which differ only slightly from each other. They are found in "Klu gnyan sa bdag gi pang skong" in Bru-ston 1974, ii:88ff., and in "Klu gnyan sa bdag gi spang skong" in Gshen Mkhas-grub 1974, ii:166ff.

between the queen and the teacher illustrates that even actions performed with the best of intentions (love and piety) may produce unanticipated and (seemingly) unwarranted misfortunes. The queen produces sickness for herself and death or injury for others.

We think that the Tibetan world view is better represented by the queen's perplexity than by the teacher's exegesis. Unlike Buddhas, ordinary people cannot perceive their friends' arrival in paradise, or even begin to imagine liberation. What they can see is the tangible suffering of life, and this they endeavor assiduously to avoid. For ordinary Tibetans the abstract idea of suffering is conceptualized in terms of *rkyen*, that is (1) any misfortune, accident, sickness, or pain, and (2) any proximal (generally demonic) causal contingency. *Rkyen* seems sometimes to imply a division of types of suffering, and sometimes to stress the unity of all types of suffering. The reader will recall that when people say an event is *rkyen*, they do not exclude the possibility that it is karma—they are simply making a different statement about the event's antecedents. It is in the latter aspect, when salience is given to a particular supernatural cause, that *rkyen* commonly assumes the role of a concrete metaphor for the philosophic concept of suffering.

This is especially clear in the case of ghosts (*gdong-'dre*, *shi-'dre*), where we find a metaphoric lesson on the theme of attachment and its attendant suffering, as preached, for instance, in Mi-la's songs quoted above. A human becomes a ghost because of attachment. For example, a person who dies prematurely, or who dies without arranging his affairs, collecting his debts, or making his will, may become a ghost. The neglect of funerary observances, with their emphasis on reassuring the departed spirit of the continued proper management of its former affairs and the use of its property for its own merit, is also likely to occasion the return of the departed spirit as a ghost. Although there are ghosts that remain behind to collect what is owed them (*sha-'khon*, *rgyu-'khon*), in general people become ghosts because they "can't die" or "can't find the path." Whereas in theory it is attachment which entrains the whole process of karma and rebirth, here we have attachment derailing karma; instead of proceeding to a normal rebirth, people remain behind, disembodied and malignant. They are too attached to the world to be able to die properly. Unable or unwilling to find their way to a new rebirth, they haunt their former friends and relatives. Dpal-sprul Rinpoche writes, "Even though they come joyfully to former friends and relatives, the latter get miseries like sickness and insanity" (1971:110). Love in excess is the opposite both of itself and of detachment.

The role of attachment to things of the previous life, and especially unfinished business, in the etiology of ghosts seems to be well illustrated in the definitions of two subtypes of ghost: *rgyal-po* and *the'u-rang*. *Rgyal-po* are the most powerful ghosts; the standard idea of *rgyal-po* is that they attain a preeminent status among ghosts by outstanding success, especially in possessing human beings. They are also especially irascible. Lamas, already being powerful in life, are likely, if they become ghosts, to become *rgyal-po*. For Tsumbas this is *the* criterion by which *rgyal-po* are distinguished from other ghosts, and the lamas who become *rgyal-po* are distinguished by greed and irascibility—inappropriate character traits for beings whose karma is supposed to be too good for such faults. This accentuates the relationship of ghosthood and a life or death which seems to mock the fulfillment of karma. The same relationship is illuminated in ideas about *the'u-rang*.

The *the'u-rang* are impish miniature goblins. Although most Tibetans do not regard them as ghosts, Tsumbas say they are the ghosts of dead children. They are not dangerous and often not considered malignant, standing among ghosts as they stood among human beings. Their excuse for ghosthood, as it were, follows the pattern of unfulfillment in life of what might be regarded as a karmic promise: the enjoyment of a human birth with a normal life-span as a reward for the virtue of previous existences.[16]

While it is clear that humans can become dangerous supernaturals by virtue of the fact that they are attached to, or unfulfilled in, the material world, even the types of *rkyen* involving territorial demons (*lha*, *gnyan*, *klu*, *sa-bdag*, *gzhi-bdag*) can be integrated to an ironic perspective. The deeds which offend them (organic functions, agricultural work, house building, etc.) are so essential to existence that even if one has the best or most pious intentions, one cannot forego them. Moreover, inadvertence enters most conspicuously into the ethical causal scheme when territorial demons are concerned, because they are typically offended by accident. This was well illustrated in the story of the queen and her edifices.

[16] It should be emphasized that the characteristics of *rgyal-po* and *the'u-rang* we give here are according to Tsumbas. Some Tibetans would not limit the production of *rgyal-po* to lamas alone. But generally, *rgyal-po* do originate from powerful, or particularly irascible, individuals. Some Tibetans also add that the demons known as *btsan* may also originate in this way.

Looking at the irony again, from the demon's point of view, there are such things as "living ghosts" (*gson-'dre*), human beings who enter the status of witch at birth rather than that of ghost at death. The peculiarity of their position with respect to karma is that the harm they do is never intentional.[17] The witch's nature is karmically inherited, but opposed to the moral power of choice which distinguishes humanity. This karmic irony is replicated in the witch's social personality. Although their personae seem to vary, they are related by the fact that they are out of control socially. On one hand, they may be pious and withdrawn from interaction, and on the other hand, they may be outstanding pests, such as neighbors with too little respect for one's privacy. In either case, as witches they possess people, damage property, injure livestock, cause illness, and in extreme cases cause people to die and even eat them.

In folklore witches are often depicted as bad wives or bad mothers who typically attempt to kill and eat their own spouses or children. Here we have the most nurturant member of the family eating the very people she is supposed to feed. For most villagers, the witch is a bad neighbor, rather than a bad wife or mother. Witches are people who, because of the stars under which they were born, unconsciously cause harm to people they think of visiting. Their souls go unaccompanied by their bodies and enter their friends' bodies. Although they are not consciously malicious, witches are bad people because of the harm they do. In the normal course of things, it is not always possible to anticipate witches' whims and see to it that they are always entertained well enough to forestall any harm they might do. Witches therefore violate the norms of friendship and hospitality, first by inverting the principle of reciprocity and causing harm to people who are good to them, and second by short-circuiting the allowances that friends make for another's practical problems when claims of friendship conflict with other requirements.

Contrasting with the witch is the Tsumbas' poisoner, who is a bad host rather than a bad guest.[18] The poisoner does not belong to the same taxonomy of supernaturals as ghosts and witches do. Poison-

[17] Other words for witches are *bdud-mo*, *sbag-mo*, and *phra-men-ma*. Some Tibetans say that while the former two have evil intentions, the latter's deeds are unconsciously perpetrated.

[18] Poisoning does not seem to have had a wide practice in Tibet. However, some regions, such as Kong-po, were notorious for this. There the reasons for poisoning were the same as we cite here: to get the victim's merit.

ing's peculiar relationship to ideas of karma is that poisoners hope to acquire their victims' merit (*bsod-nams*) by murdering them. This is the perfected materialist misinterpretation of karma, and, as it happens, Tsumbas' horror of poisoners is greater than the outrage they feel toward witches. While witches afflict only their friends and neighbors, poisoners will murder anyone—including a husband or even a dog, if their preferred victims do not appear.

While the victims of ghosts and witches are singled out because of particular (otherwise good) social relationships, the victims of poisoners—because their good karma makes targets of them—are selected on the basis of whole statuses. This is even more true of the phenomenon called *mi-kha*. Anyone who is too outstanding in any way, even in happiness, risks *mi-kha*, a type of *rkyen* such that universal gossip becomes reified somehow as a malignant agent and then must be exorcised just like a demon. A text for pacifying the effects of *mi-kha* reads:

> Doing good is seen as evil; if one is seen to have something, one must endure gossip;... whatever one says is seen as lies; whatever one does leads to discord; if one does not even have a son, one still becomes known as powerful; one might be poor and know nothing but misery, yet everyone hears one is rich; one might give all one has accumulated to others, but shameless evil things are said about one; one might sleep alone without a mate, but controversy whirls about one like the wind. (Gshen Mkhas-grub 1974, ii:339 ff.)

Mi-kha seems to be a caution against any excess in deed or fortune in a society with strong intrastratum egalitarianism, yet according to the text it may afflict anyone at all, just because of the vagaries of gossip. In any case, if it did not seem to be in fact quite rare, *mi-kha* would seem to put the cap on the idea of just happiness by entering it directly on the list of *rkyen*—in addition to all the other risks of seeking even the best goods of social existence. At this point we might add that there seems to be a significant trend to dropoutism among Tibetans, who often prefer reclusiveness and a generally low social profile to the demands of sociability—even at the cost of its greatest satisfactions.

The people who ostensibly attack this whole problem most directly are monastics. The monastic life, of course, is too often considered to be the only distinction of Tibetan or Buddhist life. By and large, Tibetans seem to concur with that opinion. From the lay point of view, the specialists are there to serve the general good both as intercessors in supernatural problems and as moral guides and surrogates. Monks and nuns are as likely to explain that their own souls' prospects benefit most from their vocation, and that, moreover, they also enjoy their freedom from the worldly cares of household life. They need only concern themselves with their individual livelihoods, which indeed they gain with less labor than is required of lay people, if only because of their vows, which disqualify them from certain kinds of labor, such as plowing or weeding. But menial labor or hard work is only part of a householder's worries. Monks need not worry about conserving and passing on to their sons an intact patrimony; for women the nunnery is a refuge from the drudgery of household routine and the dangers and pain of childbearing. Also, the tea is better.

Monastics will plainly say that the reason for becoming a monk or a nun is to be *skyid-po*, "happy," and neither the soteriological nor the social aspect seems to dominate their imaginations. But by avoiding the *duḥkha* of lay life, they do not necessarily give up the satisfactions of sociability. The clubbiness of the monastic community allows them to enjoy their fellowship in a situation which is not only more moral, but more relaxed and agreeable than in the village.

The hitch is not in the ideas behind monasticism but in the difficulty of living up to them. To pick what seems to be a real stumbling block for many people, there are always those monastics who, while appreciating the superiority of ideal fellowship in the cloister, prove susceptible to the pleasures of the flesh—especially sex. Although people who backslide are not stigmatized, particularly after reentering lay life, the forsaking of their vows is itself thought to be a type of *rkyen*, and is a source of pollution (*grib*), which must be ritually cleansed. Since people are well-informed and shrewd critics of behavior, the respect that those who remain in monasteries actually enjoy depends largely on their personal piety or learning. Because more is expected of them, people are hypercritical, and sins which are tolerated or expected in lay people are doubly disapproved in monks and nuns. Those who exhibit interest in such matters as sex, property, litigation, alcohol, and so on, are criticized on the grounds of acting too much like lay people. After all, one hears, it is not supposed to be their clothes alone which distinguishes them. Tibetans say that a lay person with good intentions is better than a monastic with bad ones.

The only people for whom this does not apply are lamas. Either incarnate or just very worthy lamas theoretically can become so perfect that they no longer generate karma by their deeds. Lay people say that nothing a lama does can stop him from being a lama. The most venerable lama may be completely mad or may even indulge in outrageously criminal behavior without losing his holiness. Moreover, by virtue of being a lama, he can bestow saving grace (*byin-rlabs*) by means which would ordinarily be polluting: touching the heads of his devotees, giving them leftovers of his food and drink, and so on. The pious may even swallow pills compounded of lamas' feces, believing in their curative powers. Such lamas are rare though, to say the least.

In discussing causes of unhappiness under the headings of karma and *rkyen*, we selected our topics so as to demonstrate our proposition that Tibetan ideas of happiness are darkly shaded by a profound and skeptical ambivalence. Dwelling on love and sociability in various forms—such as personal intimacy, converse, conviviality—as premium requirements of the good life, we have shown them emerging through accident, excess, error, and even through karma as dire afflictions. One might think of this phenomenon as the Tibetans' metaphorical rebuke of bad analogies between worldly or personal love and the bodhisattva's universal love.

The caveats applied to the ideality of monastic life can be considered in a causal framework also. Sometimes, the idea of *rkyen* applies, as is indicated in the expression *bdud chos kyi bar-chad*—"the devil is the doctrine's accident"—the idea that good invites evil, or that where Buddhism is active there is bound to be deviltry also. We have already mentioned the special types of *rkyen* associated with religious personnel: *grib* for broken vows and *rgyal-po* status for the ghost of imperfect lamas. This trend is extended in a thick vein of Tibetan humor which enriches the theme of monastic imperfection with innumerable black jokes and ironic tales. Lamas (like other religious folk) are significant to Tibetans, first because they are human, but mainly because they are different from other humans. While Tibetans recognize that lamas are above and beyond the laws of cause and effect, the ordinary man seems to collect suffering above and beyond his just deserts. There is more to this than ignorance of the uncollected effects karma or *rkyen* hold in store. Rather, there is an idea here which is foreign to karma and to supernaturalism—an idea of net loss. Backsliding monastics by their failure make the joke of normal human striving all the more pointed. Tibetans' stark refusal to have a Pollyanna attitude toward the religious life, and their idea of it as a grand opportunity too easily lost or too often wasted, is an example of something we will discuss under the heading of *la-yogs*. It is the idea of a basic flaw in karma's fabric. We have proposed to demonstrate Tibetans' acceptance of the First Noble Truth, the doctrine that all is suffering, and this becomes most clear in the meaning of *la-yogs*, which takes a karma-like conception of causation and strips it of karma's justice and optimism.

La-yogs

If one asks what *la-yogs* means, most often one hears that it is the same as karma, or else the same as sin.[19] Obviously, it cannot be both, but must have something in common with both. With only so much to go on, one might simply reflect that here is another instance of Tibetans' penchant for lumping cause and effect under the same name, or for naming one to indicate the other. (This penchant we have observed in several aspects of our discussion of karma: the whole meaning of karma being condensed into the single fact of retribution; or the merit of an act being indistinguishable from its fruit. We have also seen it in our discussion of *rkyen*.) But this explanation is not sufficient, because *la-yogs* is obviously outside or even contrary to karma. In an example somewhat reminiscent of the queen's story, one Tsumba proposed that if a man gives away everything he has and as a result winds up a pauper, then that is *la-yogs*. Of course, giving things away is no sin—quite the contrary. As always, one can append a karmic exegesis to such a tale, but that is not the point of the story. Only by considering the story in its own right can we grasp the point of *la-yogs*.

[19] It should be noted that while the other terms Tibetans use for causation gloss textually derived Sanskrit words, *la-yogs* is a primary term. The lexicographer Jäschke (1958:541) defines it as "retribution, punishments overtaking a sinner during this life." He seems to make it equivalent to the term *lan-chags*, a kind of vengeful retribution.

The lexicographer Das (1960:1202) has the following phrase: *las kyi la-(g.) yogs dang la 'khor gsungs* ("he said that retribution of one's wicked actions visit one"). Das's reference is to the famous didactic tale *Sgom chen dang rdza rtsig gi rnam thar* by 'Brong-rtse yongs-'dzin Blo-bzang-tshul-khrims (Bkra-shis-lhun-po Xylograph, folio 9). Here, we think, the term could be better rendered "comeuppance."

We have personally seen the term used only twice in other texts. In the biography of the *'das-log* Gling-bza' Chos-skyid, it is clearly used as a synonym for sinful karma (*sdig-pa'i la-yog(s) ma-byas*, "I did not commit sinful deeds"). See Patshang Lama Sonam Gyaltsen 1974:364. The term also occurs in several places on page 92 of *Rgyal bu yid 'dzin bzod pa chos kyi dbang phyug gi rnam thar* in *Two 'das-log manuscripts from the library of Lhakhang Lama*, Delhi, 1978. Here the good minister, Dge-ba-bzang-po, curses his evil counterpart, Khri-nag-mdzes, for his machinations against the king and prince: *las-kyi las (=la)-yogs sdig-blon khyod-la shog* ("May you, sinful minister, get the retribution of your action!").

According to Gorer (1938:182), the Zongu Lepchas make *la-yo(gs)* the equivalent of "sin."

If *la-yogs* has a typical story, it must be something like the following. You plan to go up into the hills and your mother warns you to dress warmly because it looks like rain. You ignore this advice but your mother turns out to be right. When you are cold and wet, this is *la-yogs*. Or: you plan to go to the city and you are warned not to because it will turn out badly, but you go anyway, and in fact it does turn out badly. This is also *la-yogs*. The queen's story is a classic example—she ignored her parents' advice and thereby caused their deaths and great suffering to all around.

Considering their respective stories, it is much easier to understand karma in terms of *la-yogs* than to understand *la-yogs* in terms of karma. The story of karma teaches that if one does the wrong thing, one will be sorry. This fits well into the story of *la-yogs*. But in the story of *la-yogs*, the wrong thing one does may be quite innocent as far as karma is concerned. It is no sin to misjudge the weather or one's friend's wisdom. If on the other hand someone tells you not to commit a sin, but you do, and then you suffer for it, that is *la-yogs*. So, if *la-yogs* involves a sin, then essentially it is the same as karma. *La-yogs* includes karma to this extent. But if someone tells you not to do a good deed, yet you do it, and then you enjoy the reward, that is still karma, but decidedly not *la-yogs*. Likewise, if someone warns you not to go to the city, but you go, and everything turns out beautifully, that is not *la-yogs*. *La-yogs* does not operate according to moral principles, and is not related in any way to the golden rule. This is what most definitely sets it apart from karma.

From the examples cited in the previous paragraphs, one might conclude that in fact the ignoring of good advice or generally the throwing away of a good thing is what really defines *la-yogs*. This is indeed very near to the heart of the affair, but *la-yogs* is not just a matter of blunders. As one nun put it, there is the *la-yogs* of bad things and there is the *la-yogs* of good things. She said that *la-yogs* of bad things is the suffering contingent upon having done something wrong. The *la-yogs* of good things is the rest of *la-yogs*, and occurs even if one does nothing. By now we have only to consider the *la-yogs* of good things.

To take a mundane but pure and affecting example, consider the case of the landlady's boots. The landlady was a well-off woman who had in recent years been going barefoot so much that her feet were cracking just as though she were destitute. In the old days she never had any trouble getting boots to wear, and even had a bootmaker living in her house. Now, she says, the fact that she has to go barefoot is *la-yogs*. If you ask why, the only answer is that the old bootmaker simply went away. No one will admit that for some particular misdeed the landlady deserves to go barefoot (as they would if they were talking about karma). This is the bootmaker's *la-yogs*, but that is not to say that it is somehow his retribution against her (as it might be if it were *rkyen*). It is simply her loss of him. The *la-yogs* (in this case) is that she craves boots and therefore suffers from barefootedness; or (in general) that craving causes suffering. There are numerous analogous examples. If the blacksmith leaves town, tools and cookware cannot be repaired, and that is *la-yogs*. When a dear friend or a just ruler is gone, one suffers, and that is *la-yogs*. According to a Tibetan noble who had servants in his homeland and who now has none in exile, that is *la-yogs*. This *la-yogs*, which initially appeared to be none other than karma itself, now resembles nothing so much as the Suffering of Change, or Conditioned Suffering.

We close our examination of karma and suffering with this discussion of *la-yogs* because, while spanning the range of human experience, the meaning of *la-yogs* seems to imply that ultimately there is no happiness in the realm of karma. Initially, we said that unhappiness was a neglected topic in the ethnography of Buddhism. We said that ostensible striving and costly ritual directed toward worldly and karmic advancement distracted from the meaning of suffering to Buddhists, and in fact could seriously distort the ethnographic view of it. We proposed not to neglect this subject in discussing karma and related subjects.

After outlining the essentials of Tibetan karma, we discussed *rkyen*, which appeared academically as a functional part of karma and colloquially as an independent system which confirmed its Buddhist character by metaphor. We pointed out that *rkyen* is at once a concept of causation and a concept of suffering. We showed that karma and *rkyen* are best distinguished along a line between this world and the next, and best related along a line between happiness and unhappiness. Most especially, we showed that *rkyen* often modifies the meaning of those very goods which are typically sought by karmic striving. *Rkyen* as a theory does not allow that a person may do better (in the long run appropriate to karmic considerations) than karma allows. Yet *rkyen* introduces the concept of unmerited suffering. Considered as a comment upon karma, *rkyen* says that well-intended actions can have bad results, and that even very good things have their bad points. Thus we found, ethnographically, some of the same philosophy we read in textual lessons on the meaning of unhappiness.

Finally, we come to *la-yogs*, which appeared intially as karma itself, or at least as sin, and finally refers to the most innocent sorts of pain and bereavement. Considered as a comment on karma, *la-yogs* says that all its goods pass away and that by wanting them we bring about our own suffering. It carries this meaning both in its generality and in its unique connotations. As we have pointed out repeatedly, both karma and *rkyen* are simultaneously concepts of causation and of suffering, but these terms refer to unhappiness by exclusion. That is, karma means suffering if one overlooks good karma, and *rkyen* means suffering if one overlooks good *rkyen*. Moreover, karma may be considered to explain only the grand contingencies and not the ordinary little joys and sorrows of life, while *rkyen* may be reserved for supernatural harm. *La-yogs* is not like this. In the first place, *la-yogs* refers to unhappiness by generalizing, not by excluding. From *la-yogs* we arrive at karma by narrowing our focus. Second, *la-yogs* is not invoked as one casts about for explanations for some mishap, but is a simple and immediate label which requires neither theory nor divination—and it may be anything from the loss of a kingdom to a rainy day in the open. *La-yogs*, for all its breadth of reference, has its own particular tone, which condenses a whole seriocomic world view. If one observes a deed and comments that it will lead to *la-yogs*, one may be simply calling it a sin and predicting that the doer will not be happy with the way it works out. But one will also be alluding to the foolishness of sinning, the deluded willfulness of it, and the waste, perhaps above all. No matter what good fortune befalls, one may enjoy it while reflecting that there is still *la-yogs* and that this will pass away, while also reflecting that this is just the way things go in the world and one were better out of it. It is with this gesture of familiar surprise that *la-yogs* gives karma its final jokelike twist. It is a Buddhist twist, we think, to give the straightforward and perhaps overly complacent idea that virtue leads to happiness. At least, it is a Tibetan twist, and we feel that it typifies the slightly ironic detachment with which Tibetans contemplate their own happiness.

References Cited

Works in English

Das, Sarat Chandra
1960 A Tibetan-English Dictionary. Alipore: West Bengal Government Press.

Epstein, Lawrence
1975 Blood and Thunder: Theories of Causation in Tibet. Tibet Society Bulletin 9:40–45.
1977 Causation in Tibetan Religion. Ph.D. dissertation. Department of Anthropology, University of Washington.
MS. Where Buddhas Fear to Tread: A Study of the 'das-log.
Gombrich, Richard F.
1971 Precept and Practice: Traditional Buddhism in the Rural Highlands of Ceylon. Oxford: Clarendon.
Gorer, Geoffrey
1938 Himalayan Village. London: Thomas Nelson & Sons.
Jäschke, H. A.
1958 A Tibetan-English Dictionary. London: Routledge and Kegan Paul.
Lichter, David
1980 Person, Action and Causation in a Bhote Ethic. Ph.D. dissertation. Department of Anthropology, Stanford University.
Nebesky-Wojkowitz, René de
1975 Oracle and Demons of Tibet. Graz: Akademische Druck- u. Verlagsanstalt.
Ortner, Sherry B.
1973 Sherpa Purity. American Anthropologist 75:49–63.
1978 Sherpas through Their Rituals. Cambridge: Cambridge University Press.
Schlagintweit, Emil
1968 Buddhism in Tibet. London: Susil Gupta.
Smith, E. Gene
1969 Preface to The Autobiographical Reminiscences of Ngag-dbang-dpal-bzang, Late Abbot of Kaḥ-thog Monastery. Ngagyur Nyingmay Sungrab, 1. Gangtok: Sonam T. Kazi.
1970 Introduction to Kongtrul's Encyclopaedia of Indo-Tibetan Culture. Śata-piṭaka, 80. New Delhi: International Academy of Indian Culture.
Spiro, Melford E.
1970 Buddhism and Society: A Great Tradition and Its Burmese Vicissitudes. New York: Harper and Row.
Waddell, L. Austine
1967 The Buddhism of Tibet. Cambridge, Eng.: W. Heffer.

Works in Tibetan

Kong-sprul Blo-gros-mtha'-yas
1970 Kongtrul's Encyclopaedia of Indo-Tibetan Culture (Shes bya kun khyab). Lokesh Chandra, ed. Śata-piṭaka, 80. New Delhi: International Academy of Indian Culture.
Chandra, Lokesh, ed.
1969 A 15th Century Tibetan Compendium of Knowledge. Śata-piṭaka, 78. New Delhi: International Academy of Indian Culture.
Lce Sgom-pa
1975 Man ngag rin chen spung pa'i dkar chag. Varanasi: Treasury of Elegant Sayings Printing Press.

Patshang Lama Sonam Gyaltsen, ed.
1974 'Das log gling bza' chos skyid kyi rnam thar. *In* Two Visionary Accounts of Returns from Death. Dolanji: Tibetan Bonpo Monastic Centre.
Dpal-sprul O-rgyan-'jigs-med-chos-kyi-dbang-po
1971 Kun bzang bla ma'i zhal lung. *In* The Collected Works of Dpal-sprul O-rgyan-'jigs-med-chos-kyi-dbang-po, vol. 5. Ngagyur Nyingmay Sungrab, 42. Gangtok: Sonam T. Kazi.
Bru-ston Rgyal-ba-g.yung-drung, compiler
1974 Gzungs 'dus. 2 vols. Dolanji: Tibetan Bonpo Monastic Centre.
Yon-tan-rgya-mtsho
1969 Yon tan rin po che'i mdzod 'grel pa nyi zla'i sgron me. Ngagyur Nyingmay Sungrab, 25. Gangtok: Sonam T. Kazi.
Gshen Mkhas-grub Tshul-khrims-rgyal-mtshan, compiler
1974 Mdo mang. Dolanji: Tibetan Bonpo Monastic Centre.
O-rgyan-rdo-rje, ed.
1975 Gshin rje chos kyi rgyal po'i gsung phrin. *In* Two Obscure Texts of the Avalokitesvara Cult from Spiti. New Delhi: n.p.

·10·

Merit-Transference in the Kammic Theory of Popular Theravāda Buddhism

Charles F. Keyes

The Doctrine of Kamma in Theravāda Buddhist Practice

The theory of *kamma* (Sanskrit *karma*), of moral action with moral consequences, holds a central place in Theravāda Buddhist doctrine. In the second Noble Truth, the Noble Truth of the Origin of Suffering, the Buddha posits the ultimate cause of suffering as "craving" or "desire" (*taṇhā*). *Taṇhā*, in turn, leads one to act, and these actions (*kamma*) have their consequences (*vipāka*; *phala*), whose character depends upon whether the act itself was morally positive (*puñña*) or morally negative (*pāpa*).

The Buddha analyzed *taṇhā* as being of two types: the first, caused by ignorance (*moha*), conduces to bad kamma; the second, the desire for existence, conduces to good kamma. The Buddhist theologian Buddhaghosa summarized this analysis as follows:

> For the Blessed One in his discourses on the round of rebirth was accustomed to choose from Dependent Origination two of the factors of being as his starting points: either, on the one hand, ignorance, as when he says, "As I have told you, O priests, the first beginning of ignorance cannot be discerned, nor can one say, 'Before a given point of time there was no ignorance, it came into being afterwards.' Nevertheless, O priests, it can be discerned that ignorance possesses a definite dependence"; or, on the other

I am indebted to Mr. Suriya Smutkupt and Professor Sommai Premchit for their assistance in translating the northern Thai text that is discussed in this essay. A grant from the Social Science Research Council made it possible for me to undertake the research upon which this study is based and to bring Professor Sommai to Seattle to work with me. Professor F.K. Lehman provided a detailed critique of an earlier version of this essay, and I have incorporated some of his suggestions into this version. I appreciated receiving his reflections on my work even when I did not always agree with them.

hand, desire for existence, as when he says, "As I have told you, O priests, the first beginning of desire for existence cannot be discerned nor can one say, 'Before a given point of time there was no desire for existence, it came into being afterwards.' Nevertheless, O priests, it can be discerned that desire for existence possesses a definite dependence."

But why was The Blessed One in his discourses on the round of rebirth accustomed to choose these two factors of being as his starting-points? Because they constitute the difference between the karma which conducts to blissful states of existence. For the cause of the karma which conducts to unhappy states of existence is ignorance. . . .

But the cause of the karma which conducts to blissful states of existence is desire for existence.[1]

Ignorance and desire for existence are basic to human nature, although these two are dependent upon sensation which comes about through contact between the individual and the physical forms of the world. From desire springs attachment to those things which fulfillment of desire brings, and it is such attachments which bind us to the samsaric world. These links in the chain of causation, subsumed under the doctrine of "dependent origination" (*paṭicca-samuppāda*), are given considerable attention in the *suttas* and in the commentaries.

The theological subtleties of the doctrine of "dependent origination" are of little interest to the ordinary practitioner of Buddhism. Rather, what he finds most meaningful is the doctrine of kamma, a doctrine that has two basic aspects. On the one hand, kammic theory provides the basis for action. If one acts in ignorance—giving vent to one's passions of greed (*lobha*), lust (*rāga*), and anger (*dosa*)—one will commit immoral acts and will suffer negative consequences. If, on the other hand, one acts with awareness, suppressing the impurities (*kilesa*) of one's nature and following the desire to reduce or eliminate suffering, one will perform moral acts and experience positive consequences.

Kammic theory is predicated upon a simple formula known to every Buddhist from early childhood. The following version of the formula from the *Samyutta Nikāya* is widely quoted among Buddhists:

> According to the seed that's sown
> So is the fruit ye reap therefrom
> Doer of good will gather good,
> Doer of evil, evil reaps.
> Sown is the seed, and thou shalt taste
> The fruit thereof.

[1] *Vissuddhimagga*, chap. 17; translation by Warren (1953:171–172).

The formula is often made simpler still, as in this Thai saying: do good, receive good; do evil, receive evil (*tham dī dai dī*; *tham chūa dai chūa*). This theory serves, in the first instance, to provide a framework for interpreting the differences in suffering that are observable by humans in the world. For example, in *Anguttara Nikāya* the Buddha tells Mallikā, the queen, why some women are "beautiful, attractive, pleasing, and possessed of surpassing loveliness," whereas others are "ugly, of a bad figure, and horrible to look at," and why some are "rich, wealthy, affluent, and high in the social scale," whereas others are "indigent, poor, needy and low in the social scale." The Buddha says that anger has been the cause of ugliness and that the lack of anger, despite provocation, has been the cause of beauty. Greed is the cause of poverty, while generosity, including giving alms to monks and Brahmins, is the cause of wealth and high status (Warren 1953:171–172).

A number of popular texts known throughout Buddhist Southeast Asia contain extended discussions of how the characteristics that differentiate humans as to their relative degree of suffering can be traced to moral acts performed in prior lives. The most systematic of such texts is a fourteenth-century treatise written in Thai, the *Trai Phūm* (*Traibhūmi kathā*), the "Three Worlds," compiled by Phya Lithai, a future king of the Siamese statelet of Sukhothai. To take one example, the *Trai Phūm* offers the following explanation of why some women are barren:

> The reason why some women do not have children is because of the effect of the evil deeds of those who are to be born. This generates a force like a wind that acts in the woman's abdomen and destroys the embryo.[2]

The *Trai Phūm* also considers the reasons why there are social inequalities among humans:

> There are three kinds of children; the children of superior birth, the children of similar birth, and the children of inferior birth. The children of superior birth are the kind of children who are wiser than their parents. They have more of the knowledge of the wise men than their parents have. They have a better appearance, are richer, attain a higher status, and are stronger than their parents. The children who are better than their parents in such ways are called children of superior birth. The children who are born equal to their parents in knowledge, strength and appearance are called children of similar

[2] This and the following passage from the *Trai Phūm* are taken from the translation by Frank E. and Mani B. Reynolds (forthcoming).

birth. Those who are less gifted than their parents in every way are called children of inferior birth.

In the latter passage we have an interpretation of social inequalities that takes into account social mobility. Unlike the Indian theory of karma, which asserts that every person is born into a caste which he cannot move out of during his or her lifetime, and unlike the Sinhalese Buddhist theory of kamma, which posits much the same thing (since there are castes in Sri Lanka), the Thai author of this fourteenth-century text allows for children who rise to higher status than their parents and for those who sink into lower statuses. It is the individual who inherits a kammic legacy from a previous existence, not an aggregate of individuals. Nonetheless, it is true that even in Southeast Asia those born to royal status were considered to be fixed in a hierarchy of social inequality.

There are yet other differences among humans that are explained in kammic terms. The same text speaks of those who are born with physical deformities as "hell-men" who suffer the consequences of having killed work animals in previous existences. Those who are exceedingly poor and lack both clothing and food to eat are those who committed no positive acts in previous existences. On the other hand, the wealthy man enjoys benefits of generosity in a previous life. And the universal monarch, the Cakkavatti king, is one who has gained his status through a kammic legacy born of actions which were supremely moral—which, in fact, were the very perfections which the Buddha himself attained prior to becoming the Buddha.

Kammic theory not only explains those physical and social differences among humans that are apparent at birth (or that can be deduced to have existed from birth), but it also is used to explain conditions which emerge during the course of a lifetime. That a woman proves to be barren is explained as a consequence of kamma (although, as was noted above, not her kamma alone). If a person dies a premature death, this too is explained by kamma. That such conditions are explained with reference to kammic theory would seem to suggest that the theory is fatalistic—that is, that one's situation (albeit constantly changing) has been foreordained by one's actions in a previous existence, the consequences of which are successively being realized.

Despite such arguments, kammic theory is fatalistic neither in practice nor in doctrine. As Obeyesekere has said, writing of Sri Lanka:

From a logical point of view *karma* is a highly deterministic theory of causation, but *karma* must be distinguished from Fate. A fatalistic theory of causation strictly implies that whatever one does has been preordained by an impersonal agency. By contrast, the Buddhist theory places responsibility for each individual's present fate quite squarely on the individual himself—albeit in his past births. Since the quality of my current action will, with some leeway, determine my future birth, I am in control of my own destiny. (1968:21)

Gombrich, writing both of the doctrinal position and of what he discovered was believed among practicing Buddhists in Sri Lanka, makes the point even stronger:

The doctrine is logically very far from fatalism; indeed it might be said to go to the other extreme. On one level the imprecision of linguistic usage is misleading. When a villager meets with misfortune he is liable to say, "It's *karma*" ('*Karumē*'), by which he means—and will, I think, say so if questioned—that the misfortune is the *result* of his former bad actions. To this extent "it can't be helped," but that does not mean that it is not his fault, or that he is not responsible. Determinism is a heresy.... Moreover, *karma* is not necessarily responsible even for everything that happens to you: it operates, if I may so put it, in a gross way. One monk said that *karma* determines the station in which you are born, and your luck (*vāsanāva*); after that, it is up to you—the present you. (1971a:145)

In order to be able to engage in acts which can be *either* morally positive or morally negative, it is essential that kammic theory not be construed by those who follow it as being fatalistic. In practice, a balance must be struck between an interpretation of one's present situation as having been brought about as a consequence of the ripening of the consequences of past kamma and an interpretation of one's present situation as being undetermined so that one has the choice to act in a positive or negative moral sense.[3]

In popular Buddhism, that is, among practicing Theravāda Buddhists, kamma is invoked as an explanation of conditions that have emerged in one's lifetime only on rare occasions. Indeed, the term kamma—*karumē* in Sinhalese, *kan* in Burmese, *kam* in Thai and Lao, *kamma* in Khmer—is restricted in usage to apply precisely to certain conditions for which there is no other explanation—that is, for conditions which must be accepted because there is nothing one can do

[3] I have discussed the two-sided nature of karmic theory at somewhat greater length in the Introduction.

about them. (On this usage, see Gombrich 1971a:145 and Spiro 1970:114–115.) This does not mean, as Gombrich has suggested, that "on the affective level the villager may not accept the total responsibility which he admits cognitively" (Gombrich 1971a:145–146). On the contrary, Buddhists in all the countries of Theravāda Buddhist South and Southeast Asia tend to act as though they had control over their lives unless something occurs that clearly is beyond their ability to control or do anything about. Since the results of previous kamma are, as Obeyesekere (1968:21) has said, "psychologically indeterminate," and I would add also cognitively indeterminate, that is, since they cannot be in fact known until they have actually manifested themselves, a person can assume that he has freedom to act—admittedly this freedom is conditioned by his "gross" kammic heritage.

This understanding of kamma permits us to explain the apparent anomaly that is reported from all Buddhist societies of Buddhists accepting several theories of causation in addition to that of kamma. In particular, it has been noted that all Buddhists believe that some of their misfortunes may be caused by spirits, not by kamma. Spiro has interpreted this fact as suggesting that Burmese Buddhists, at least, are denying kammic theory when they resort to explanations of events as having been caused by spirits—called *nats* in Burma.

> For, although as Buddhists they profess to believe in the karmic law—and, indeed, they perform numerous meritorious acts with the intention of enhancing their karma—as nat cultists they deny, at least by implication, its inevitability. (Spiro 1970:21)

This implies that kammic theory is fatalistic, whereas, as we have shown, it is not. Yet, although Spiro misinterprets kammic theory in this regard, he is correct in the reason for why a spirit-cause explanation is chosen over a kammic explanation for a particular misfortune:

> Since according to this doctrine [of kamma], present suffering is the karmic consequence of previous sinning, one can do nothing to avoid it. If, on the other hand, suffering is caused by nats and other harmful supernaturals, one can combat suffering, rather than acquiescing in it, by proper propitiation of these supernaturals. (Spiro 1978:256)

It is only when a condition is clearly beyond the ability of anyone to do anything to rectify it—and such conditions are actually rarely accepted outside of death—that one interprets it as having been a consequence of previous kamma. Kammic theory, insofar as it involves utilizing supposed previous actions to explain present conditions, is drawn upon only for ultimate explanations—for an explanation that can be used when no other explanation (scientific or magical) satisfies.[4]

Kammic theory provides practicing Buddhists not only with a means to explain conditions that are susceptible to neither natural nor supernatural (magical) explanation or control, but also, and of at least equal importance, with an orientation for action, that is, an ethos. The kammic ethos finds expression in the discourse of Buddhists of the Theravādin tradition rarely under the rubric of kamma but more commonly in language used to speak of the quest for merit (Pāli *puñña*, *kusala*; Sinhalese *pin*; Burmese *kutho*; Thai and Lao *bun*; Khmer *bon*) and the avoiding of actions that produce demerit (Pāli *pāpa*, *akusala*; Sinhalese *pav*; Burmese *akutho*; Thai, Lao, and Khmer *bāp*). Demerit does not receive equal billing in this theory of action; this reflects the interpretation that the avoiding of demerit produces merit. The kammic theory of action centers thus on merit-making.

For the majority of Theravāda Buddhists throughout South and Southeast Asia, merit-making is equated with religious action. It is not that these Buddhists lack knowledge of the other modes of the Path taught by the Buddha—that is, of *paññā*, "wisdom," and *samādhi*, "mental discipline," as well as *sīla*, "morality"—but that most people conceive of themselves as being unable to pursue these other modes of action to any significant degree. Even most Buddhist monks look upon their own actions, including those of adhering to the discipline (*vinaya*) and disseminating the teaching (*dhamma*), as aspects of merit-making. The centrality of merit-making to the practice of Theravāda Buddhism has made of merit a complex symbol to which many meanings adhere.

There are two meanings that are fundamental and are understood in much the same way by Buddhists everywhere. First, merit is seen as a form of spiritual insurance, an investment made with the expectation that in the future—and probably in a future existence—one will enjoy a relatively prolonged state without suffering. What villagers told Tambiah in a community in northeastern Thailand could be duplicated in most communities throughout the Theravādin world: "It is

[4] On this question of the relationship between kammic theory and other explanatory theories, see Tambiah (1970:41).

said that one's fund of merit accumulated in this life will ensure a rebirth blessed with happiness, prosperity, and wealth" (Tambiah 1968a:49). One's state in the next life is of significant concern primarily in situations in which one is conscious of one's inevitable death. Many merit-activities take place, however, without allusions to death and at times when few people are acutely aware of death.

A strong positive value still attaches to the quest for merit even when the concern about the future life is not present. In its second fundamental meaning, merit is also valued for the quality of virtue that a person acquires in the eyes of others through his or her acts of merit-making. Again, as northeastern Thai villagers told Tambiah: "While merit-making is . . . given ideological direction in terms of somehow immunizing the consequences of death and ensuring a prosperous rebirth, villagers also say it has certain consequences in this life: the giving of gifts to monks [the act of merit-making par excellence] produces a happy and virtuous state of mind" (loc. cit.). I argue that it is not the state of mind that is significant, although this may also be present, but the social recognition of being a person of virtue.

The virtue that accrues to the person who has accumulated merit has at least two different manifestations. At one level, virtue may be its own reward. Such an interpretation of virtue is evident among the Burmese when they speak of a person as having *gon*, a term derived from the Pāli term *guṇa*, meaning "virtue, good quality." As Nash has said: "The notion of *gon* . . . connotes a sterling personal character, special religious learning or piety, or even the trait of impartiality in dispute" (1965:76). Burmese also distinguish among several types of *gon* correlated with the three divisions of the Path: "The major forms of village *gon* are (1) *thila* [Pāli *sīla*] *gon*, morality and good character, (2) *thamadhi* [Pāli *samādhi*] *gon*, an incorruptible person, beyond bribe or self-interest, and (3) *pyinya* [Pāli *paññā*] *gon*, wisdom or learning (Nash 1965:271). Writing of Laos, Zago (1972:115) notes how the acquisition of merit becomes transformed into social prestige. Lao and Thai also speak of a person having *khun*, a cognate word to the Burmese *gon*, derived from the Pāli *guṇa*, to designate the intrinsic virtue acquired by the person through his moral actions.

On another level, the person who has accumulated merit may not only be one who radiates virtue in this narrow sense, but may also be a person who has enhanced efficacy in social action. The Burmese distinguish between such efficacy, known under the label of *pon*,[5] from simple virtue, *gon*. Nash says: "*Pon* is charisma (in the secular realm) and glory (in the sacred realm). *Pon* describes any power, moral or not, and *pon* is a mystic quality tied to *kan* [*kamma*], to *kutho* [merit], to drive, to ambition, and to the horoscope" (1965:272). One's *pon* is interpreted as being a function of one's kammic legacy, that is, of merit accumulated in previous lives. It is also something that can be cultivated either through moral actions or through actions that evidence one's ability to control events and other people. The supreme exemplar of the moral cultivator of *pon* is the monk, known in Burma as the *pongyi*, "great glory."[6] A man of *pon* need not, however, be a monk; he may also be a secular leader:

> Pon is a matter of personal achievement and in the village [in Burma] there are tides of competition to define a man of power. The idea of pon is mystical; it is close to the idea of grace, charity, election, destiny. The presence of great amounts of pon (all males have some) is a fact of social inference. It depends upon the meshing of community opinion, on the one side, and the mundane success and power of a man, on the other. . . . Such a mystic power is not a continually present thing. A leader must continually show his credentials to pon by being successful in this life, by being heeded by his fellow villagers, by getting respect from people outside of the village, and by being consulted by persons higher in official structure of political power. (Nash 1965:76–77)

The Thai and Lao call the equivalent to the Burmese man of *pon* a man who "has merit" (*mī bun*). While Thai and Lao recognize that everyone has a certain store of merit from one's past kamma and that everyone is capable of accumulating more merit, they speak only of the rare individual as being one who "has merit." Typically, these persons display unusual ability in the exercise of power; but it is not merely power itself that defines one as "having merit"; one must also have harnessed that power to moral ends. Past membership in the

[5] F. K. Lehman (personal communication) informs me that a more correct transliteration of this word is *hpon*, "spelt, in Burmese, *bhun*."

[6] According to Lehman (personal communication), the *hpon* of the *hpongyi* derives not from his own merit, but from that of the king, "the paramount traditional patron of the sangha as a whole; for the king, the entire sangha (of the kingdom) is his field of merit, which lets him make more merit than any other secular person." There is authoritative precedent for Nash's gloss (see, for example, Shway Yoe/Scott 1963:108–109), and one should, I believe, see Lehman's interpretation as an extension rather than as an alternative to that offered by Nash.

Buddhist Sangha or some extraordinary acts of merit-making are probably the most important demonstration that one's great kammic legacy has been used for moral purposes.

The "man-of-merit" to whom Thai and Lao have historically been most likely to point has been a king. Insofar as a king tempered his rule with moral imperatives and displayed his support of the faith through conspicuous and significant acts of merit-making, then he was likely to be recognized as having merit (see Akin Rabibhadana 1969:46–47; Keyes 1973 and 1977). In addition to kings, Thai and Lao may also recognize certain monks—those who have demonstrated extraordinary qualities—as persons who have particularly large stores of merit. And they may also recognize secular charismatics, particularly former monks, who become the centers of cults of politicoreligious movements as being men with merit.

Throughout Buddhist Southeast Asia, although perhaps not to the same extent in Sri Lanka,[7] merit is conceived almost as a substance that can be possessed in variable quantities and that can be translated into this-worldly virtue or power as well as stored up to be used at death to ensure a good rebirth. Merit is interpreted as deriving, in part, from the individual person's kammic legacy from previous incarnations and, in part, from the individual ongoing moral acts.

Merit is not only a good that can be used to benefit, either now or in a future existence, the individual. It is also something that can be shared in part or in whole with other people and used by them for their benefit. The idea of merit-transference, so important in the popular Buddhist traditions, appears, at first blush, to represent a significant departure from orthodox Theravāda Buddhism. Doctrinally, one is supposed to be morally responsible for one's own actions. In the famous words of the *Dhammapada*:

> By oneself alone is evil done,
> By oneself is one defiled,
> By oneself is evil left undone,
> By oneself alone is one purified;
> Both purity, impurity depend upon oneself
> And nobody is found who can purify another.[8]

[7] The concept of merit is given far less attention in the literature of popular Buddhism in Sri Lanka than it is in the comparable literature of Southeast Asia. This suggests that there may be a fundamental difference in the significance ascribed to merit in the Sinhalese tradition as compared with the Buddhist traditions of Southeast Asia. The question requires further inquiry.

[8] The translation is that of Bhikkhu Khantipalo (1966:12).

Yet, as Spiro has observed: "In the very face of the normative theory which insists that the karmic consequences of merit can attach only to the actor himself, Buddhism has long sanctioned. . . practices which significantly qualify this theory. . . . I am referring, of course, to the sharing and transfer of merit, practices in which the merit acquired by one person can be used to enhance the karma of another" (Spiro 1970:124).[9]

All of the popular Theravādin traditions of South and Southeast Asia are associated with manifold practices believed to effect the transfer of merit from one party to another.[10] While these practices do have, as Spiro has noted, an ancient lineage in Theravāda Buddhism—a fact to which I will return—their significance lies, I maintain, in making it possible for people who live within a social order—who have not, in other words, renounced the world—to adhere to the Buddhist theory of kamma. Without the inclusion of the conception of merit-transfer within the theory of karma, it would be difficult, if not impossible, for those who lead the lives of householders—as distinct from the life of the *bhikkhu*—to make kammic theory the basis of an ethos or orientation toward action. Before I pursue this argument, I will consider the formulations of the idea of merit-transference as contained in a ritual text from northern Thailand. This text permits one to grapple concretely with the social implications of the idea of merit-transference. I will then return, in the last part of the essay, to consider the question of the genesis of the concept of merit-transference and then conclude with some reflections on the place of the concept in the kammic theory of popular Theravāda Buddhism.

Text and Ritual in the Formulation of Religious Dogma

All religious worldviews are predicated upon a set of axiomatic dogmas about the nature of ultimate reality. These dogmas are the grounding, the bedrock, for all interpretations which people utilize in informing their experiences. In recent years, a number of anthropologists have begun to examine, in particular cases, the cultural sources from which specific peoples gain their understanding of dogmatic

[9] I have left out of this quotation Spiro's specification of these practices as being of two types because I see no justification in distinguishing between merit-transfer and merit-sharing.

[10] For discussions of these practices in the various Theravādin societies, see Gombrich (1971a:227–243 and 1971b), Malalasekere (1967), Obeyesekere (1968:25–26), Spiro (1970:124–128), Tambiah (1968a and 1970), Zago (1972:122–128), and Leclère (1899:274–275).

formulations. Victor Turner (1967:123, 128) has demonstrated, in great detail, that for the Ndembu, a nonliterate African people, ritual provides a powerful context in which the "communication of the sacra" takes place. Ritual, as Tambiah (1968b; 1970) has shown for a village in northeastern Thailand, remains important in societies in which at least a part of the populace, and especially religious specialists, are literate. Literacy adds, however, a new dimension to the sources of a religious worldview in that formulations of dogma may also be contained in texts.

The relevance of texts to religious dogma in the worldview of any people cannot be assumed simply because some set of texts have been recognized as belonging to a particular religious tradition. It is necessary, in every particular case, to identify those texts that can be shown to be the sources of dogmatic formulations that are being communicated to the people through some medium. There is no single integrated textual tradition based on a "canon" to the exclusion of all other texts (cf. Tambiah 1970:371). What Gombrich has said about the textual tradition of Theravāda Buddhism could be applied to any historic religion: "The Pali canon as we have it was not compiled at one time. Therefore. . . it cannot reflect the state of Buddhist religion at one given moment; nor indeed is it likely that so large and heterogeneous a body of material should be entirely free from contradictions" (1971a:42). The very size and complexity of a canon leads those who use it to give differential emphasis to its component texts. Moreover, even those for whom a defined set of scriptures exists will employ as sources of religious ideas many texts which do not belong to a canon. For example, the evidence from monastery libraries in Laos and Thailand (see Finot 1917; Tambiah 1968b; Keyes 1970; Sommai Premchit 1974–1975) reveal that what constitutes the Theravādin *dhamma* for people in these areas includes only a small portion of the total *Tipiṭaka*, some semi-canonical commentaries such as Buddhaghosa's *Vissudhimagga*, a large number of pseudo-*jātaka* and other pseudo-canonical works, histories of shrines and other sacred histories, liturgical works, and popular commentaries. Moreover, for any particular temple-monastery in Thailand or Laos, the collection of texts available to the people in the associated community are not exactly the same as those found in another temple-monastery. In brief, the relevance of textual formulations to religious dogma in popular worldviews is problematic in each specific case.

I assume, following the work of Tambiah, that textual constructions of religious ideas serve to formulate dogma for a community of people only if these constructions fit into a total religious field of meaning. Although individuals may be able to evolve their own personal religious worldviews through the study in private of esoteric texts, popular religion depends upon the public display and communication of religious messages. In traditional societies where structured education, formal or informal, was quite limited, the most important way in which religious ideas were communicated was through ritual. It follows that for these societies the most important texts are those which have an inherent relationship with particular rituals. In such cases, texts are invested by a people with a timelessness whose message becomes translated in ritual into meanings that inform ongoing social experience. In turn, the relevance of texts often depends upon the persistence of the rituals with which they are linked. In other words, there often exists a dialectical interconnection between texts and rituals in traditional societies which is comparable to the dialectical interrelationship between oral myth and ritual in preliterate societies (see Munn 1969 and Turner 1969).

For religions in which orthodoxy is important, certain rituals and their associated texts become critical sources of authority regarding fundamental dogma. While I cannot develop the point fully here, I assert that in Theravāda Buddhist societies there are two core rituals upon which the religion is predicated. The first ritual—or, more properly, set of rituals—is that in which suffering in its most profound form, that is, death, is subjected to Buddhist interpretation and juxtaposed with a course of action that moves people away from the abyss of meaninglessness to which ultimate suffering carries one. The problem of suffering is central to all religions, although not always so explicitly as it is in Buddhism, whose theology begins with the premise that all sentient existence is suffering (*dukkha*). The second ritual that lies at the foundation of Theravāda Buddhism as it is actually practiced is the ordination ritual wherein males are initiated into the Buddhist Order, the Sangha, as either *bhikkhus* ("monks") or *sāmaṇeras* ("novices"). Without a Sangha the religion (*sāsanā*) could not exist, for in addition to being of the Triple Gems (along with the Buddha and the Dhamma), the Sangha also functions to perpetuate the teachings of the Buddha.

Death rituals found in the various Theravāda Buddhist societies have already been shown to give expression to ideas of merit-transference (see Malalasekere 1967; Gombrich 1971b; Anusaraṇaśāsanakiarti and Keyes 1980). To my knowledge, only passing reference has been made to how these ideas also find expression in the Buddhist ordination ritual (Malalasekere 1967:89 and Gombrich 1971b:205). Indeed, insofar as the ordination ritual is considered to consist entirely of the enactment of actions specified in the standardized liturgical texts, texts that have a clear canonical basis,[11] then it would appear that merit-transference could be only a very minor theme of the ordination ritual. In no society, however, is the ordination ritual restricted to this enactment alone.

The essence of the ordination ritual involves the "going forth" of a male from the world and the assumption by him of a new life bound to the *vinaya*, the discipline. This renunciation of the world involves a fundamental dilemma for the society from which the world-renouncer has come. Tambiah has phrased this problem in the following way: "A question that puzzles the student of popular religion is how a lay public rooted in this world can adhere to a religion committed to the renunciation of the world" (Tambiah 1968a:41). This question is resolved in all Theravāda Buddhist societies through the construal of the role of the Sangha as being a source of merit rather than being (except in very rare instances) a means to the attainment of ultimate salvation, *Nibbana*. The man who becomes a monk or a novice accumulates great merit for himself; he also serves as a "field of merit" for the laity in that the offerings made by the laity to the Sangha are defined in all Theravādin traditions as being the supreme moral acts through which the laity acquires merit; and, at least in some cases, he generates merit that can be transferred to others. As a "field of merit" the member of the Sangha serves a general social function in the community where he resides. As one who is capable of transferring significant merit to others, he is able to strengthen specific social bonds, such as those linking him to his parents.

While the canonically based ordination texts make no direct mention of merit-transference from the member of the Sangha to his parents,[12] I have found a northern Thai ritual text connected with the

[11] For the Pāli text of the ordination procedure, together with an English translation, see Prince Vajirañāṇa Vovorasa (1973). For a translation of the canonical source (*Vinaya-piṭaka*, *Mahāvagga* I), see Rhys Davids and Oldenberg (1968, Part I, pp. 73–238).

[12] F.K. Lehman (personal communication) informs me that there is some canonical basis for the notion of merit-transference to parents by one who is ordained. The "Buddha is said to have preached to and otherwise made every effort to ensure the good *kamma* of his mother. The case is not, I admit, very direct, but we must not, in these matters of religion, discount analogical reasoning and its extensions. The canon here is certainly, and not implausibly, interpreted as allowing for merit transfer."

ordination ritual that makes this idea central. This same text is also associated with the ordination tradition found among Lao-speaking peoples in Laos and northeastern Thailand. I suspect that counterparts to this text, or at least to symbolic acts that convey the same message in the ritual, could be found in ordination rituals throughout Buddhist Southeast Asia.[13] The formulation of the idea of merit-transference contained in the text that I will now consider is similar in many respects to formulations found in association with death rites. Yet, there are also differences, derived, as was already noted, from the interpretation given in popular Buddhism to the role of the Sangha. These similarities and differences will become clear once we have considered the contents of the text in some detail.

The "Blessings of Ordination"

In 1967 and 1968, while I was engaged in anthropological field research in Mae Sariang district, northwestern Thailand, I had the opportunity to observe a number of ordinations of both novices and monks. At the conclusion of the ordination ritual proper, it was the custom for one of the new monks or novices to present a sermon, an act which was explicitly likened by some informants to the act of the Buddha giving his first sermon following his enlightenment. However, the analogy was not carried to the substance of the sermon itself, since the sermon, always involving the reading of a text, was not a version of the *Dhamma-cakka sutta*, the sermon of "setting the wheel of the law in motion." In most cases, the new member of the Sangha read a sermon entitled in northern Thai *ānisong būat* (Pāli *ānisaṁsa pavaja*),[14] "the blessings of ordination."

The term *ānisong* (abbreviated as *song* in some contexts) is used as a label for a category of texts found throughout a large area populated by Tai-speaking people in northern Thailand and in neighboring areas in Burma, Yunnan, Laos, and northeastern Thailand. Although there is no firm evidence, it appears that the tradition of composing *ānisong*

[13]There is reason to suppose that ideas of merit-transference may not be associated with ordinations in Sri Lanka. In Sinhalese society far fewer men go through the ordination ritual than do men in Southeast Asia where ordination is a rite of passage. Moreover, ordination rituals in Sri Lanka are not community rituals as they are in Southeast Asia, but are performed only at the headquarters of the several Sinhalese sects.

[14] Although the Thai spelling yields this version of the Pāli word, the more correct Pāli form, as F.K. Lehman reminds me, is *pabbaja*.

probably began in northern Thailand. All of these texts are commentaries or interpretations, presented in mythological form, of important merit-making rituals (see Finot 1917:72 and Keyes 1970:227). They all appear to incorporate materials from Jātaka tales or from other Buddhist legends. These texts have been written in the vernacular rather than in Pāli and are, therefore, directly comprehensible to the people.[15] All *ānisong* texts appear to have been read in the context of the rituals with which they are associated.

Palm-leaf manuscript versions of the *ānisong būat* have been reported from Luang Prabang in Laos (Finot 1917:205) and from Chiang Mai in northern Thailand (Sommai Premchit 1974–1975, Part I, p. 11). The text has been important in the northern Thai tradition of Mae Sariang for at least two hundred years (and probably much longer), for a copy of the text bearing a date of 1770/1771 was found among a collection of manuscripts which had been hidden in a cave near the Salween River in Mae Sariang district (Keyes 1970:237).

In recent years, the practice of copying manuscripts by hand onto palm-leaf has begun to disappear as a consequence of the availability of printed works. In northern Thailand several printer-publishers have printed important religious texts, often in a form quite similar in shape to traditional palm-leaf manuscripts. In the ordination rituals that I observed in Mae Sariang, versions of *ānisong būat* that had been printed in Chiang Mai were used even though several temple-monasteries had palm-leaf versions in their libraries. For purposes of analysis I have used a recension, printed in Chiang Mai (*Ānisong Būat*, n.d.).

The text relates a story, purportedly told by the Buddha himself when he was living near Savatthi, of a young man, Prince Mahinda (*Mahinda kumāra*), who wanted to be a monk. However, his parents held false beliefs (*micchādiṭṭhika*), and his father, in particular, was a hunter and a cruel man who had no faith in the Three Gems. Denied his parents' permission to become a *bhikkhu* on every occasion that he asked, the young man became very despondent and went on a fast.

[15] As no one has yet done a systematic comparison of *ānisong* texts from different parts of the area, it is not possible to be definitive about the types of language and script used. I have seen texts written in Yuan script, a script traditionally used in northern Thailand, parts of the Shan States, and in some areas of Yunnan and Laos, in *tūa tham* ("*dhammic* script"), a closely related orthographic system used in Laos and northeastern Thailand, and Thai, the national script of Thailand and pre-modern Siam. I suspect that there is little variation in vocabulary or style in texts from throughout the area, since all versions I have examined strike me as using what might be termed "archaic" forms.

After seven days, his mother could no longer remain passive at the sight of her son wasting away and so she showed mercy (*NT indū*) on him and granted him permission to be ordained. The son immediately became happy and asked that his mother take him to enter the religion under the direction of a learned *bhikkhu* (*NT khrūbā phikkhu song*).

The next part of the text concerns the preparations of the young man for entering the Sangha and his transformation into a *sāmaṇera*, a novice. While her son was in the process of becoming a member of the Order, his mother continued about her everyday tasks.

One day while in the woods gathering firewood, she grew tired and stopped to take a rest. She fell asleep, and while in that state she was visited by a servant of Yama, the Lord of Hell (*naraka*). He asked her if she had done any acts of merit (*puñña*) while in the human world. When she responded that she had not, the servant of Yama tied her up and told her he would take her to Hell. When she saw the flames of Hell she said that they were a beautiful yellow like her son's robes when he entered the Sangha.

Lord Yama consulted the documents and found that the woman had committed the actions of demerit (*pāpa*) by holding to false views (*micchādiṭṭhi*). He then struck her mouth three times with a piece of wood and then took her and cast her toward Hell. Just at that moment there appeared a beautiful golden lotus as big as a cart wheel that spread out to catch her. Seeing her protected from the fires of Hell, Lord Yama was truly amazed. He brought her back and said that he could not understand, since the documents showed that she had acted demeritoriously and he had tried to place her in Hell. Why then have you not suffered? he asked. You must tell me, he said, whether in fact you did any meritorious acts in your lifetime.

The woman then addressed Lord Yama in a respectful manner and said: I neither did any act of merit nor observed any of the moral precepts (*sīla*) while in the human world. I do have one astute jewel-like son who entered the religion (*sāsana*) of the Buddha and has become a mendicant (*samaṇa*) and intends to become a *bhikkhu*. He lives in the great city of Savatthi. I have told you all my kamma, she concluded.

The woman was returned to the human world and she then reported what had happened to her son. He realized that having gone forth as a novice, he was able to show compassion and help (*NT phōt*) his mother. Then, he thought, I will become a monk in order to help my father.

After being ordained as a *bhikkhu*, he undertook to follow the practice by observing strictly all of the virtues incumbent upon a monk, by study of the scriptures, and by meditation. Shortly after the young man's ordination, his father died. Because of his demeritorious action, the father became a ghost (*petta visaya*). He made his state known to his son, who then undertook to extend compassion (*metta*) toward his father. After receiving morning alms, he transferred the merit of the alms to his parents through the pouring of a libation (*NT yāt nam*).

As the result of these acts, his father was immediately released from his loathsome state (*NT pēt*) and was reborn a *deva* in heaven (*NT mų̄ang fā*) and lived in a palace fifteen *yōjanas* high. His mother through merit-building also attained the same place, that is, in the Tāvatiṁsa heaven. The merit which attached to the parents ensured that they lived for a long time.

The text continues by pointing out that just as these effects happened then, so now the same benefits (*ānisaṁsa*) follow from ordination. Anyone who sponsors the ordination of their son as a novice will gain the benefits for four *kappa*,[16] and for ordination as a *bhikkhu* will gain the benefits for eight *kappa*. If one sponsors the ordination of someone else's son, one will receive the same benefits. If one sponsors the ordination of a slave as a novice, he will receive benefits for two *kappa*, and if the slave is ordained as a *bhikkhu*, he will gain benefits for four *kappa*. A wife who allows her husband to become a *sāmaṇera* will receive benefits for eight *kappa*, and if her husband becomes a monk she will realize benefits for sixteen *kappa*. As for the individual himself, he will realize benefits for sixteen *kappa* if he becomes a novice and for thirty-two *kappa* if he becomes a monk. Each *kappa* can be thought of in terms of the time it would take for a rough rock 1,000 *wa* high (about 2,000 meters) to become smooth if it is wiped with a divine cloth every hundred years by the *devas*.

The text concludes by having the Buddha say that the man who was ordained in this story practiced meditation and was reborn as Mahinda Thera. Those who heard the sermon given by the Buddha were said to have advanced along the road to *Nibbana*, the distance moved being a function of past kamma.

[16]A *kappa* (Skt. *kalpa*) is postulated in some sources to be equal to 4,320,000,000 years (see McFarland 1960:88).

Conclusions

In this text we are presented with a myth, and all myths, as Lévi-Strauss has shown us, turn on fundamental contradictions encountered by people in their experiences. Here the contradiction stems from the fact that a person who has entailed social responsibilities by virtue of being a son and a member of society more generally must renounce those responsibilities when he becomes a member of the Sangha. The contradiction is resolved in the myth, as in the ritual of ordination itself,[17] by the positing of a merit-transference from son to parents or to others who are linked to him as patron, master, or wife as a consequence of the merit made through the action of ordination. To put the point in somewhat different terms, without the idea of merit-transference there would be an irresoluble conflict between the demands of lay society and the demands of following the Path of the Buddha according to the Vinaya. Why should parents forego their son's labor and renounce his sexual potential to produce heirs? Or, if a man is married, why should his wife allow her husband to end his responsibilities for supporting her and his children? Why should a master release his slave? Why should anyone seek to sponsor a person in renouncing the world, since in so doing the person so patronized would not be in a position to repay his patron with tangible benefits? The text answers these implicit questions by stressing that all those who release a man from his social obligations in order that he might become a member of the Sangha will receive transcendent benefits, a reward of great merit (*puñña*), thereby ensuring a decrease in suffering in the future.

More than positing an abstract notion of merit-transference, the text also formulates very specific notions about the relative quantity of merit gained from releasing a person from his social obligations to become a member of the order, and it also specifies in concrete, albeit mythical, terms the consequences of such merit. The first part of the text treats the relationships in a family in which there is but a single son, a situation that makes understandable the great reluctance that the parents have in permitting their son to renounce the world. In the myth, the mother is depicted as having never performed any meritorious action on her own behalf and having in fact committed the great

[17]For a preliminary analysis of the ordination ritual in northern Thailand, see Keyes (1978).

act of demerit by holding false views. Her own kamma should ensure that she be reborn in Hell. Thus, Lord Yama is truly amazed when he finds that he cannot cast her into Hell. It is the merit made by her son's ordination as a novice, symbolized by the wheel which is also a lotus, and the transfer of that merit to his mother, which ensures that she does not end up in Hell. The father, on the other hand, has such negative kamma as a result of having been a hunter and a cruel man that he cannot escape being reborn as a ghost. Nonetheless, his son again comes to his aid, and through being ordained as a monk and following the discipline he is able to make sufficient merit which, after its transfer to his deceased father, leads to his father's being reborn in a heavenly state. In other words, the myth shows that even those whose personal kamma is very bad can benefit greatly by the merit transferred to them by their son through his actions of being ordained successively as a novice and then as a monk. Moreover, the episode involving the father also asserts that merit can be transferred to the dead; this is a theme which appears more developed in rituals and associated texts connected with death.

It should be pointed out here that in northern Thailand, where this text comes from, the normal practice is for most young men to be ordained as novices and only very rarely as monks. It is commonly said that one is ordained as a novice in order to make merit for one's mother, who cannot herself be ordained.

The text also recognizes social connections other than those that obtain between parents and son. Interestingly, in the relative numerical weighting given to the merit acquired through transference from one who has been ordained, wives are said to benefit more than parents. Despite this quantitative superiority of the merit transferred to a wife over that transferred to parents, the text clearly emphasizes the latter transfer. The apparent discrepancy probably reflects the fact that although men are rarely ordained after marriage, when they are ordained at this stage the renunciation of social obligations results in much greater hardships for those to whom ties have been severed. The text also specifies that a man who releases a slave for the purposes of ordination also gains merit by transfer. It should be noted that slavery has been outlawed in Thailand for over a hundred years, and so the formulation here is of only theoretical interest today. Finally, the text adduces that a person who sponsors an ordination can obtain merit equal to that obtained by parents. Ordination rituals often involve heavy expenditures on the part of the sponsors, primarily as a result of the costs of feasting large numbers of guests. Poor families might not be able to raise the wealth necessary to sponsor an ordination. The promise of great merit for the sponsor of an ordination thus becomes an important incentive for those who are approached by poor people (usually kinsmen) to serve as sponsors.

Although the text considered here is clearly post-canonical, even if northern Thai subsume it under the general rubric of "*dhamma*,"[18] and although the formulation of the idea of merit-transference contained within it is in an idiom that can be comprehended by those who adhere to the cultural tradition of northern Thailand, the idea itself is not original with the northern Thai. As was already noted, this idea finds expression in other ritual contexts—notably in those connected with death—among all Theravādins. Indeed, there is clear evidence that the idea of merit-transference is to be found in early Buddhism, even if subject to dispute and accepted only grudgingly, as McDermott (1980:191) has noted. (Also see McDermott 1974, and compare Woodward 1914, Malalasekere 1967, and Gombrich 1971b.) The Buddhist conception of merit-transference represents a reworking of the pre-Buddhist Indian practice of *śraddhā* (Pāli *saddhā*), entailing the offering of food and other goods for use by the dead (Law 1936, Gombrich 1971a:210–214, McDermott 1980:190–191; O'Flaherty 1980a:xv and 1980b:10–13; also see Knipe's [1977] discussion of the relationship between Hindu *śraddhā* practices and the development of ideas of merit-transference).[19] In the Buddhist reformulation, the substance of food was replaced by a more intangible quality, that of merit. As Gombrich has said, "whatever the date of the final victory of orthodoxy, it is clear that sensible Theravādin monks decided that food being visibly consumed by a monk could not possibly be eaten by someone else, so that, if people persisted in their habit of feeding

[18] The "*dhammic*" label is applied by northern Thai—and by other Buddhists in Southeast Asia—to any text that has long been associated with accepted Buddhist practice. The "*dhamma*" of the northern Thai tradition thus includes many pseudo-canonical and non-canonical as well as canonical texts. For further discussion of this label, see Finot (1917).

[19] The idea of merit-transference also finds a place in Hindu thought, but as O'Flaherty notes, the Buddhists developed "the idea of merit transfer far more strongly than Hindus ever did themselves" (O'Flaherty 1980b:10). The relative unimportance of the idea of merit-transference in Hinduism is reflected in the conclusion—albeit overstated—reached by Ursula Sharma in her essay "Theodicy and the Doctrine of Karma." Sharma says that in popular Hinduism the idea of merit-transference "receives neither ritual institutionalization (unless we regard some of the rites honouring the dead, such as Shraddha, in this way) nor textual elaboration, to the best of my knowledge" (Sharma 1973:363n).

dead relatives, the custom required reinterpretation. What the relatives were really getting was something else—merit" (Gombrich 1971b:213-214).

Such a reinterpretation posed a serious theological problem in Theravāda Buddhism: how could the belief that the merit made by one person could be utilized for the benefit of another be accommodated to the basic doctrine that each person reaps the positive and negative consequences of only his or her own kamma? McDermott has shown that one solution to this problem, found in the *Sādhīna Jātaka*, was to insist on the correctness of individual responsibility for one's own kamma for monks even if not accepted by the laity:

> We take this *Jātaka* as representative of a period in Theravāda history when the inconsistency between the Buddha's teachings on *kamma* and belief in the transfer of merit was recognized in some monastic circles, but when the popular belief in the possibility of merit transference as demonstrated in popular religious practice was too strong any longer to be denied. If the possibility of merit transference could not be denied practically, at least the practice which supported the belief could be discouraged by the monks who wished to remain true to the earlier tradition. (McDermott 1974:386)

This solution remains possible even today for some monks who decline to participate in rites involving the idea of merit-transference. But such individuals have probably always been extremely rare. Most monks have been too much drawn into the ambience of the social order and have accepted their roles as sources of merit.

The more common theological solution, according to Gombrich, consists of a harmonization of practice with canonical theory, "although not without becoming exceedingly tortuous (and philologically barbarous)" (Gombrich 1971b:219). The theological efforts to save the purity of the doctrine of individual responsibility for one's own kamma appear in Gombrich's accounts to be relatively well known to Sinhalese monks. The explicitness of the merit-transference ideas in the "Blessings of Ordination" (and in other texts) make it less likely that Theravādin monks in Southeast Asia were quite so aware of these efforts. In Southeast Asia, contrary to the situation in Sri Lanka as described by Gombrich, the idea that merit can be generated by one person and transferred to another is accepted at the cognitive as well as the affective level.[20]

[20]The distinction between cognitive and affective beliefs is developed at some length by Gombrich (1971a and 1971b) in his studies of Sinhalese Buddhism.

Gombrich has suggested a reason why merit-transference is an essential element in the doctrine of kamma in popular Buddhism: "A sociologist might add that, although the Buddhist doctrine of karma is purely individualistic, merit-transference can make merit appear as the common property of a social group, so that *patti* [proferring merit to others] is functional for kinship solidarity" (1971b:219). A totally individualistic ethic whereby the individual works out his own salvation through assuming sole responsibility for both his actions and the positive and negative consequences of his actions would undermine any dependence of the individual on society. Popular Buddhism, unlike the Buddhism of the religious virtuoso, is adhered to by people who have, *au contraire*, committed themselves to living within specific social orders. Thus, while they have accepted the Buddhist doctrine of kamma, they have come to conceive of merit as having the character of a "spiritual currency," to use Gombrich's term (1971b:216–217), that is a transferable commodity. The importance of this commodity is stressed primarily in those situations when there is a rupture in the social order: that is, when a person dies and when a person renounces ordinary social life in order to become a member of the Buddhist Sangha. Yet another rupture, one that has not been given attention here, occurs when there is a crisis of political legitimacy (Keyes 1977). The flow of the currency of merit serves, in the practice of popular Buddhism, to repair the rupture.[21] In other circumstances, those who adhere to popular Buddhism are willing to accept the more orthodox interpretations of the doctrine of kamma. The individual's personal place in the hierarchy of suffering has been, to his mind, conditioned by past kamma. The individual also can act in morally responsible ways to enhance his virtue or power and to ensure a good rebirth. But as a committed member of society, the individual has foisted upon himself or herself a social imperative. The idea of merit-transference makes possible the accommodation of the Buddhist theory of kamma to this social imperative. I would stress that in so concluding, I am not implying, as F. K. Lehman (personal communication) suggests, that the imperatives of social life account for people's belief in merit-transference. Rather, I am saying that kammic doctrines have made

[21] The argument here is not obviated by the fact—as F.K. Lehman (personal communication) reminds me—that the most common ritual act that entails transfer of merit is one in which the merit that one has made is shared with all sentient beings. The pouring of a libation at the end of a ritual act of merit-making to effect such a transfer is but a leitmotif, signifying (as do other ritual elements) that as a moral actor, one is part of a larger moral universe. By way of contrast, the merit-transference to parents and other significant persons occupies a central place in ordination rituals, funerary rites, and charismatic movements.

sense to those who have articulated a Theravāda Buddhist worldview with the totality of social experience only in formulations that have incorporated ideas of merit-transference.

References Cited

Akin Rabibhadana
1969 The Organization of Thai Society in the Early Bangkok Period, 1782–1873. Ithaca, N.Y.: Cornell University Southeast Asia Program, Data Paper, 74.

Ānisong Būat
n.d. Ānisong Būat (The Blessings of Ordination). Chiang Mai: Thān Thōng Kānphim. (Probably printed in the mid-1960s.)

Anusaraṇaśāsanakiarti, Phra Khru, and Charles F. Keyes
1980 Funerary Rites and the Buddhist Meaning of Death: An Interpretative Text from Northern Thailand. Journal of the Siam Society 68(1):1–28.

Dhammapada
1966 Growing the Bodhi Tree in the Garden of the Heart, Being the Verses of the Dhammapada. Bhikkhu Khantipalo, trans. Bangkok: Buddhist Association of Thailand.

Finot, Louis
1917 Recherches sur la littérature laotienne. Bulletin de l'École Française d'Extrême-Orient 17(5):1–219.

Gombrich, Richard
1971a Precept and Practice: Traditional Buddhism in the Rural Highlands of Ceylon. Oxford: Clarendon Press.
1971b "Merit-Transference" in Sinhalese Buddhism: A Case Study of the Interaction between Doctrine and Practice. History of Religions 11:203–219.

Keyes, Charles F.
1970 New Evidence on Northern Thai Frontier History. *In* In Memoriam Phya Anuman. Tej Bunnag and Michael Smithies, eds. Bangkok: The Siam Society. Pp. 221–250.
1973 The Power of Merit. Visakha Puja B. E. 2516 (Bangkok). Pp. 95–102.
1977 Millennialism, Theravāda Buddhism, and Thai Society. Journal of Asian Studies 36(2):283–302.
1978 Donning the Yellow Robes: Theravada Buddhist Ordination Rituals in Northern Thailand, Visakha Puja B. E. 2521 (Bangkok). Pp. 36–50.

Knipe, David M.
1977 *Sapiṇḍīkaraṇa*: The Hindu Rite of Entry into Heaven. *In* Religious Encounters with Death. Frank Reynolds and Earle Waugh, eds. University Park: Pennsylvania State University Press. Pp. 111–124.

Law, B. C.
1936 The Buddhist Conception of Spirits. London: Luzac.

Leclère, Adhemard
1899 Le Buddhisme au Cambodge. Paris: Ernest Leroux.
McDermott, James P.
1974 Sādhina Jātaka: A Case Against the Transfer of Merit. Journal of the American Oriental Society 94(3):385–387.
1980 Karma and Rebirth in Early Buddhism. *In* Karma and Rebirth in Classical Indian Traditions. Wendy Doniger O'Flaherty, ed. Pp. 165–192.
McFarland, G. B.
1960 Thai-English Dictionary. Stanford: Stanford University Press.
Malalasekere, G. P.
1967 "Transference of Merit" in Ceylonese Buddhism. Philosophy East and West 17:85–90.
Munn, Nancy D.
1969 The Effectiveness of Symbols in Murngin Rite and Myth. *In* Forms of Symbolic Action. Robert F. Spencer, ed. Seattle, Wash.: American Ethnological Society, Proceedings. Pp. 178–207.
Nash, Manning
1965 The Golden Road to Modernity: Village Life in Contemporary Burma. New York: Wiley.
Obeyesekere, Gananath
1968 Theodicy, Sin and Salvation in a Sociology of Buddhism. *In* Dialectic in Practical Religion. E. R. Leach, ed. Cambridge: Cambridge University Press. Pp. 7–40.
O'Flaherty, Wendy Doniger
1980a Introduction. *In* Karma and Rebirth in Classical Indian Traditions. Wendy Doniger O'Flaherty, ed. Berkeley: University of California Press. Pp. ix–xxv.
1980b Karma and Rebirth in the Vedas and Purāṇas. *In* Karma and Rebirth in Classical Indian Traditions. Wendy Doniger O'Flaherty, ed. Berkeley: University of California Press. Pp. 3–37.
Rhys Davids, T. W., and Hermann Oldenberg, trans.
1968 Vinaya Texts. Delhi: Motilal Banarasidass.
Sharma, Ursula
1973 Theodicy and the Doctrine of Karma. Man 8:347–364.
Shway Yoe (Sir James George Scott)
1963 The Burman: His Life and Notions. New York: W. W. Norton.
Sommai Premchit
1974–1975 Pramūan rāichų khamphī bailān lae samut khọi nai khēt amphōē mųang Chiang Mai, phāk 1, 2, 3 (Catalogue of Manuscripts in the Mųang District, Chiang Mai, Parts 1, 2, 3). Chiang Mai: Chiang Mai University, Faculty of Social Sciences, Department of Sociology and Anthropology.
Spiro, M. E.
1970 Buddhism and Society. New York: Harper and Row.
1978 Burmese Supernaturalism. Expanded edition. Philadelphia: Institute for the Study of Human Issues.
Tambiah, S. J.
1968a The Ideology of Merit and the Social Correlates of Buddhism in a

Thai Village. *In* Dialectic in Practical Religion. E. R. Leach, ed. Cambridge: Cambridge University Press. Pp. 41–121.
1968b Literacy in a Buddhist Village in North-East Thailand. *In* Literacy in Traditional Societies. Jack Goody, ed. Cambridge: Cambridge University Press. Pp. 86–131.
1970 Buddhism and the Spirit Cults in North-east Thailand. Cambridge: Cambridge University Press.

Trai Phūm (Traibhūmi kāthā)
Forthcoming The Three Worlds According to King Ruang: A Thai Buddhist Cosmology. Translated and with an introduction by Frank E. and Mani B. Reynolds. Berkeley: Lancaster and Miller. Berkeley Buddhist Research Series.

Turner, Victor
1967 The Forest of Symbols. Ithaca, N.Y.: Cornell University Press.
1969 Forms of Symbolic Action: Introduction. *In* Forms of Symbolic Action. Robert F. Spencer, ed. Seattle, Wash.: American Ethnological Society, Proceedings. Pp. 3–25.

Vajirañāṇa Vovorasa, Prince
1973 Ordination Procedure. Bangkok: Mahāmakuṭarājavidhyālaya.

Warren, Henry Clarke
1953 Buddhism in Translations. Cambridge: Harvard University Press.

Woodward, F. L.
1914 The Buddhist Doctrine of Reversible Merit. The Buddhist Review (London) 6:38–50.

Zago, Marcel
1972 Rites et cérémonies en milieu bouddhiste Lao. Rome: Università Gregoriana Editrice.

Conclusion: Karma, the Uses of an Idea

E. Valentine Daniel

The contributors to this volume are all primarily anthropologists, and it may be noted that none are Indologists. Nevertheless, much like the Indologists who are interested in the subject of karma, we too have asked, "What does karma mean?"[1] However, what we mean by meaning is somewhat different from what they mean by meaning; and as for the karma of karma in these somewhat different meanings of meaning it is perhaps too early to foretell. The differences between our two approaches to the study of karma may be best illustrated by analogy to the two approaches to the issue of meaning we find in linguistics, namely, semantics and pragmatics.[2] For the semanticist, meaning is essentially referential; it can be traced to and located in a lexicon; it is a function of a grammar which is by and large context-free. For the pragmatist the meaning of a message is a function of a grammar which is expressible only as a function of any number of pragmatic factors, such as speaker, audience, referent, location, time, and so on, and includes the more delimited semantic or context-free grammar which for the semanticists constitute the sole meaning of the message. The analogy, granted, is not flawless; it is intended, however, to highlight our quest in this volume, which has been to locate the meaning of karma *in use*, as it pragmatically expresses itself, embedded in a cultural context.

[1] See, for example, the companion volume edited by Wendy O'Flaherty (1980).

[2] See Michael Silverstein (1976) for a lucid discussion of the two and the implications of the difference for anthropology.

Thus culture is a message pragmatically communicated to us, communicated in its context of use.[3] The anthropologist's task is to ferret out this message, understand it, and make it conceptually available as well as accessible to a different, usually Western scholarly public. This responsibility or task entails two goals. One is to understand a culture or a given aspect of a culture in its own terms and for its own sake. The second is to interpret or translate what has been thus understood into one's own (usually Western) terms. These two goals are neither always complementary nor consonant with each other, and the fate of culture in interpretation is not unlike that of poetry in translation. And yet we have reason to be encouraged in realizing that when we do approach the study of culture from a pragmatic point of view the dichotomy between the interpreter and the object of interpretation is dialectically subsumed in the interpretation itself. For the anthropologist, as field worker, ethnographer, and interpreter, finds himself to be a part of the very pragmatic equation he proposes to study. By interpreter I intend to include the very means employed by the anthropologist for effecting interpretation, namely, the culture-concept and its attendant assumptions of a certain mode of signification which is in itself the product of an epistemology that is non-Indian. The meaning contained in a pragmatic equation thus constituted becomes the locus classicus of interpretation. And this interpretation, which is intersubjective rather than objective, is the essence of culture. To paraphrase Habermas, culture by definition becomes dialogic and cannot be monologic (see McCarthy 1978).

If, however, the object of interpretation as well as the interpreter become dialectically subsumed in the interpretation that is intersubjectively generated, the dialectical tension between the object of interpretation and the interpreter is never completely neutralized, nor should it be. The anthropologist's task vis-à-vis this dialectical tension is twofold. On the one hand, he must strain interpretation to its limit —that is, stop short of subjecting it to a total collapse of meaning— by pushing it in the direction of the interpretive object with the hope of apperceiving it in its near-pristine state. On the other hand, he must self-consciously hold tight to the reins of self-reflection and awareness of his own place and role as interpreter in the pragmatic equation of cultural meaning. In other words, the tension inherent in interpreta-

[3] By "culture," in this essay, I refer to the general concept of culture, to the particular cultures—Indian, Tibetan, Thai, or Balinese—on which these essays are based, and to karma (that aspect of culture which is under scrutiny).

tion is one of push and pull, the former favoring the interpretive object, the latter the interpreting subject.

Given that most of our essays (with the possible exception of Boon's) have been written in the push-spirit, so to speak, I shall devote the greater part of this essay to examining the pull side of this tension. I shall return briefly at the end to suggest that perhaps there is more room, if not need, for pushing. With this in mind it might serve us well to meet again with Indologists at a different level of abstraction to discourse upon the potential for enlightenment that we are likely to find in Hindu, Buddhist, or Jaina epistemology; or even more appropriately, in an Indic semiotic. Such a finding will not only enhance our understanding of karma but also enhance and enrich our concept of culture.

To begin with, the true character of a summary essay requires me to identify a common premise which all the contributors to this volume share apart from our common problem, karma. This common premise, as I have already implicitly assumed, is the concept of culture; but here is where simplicity for anthropology begins and ends. For given the oxymoron that "culture" is, its fruitfulness not withstanding (Boon 1973), it is possible for every one of us to smuggle into his or her respective study—smuggle into his or her pragmatic equation—his or her own idiosyncratic definition of culture. However, I shall make yet another assumption, namely, that all of us see culture as being, among other things (if not solely), a system of signs[4]—an assumption made safe by the knowledge that at least none of our contributors are dyed-in-the-wool adaptationists (see Keesing 1974). Insofar as all of us subscribe to the notion that culture redescribes reality through a system of signs, my attempt to examine the content of the essays in this volume under a tropologically formulated system of redescription will not be out of place.

In this volume and in many other works karma has been characterized as a doctrine or a theory. I do not know whether this is a fair characterization from an Indological point of view. Assuming that it is, I shall make a series of defensible reductions which I shall not defend here but instead use to proceed to the main argument. The most famous treatment of karma as doctrine if not theory in the annals of the social sciences is that of Max Weber, who gave karma that

[4]I say "sign" rather than "symbol" because I wish to preserve the useful Peircean trichotomy according to which "symbol" is but one of three kinds of signs, the other two being icon and index.

dubious distinction of being the most airtight response extant to the question of theodicy. Weber's view of karma as doctrine or theory constitutive of action is consonant with Geertz's understanding of culture as a model for and of behavior (1966). By reducing doctrine as theory to model I do not wish to trivialize the significant differences that obtain between theory or doctrine, on the one hand, and model, on the other. But that at the core of every theory or every doctrine there lies a model, as a means of or mode for representation, is a defensible claim. The next reduction I wish to make is by means of a link to one already made by Max Black (1962), namely, that metaphor is to poetic language what model is to scientific language. Ricoeur (1975:241–243) citing Hesse (1970) observes that a model and a metaphor are alike in that they are both instruments of redescription. Even though the model that Black, Hesse, and Ricoeur have in mind is the scientific one whose metaphoric essence they are keen on exposing, the cultural model of Geertz is no different. By this token, then, karma as a cultural doctrine or model—one may even call it an ethnoscientific model—redescribes a certain "reality." Different metaphors shed different shades as well as different intensities of light and exploit different shadows of the explanandum for illuminating.

However, a cultural theory, a model for and of behavior which a culture constructs for itself—in short, a macro-sign complex—need not be seen as functioning exclusively as a metaphor or an extended metaphor. "Metaphor" is being employed here more in its tropological sense than in the structural linguistic sense formulated by Jakobson (1960) and used so imaginatively by Lévi-Strauss (1966). A cultural theory's dominant mode of expression might well belong to one of the other major tropes, namely, metonymy, synecdoche, or even irony. Different cultures or different subsystems within a culture may well favor one tropological mode or representation over another. The point has already been made for the genre of poetry among the ancient Tamils, wherein the dominant mode of expression is metonymy, with metaphor playing the subdominant one (Ramanujan 1967).

Let us take metaphor first: karma as metaphor. In so far as karma is a doctrine, it represents "reality" as a theory. This is certainly a metaphoric function. However, a close examination of the essays in this volume display the metaphoric functions of karma in many more interesting ways.

James Boon's paper is unique not only because it is a study of a culture so far removed from India, but also because—in terms of our immediate subject matter, karma—it is the only one that concerns itself with the characteristic absence of a full-blown ethicized karma doctrine rather than with its presence. Boon's finding is made even more vivid when set against Babb's admirably comprehensive account of karma in popular Hinduism in India. In Bali, even when ethical karma is presented, as in the writings of reform-minded Balinese literati, its "outlandishness" cannot be missed. In Hindu India by contrast, even when and where karma is denied, is belittled, or is absent, its presence and perfusion in the larger cultural matrix as a fully assimilated indigenous a priori cannot be missed. To the extent that karma may be said to have penetrated Bali, all it has done is to have merged with if not transformed into a "parental karma," its status within the symbolically mutilayered structure of Balinese cultural systems of myth, ritual, and marriage remaining more as a suspended compromise rather than a solution of complementarity. The metaphorical (analogical) representation of such a complementarity of extremes with its included middle (which Boon reminds us is not the average of the two) is vividly replicated in several other cultural domains. Prominent in all these replicates is, from the "ideal-typical Indian point of view," a lacuna created by the absence of a full-blown ethicized karma or its structural analogues. I stress the Indian point of view because in it (represented more or less in all the essays excepting Boon's) karma, once having injected itself into a causal system, reconstitutes the logic of causal relations in such a manner that its (karma's) presence seems inevitable if not indispensible. This Indian perspective sets Balinese culture in clear relief as one whose world-view holds together quite coherently in spite of the unambiguously opted rejection of karma as something superfluous at best, the protestations of the reform-minded literati not withstanding.

But what of Tibet, which lies at the edge of South Asia? And what is the status of the ideal-typical Indian point of view in popular Tibetan Buddhism? To begin with, "for rank and file Tibetans, karma is not so much an abstract theory pursued to logical extremes as it is a certain sort of a hypothetical story with a moral" (see Lichter and Epstein, this volume). If indeed the metaphorical aspect of an abstract theory is latent, that of a hypothetical story with a moral in it is not.

Even more obvious, from our point of view, is the systemic analogy that inheres between karma and *rkyen*. For the average Tibetan, karma and *rkyen* seem to describe distinct realities. Thus, karma becomes a metaphor of reality R^1 and *rkyen* a metaphor of reality R^2. Nevertheless, Tibetan academic exegesis readily reduces R^2 to the status of being but an aspect of R^1, and correspondingly *rkyen* becomes but an aspect of karma. Even though the essentially comprehensive view of karma constricts *rkyen* into a metonymic relationship (see below) with karma, there is a corresponding set of beliefs concerning karma that holds that even karma needs the right conditions to come to fruition. Furthermore, Lichter and Epstein point out "that these cooperating causes are accepted as part of karma is a matter of opinion." This fact not only makes karma less than comprehensive but also enables it to enter into an object-object, metaphoric relationship with other causal systems such as *rkyen*.

While Lichter and Epstein's relatively comprehensive notion of the good life delineates in great detail the different kinds of causal nexes, causes, and effects apart from that of karma, Beck's is the only essay in the present collection on Hindu India which attempts to carry out a similar differentiation systematically in her study of *viti* in contradistinction to karma. However, Babb and Hiebert in their more general essays also remind us with many an example that karma is not everything, and Wadley raises a distinction worth pursuing further, namely, that between karma and *bhāgya*.

In spite of the existence of such differences, karma looms large, if not in the open, then in the shadows, and is ever ready to overwhelm cognitively and affectively.[5] Beck's study, based on a contemporary folk epic, does distinguish clearly between "divine action" (*viti*) and "human action" (karma). But even in this very study of delineation the two planes of causation are seen to merge. Furthermore, the widely held belief among Tamils that even the gods have their own *karmam* to live out and act out would leave one to conclude that at a higher level if not a grosser level, it is karma that determines. This is even true of the culturally more finely categorized case of Tibetan Buddhism. Keyes makes the same point for Thai Buddhism and (citing Gombrich and Obeysekere) for Sri Lankan Theravāda Buddhism, wherein karma is not directly responsible for everything and anything that happens to a person but "operates . . . in a gross way. . . . Karma determines the station in which you are born, and your luck; after that, it is up to you."

Seen in this light then, the papers of S. Daniel, E.V. Daniel, and Pugh present or re-present karma as being in some sense the ultimate point of reference or reduction complementing rather than contradicting the other more pluralistic views. Given that these cultures have incorporated ethicization into their textures, it is easy to see why

[5] See Gombrich (1971) for a detailed discussion of the difference.

karma, if not actually, then with imminent potentiality, provides a doctrinal locus to which all else in the active universe of cause and effect may be reduced. In tropological terms, karma becomes more metonym than metaphor. It is metonymic in two senses. As a doctrine, theory, or law it is still a part of the universe it tries to represent. This use of metonym is also in keeping with the structuralist sense of the term. In the more conventional, tropological sense, metonymy need not be viewed as *necessarily* being composed of a part-whole relationship but may be a part-part relationship, provided that it is such that "one can effect the reduction of one of the parts to the status of an aspect or function of the other" (White 1973:34 n.). White uses the figurative expression "fifty sail" to indicate "fifty ships" as an example.[6] In metonymy, as can be seen from this example, two operations take place. First, two different objects are being implicitly compared. But this is not all, for if it were to end here, it would be metaphor. The second, more distinctive operation is one of reduction in which the "whole"—the ship—is reduced to one of its parts. However, as White points out, "the modality of this relationship, . . . is not that of a microcosm-macrocosm"—that would be synecdoche. From a metonymic point of view then, the ship as a "whole" is in a sense a kind of part, making the ship-to-sail reduction a part-to-part reduction rather than a whole-to-part one.

Of course, the kind of reduction effected in karma is one of cause and effect, and this cause-effect structure of metonymy needs to be explicated. To quote White on this again:

> [In] the [metonymical] expression "the roar of thunder" the whole process by which the sound of thunder is produced is first divided into two kinds of phenomena: that of cause on the one hand (the thunder); and that of effect on the other (the roar). Thus this reduction having been made, the thunder is related to the roar in the modality of a cause-effect reduction. The sound signified by the term "thunder" is endowed with the aspect of "roar" (a particular kind of sound). (White 1973:35)

In the Hindu/Buddhist world of causality, for instance, either *viti* and karma or *rkyen* and karma can be seen as two parts, both similar and

[6] My inspiration for applying the theory of tropes to enhance our understanding of the karma concept derives from Hayden White's study of the historical imagination of 19th-century Europe in which the theory of tropes is employed to understand the "stylistic" elements of historiography (1973). My invoking the theory of tropes is obviously directed toward different ends. But since White's exposition of the classical tropes in his Introduction can hardly be improved on, I shall quote or readapt his presentation and illustrations rather freely.

different at the same time, to a totality of a causal nexus. However, the cause-to-effect reduction moves from karma to *viti* or karma to *rkyen*. *Viti* and *rkyen* are partial expressions of karma, not unlike the heavens in Pugh's essay which make the unseen karma visible. *Viti* and *rkyen*, like the stars, are seen as indexing (i.e., as signifying an inevitable contiguity, even as smoke indexes fire) the presence if not the truth of karma.

In metaphor, object is related to object by arbitrary convention. In other words, the dominant mode of metaphoric expression is *symbolic*.[7] In metonymy part is related to part as a function of their contiguity in which the representamen *indexes* the object.

Do these two tropes exhaust the various cultural expressions of karma (or fate) which, as Pugh so succinctly puts it, ought to be seen "as a holistic quality of life, . . . an emergent phenomenon whose subjective reality arises from the congeries of culturally informed experiences in the various milieus of the life-world of the person"? Can the extrinsically expressed relationship in which karma has been seen first as metaphor and then as metonym be re-presented and recast so as to express the intrinsic relationship of shared qualities that inhere between one causal nexus and another, between cause and effect, between actor and action? The integrative trope, the synecdoche does offer us direction. Unlike metaphor, which re-presents, and metonym, which reduces, in synecdoche a part is employed to signify "some *quality* presumed to inhere in the totality" (White 1973:34). White's example is the expression "He is all heart." By an integrative operation what is signified is that the person in question "possesses some quality (generosity, compassion, etc. [that is figuratively expressed by the term 'heart']) that suffuses and constitutes the essential nature" of his whole being (ibid.).

Karma, when forced by context or design to assume its logically endowed power, integrates cause and effect, act and agent, in much the same way as does a synecdoche. In this integrative mode of synecdoche one part merges with the other, and they perfuse each other, so to speak. The same operation takes place in the case of cause and effect within karma, so that cause *is* effect, action *is* actor, and process *is* the processed.

Karma does compel us, however, to go beyond synecdoche. In

[7] There are obviously iconic and indexical functions that can be prescinded from a metaphor. Taken as a whole, however, and seen in relation to metonymy and synecdoche, a metaphor is symbolic.

synecdoche object and representation are *iconically* connected—they are connected or related by a shared quality. That this significant relationship, unlike the extrinsically constituted metaphor and metonym, is an intrinsic one must be granted. However, insofar as the connection between representamen and object remains a figurative one in spite of its intrinsic quality and in spite of its iconicity, it still falls short of comprehensively accounting for the dynamics of karma. Karma goes beyond figurative representation made available to us in both tropology and semiotics. Ranging from the Tibetan's stored-up merit of *bsod-nams*, through the Thai concept of merit transfer, down to the Tamil cases studied by the Daniels (this volume), karma becomes substantive. At one level, at the level at which we define culture and try to understand phenomena in *cultural* terms, karma substantiated is still symbolic. However, to conclude that culture so defined exhaustively accounts for karma in all its contextual and cognitive manifestations might well be naive. Anyone who has carried out field work in South Asia is aware that between what we categorize as symbolic (significant) and literal there is an interstitial region which we have never quite been able to hold down and examine and understand in terms of the epistemological categories at our disposal. Oberoi (1978) ascribes this conceptual limitation on the part of Western science to post-Zwinglian dualism, which has generated a whole series of absolute dichotomies, of which the literal-symbolic is but one—fact vs. value, theory vs. praxis, being some of the others. At a point such as this it becomes cogent to turn once again to the Indologists, who perhaps could introduce us to an epistemology if not a semiotic that will be able to provide us with a clearer perspective on a part of "reality," on that aspect of an explanandum which we now only perceive dimly, dualistically.

Perhaps once we have at our disposal such an epistemology or semiotic, the "parental karma" of Bali and the ethicized karma of India, Sri Lanka, Tibet, and Thailand may not appear to be as different as they do now. Neither will the "social mobility" of the individual in Thai society be seen as different from the "apparent" immobility of the Hindu born into a *jāti*, as Keyes sees it in his essay in this volume.[8] Furthermore, what appears to be basically a cognitive-cum-social paradox (how can a man with social responsibilities as son or father

[8] See Marriott (1977) wherein the fixed nature of *jāti*-status has already been brought into doubt in terms of what he claims to be based on a pervasive nondualism in Hindu culture, a position with which this essay concurs.

renounce these responsibilities for monkhood?) is resolved in essentially substantive terms of merit transference. Keyes observes this of the novice:

> [The novice] serves as a "field of merit" for the laity in that the offerings made by the laity to the Sangha are defined in all Theravādin traditions as being the supreme moral acts through which the laity acquires merit; and, at least in some cases, he generates merit that can be transferred to others.

The homology between this and what goes on in the offering of foods to the gods in the Hindu ritual of *pūjā* is compelling (see Babb 1970; Marriott and Inden 1974). Nonetheless, one cannot miss the cognitive continuum that stretches between Hinduism and Buddhism as being characterized by a movement from gross substantial representations to subtle ones, from the more concrete to the more abstract.

In introducing the tropological scheme in the beginning of this essay, I listed irony as one of the tropes I wished to consider. Perhaps irony is, as White observes (1973), as much metatrope as trope, standing above the rest, assuming a stance both self-conscious and critical. When Weber described karma as a solution to the question of theodicy, he clearly saw its function as that of relieving evil of its irony. As Lichter and Epstein have so perceptively observed for Tibetan Buddhism, evil's loss has become the "good life's gain," and ironically, karma is its benefactor. For those of us who have found the good life of understanding in "culture," we had hoped to understand "karma" by means of it. It would indeed be ironic if instead, by a peculiarly anthropological twist, karma helped us enhance our understanding of "culture." To me at least, this would be a welcome irony. But irony also persists in yet another form in the Tibetan idea of *la-yogs*, an idea that is the most elusive and enigmatic of all the ideas and concepts that have been considered in the present collection of essays. *La-yogs* is the embodiment of a pervasive irony which is co-present with karma wherever the latter exists. *La-yogs* in its most articulate form happens to be present among the Tibetans. Closer examination of the non-Tibetan systems, however, reveals that even here "*la-yogs*" is present even though in more subdued and subjunctive tones.

In one sense, of course, in an extreme sense, one might say, with Lichter and Epstein, "every color of the peacock's tail is determined by its own karma." Or, as Lichter and Epstein comment following the rendition of a typical *la-yogs* story, "As always one can append a karmic exegesis to such a tale." In this sense the relationship between *la-yogs* and karma becomes a non-ironic, metonymic one. But there is another more significant and more conscious sense in which *la-yogs* is used and understood in the daily lives of ordinary Tibetans. According to this view, *la-yogs* seems to have an ontogeny all its own. In fact one might even say that ultimately it is the irrational *la-yogs* that sets the stage for the enactment of the rational, ethicized, rule-governed drama of karma.

Explanations that resort exclusively to karmic reductionism do not exist in any of the ethnographic areas represented in these essays. Hiebert reminds us that there is provision in any explanation tradition for making selections from among several theories. Nevertheless, karma does secure for itself a special status among competing if not complementary theories of explanation. As Hiebert indicates, karma entails lower systems of explanation. Or as Babb reminds us, citing Sharma, that "while karma is rarely the first explanation a villager might give for misfortune, 'it is generally the last which he will abandon.'" In other words, karma's sheer comprehensiveness makes it, if not actually then potentially, an explanation to which everything could be reduced. And I do believe that some cultures are more prone to make such a reduction in a far greater number of contexts than others. The Veḷḷāḷa villagers of Kalappūr, the Tamil village studied by Sherry and Valentine Daniel, is such a case in point. This is clearly reflected in their essays, especially when karma is invoked to explain the present in terms of the past rather than when relating present to future. The significant question to be asked, then, is this: given the ever present possibility of karmic reduction in the Tamil case, is it possible to find therein also the equivalent of *la-yogs* considering that *la-yogs* flies in the face of any form of karmic reductionism or even karmic comprehensiveness?

At first glance, *viti* presents itself as a possible candidate in that it, like *la-yogs*, is invoked to describe negative events. The similarity ends there, however. In fact, *viti* has more in common with *rkyen* in that both invoke nonhuman causative agents, even though it is worth noticing that the agent involved in *viti* is a major god or even God, whereas *rkyen* includes all manner of lesser supernatural agents, such as ghosts and spooks. It is interesting to note that *viti* by being relatively abstract and hence closer to the even more abstract *karmam* tends to "contaminate" the latter with its less abstract connotations. For this reason karma and *viti* are often used interchangeably by Tamil speakers. In the Buddhist tradition, the abstract, purely law-like quality of karma is preserved, and causative systems such as *rkyen* are so far removed from the abstractness of karma that they could never be used interchangeably as *viti* and karma are. What then is *la-yogs'* Tamil counterpart? I believe that it is to be found buried in the following "Advaitic" version of the creation myth obtained from several of some of the same informants who gave us much of the data on karma in the village of Kalappūr. I shall present it here in its ample pragmatic context.

> Kaṭavuḷ [Śivan] was everything. In Him were the five elements of fire, water, earth, *akāsam* ["ether"] and wind. These five elements were uniformly spread throughout the three humors, *kabam* [phlegm], *pittam* [bile], and *vāyu* [wind]. They were so evenly distributed that even to say that there was *kapam*, *pittam*, and *vāyu* would be wrong. Let us say that they were indistinguishable, or even nonexistent. Similarly, the three *kuṇams* of *rajasa*, *tāmatam*, and *cātvīgam* neither existed nor did not exist. That is why we still call God Kuṇātītan [He who is above all *kuṇams*]. The question as to their existence did not arise. Then something happened. The five elements started to move around as if they were dissatisfied, as if they were disturbed. Now, as to who disturbed those five elements, or why they were disturbed, no one knows.

At this point, a second villager interrupted the narrator to suggest that the one who caused this mysterious disburbance was Kāma, the god of lust. The narrator found his suggestion unacceptable, since Kāma had not even come into existence at that time. But his friend insisted that Kāma himself was distributed throughout Śiva's body like the humors, the elements, and the *kuṇams*. After considerable debate, it was agreed that it did not make sense to speak of Kāma existing when he was as evenly distributed throughout Kaṭavuḷ's body as floating *aṇūs* (atoms). Then the narrator continued.

> Let us say that what disturbed them was their *talai eṛuttu* ["codes for action" or, literally, "headwriting"].[9] When the elements started moving around, the humors started separating from each other and recombining in new proportions [*aḷavukaḷ*]. These new combinations resulted in three *kuṇams*. Now, the *kuṇams* and humors and elements all started to move hither and thither. Then came the separation as in an explosion and all the *jātis* of the world—male *jātis*, female *jātis*, vegetable *jātis*, tree *jātis*, animal *jātis*, Veḷḷāḷa *jātis*, Para *jātis*—were formed and they started meeting and mating and procreating. This is how the world came into being. (E.V. Daniel 1979:3–4)

[9] Tamils believe that at the time of birth Kaṭavuḷ writes a script on every individual's head and that the course that each individual's life takes, to the very last detail, is determined by this script. This script, or writing of God on one's head, is known as *talai eṛuttu*. In this narration, my informant ascribes "headwriting" even to the particles that constituted the primordial Being (Kaṭavuḷ) (Daniel 1979: 3–4).

The very first "act," the primordial "action" or *karmam*, was the action of movement. "Desire" is momentarily suggested as having been the motivating force behind this movement, but we are quickly reminded that "desire" itself is (or was) part of that which was moved. Nonetheless, the same desire reappears in Buddhist dogma as "craving" (*taṇhā*), the root of all sorrow and all suffering. In the above Tamil version of the creation myth, desire, if allowed to stand, becomes synonymous with the degenerative process of creation with the ensuing consequences of *saṃsāra*, karma, and *dharma*, from which liberation is sought. But why did "desire," this misery- and sorrow-triggering agent, differentiate itself from the serenity of oneness in the first place? The narrator ascribes "headwriting" to the very particles that were in the primordial state of equipoise. One might say, it was written. But why? There is no reason, ethical or logical, that could justify this event. This creation myth, then, may be seen as harboring in its bosom, as either vestige or rudiment, that paradigmatic irony, *la-yogs*. The Tamils may not have a special term for *la-yogs*. But I do believe that even when they use the term *karma* to describe or characterize a particular misfortune for which no plausible explanation is possible, what comes to their minds is not a whole series of ethicized causal reasoning but a sense of the "meaninglessness of it all," a sense of *la-yogs*. In any event, *la-yogs* or its cryptotypic equivalent seems to be both logically as well as ontologically prior to an ethicized karma. Paradoxically though, logic, any logic whatsoever, becomes possible only after the a priori of karma is admitted into the scheme of things. This indeed is the final irony.

References Cited

Babb, Lawrence A.
1970 The Food of the Gods in Chhattisgarh: Some Structural Features of Hindu Ritual. Southwestern Journal of Anthropology 26:287–304.

Black, Max
1962 Models and Metaphors. Ithaca, N.Y.: Cornell University Press.

Boon, James
1973 Further Operations of Culture in Anthropology: A Synthesis of and for Debate. *In* The Idea of Culture in the Social Sciences. Louis Schneider and Charles Bonjean, eds. New York: Cambridge University Press.

Daniel, E. Valentine
1979 From Compatibility to Equipoise: The Nature of Substance in Tamil Culture. Ph.D. dissertation, University of Chicago.

Geertz, Clifford
1966 Religion as a Cultural System. *In* Anthropological Approaches to the Study of Religion. Michael Banton, ed. London: Tavistock.
Gombrich, Richard
1971 Precept and Practice: Traditional Buddhism in the Rural Highlands of Ceylon. Oxford: Clarendon Press.
Hesse, Mary B.
1970 The Explanatory Function of Metaphor. Models and Analogies in Science. Notre Dame, Indiana: University of Notre Dame Press.
Jakobson, Roman
1960 Closing Statements: Linguistics and Poetics. *In* Style in Language. T. A. Sebeok, ed. Cambridge: MIT Press.
Keesing, Roger
1974 Theories of Culture. Annual Review of Anthropology 3:73–97.
Lévi-Strauss, Claude
1961 Tristes Tropiques. New York: Criterion Books.
1966 The Savage Mind. Chicago: University of Chicago Press.
McCarthy, Thomas
1978 The Critical Theory of Jurgen Habermas. Cambridge: MIT Press.
Marriott, McKim
1977 Hindu Transactions: Diversity Without Dualism. *In* Transaction and Meaning: Directions in the Anthropology of Exchange and Symbolic Behavior. Bruce Kapferer, ed. Philadelphia: Institute for the Study of Human Issues.
Marriott, McKim, and Ronald Inden
1974 Caste Systems. Encyclopaedia Britannica 3:982–991.
Oberoi, J. S.
1978 Culture and Science. New Delhi: Oxford University Press.
O'Flaherty, Wendy D., ed.
1980 Karma and Rebirth in Classical Indian Traditions. Berkeley: University of California Press.
Ramanujan, A. K.
1967 The Interior Landscape. Bloomington: Indiana University Press.
Ricoeur, Paul
1975 The Rule of Metaphor. Toronto: University of Toronto Press.
Silverstein, Michael
1976 Shifters, Linguistic Categories and Cultural Description. *In* Meaning in Anthropology. Keith H. Basso and Henry A. Selby, eds. Albuquerque: University of New Mexico Press.
Singer, Milton
1979 For a Semiotic Anthropology. *In* Sight, Sound and Sense. T. A. Sebeok, ed. Bloomington: Indiana University Press.
White, Hayden
1973 Metahistory. The Historical Imagination in Nineteenth-Century Europe. Baltimore: Johns Hopkins University Press.

Index and Glossary

Words from Sanskrit have not been identified as to source language except when the same word is also found in another language in the same form; then the abbreviation *Skt* is used. For words from other languages, the following abbreviations are employed: *P*, Pāli; *H*, Hindi; *U*, Urdu; *T*, Tamil; *Tib*, Tibetan; *Th*, Thai; *NT*, Northern Thai; *B*, Balinese. For all other words for which a source language is indicated, the full name of the language is used.

Acchāgraha dashā (H), "good planetary condition," 143, 144
Account books and keepers, 64, 66, 73
Actor-action identity, 107
Adṛṣṭa karma, "invisible karma," 134
Advaita, "non-dualism," 298
Agni, god of fire, 88
Aiyangar, M.V. Rangaswani, 148
Akin Rabibhadana, 270
Akusala (P), "sin, demerit," 267. Also see *Pāpa*
Akutho (Burmese), "sin, demerit," 267
Āḷ (T), "person," 30
Alberuni, 133
Allah, 136, 137, 138
Allen, Richard H., 134
Alliance: marriage, 190–199, 203, 207, 215, 218; power, 191, 196. *Also see* Marriage
Allison, Charlene, 57
Almanacs, 64, 131, 138, 144
Amarasingham, Lorna, 52
Ancestors, 30, 65, 121, 187, 188, 191, 201, 214, 216
Ancestral spirits, 88
Anderson, Ben, 210
Andhra Pradesh, 165
Anger, 234, 262
Anguttara Nikāya, 263
Ānisaṁsa (P), "benefit," 278. Also see *Ānisong*
Ānisong (Th, NT), a category of vernacular texts in which the "benefits" of Buddhist ritual action are discussed, 275, 276
Ānisong būat, text, "The Blessings of Ordination," 275–278
Anusaraṇaśāsanākiarti, Phra Khrū, 273
Arabic system of astrology, 133
Arjuna, a prince in the *Mahābhārata*, 72, 74
Artha, "force, wordly power," 187, 191, 198, 202, 206
Aruchalam, M., 71
Āsārī (T), smith-caste, 85, 86
Asceticism, 4, 55, 88, 119, 126–127, 186, 187
Asterisms, 134
Astrologers, 17, 47, 49, 65, 67, 131, 132, 133, 134, 135, 136–139, 140, 142, 144, 145
Astrological: anomalies, 113; codes, 16; prediction, 44–50; texts 133, 142
Astrology, 44, 77, 90, 113, 121, 125, 129, 130, 131–146, 240; and applied science, 133–134. *Also see* Astrologers; Astrological; Constellations; Horoscope; Planets; Stars
Atjehnese Muslims, 137
Ātma, *ātman* (Skt, P), "soul," 54, 55, 140
Auspiciousness, 89-91, 94, 100, 142–143
Austerities, 70, 149, 178, 236. *Also see* Penance; Sacrifice; *Vrat*; Vows
Authority, 12, 273; religious, 4; legitimate, 4: of text 4, 9, 10, 12, 150; of tradition 4, 9; of mystical experience, 4, 5
Ayurveda, branch of Indian medicine, 86

Babb, Lawrence A., 3, 13, 88, 120, 124, 130, 165, 291, 292, 296, 297
Bad deeds. *See* Misbehavior
Bāddhā, "obstruction," 142, 143
Bahut kharābgraha dashā (H), "very bad planetary condition," 143, 144
Balance, 72, 87, 90. *Also see* Equilibrium; *Līlā*
Bali, 7, 10, 12, 13, 14, 18, 20, 185–219, 288, 291, 295
Balinese culture, 190, 214, 215

170–171, 176; referential, 287; systems of, 2, 3, 13; ultimate, 3, 18, 122, 127
Medicine, 52, 86, 127
Meditation, 119, 278. Also see *Samādhi*
Menstruation, 87–88, 90, 190
Merdah (B), servant-clown in Indonesian Ramāyaṇa, 209, 210, 211, 212
Merit, 6, 13–14, 18, 39, 71, 149, 150, 216, 230, 235, 240, 242, 247, 248, 250, 254, 261, 267, 268, 269, 270, 271, 274, 277, 279–280, 281–283, 295; field of, 274, 296; intergenerational transfer of, 159; making, 19, 223, 267, 268, 270, 276, 280; "man-of-," 269–270; as substance, 270; quest for, 268; sangha as source of, 274, 296; transference of, 9, 14, 18, 19, 20, 158–159, 186, 236, 261, 270, 274, 278–284, 295, 296. Also see *Bon*; *Bsod-bde*; *Bun*; *Kusala*; *Kutho*; *Phan-yon*; *Pin*; *Puñña*; *Puṇyam*; *Tham bun*
Metaphor, 2, 71, 196, 236, 237, 253, 256, 290–291, 291, 292, 293, 294
Metonymy, 2, 196, 290, 292, 293, 294, 297
Metta (P), "compassion," 278
Mī bun (Th, Lao), "has merit," 269
Micchādiṭṭhi(ka) (P), "false beliefs, views," 276, 277
Microcosm/macrocosm, 189, 197, 210, 293
Mi-dge-ba bcu (Tib), "the ten vices," 232
Mi-kha (Tib), "gossip," 251
Mi-la-ras-pa, Tibetan poet-saint, 230, 248
Miller, Barbara D., 151
Mind, 135, 140. *Also see* Intentionality
Misbehavior, 67, 68, 69–70, 72, 172. *Also see* Sin
Misfortune, 3, 14, 15, 16, 17, 20, 65, 67, 78, 158, 160, 161, 165–180, 238, 239, 248, 257, 265. *Also see* Suffering
Mishra, V. B., 148
Moha (P), "ignorance," 261
Mokṣa, *moksha*, "release," 119, 154, 155, 156, 159
Monism/dualism, 189
Monistic perspective (non-dualism), 55, 57
Monk/lay distinction, 11–12, 216, 224, 251–254
Monkeys, 12, 208, 218
Monks and monasticism, 4, 11, 12, 19, 202, 213–218, 225, 233, 235, 251–254, 268, 270, 271, 273, 276–278, 282. Also see *Bhikkhu*; *Samaṇa*; *Sāmaṇera*
Moore, Charles A., 132
Morality, 177–180, 267, 268, 277; vs. destiny, 275–278
Mōṭccam (T), "salvation, release," 55. Also see *Mokṣa*
Mother Earth, in Bali, 195, 198
Mukur (B), "second cremation," 211, 212
Mūḷai (T), "brain," 31, 32, 33, 34, 35
Munn, Nancy, 273
Murayāna karmam (T), "appropriate action," 95
Murugan, 94–95
Muslims, 131–146 *passim*. *Also see* Islamic theology
Myrdal, Gunnar, 163
Mystical experience and insight, 4. *Also see* authority
Myth, 10–11, 12, 36, 48, 52, 54, 55, 122, 125, 126, 127, 129, 150, 185, 189, 190, 198, 199, 201, 202, 214, 218, 246–247, 276, 279, 280; and ritual, 119, 273; of Kalappūr creation, 298; of origin of sweeper, 166. Also see *Kathā*

Najūm (Urdu), "astrology," 137
Naradjī, the sage Narad, 152–154
Naraka (P), "hell," 277
Nāsh (H), "destruction," 142, 143
Nash, Manning, 268, 269
Nasr, S. H., 133
Nat (Burmese), "supernatural being," 16, 266
Ndembu, 105, 272
Nebesky-Wojkowitz, René de, 225
Neethishstramu, text, 127
Nepal, 223, 224
Nibbāna (P), "Nirvāṇa," 274, 278
Nicholas, Ralph W., 110, 134
Nirvāṇa, 189
Northern India, 17, 131–146
Novices, 273, 277, 296

Oberoi, J. S., 295
Obeyesekere, Gananath, 5, 6, 21, 155, 167, 175, 264–265, 266, 271, 292
Oceania, 199, 200, 201
O'Flaherty, Wendy, 3, 4, 6, 11, 15, 18, 19, 52, 55, 99, 155, 186, 187, 201, 202, 214, 215, 281, 287
Oldenberg, H., 274
Opportunism, 60
Ordination, Buddhist, 273–278
"Organic-mechanical" continuum, 120
Organic solidarity, 11, 189, 216

Compositor:	Trigraph, Inc.
Printer:	Braun-Brumfield, Inc.
Binder:	Braun-Brumfield, Inc.
Text:	11/13 Bembo
Display:	Bembo